Cranes Ever Flying
Introductions to
Asian Christian History and Theology

Cranes Ever Flying
Introductions to
Asian Christian History and Theology

John C. England

2020

Cranes Ever Flying: Introductions to Asian Christian History and Theology —
published by the Indian Society for Promoting Christian Knowledge (ISPCK),
Post Box 1585, Kashmere Gate, Delhi-110006.

© Author, 2020

All rights reserved. No part of this book may be reproduced or transmitted in any form or by any means, electronic, mechanical, photocopying, recording, or by any information storage and retrieval system, without the prior permission in writing from the publisher.

The views expressed in the book are those of the author and the publisher takes no responsibility for any of the statements.

Online order: http://ispck.org.in/book.php

Also available on amazon.in

ISBN: 978-93-88945-67-7

First edition, here revised and enlarged, published by Association for Theological Education Myanmar, for Programme for Theology and Cultures in Asia, PTCA Series No. 14, 2018.

Laser typeset by
ISPCK, Post Box 1585, 1654, Madarsa Road, Kashmere Gate, Delhi-110006
• *Tel:* 23866323

e-mail: ashish@ispck.org.in • ella@ispck.org.in
website: www.ispck.org.in

Contents

Foreword	...	vii
Acknowledgements	...	xi

PART ONE

Chapter - 1
Reclaiming Christian History for Over Half the World ... 3

Chapter - 2
Ecumenical Movements in Asia since the 3rd Century ... 32

Chapter - 3
The Early Christian Art of Asian Peoples ... 55

Chapter - 4
Bamboo Groves in Winds from the West: Indigenous Faith and Western Influence in Asian Christian Writings of 16th-18th Centuries ... 86

Chapter - 5
Cranes Ever Flying: Creativity and Continuity in Contextual Asian Theologies ... 103

Chapter - 6
Within our Movements and Histories:
The Crane is Ever Flying ... 131

Chapter - 7
Doing Theology in Asian Ways ... 155

Chapter - 8
Watershed Theologians ... 182

1. Wu Yao Zong (Y. T. Woo) (China: 1893-1979)
   Love as Practice for Change ... 183

2. Kim Jae-Joon (Korea: 1901-1987)
   Human History in the Third day ... 195

3. Daniel T. Niles (Sri Lanka: 1908-1970)
   Christian Selfhood and Secular Engagement ... 206

4. Hwang Chiong-Hui (Shoki Coe) (Taiwan: 1914-1988)
   Today's Gospel and Context ... 216

5. Madathilparampil Mamen Thomas (1916-1996)
   Living Theology in Action ... 231

6. Horacio de la Costa sj (1916-1977)
   Identity and a Liberating Theology ... 244

7. Lee Park, Sun-Ai (1930-1999)
   Women's Story in Future Theologies ... 254

8. D.S. Amalorpavadass (India: 1932-1990)
   Vision of Universal Salvation ... 264

PART TWO
For a 21st Century Praxis and Study

I. The Foundational Way – The Human Life of Jesus ... 273

II. Choosing Approaches & Sources
    for Asian Christian Studies ... 283

III. Towards a Charting of Asian
     Church Histories and Theologies ... 296

Foreword

Writings on the history of Asian Christianity and on the theologies of Asia have greatly multiplied in recent decades and I have hesitated to add to them. I have however been persuaded to prepare this collection in order to provide a survey of largely unknown materials for the history, arts, ecumenism and indigenous theologies of Asian Christianities – a survey which might in fact serve as an introductory text-book for courses in their study. (See Part Two, II and III below). There is at present no such volume which serves as an introduction not only to the early history of Christianity in Asian regions but also to ecumenical and theological movements since the 2nd century, as well as to the history of Christian art in the same periods. Nor is there any basic outline of the sources for such study in each region – in south, southeast, east and northeast, west and inner Asia - that is, in 'more than half the world', from the Ural mountains and the Mediterranean Sea in the west to Kamchatka in the northeast, and to Arabia, India and Indonesia in the south.

The first three chapters provide introductory outlines of the history, ecumenical mission and art-forms of Christian communities in the Asian region until the 16th century (chapters 1 and 3) or the 19th century (chapter 2) – the periods and subject areas which are less often (if ever) studied in today's colleges and universities. The intent here is to present not a history of the 'church as institution' but the Christian community as a movement, or indeed movements, with their own dynamic characteristics. (See further on 'the church as movement' in chapter 6). To these I have added groups of case-studies in church history and theology from particular periods between the 17th and the 20th centuries, in order to take further the historical outline as well as to sharpen focus upon particular significant individuals and groups. No attempt has been made to include here more well-known movements such as Dalit, Minjung, Struggle or Homeland theologies as these are well covered in other volumes (Refer chapter 7 and bibliographies to Part Two, II and III below).

Focus is further sharpened by considering the methods and models used by representative theologians across the region in the 'doing of theology' over the last century. I have included lesser-known personalities here also, in order to introduce the range of diverse approaches taken in the region's 'living theologies' since the 16th century. This is followed by studies of selected 'watershed' or path-breaking theologians who have shaped much of Asia's living, contextual theologies since the early 20th century. Concluding chapters present more fully the imageries and interpretations for the 'life-of-Jesus-with-others' which has emerged from many of these theologies, along with a final presentation of the basic approaches and sources being employed in Asian Christian sources. Particular attention has been given throughout to bibliographical materials to be used in further study.

In presenting such an outline the chapters which follow are shaped by the convictions that there is one Great Spirit of all peoples, places and times; that all living theologies are therefore responsive and contextualizing – responding to the discerned presence of God, within a particular people's culture and history; and that living theology arises in the interactive relationship of Christian faith with the particular realities of history, geography, society, culture and other living faiths. For such 'theology' (or 'theodao/dharma') Christianity in Asia has possessed from the earliest centuries its own distinctive identities and autonomous traditions in life and thought. Christian communities in each region have been shaped by particular cultural, religious and political contexts and have demonstrated their self-hood in expressing their faith, in dialogue with those of other living faiths as well as in their 'secular engagement' (D.T. Niles). I believe this forms a dynamic basis for coming forms of church life and devotion as well as for critical reflection, writing and teaching. These are beliefs only strengthened through over 50 years of collegial work when I have been privileged to have the generous companionship and teaching of colleagues in a score of Asian countries.

The chapters following, many of which have been previously published in earlier versions, are here however fully revised and extended. They are selected for their more direct contemporary relevance from many articles originally written in the course of ecumenical programmes for theological education and action conducted in various parts of the region over many years. It is hoped that in their present form they together provide an introductory volume for the study of 'Asian church history and theology'. Some of these materials arose firstly as part of the CCA's (Christian Conference of Asia) Asia-wide activity in laity formation and theological education, others were part of similar work based at Tao Fong Shan Ecumenical Centre (Hong Kong), and later in the annual courses and publications of PTCA (Programme for Theology and Cultures in Asia) for staff members of theological colleges and faculties from 1983. As noted below some of these papers were originally journal articles, or parts of symposia, or were developed in later collections or monographs.

Note: The terms 'theodao' and 'theodharma' - (in briefest terms the 'way of communion with all things' and ‹the universal law and teaching) - are often used by Asian writers/activists to represent the alternatives to 'theo-logy', as they replace studies which are shaped largely by Graeco-Latin tradition with approaches shaped by the major traditions of South Asia (as with 'Dharma') or East Asia (as with 'Dao). See for example Somen Das *Dharma of the Twenty-First Century*. (Punthi Pustak, 1996) and Kim Heup Young *A Theology of Tao* (Orbis, 2017).

Acknowledgements

Earlier writings which outline the initial approaches I and my colleagues have taken on these subjects can be found in *Theology in Action* (with Oh Jae Shik, 2nd ed. EACC 1973), *Living Theology in Asia* (SCM & Orbis 1981), *Doing Theology with Asian Resources* (With Yeow Choo Lak, Annual vols. of the Association for Theological Education in South East Asia *Occasional Papers* (ATESEA, 1984-1994); "Towards a Charting of Asian Theologies" (*InterReligio* 12, Winter, 1988; also published in *Indian Theological Studies* and other journals); and with Rita M. England in *Ministering Asian Faith and Wisdom* (New Day & ISPCK, 2001). The Research Guide to *Asian Christian Theologies,* for which I was chief editor and writer (with Jose Kuttianimattathil sdb, John M. Prior svd, Julita A. Quintos rc, David Suh Kwang-sun, and Janice Wickeri, 3 vols. ISPCK, Claretian, Orbis, 2001-2004) also illustrates these approaches as taken by many other colleagues in each country of the region.

For chapter 1, a fuller treatment is found in *The Hidden History of Christianity in Asia: The Churches of the East before the year 1500* (ISPCK & CCA, 1998, 2002) and is updated in chapters of this volume. Chapter 2 was first prepared to outline the long history of ecumenism in Asia for the *Re-Routing* Consultations held prior to the CCA's Golden Jubilee (1997). It was published in part in *They Left by Another Road – Rerouting Mission and Ecumenism in Asia* edited by A. Wati Longchar et al. (CCA, 2007), and in Hope S. Antone, et al. (eds.) *Asia Handbook for Theological Education.* (Wipf & Stock, Regnum, 2013). Chapter 3 outlines the long story of Christian Art in the region for which a short article was first published in *Image* (Asian Christian Art Assoc., Sept. 1997).

Chapters 4, 5, and 6 explore further particular movements in Asian theology and Church history. A version of chapter 4 on indigenous responses to western missions was first published in Klaus Koschorke, (ed.) *Christen und Gewurze*. (Vandenhoeck & Ruprecht, 1998). Chapter 5 continues the stories of Asian Theologies with case studies from selected countries. It was first published in part in the *Asia Journal of Theology* (23.2, 2009). Chapter 6 presents Church History as the story of creative theological movements in the region and first appeared in part in the *Asian Christian Review* (7.1, 2014). Parts of chapter 7, here much extended, have appeared in *Theology in Action* (EACC, 1973), *East Asia Journal of Theology* (vol. 3.2, 1985) and *ATESEA Occasional Papers* No.12 (ATESEA 1993).

Chapter 8 gives a selection, extensively revised, from the series of studies of 'Watershed Theologians' which were published in part in *ATESEA Occasional Papers* (10, 1990) and in *Indian Theological Studies* (27.2, 1990). Part Two, section I gives a selection of basic approaches to *living* our theology contextually when this is centred on the *life-of-Jesus-with-others* (Shoki Coe's phrase). This has now evolved as supplementary to sections of my life-prayer manual *Wagering to Live* (ISPCK, 2017). The final sections on "Approaches to Asian Christian Studies", have developed from sessions introducing studies of Asian History, Church History and Theology to scholars and students in many different contexts.

All chapters draw also on the resources assembled for the Research Guide to *Asian Christian Theologies*, and on my book reviews subsequently published in *Asia Journal of Theology*. It is hardly necessary to say of these papers that just as they have arisen in co-operative research and action so also they are part of the on-going recoveries, discussions and joint endeavours now being shared in the region. These form a continuing and vital appropriation of indigenous history and current Christian endeavour which – along with the contextual experience of culture, social history and religion – give resources and shape to Asian Christian identity and autonomous creativity.

Clearly all chapters owe most to co-workers in each of the networks and centres in which I have worked, as well as to many colleagues across the region with whom I have lived and worked over many years. For I have been favoured with the generous friendship of companions in theological colleges and university faculties, in lay institutes and social action centres, in people movements, research centres and mission agencies.[1] To all these colleagues I am indebted for assistance and team-work in not only research and planning, but also through continuing stimulus, support, and friendship. To them I give my warmest thanks. Names of those colleagues who have most inspired and challenged me are shown in citations and the references included in the above chapters, especially those in chapters 7 and 9. Amongst these I wish to particularly acknowledge the inspiration, support and/or friendship of Daniel T. Niles, M.M. Thomas, Liem Khiem Yang, Song Choan Seng, Masao Takenaka, Yohan Devananda, Somen Das, Oh Jae Shik, Jose Kuttianimattathil sdb Janice and Philip Wickeri, John Mansford Prior svd and David Suh Kwang-Sun.

Special acknowledgement must be made of the contribution to all my work, research and writing of my late wife Rita. As loving partner she devotedly shared in every aspect of our joint calling, studies and publishing, 'walking and bearing every mile' of those journeys with me over many years. To her I owe deepest gratitude.

More recently I have received full support and encouragement from my present wife Helen who in every way continues to 'walk mindfully' with me in these latter years. To her also I owe deepest gratitude. "The road goes ever on".

Note – The title and cover illustration for this volume have been chosen for the strong symbolism long- associated with the crane species in Asian religion and culture. By their high and steady flight they have often symbolised sure purpose and quest; flight so constant and extensive that they have been thought to even 'reach heaven'. This has then come to often signify longevity and immortality. The flight of white cranes in particular has also symbolised both purity and the 'freedom from all bonds' so that in many Asian countries they have become symbols of justice and peace.

Endnotes

[1] Any partial listing would include, apart from the extensive fellowships of the EACC/CCA and the FABC, colleagues in the Association for Theological Education in Southeast Asia (ATESEA), in the National Christian Councils of the Asian region, in the Chinese University of Hong Kong and Doshisha University Kyoto, in the former Selly Oak Colleges and the Chicago Cluster of Theological Schools, and not least in the teams that developed in PTCA programmes and for the preparation of the Research Guide to *Asian Christian Theologies* (ISPCK, Claretian, Orbis, 2001-2004), along with the projects of PTCA since 2005.

PART ONE

Chapter - 1

Reclaiming Christian History for Over Half the World

"They pitched their tents in the camps of the wandering Tartar ... they stood in the rice-fields of the Punjab and taught fishermen by the Sea of Aral, they struggled through the vast deserts of Mongolia ... Hsien-fu attests their victories in China. In India the Zamorin (of Callicut) himself respected their authority".[1]

The history of Christianity in Asia is often portrayed as belonging to only the last few centuries, when European or North American missionary movements entered the region, sometimes under the protection of western mercantile or even military presence. Unfortunately only a few Christian communities in the region have retained a strong sense that their history began long before in the earliest centuries of the Christian era. Yet we now know that this is true not only for churches in South India and China but for many countries throughout the region. These stories of the Christian movement in Asia began in the first and second century spread of Palestinian and Syrian churches eastward into Mesopotamia, as well as to central, south and east Asia.[2] The consequent missions of the *Churches of the East* (sometimes misnamed "Nestorian") and of the Syrian Orthodox Church, reached to a 'dozen countries east of Persia by the 8th century'; later leaving active churches in a number of countries for even the first Roman Catholic missionaries to discover. By the 9th-11th centuries these communities numbered more than those of the Latin and Byzantine traditions combined.

Christianity is therefore an ancient Asian religion not just because of its origins in west Asian cultures and in the life and death of an astounding Palestinian Jew, nor just because of the Asian form of its foundation scriptures. Christianity in its central features also remains indelibly Asian because of this long and diverse presence from the earliest centuries throughout central, south, south-east and north-east Asian countries. This is the tradition in which Asian, and indeed all Christians stand; the often neglected 'other half' of world Christian history. This is therefore our own Christian history and a most rich resource for present tasks of mission and theological education in each of our countries.

Clearly such a history has been consistently disregarded – and our understanding of Christian presence and identity within the particular histories and cultures of the region massively distorted – often for doctrinal, ideological or even imperialistic reasons. Church history is still often taught as if anything east of Antioch was 'heretical' from the second century on, and unworthy of study even if it did survive! Once assume that the evidence is marginal, fragmentary or non-existent there is no reason to recognise the very extensive materials available, nor the rich heritage which retains lasting significance for our own self-understanding. Ethnocentric assumptions regarding orthodoxy and heresy, along with culturally confined criteria in scholarship, then often prevent any adequate study of Eastern Christianity in terms of its own historical and cultural setting. Yet any view of Christian history which regards the post-Nicene history of Europe as universally normative, while largely ignoring the equally rich history 'East of Antioch' (pre- and post-Nicaea) can no more be sustained than the doctrinal and ideological assumptions on which such a view rests.[3]

In order to reconstruct a map of early and medieval Christianity in Asia and the diverse stories of the Christian movement it represents, many technical and critical problems must be recognised. Changes in terrain and climate, as well as most turbulent histories have fragmented much of the manuscript and other evidence, making it necessary to employ a wide range of investigative methods. Texts are extant in an unusually wide range of ancient and medieval languages, with secondary sources in almost every major European or Asian language, making necessary a high degree of co-operative and inter-disciplinary study. Geographical and theological terminologies in particular have been confused, often for polemical reasons; terms such as 'Arab', 'Syrian', or 'Persian', we now know, can refer in the earliest south-east Asian records, to many localities in west, central, or southern Asia. 'India' or 'Indian' can be used variously to indicate almost any territories east and south of Iran, or in mainland or archipelago south-east Asia.[4] Similarly "Nestorian", long used to denounce many non-western traditions, is both misleading and pejorative in describing the doctrine or traditions of 'the Church of the East', to which it is often applied. The teachings of Nestorius were in any case most often formerly much misrepresented.[5] The two largest non-Latin/Greek Christian traditions widely present across the Asian regions, are more correctly named Church of the East ('Assyrian' or 'Chaldean') and Syrian Orthodox ('Monophysite' or 'Jacobite'). Both reject the definitions of Christian faith which were decided at the Council of Chalcedon in 451.

The Range of Evidence

Taking account of these and similar issues, and drawing on the range of evidence now available to us, it is possible to outline the presence of Christian communities from Syria in the west to Japan in the north-east and as far as Java in the south-east by the first half of the 8th century. The accompanying map traces their extent by naming only those locations where material remains have been discovered; i.e. notably inscriptions and sculpture, individual crosses and tombs, frescoes and paintings, buildings and ruins, coins and seals, along with contemporary manuscript evidence. Much of the evidence now available is the work of scholars in ancient Syriac, Arabic or Turkic dialects, or of historians studying late antique history and the early trade routes linking west Asia and east Asia by land or sea.[6] Unfortunately only a few comprehensive outlines or collections of the many studies are yet available, and few specialist papers referring to them have so far appeared in the region.

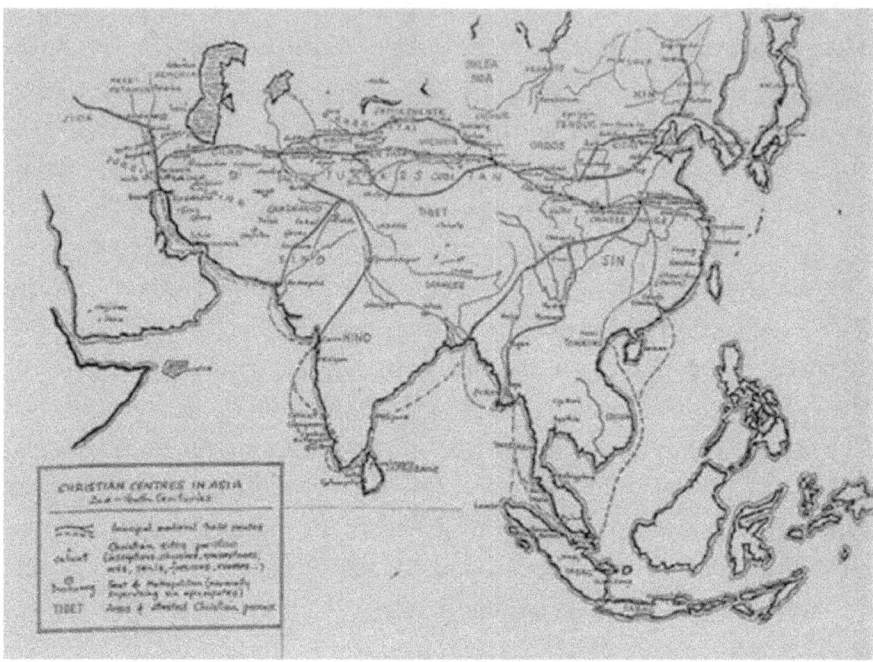

The densest concentration of centres – only a few of which are here included – occurs in the Mesopotamian, Central and South Asian regions and represents the many dioceses of the Syrian, Persian, Turkistani and Indian churches. Almost all these suffered frequent persecution as Rome, Persia and nearby principalities jostled for dominance throughout West Asia and beyond. Originating in exchanges between Jerusalem, Antioch and Damascus the churches had grown largely from house churches and 'occupational' groups, synagogue and proselyte communities; from refugee encampments or from groups settled in oases, trading-posts or townships.[7] In 280 C.E. Seleucia-Ctesiphon, became the seat for the Patriarch but the traditions, life and mission of the Church of the East were then penetrating throughout all regions of Asia. Extending rapidly throughout the Persian empire, and along both the land and marine 'silk routes', they had become established in north and south India and east

China in the 1st century, Bactria and inner Asia by the late 2nd century, northern regions of central Asia by the 5th century, Sumatra, Korea and Japan by the 8th century, and Burma, Mongolia, Tibet and Java by the 12th century.[8] European traditions would follow in most countries of the region by the 17th century.

Marks of the Movement
Behind such bald statements lies a wealth of data and histories for which we have evidence across the region and which is only now being widely recognised and studied. Amongst them we have the earliest life of Jesus, the *Diatesseron*,[9] a harmony of the Gospels written by Tatian c.165 CE, which remained virtually the only version of the gospels used across Asian regions for almost 250 years. There is also the first non-Greek version of all the scriptures, the *Peshitta*, which has recently been re-issued in a complete critical edition.[10] Many other 'firsts' for Christian history are found in records for the Churches of the East. What has been named the first Christian hymnbook, 'The Odes of Solomon' has been dated to the late 1st /early 2nd cent.[11] Remains of the oldest extant Church building anywhere found, have been restored at Dura-Europas (Mesopotamia, (235 C.E.).[12] The first theological college we know of anywhere in the world, was established at Nisibis, (ca.350), later moving to Edessa,[13] with the first 'medical college' (later university, now extended) being established at Gondishapur (Jundishapur) in the 5th century. Other important schools were soon established at Seleucia-Ctesiphon (later Baghdad) and Merv. In this tradition also the earliest translations of Greek classical writings were made in this region, firstly to Syriac and later (8th century and on) to Arabic.[14]

It has long been known that traders, refugees, envoys and monks from west Asia diligently travelled the land routes to 'further India' and Cathay, from as early as the 2nd century (BCE). This cavalcade followed the many routes by which textiles and spices, grain, vegetables and fruit, animal hides and tools, wood work and metal work, religious objects, art work, precious stones and slaves were carried and traded. Here too the traditions and writings of many living faiths were also spread in this way across these vast territories. But although many early settlements, hospices, churches or monasteries may have been founded by Buddhists, Hindus, Zoroastrians or Manicheans, it is now clear that many were the work of Eastern Christians. Early eastern monastic communities also are dated to at the latest, the early 4th century and may have pre-dated those in Egypt, for these centres grew wherever 'Persian', 'Arab', Chinese or 'Indian' trade had become established in central, south, east or south-east Asia. [15]

Significantly for us we then have the surprising stories of an amazing missionary endeavour, which saw monks and merchants, travellers, priests, traders and physicians carrying the 'pearl of the Gospel' across all the trade routes on ancient and medieval Asia. This meant journeys of often at least a year long, by camel, mule or even by foot, across the many tracks of the 'Silk Routes', or by lengthy sea-trips, along the many routes of Arab, Sogdian or Indian traders.[16] Such journeyings must also be seen as part of a larger pattern of visits, temporary settlement, semi-permanent residence or, in some cases, permanent domicile in settlements or cities, at oases or fortified towns. There were also communities based in caravanserais, in temples or churches, in shrines, monasteries or libraries. All this was to be found from the late antique to medieval periods anywhere in the vast region between Syria in the west, Mongolia in the north and 'the Indies' in the south.[17]

Ascetic traditions were always strong within the Eastern churches, yet in contrast to many Egyptian traditions, in the very earliest Christian documents of the east (i.e. in Syria) the call to ascetic self-denial is almost always associated with the call to go and preach and serve.[18] This would be a distinctive mark of Eastern monasticism as it spread throughout Asian lands. It would also be one of the underlying reasons for the wide-spread growth of Christian communities across the region which has always amazed historians. The closing words of the *Xian-Fu Stele* witness to a holistic Christian presence and service which can be observed especially in the many monasteries of the Church of the East across the region:

.......'the hungry came and were fed,
the cold came and they were clothed,
the sick were healed and raised up,
the dead were buried and laid to rest'.

In case it is assumed that such endeavours were the work of men only, it must be stressed that women too were very significant leaders in these diverse communities. They were in fact recognised from the earliest centuries as prophets, and abbesses, teachers and ascetics, priests, confessors and martyrs. We have biographies for them from the 3rd century on, with letters, poems, prayers, chronicles, along with accounts such as those recorded for 'the Syrian Orient' (3rd-6th cents.): those such as Martha and Thecla, Tarbo and Anahid, the Mmes, Macrina, Mary and Euphemia, (Euphemia herself being a remarkable prophet).[19] Egeria produced her wide-ranging journal of pilgrimage in the 4th century recording the work of many women in the Levant.[20] There are also fragmentary accounts such as those of Rashid Al-Din, the famous Persian historian. When speaking for example, of Sorgaqtani the Christian mother of Kublai Khan, he wrote that she is 'extremely intelligent and able and towering above all the women in the world... If I were to see among the race of women another woman like this I would say that [they] are far superior to men!'[21] Other noteworthy Christian wives of Khans included - amongst others – Dorqas Khaton and Cotota Khaton. [22] As in other regions such roles and recognition would be quickly eroded by male leaders who too often failed to recognise that the 'apostles' of the New Testament included named women, or who were fearful of losing authority and leadership in the burgeoning Christian communities.

Diversity and Extent: Some of the Stories

We know from Tertullian of many bishoprics established throughout the Persian empire by the year 220, this was despite Christians being suspect to Zoroastrian rulers, especially following Constantine's declaration that Christianity was the official religion of the Roman Empire (325). This, along with the policies of some Zoroastrian rulers in Sassanid

Persia, would lead to periods of severe persecution and thousands of martyrdoms in Persian lands in the 4th and 6th centuries in particular. Yet more Christian communities were soon being established to the north in territories of Turkish or Mongol tribes, as well as eastwards as far as south China. There is now agreement that there are many episcopal and metropolitan sees recorded later for the Churches of the East, as existing within the far-flung Persian Patriarchate from the 4th until even the 16th centuries.

By the 8th/9th centuries these would number eighteen Metropolitans, with scores of Bishops also being appointed. These included bishoprics for territories identified as being in today's Syria, Iran and Iraq, former Soviet states of Central Asia, Arabia and Socotra, Afghanistan, Tibet, Pakistan and India, China, Indo-China and Burma, Thailand, Malaysia and Indonesia, Mongolia, Korea and Japan.[23] For some peoples there were mass Christian movements, from that of Armenians to form the first Christian state in 301 CE to that of Kerait Turks in 1007-8, and later conversions of Mongol tribes in the following century. [24] The history of these countless Persian, Turkish, Indian and other Christian communities shows some to be nomadic, some monastic, some largely expatriate at first, many flourishing in cosmopolitan ports or trading centres, some in the households of tribal Khans, local or imperial rulers, some in remotest valleys or desert oases.

It is a long history of surviving, despite often hostile state power and frequent martyrdoms; a mission largely by 'lay' people through their work in education, medical care, state service and trade. It is also a history of friendly coexistence – even mutual borrowing – with in particular, Buddhists, Manicheans and Muslims. The story is not so fragmentary as has been often thought, either in India, where the early traditions were preserved until the Portuguese arrived, nor in lands of west Asia where significant Christian communities remain in half a dozen countries (although now sadly under great threat). Nor was it so in China where there is evidence of Christian presence in the north and east from the first century (see below) even through the 10th to the 12th centuries, which are sometimes thought to be a complete gap in Chinese Christian history.[25]

Something of the diversity and extent of such Christian presence can be seen in stories from west China, Kyrgyzstan and south India. Shui-pang is a small town on one of the many routes of the old Silk Routes, near Balayik, Turfan, in Turkestan. And if we had been among the many travellers seeking rest or trade there, a thousand years ago, we would have come upon a fruitful oasis with farms, hostelries and monasteries, both Buddhist and Christian (as throughout many of the Silk routes). We would find too, an earth and stone church with a stupa tower, along with 'Nestorian' crosses and murals reminiscent of Byzantine art. Here we could attend worship led by a Syrian priest, reading the *Peshitta* version of the scriptures and celebrating the ancient Syriac liturgy. Our co-worshippers would be merchants and traders from Persia or China or any country in between, a few farmers and families, soldiers, traders and muleteers, most of whom would understand Syriac, which was closely related to Aramaic, as well as either Sogdian, Mongol or Turkic languages.

And if we stayed behind in the coolness to leaf through the collection of prayer books and scriptures used there, we might be surprised to discover among them a Psalter in the Pahlavi text of the 5th century; a translation in mid-Turkish of the *Georgios* legend as well as Christian apocalyptic writings. In Sogdian and other scripts, would be parts of the Nicene Creed, the Gospel of St Matthew, the legend of Helena and the Holy Cross; and in Syriac, liturgical and other manuscripts of the Church of the East, between them all, spanning many centuries and written in 24 different languages.[26]

The story of Christian settlements near the salt lake of Issyk-kul – now in Kyrgyzstan – is yet to be fully told, but its fascinating outlines emerge from the two ancient cemeteries there at Bishkek and Tokmak, each containing many hundreds of cross-engraved tombstones. The oldest date given for these is 858 and the latest 1342. The inscriptions on many were in the Syriac script but the names indicate that these people were native converts. One inscription reads, "This is the grave of Pasak : 'The aim of life is Jesus, our Redeemer.'" Another states, "This is the tomb of Shliha, the famous Exegete and Preacher who enlightened all the cloisters with Light, being the son of Exegete Peter. He was famous for his wisdom, and when preaching his voice sounded like a trumpet." There is also "The charming maiden Julia, betrothed of the Chorepiscopus (suffragan Bishop) Johanan". Among the names are those of "nine Archdeacons, eight doctors of ecclesiastical jurisprudence and of biblical interpretation, twenty-two (official) Visitors, three commentators, forty-six scholastics, two preachers and an imposing number of priests." [27] Evidence indeed of extensive Christian activities, institutions and settlements over many centuries.

The stories of St Thomas Christians of Kerala, co-existing peacefully with Hindu and Jewish neighbours from the 1st century on are to some extent well-known. We now have many accounts of the earliest Christian presence in Kerala; its apostolic foundation and favoured role under local Hindu rulers; early visits by Pantaneus (ca.180) and Cosmas Indicopleustes (ca.540); and the relations with Persia maintained by personal encounters and migration in the 8th century and later.[28] Too little attention has yet been given however to the accumulated evidence for the apostolic foundation of Indian Churches in not only the south but the north also.[29] Moffett concludes that Thomas "was the apostle to all India" and T.V. Philip summarises the evidence by saying that the evidence therefore "indicates that there were Christian communities scattered throughout the country in the early period." [30]

Also well-known is the 'Nestorian', or *Hsien-Fu* Monument which records in deeply contextualized form Christian presence in central China from the 6th century. The full story of that presence has however yet to be assembled. This begins with the remarkable and extensive evidence recently uncovered for Christian presence in China from as early as the first century; continues with other communities in the 3rd and 5th centuries,[31] the established institutions recorded in the Sian-fu Monument following the Edict of Toleration for Christians of the Emperor T'ai-tsung in 638 CE, and the foundation of scores of churches and monasteries in following centuries.[32] Although sometimes previously written off as legend this evidence has placed foundation of the Chinese church to be almost as early as that of the Indian churches. It also corroborates the accounts for other remains throughout China, parallel to, and enlarging, the story of Eastern Christians there.[33]

'Further India' and Beyond

For south-east and north-east Asia, I have outlined the evidence elsewhere,[34] yet even a brief summary must present at least some examples from the many records, some of which are still emerging. These would include documented accounts of Christian officers at the service of Sinhala Kings ('Ceylon') in the 5th and 6th centuries; evidence of Christian Indian and Persian traders in peninsular Malaya from the 7th century, and others at the medieval courts of Buddhist or Hindu rulers in Sumatran and Javanese kingdoms; records of churches growing from the work of Syrian and Persian missionaries in 8th century Korea and Japan. To the north and east were the established Christian settlements in such localities as Samarkand, Bukhara and Merv,[35] Tokmak and Bishkek, Turfan and Dunhuang, as well as amongst tribal groupings of the steppes.[36] Epigraphical, manuscript and artefact evidence is particularly extensive from the 9th– 11th centuries in many of these areas.[37]

For the later period there is evidence that in the Mongol Empire, Christians were present in all the four khanates: the Golden Horde in the northwest, the Chagatai Khanate in the centre, the Ilkhanate in the southwest, and the Yuan dynasty in the east based in Khanbaliq (modern-day Beijing). It is well-known that Marco Polo also found Christians amongst Kurds, Arabs and Turks, in Samarkand, Kashgar, and Yarkand, in Chinese cities further east, as well as in Malabar and Quilon in India, and in the Maldives and Socotra. Many such Christians were acting, as in previous centuries, as scribes or administrators, physicians, interpreters, viziers and astronomers.[38] We know that family members of the khans were Christian and that Christians were in any case accorded tolerance and recognition in the courts of the khans, and in the case of such families as that of the Bukhtishu or of Ai Xieh, appointed to the highest administrative positions. Some of the khans such as Guyuk (d.1248) and Hulagu (d.1265), showed on occasion marked sympathy to Christians even in their military policies.[39]

So the evidence, and the stories, of Christian presence and activity is found not only in rare manuscripts, but also in church buildings, some now partially restored on site; in priceless frescoes and silk paintings scattered now in more than twenty museums (though in a few cases still to be seen in cave, chapel or ruined temple e.g. in the Tien Shan and Gobi regions); in the extensive village ruins or cemeteries remaining from Christian settlements or graves in many centres in for example, eastern Turkestan and Mongolia; and in collections of inscriptions, crosses, texts and seals in southern India, central and eastern China, and throughout north-east and south-east Asia.[40]

To underline the fact that here we are handling the story of an Asia-wide movement which has left tangible evidence of widespread exchanges and genuinely contextual Christian thought, we should note that one of the Japanese manuscripts, now held in the *Nishi-Hoganji* temple in Kyoto is *'The Lord of the Universe' Discourse on Alms-giving*'[41], a copy of the manuscript discovered originally in Dunhuang, west China. This preserves the Sermon on the Mount and other Matthaean passages. To show yet another international linkage it is translated in the language and thought-forms of 9th century Turkestan. This is not surprising when we remember that the cities of Nara, and later Kyoto, were two of the final destinations for many travellers on early and medieval trade routes. Many relics of that long continued trade and travel are held there, in particular in the Shoso Repository of Todai Temple at Nara. Then there are the two carved Sogdian silver dishes of the $9^{th}/10^{th}$ centuries, which utilise the Buddhist pattern of consecutive medallions to depict, in one, incidents in the battle for Jericho, and in the other, the crucifixion, burial and resurrection of Christ. These seem to have been crafted in northern Turkestan but show the craftsmanship of Persian Sasanian artists; they were discovered far to the west in the Ural mountain region, but can now be seen even further west in the Hermitage Museum, St Petersburg. Clear evidence of wide international and inter-faith exchanges and participation.[42]

There are also the eleven libraries of Syriac manuscripts held now in Trichur and other centres of South India[43] – many inscribed by and received from Persian Christians. There are also the early relics from *Xuzhou, Xian* and *Da Quin* China along with Chinese manuscripts from east Turkestan and coastal China.[44] And then there are the range of seals and inscriptions discovered across the whole area of the Mongol Empire.[45] These all give similar evidence of widespread yet localized Christian creativity. Across the region have been found other manuscripts, artefacts or carvings found in ruins, paintings and frescoes (often located in large caves), grave-stones, collections of Christin coins, tablets and seals. Many of these are still being discovered as archaeologists, historians (or developers!) continue to uncover ancient sites or ruins. A large number of the texts and scrolls discovered over a century ago in localities such as Turfan or Dunhuang, and now held in more than thirty libraries and museums across the world, are yet to be identified or interpreted.

Key Figures and Characteristics of the Tradition

If we attempt a spectrum of key theological figures of the 2nd to 6th centuries these would include, in the briefest listing along with Tatian, the eclectic philosopher Bardaisan (d.222), the 'Persian Sage' Aphrahat (d.345), the orthodox defender and hymn-writer Ephrem Syrus (d.373), the pilgrim author Lady Egeria (4th cent.), along with theologians of the humanity of Christ, Theodore of Mopsuestia (d.428) and his student Nestorius (d.451). Amongst many other leading figures from across the Asia region, these were followed by the exegete and poet Narsai (d.ca.503), lady prophet Euphemia (6th cent.), geographer Cosmas Indicopleustes (6th cent.), the 'Theolologian' Mar Babai (d.628), missionary to China A-Lo-Pen (fl.635), linguist and author Adam Ching-Ching (7th cent), the polymath Jacob of Edessa (d.708), founder of monasteries in China Mar Sergius, (8th cent.),administrative reformer and scholar Patriarch Timothy 1 (d.823), Arab linguist and physician Hunayn ibn Ishaq (d.873), the Syrian physician and astronomer Qusta ibn Luqa (d.912), the "Nestorian" chronicler Mari (fl.1140), scientific author Jacob bar Sakko (d.1241), leading mother of four Khans Sorghaghtani (d. 1252), Chancellor to Kubilai Khan Ai Xieh (d.1308), Persian historian and philosopher Bar Hebraeus (d.1286), Mongol envoy to Europe Rabban Sauma (d.1294), Patriarch Shim'un bar Mama (d. 1551), and Bishop Mar Jacob of Malabar (d.1552).

The theology of these forebears in the faith was initially rooted in Antiochene traditions which stressed a more historical, 'rational' and 'simple' exegesis of the scriptures, and of the humanity of Jesus. This was in contrast to the stronger emphasis upon his 'divinity' found in the allegorical approaches of the Alexandrians. This preserved many of the features of Semitic monotheism and of Syrian Christology along with a less ontological view of the Trinity.[46] This was sometimes understood to be largely an 'economic' understanding of the Godhead, and an 'adoptive' understanding of Christ's person, stressing complementary function rather than the absolutes (and speculations) of later philosophical categories.[47] The humanity of Jesus, which was nonetheless revealing God, was strongly emphasized in many of their traditions and this was later to develop in richly symbolic theologies of Christ and the church.[48] Theodore, Nestorius and their colleagues especially, tended to see Christ, not as the God-man, but a 'man indwelt by God'. Many in the early churches of the east were therefore either untouched by the controversies of Nicaea or Chalcedon or rejected such definitions and also in consequence frequently suffered persecution for such deviance.

Some of their scholars have in fact left the results of extensive critical study of the Bible, recognising different values for various sections or authors, which long pre-date some methodologies we sometimes class as 'modern'. Doctrines that exalted the mother of Jesus to be more than mother of his humanity, or others such as that of 'original sin', or what was later termed 'substitutionary atonement', were unrecognised by most of those named above or below. There was of course no imposition of the crucified body of Jesus upon any of the richly diverse images of the cross.[49]

The rich language and symbolism of early eastern Christian literatures which have so far been discovered and translated, still surprise us as well as providing exciting imagery that is accessible to us today. A few examples from many would include: the whole creation being pictured as "an arrow kept in flight by the power of God"; the name of God given as the "Lord of Heaven who is constantly present everywhere"; the Holy Spirit being described as the "pure cool wind" (in hot or tropical lands); portrayal of Jesus' earthly life as being "for the sake of all humankind"; the relation between earthy life and life hereafter being imaged as "what the mother's womb is to her child so this world is to the eternal world..."; and salvation being pictured as "the saving dew" (for desert communities), or as "the safe raft on a sea of fire"(originally a Buddhist image).[50]

In the Indian traditions which were to influence those further east, it is clear from inscriptions, documents and songs, and from the surviving libraries, that Syriac traditions were formative and that direct personal links were maintained over some centuries with parent churches in Persia. The empty cross remained central to devotion[51] as did the loving concern of Christ known directly in human affairs. There is also evidence that for these traditions the faith was expressed in daily work and social justice as well as in missionary outreach to (for example) China and Central Asia.[52]

Their liturgies, which are still in use in many communities between Syria, south India, and Japan, enshrine early Syrian and Semitic forms, such as those in the Liturgy of *SS. Adai and Mari*. Here can be recognised a strong focus upon the experience of salvation received, as well as on the presence of Christ in the Eucharist to re-create the world, establish the Kingdom and fulfil all things.[53] We have here a full Eucharistic order that does not include any of the terms that focus upon vicarious suffering, whether this be 'sacrifice', 'propitiation', 'expiation' or the shedding of blood. The purpose of this worship, as of the life which it celebrates is rather the 'restoration of the world' and the transformation of all life. The Eucharist, along with sacraments for Initiation (when the whole body was anointed) and Ordination (by laying on of hands), all gave central place also to the transforming power of the Holy Spirit. [54]

Some patterns of their piety were often strongly ascetic, and grew from strong monastic movements, both in Persia and also in China, Turkestan and India. Yet it was a piety which nourished the trader and traveller, the artisan and physician, teacher, presbyter and administrator. Many of these spent a period in one of the many colleges or monasteries famous for their missionary outreach. The scholars of this tradition, often also themselves traders or pilgrims, monks, physicians or administrators, were responsible for the first extensive translation of the classical corpus of Greece and Rome, through which theologians in European contexts would in turn first encounter the philosophies and literatures of the ancient world. Many of these scholars also held high rank in the Caliphate – being physicians or Viziers to various Caliphs, or in the administration of kingdoms in central Asia, or in the courts of Khans or Chieftains.[55] We have evidence that Christians continued to fill these roles throughout much of the region until the 10th century and beyond.[56]

Perhaps most surprising to us will be the attitude of these Christian forebears to those of other faiths, for the judgment of Mundadan regarding St Thomas Christians could be made also of those in Turkestan and much of China: "...the Indian Christians had already been living for centuries in a positive encounter with the high-caste Hindus and had developed a theological vision of the Hindu religion which was more positive and liberal."[57] It is only necessary to consider the writings we have now from such centres as Dunhuang or Turfan to see that the accepted co-existence and collegial encounter between Christians and those of other faiths easily led to mutual exchange and borrowing, both of terms and concepts.[58]

The case of Islam is somewhat different yet we have records of significant Christian-Muslim dialogues that sometimes involved the caliph himself.[59] In the wake of Muslim conquests diverse controls and compromises were imposed on Christian communities by different Caliphs and Khans. By some of these rulers, Christians – but not churches or monasteries – were required to pay special tribute taxes, especially in lieu of military service. On one hand Christians might be excused from public office and 'encouraged to convert' to Islam (Umar II), while by other caliphs church-building would be banned and the branding of all Christians proposed (Mansur)! Yet although under these and other sustained pressures and taxation many tribal groupings would become Muslim, we also see prominent Christians often engaging in debate, and sometimes dialogue, with Muslim scholars. These encounters were to include such leading Christians as the polymath John of Damascus, the Patriarch Timothy I, Theodore Abu Qurrah, Ishoyab b. Malkam, Abd al-Masih ibn Ishaq al-Kindi, Yayha b.'Adi and later those such as Barhebraeus.[60]

Implications of the Legacy

Clearly, we have yet to take seriously the extensive bodies of literature which have been left to us from the many-sided life and mission of these early Christians. As *Shui-pang* and other sites show, these are not only diverse in content but also in form and language. The largest bodies extant are found in Syriac and Sogdian, which over many centuries were used as far east as coastal China, as far north as Korea and as far south as Kerala, India. But collections have survived also in such languages as various Turkic, Chinese and Indian dialects.[61] These Asian Christian writings include hymns and poetry, treatises, homilies and chronicles, scholia (commentaries), letters, liturgies, parables, biographies and epitaphs and of course Bible translations. Many of these have yet to be catalogued or translated into contemporary vernaculars as well as to be freed from the misunderstandings imposed by later Roman Catholic and Protestant interpreters.

It must be stressed again that this is part of our own history – the 'other half' of Christian history that is so often ignored. The stories of early 'Nestorian', 'Jacobite', 'Monophysite', Orthodox, 'Assyrian' or Armenian Christians in our countries are our forebears' stories and part of the story of the Christian movement in over half the world. It must also be recognised that the stories include not only those of survival but also those of slow decline; not only of 'success' in mission but also 'failure', and this for many political or even military reasons. [62] The devastations resulting from Mongol invasions were particularly destructive of both pasturage and water supplies but also of countless communities themselves. Eventually the local divergences too, partly because of communication over great distances, became very wide and the administration centralized on Persia, less and less effective. Rapid changes in state policy, or in nomadic and migrant communities sometimes greatly weakened the churches so that it became possible for their creative traditions and history to be largely absorbed by later Roman Catholic, Orthodox, or Protestant missions.

We are not however to conclude that the Christian community in Asian lands disappeared entirely from this or that people's life. The examples of persistent presence in countries such as India, China or more recently Japan show this to be in error. In any case we can see that this far-flung network of Christian churches remained largely in place over immense distances for at least more than 12 centuries. Evidence still emerging shows also that at least scattered communities or their traditions survived much longer. And this in itself carries deep significance for our own work in education, theology, and mission. Rich resources for the present life and thought of all would-be Christians are offered in their courageous endeavours to live the faith, in their spirituality and monastic movements, their services to state administration, education and medical care, their thought and writings which are surprisingly contemporary. Especially significant for us is their mutually beneficial co-existence with neighbours of other faiths, as well as their survival despite often brutal repression and persecution.

And whatever access we may have to some of the primary materials, we can now study their legacy in many sources. (Refer Select Bibliography below). The literature from Tatian to Bar Hebraeus, and on to Yabh-alaha has been presented by scholars like Wright, Budge, Murray, Aprem, and Keelathu; the tradition of monastic and missionary education by Wensinck, Voobus, Latourette, and Colless amongst others. The emerging continuity within the larger Church history of Asian countries is dealt with by J. Foster, W. Young, B. Colless, S.H. Moffett, I. Gillman & H-J. Klimkeit, T.V. Philip, J.C. England, Valentino Sitoy, W. Baum & D.W. Winkler, C. Baumer, and others. The holistic character of faith and witness which embraced in these traditions the life of monastic and lay person, craftsman, merchant and government servant, appears in J. Stewart, B. Colless, Gillman & Klimkeit, C. Baumer, and many others. The surprising degree of co-existence and exchange, possibly 'dialogue', between Christians and their neighbours in early pluralistic communities, is treated by others like E.A. Gordon, W. Barthold, Gillman & Klimkeit, S. Lieu, D.S.Lopez & S.C. Rockefeller, G. Khodr, Li Tang & D.W. Winkler, and P. Perrier.

The conclusion to be drawn, that for us as for our ancient forebears, western Christianity is not normative, and that our theologies are to grow from our own particular contexts, is very clearly applied by many recent scholars, among them such as Kim Yong Bock, M.M. Thomas, S. Kappen, C.S. Song, A. Pieris, Suh Kwang Sun, Inoue Yoji, Edicio de la Torre and C.L. Wickremasinghe – to mention only a few contemporary Asian writers. And many of these, notably Song and Pieris, have published extensively on the theological leap from Israel to Asia in which Asian theologies – and church historiography – are engaged.[63]

The simplest conclusions for our personal understanding and life then, if we were to fully recognise such a rich history, would include a greater consciousness of, and response to:

i) the historical and contemporary *Asian* character of Christian faith – enriching our own sense of Asian Christian identity;

ii) the context for all Christian life of the world company of Christians and our active membership of the world church;

iii) the deep unity of worship and prayer with most diverse life experiences – of learning to the offering of daily work and life-with-others as themselves being worship;

iv) the resources for church and community in inter-faith co-existence – where the creative elements of each living faith are shared and understood;

v) the acceptance that life in faith communities is life as minorities – as it always has been in Asian Christian history, and is in almost all our present contexts;

vi) the rich heritage for us in the humanist study, writing and art, social participation and service of Asian Christians in our histories.

These then are some of the implications of the history and its wealth of stories - as they are of the more recent stories of the Christian movements where they are rooted in the life situations and cultures of particular peoples. This is the other half of Christian traditions in which we stand, and which we must each rediscover and amplify as we seek to be participants in the Christian movement in Asia, or indeed in any country.

Endnotes

[1] Neale 1847, 1:3.

[2] Amongst many works on this history see for example, A.S.Atiya 1991; S.H.Moffett 1992; J.C.England 1998; T.V.Philip 1998); I.Gillman & H-J. Klimkeit 1999; Mar Abraham 2000; Baum, W. & D.W. Winkler, 2003; C.Baumer, 2006; Li Tang & D.W.Winkler 2013.

The attempt is made in this chapter to learn from but avoid employing earlier 'orientalist', 'modernizing' or 'neo-orientalist' assumptions in studying histories of Christianity in the Asian region.

[3] See Foster 1972, 85ff.; Young 1969, passim; Gillman & Klimkeit 1998, pp.1-6; England 2002 pp.1-11;

[4] Colless 1969, 34f.; Leslie 1981-83, 276-295.

[5] As in Braaten 1963.

[6] As examples of early historical studies see G.Assemani 1719; Yule-Cordier 1866; Abu Salih 1894-5; Mingana 1926; Pelliot 1930; Moule, 1930.

[7] See Gibson 1965, 14f.; Atiya 1991(1968), 255ff.; Latourette 1971.I, 101ff.; Brock 1979; Neusner 1985, 16ff.

[8] Refer in particular to Mingana 1926; Pelliot 1930; Dauvillier 1948, 1983; Saeki 1951, A.S.Atiya 1991 (1968), Gillman & Klimkeit 1999, Halbertsma 2008; Li Tang and Winkler 2013.

[9] *The Diatessaron, which Titianus Compiled from the Four Gospels* (Vatican Library 1888, latest version *The Diatessaron - A Harmony of the Gospels* - Taschenbuch 2009). Translations of this have been found in Armenian, Arabic, Old Georgian, Persian, Syriac, Greek and Latin. Refer Moffett 1.73f.

[10] Oldest Biblical Manuscripts (Aramaic, 5th cent.) are held in the British Museum. The *Peshitta* is now being published as the *Antioch Bible* by Gorgias Press.

[11] J. H. Charlesworth, 2009.

[12] See further in illustrations for chap. 3 "The Early Christian Art of Asian People".

[13] Voobus, 1965: There had most likely been Christians at Edessa by beginning of the 2nd cent. See Mark Cartwright www.ancient.eu/edessa/ - 25 September 2018.

[14] See e.g. O'Leary *1949; Starr,* 2013.

[15] As in Tibbetts 1957, 5-7; Wolters 1967, 73; Colless 1969, 13; See also e.g. Atiya 256f.,287; Moffett 1992 1.144;

[16] Yule-Cordier 1866.I, 101ff.; Colless 1969-77 passim.

[17] Amongst many sources see Mingana 1925, 320-336; Foster 1939, 61 f.; Grousset 1970, 125; Barthold 1977, 38ff.; Hopkirk 1980, 27, 61, 123, 130, 184; Hickley 1980, 9, 14, 21; Colless 1969, Vol.IX: 31 f.; Klimkeit 1985; Baumer 2006; Li Tang and Winkler 2013.

[18] See Voobus 1958; Gillman & Klimkeit 1999, 56ff., 148ff., 295ff.; Palmer 2001, 11-38; Baumer 2006, 93, 111ff., 126ff.

[19] Brock and Harvey 1998. See also Wilkinson 2006.

[20] A number of examples of 'women of the east' are included in such studies as Catherine Kroeger 1988; R.S. Kraemer R.S. & Mary Rose D'Angelo 1999; Lynn H. Cohick 2009; Karen King 1998.

[21] Cited in Rossabi 1992. See also Weatherford 2010; Li, Tang "Sorkaktani Beki: A prominent 'Nestorian' woman at the Mongol Court", in Malek & Hofrichter, 2004.

[22] See Weatherford 2010.

²³ See e.g. Mingana 1926,; Vine 1937, 112ff.; Atiya 1991(1968), 265f.; Gillman and Klimkeit 1999; Baum and Winkler 2003; K. Parry, 2006; C.Baumer 2006; D. Wilmshurst, D., 2011; Li and Winkler 2013.

²⁴ Stewart 143f., and in the 10th- 12th cents. these would be followed by Onguts, Uighurs, Buriyats, Naimans and Kang-li.

²⁵ See Renaudet 1733, 121;; Vine 1937, 135; Dauvillier 1948, 298f.; Hajjar 1986, 3-20; Atiya 1991(1968), 262f. Saeki 1951, 369; Ding Wang 2004; Johnson 2011, 80.

²⁶ For example von le Coq, 1928, 1958, 100; Palmer 2001; Riegert & Moore, 2003; Sims-Williams, 2007; Hunter 2012.

²⁷ Chwolson 1896 I-III cited Mingana 1925, 40f.; Stewart 1928, 206f.; Atiya 261, Grousset 1970, 80ff.,115.

²⁸ See e.g. Mundadan 1984, 64; Mar Aprem 1976, 77ff.; England 1998, chap 4; Philip 1998, chap. 7; Zacharia, 2016; Gillman & Klimkeit 1999, 162ff.

²⁹ Stewart 1928, 85; Menachery 1973 vol.1 "The First Centuries"; Philip 1998, 101f., 116f., 122ff.; see also https://orthodoxwiki.org/Timeline_of_Oriental_Orthodoxy_in_India.

³⁰ Moffett 1992, vol.1 36; Philip 1998, 124.

³¹ Refer Irving 1919, 528; Budge 1928, 32; McCullough 1982, 180; Wang 2003, Perrier & Walter 2008, chaps.VI-CIII.

³² See Moule 1930, 86ff., Foster 1939, 61; Saeki 1951, 53, Leslie 1983, 281ff.; England 1998, 69-87; Wang Weifan 2003. See also the Exhibition "Christianity in Asia: Sacred Art and Visual Splendour" (*Asian Civilisations Museum*, Singapore, May 2016); Pierre Perrier and Xavier Walter 2008 . See also Perrier, 2012 and 2015; Hunter 2012.

³³ Gordon 1914, 17ff.; Moule 1930, 82,129ff., 1939, 61; Foster 1954, 1-25; Leslie 1981-83, 281ff.; Saeki 1951, 429ff.; Palmer 2001, chaps.6-8.

³⁴ England 1998.

³⁵ Recently added in many sources including Baumer 2006, 169.

³⁶ Gillman & Klimkeit 1999, 212ff. 220f.

³⁷ England 1998, chaps 3-7; McCrindle 1897, 118ff, 363f.; Arasaratnam 1964, 52f., 57; Colless 1969-1977, IV.121; Holdcroft 1972, 80f.; Oh Yoon Rae 1973, 242-290; Young 1984, 19; Schafer 1985, 2; Quéré 1987, 133ff., 137f.,144; also Grayson 1989.

³⁸ In many sources including Moffett 1992 382f.; Baumer 2006, 152f., 157f.

³⁹ England 1998 77ff.; Gillman & Klimkeit 1999, 287ff.; Halbertsma 2008 and Weatherford 2010, passim.

⁴⁰ See chapter 3, 'Early Christian Art along the Old Silk Roads' in this volume.

⁴¹ Saeki 1951, 206-247.

⁴² Gillman & Klimkeit 1999 plate 21. See also chap. 3 below.

⁴³ Van der Ploeg 1983 provides a full study of these sources.

⁴⁴ Saeki 1951; Palmer 2001; Wang Weifan 2003.

⁴⁵ See Halbertsma 2008.

[46] See fuller notes on this in chap.7 of this volume.

[47] Refer Baker 1908; Loofs 1914; Vine, 1948; Greer 1961; Norris 1963; Wallace-Hadrill 1982; also refs. in *The Oxford Dictionary of the Christian Church* (3 rev. ed.) 2009, 78f.

[48] Murray 1975, 2 and passim.; Baumer 2006, 115ff.

[49] Introduction of the crucifix, and the 'atonement' theologies on which it was based was only a later western practice. For a fine treatment of these issues see Brock & Parker 2008, chap 10 especially 267-68, 292-3.

[50] Many of these were first given fully in Saeki 1951, chaps. IV-XVII, but more recent translations, by e.g. Sims-Williams, 2007, and Hunter 2012 greatly expand the vocabulary.

[51] See 'Early Christian Art...' in this volume.

[52] Kuriakose 1982, 9,21ff.,73f.; Moule 1930, 228ff.; T.V. Philip 1998, 128f.

[53] Dix 1949, 183ff.; Baumer 2006, 117.

[54] Murray 1975, 21f.

[55] See e.g. Frankopan (2015) 97f. re Bukhtishu dynasty of Gundeshapur of the 8th and 9th centuries; Moule 1930 et seq. regarding Ai Xieh's dynasty of administrators for the Mongol Khans. See also Gillman & Klimkeit 1999, 101f., 130, 146; Winkler 2010, 88f., 95f.; Rossabi, passim. 1992.

[56] Bretschneider 1987 (1910), I.180-191; Gillman & Klimkeit 1999, 68, 139..

[57] Mundadan 1984, 494.

[58] See Saeki op.cit. 1951, chaps IV-XVII.

[59] Gillman & Klimkeit 1999, 87; Winkler 2010, 100ff. 110ff..

[60] See Muir 1887; Samir & Nielsen 1994, chaps. 1-3,5,7; Gillman & Klimkeit 1999, 67ff., 84f., 131ff.; Griffith 2008, chaps. 1-5; Winkler 2010, chaps 2-5.

[61] Wright 1894; Aprem 1982, 1983; Saeki 1951 53 & passim.

[62] Reasons given by Browne 1933 and echoed by others show inadequate attention to sources and contexts..

[63] See Song 1974 , and Pieris 1988 et al. above

Select Bibliography for further study

Abu Salih *Description of Churches and Monasteries of Egypt and Some Neighbouring Countries.* B.T.A. Evetts, trans. Oxford University Press, 1894-95.

Aprem, Mar *'Nestorian' Missions.* Mar Nasai Press, 1976.

_____. *A 'Nestorian' Bibliography.* Mar Nasai Press, 1982.

_____. 'Syriac Manuscripts in Trichur'. *Orientalia Christiana Analecta* 221: 355-374, 1983.

Assemani, Giuseppe *Bibliotheca orientalis Clementino-Vaticana.* Vatican, 1719.

Atiya, Aziz S. *A History of Eastern Christianity.* Methuen, Kraus, 1991 (1968).

Baker, J F Bethune *Nestorius and His Teaching.* Cambridge, 1908.

Barthold, W. *Turkestan to the Mongol Invasion* (4th ed.). E.J.W.Gibb Memorial Trust, 1977.

Baumer, C. *The Church of the East. An Illustrated History of Assyrian Christianity.* Tauris, 2006.

Ba Than Win 'Christians of the First Burmese Dynasty (1044-1300)'. Yangon: Ba Than Win, 1982.

Baum, W. & D.W. Winkler *The Church of the East.* Routledge Curzon, 2003.

Baumer, C. *The Church of the East. An Illustrated History of Assyrian Christianity.* Tauris, 2006.

Braaten, C. 'Modern Interpretations of Nestorius'. *Church History* 32(3) 251-267, 1963.

Bretschneider, E. *Mediaeval Researches from Eastern Asiatic Sources.* Biblio Verlag, 1987 (London, 1910).

Brock, S. (Intro. & trans.) *The Syriac Fathers on Prayer and the Spiritual Life.* Cistercian Publications, 1987.

_____. *Spirituality in the Syriac Tradition.* Moran 'Etho series 2. St Ephraim Ecumenical Research Institute, 1989.

_____. *The Bible in the Syrian Tradition.* SEERI Correspondence Course (SCC) on Syrian Christian Heritage. St Ephrem Ecumenical Research Institute, [?1989]

_____. *The luminous eye : the spiritual world vision of Saint Ephrem* (Rev. ed.). Cistercian Publications, 1992.

_____ & Harvey, Susan A. *Holy Women of the Syrian Orient.* University of California Press, 1998.

_____ et al. (eds.) *Gorgias Encyclopedic Dictionary of the Syriac Heritage.* Gorgias, 2011.

Brock, Rita N. & Rebecca A. Parker *Saving Paradise; How Christianity Traded Love of this World for Crucifixion and Empire.* Beacon Press, 2008.

Browne, L. E. *The Eclipse of Christianity in Asia.* Cambridge, 1933

Budge, E.A.W. *The Monks of Kublai Khan Emperor of China.* Religious Tract Society, 1928.

Burkitt, F.C. *Early Christianity Outside The Roman Empire.* John Murray, 1899.

_____. *Early Eastern Christianity.* John Murray, 1904.

Butler, J.F. 'The Iconography of the Ancient South Indian Incised Crosses'. *Indian Church History Review* 3(2) 83-95, 1969.

Charlesworth, J. H. *The Earliest Christian Hymnbook.* Cascade, 2009.

Cheryan, C.V. *A History of Christianity in Kerala.* Kerala Historical Society & C.M.S. Press, 1970.

Cohick, Lynn H. *Women in the World of the Earliest Christians* (Baker Academic, 2009).

Colless, B. 'Persian Markets and Missionaries in Medieval Malaya'. *Journal of the Malayan Branch of the Royal Asiatic Society* 42(2) 10-47, 1969.

_____. 'The Traders of the Pearl: The Mercantile and Missionary Activities of Persian and Armenian Christians in South East Asia'. Article series *Abr-Nahrain*, vols. 9-17, 1969-77.

Dauvillier, J. 'Les provinces chaldéenes 'de l'extérieur' au moyen age', in *Melanges Offerts au R.P. Ferd. Cavallera*. Institut Catholique de Toulouse 260-316, 1948.

_____. *Histoire et institutions des Eglises orientales au Moyen Age*. Collected Studies series. Variorum Reprints, 1983.

Dickens, M. www.academia.edu/398258/Nestorian_Christianity_In_Central_Asia

Ding Wang 'Remnants of Christianity from Chinese Central Asia in Medieval Ages' in R. Malek & P. Hofrichter (eds.) *Jingjiao: Church of the East in China and Central Asia*. Steyler Verlag, 2006.

Dix, G. *The Shape of the Liturgy*. Dacre Press, 1949.

England, John C. *The Hidden History of Christianity in Asia; the Churches of the East before 1500*. (2nd ed.) ISPCK, 1998.

Fernando, M. (ed.) *Visionary Wisdom of a People's Bishop : Selected Texts Rt.Revd. C. Lakshman Wickremasinghe.*: Ecumenical Institute for Study and Dialogue, 2009.

Foltz, R. *Religions of the Silk Road : premodern patterns of globalization*. Palgrave Macmillan, 2010.

Foster, J. *The 'Nestorian' Monument and Hymn*. S.P.C.K., 1938.

_____. *The Church of the Tang Dynasty*. S.P.C.K., 1939.

_____. *The First Advance : Church History I, 29-500* C.E. Theological Education Fund & S.P.C.K., 1972.

Frankopan, P. *The Silk Roads. A New History of the World*. Bloomsbury, 2015.

Gibson, J.C.L. 'From Qumran to Edessa'. *New College Bulletin*: 2(2) 9-20, 1965.

Gillman, I. & H-J. Klimkeit *Christians in Asia before 1500* . Curzon, 1999.

Gordon, E.A. *World Healers, of the Lotus Gospel and its Bodhisattvas*. Maruzen, SPCK & Morice. 1914.

Greer, R.A. *Theodore of Mopsuestia*. Faith Press, 1961

Grierson, G.A. 'Modern Hinduism and its debt to the 'Nestorian's'. *Journal of Royal Asiatic Society*. April: 311-335 (Offprint No. 476), 1907.

Griffith, S. H. *The Church in the Shadow of the Mosque. Christians & Muslims in the World of Islam*. Princeton Univ. Press, 2008.

Grousset, R. *The Empire of the Steppes: A History of Central Asia*. Rutgers University Press, 1970.

Hajjar, Yousef (ed.) *Arab Christianity*. Geneva: *WSCF Journal - Special issue*, 1986.

Halbertsma, T.H.F. *Early Christian Remains of Inner Mongolia* (Brill, 2008).

Hall, D.G.E. *A History of South-east Asia*. 4th ed. MacMillan, 1985.

Hambye, E.R. 'Some Fresh Documentation on Medieval Christianity in India & Further India'. *Indian Church History Review*. Dec. 3(2) 97-101, 1969.

Hickley, D. *The First Christians in China*. China Study Project, 1980.

History of Nestorian Church www.nestorian.org/history_of_the_nestorian_church.html

Holdcroft, J.G. *Into All The World*. Independent Board for Presbyterian Foreign Missions, 1972.

Hopkirk, P. *Foreign Devils on the Silk Road : The Search for Lost Cities and Treasures of Chinese Central Asia*. Oxford University Press, 1980.

Hourani, G.F. *Arab Seafaring in the Indian Ocean in Ancient and Early Medieval Times*. Princeton University Press, 1951.

Hunter, Erica 'The Christian Library at Turfan'. *Hugoye* 15.2, 2012.

Inoue, Yoji *The Face of Jesus in Japan*. Kindai-Bungeisha, 1994.

Irving, C. "A Chinese temple of the Cross". *New China Review* 1:522-533.

Johnson, D.A. *Asian Jesus in China* New Sinai, 2011.

Kappen, S. *Jesus and Cultural Revolution: An Asia Perspective*. BUILD, (1982)

KeeLathu, J.J. 'The History of Syriac Literature' https://www.academia.edu/4977931/

Khodr, G. 'Christianity in a Pluralistic World - Economy of the Holy Spirit'. in *Living Faiths and the Ecumenical Movement*, S.J. Samartha, ed. Geneva, W.C.C. 131-142, 1971

Kidd, B.J. *History of the Church to C.E. 461*. Faith Press, 1927.

Kim Yong Bock *Minjung Theology: People as the Subject of History*. CCA-CTC, 1981.

King, Karen "Women in Ancient Christianity: the New Discoveries" at www.pbs.org/wgbh/pages/frontline/shows/religion/first/women.html April 1998.

Klimkeit, H-J. 'Christian-Buddhist Encounter in Medieval Central Asia'. in *The Cross and the Lotus*. G.W. Houston, ed. Motilal Banarsidass. 6-24, 1985.

Kraemer, R.S. & Mary Rose D'Angelo (eds.) *Women and Christian Origins* (Oxford University Press, 1999)

Catherine Kroeger "The Neglected History of Women in the Early Church" (*Christian History* Vol. #17 1988).

Kuriakose, M.K *History of Christianity in India: Source Materials*. Senate of Serampore College & Christian Literature Society, 1982.

Labourt, J. *Le Christianisme dans L'Empire Perse sous la Dynastie Sassanide*. Paris, 1904.

Latourette, K. *History of the Expansion of Christianity* (7 vols.) Eyre and Spottiswood, 1945-47.

Legge, J. *The Nestorian Monument of Shian Fu in Shensi*. Trubner & Co. 1888.

Leslie, D.D. 'Persian Temples in Tang China'. *Monumenta Serica* 35: 276-295, 1981-83.

Li, Tang "Sorkaktani Beki: A prominent 'Nestorian' woman at the Mongol Court", in Malek,& Hofrichter, 2004.

_____ & Dietmar W.Winkler (eds.) *From the Oxus River to the Chinese Shores.* LIT Verlag, 2013.

_____ & Dietmar W. Winkler (eds.) *Winds of Jingjiao.* LIT Verlag 2016.

Lieu, S.N.C. *Manichaeism in the Later Roman Empire and Medieval China: A Historical Survey.* Manchester University Press, 1985.

Loofs, R. *Nestorius and his place in the History of Christian doctrine.* Cambridge, 1914;

Lopez D.S. Jr. & Steven C. Rockefeller (eds.) *The Christ and the Bodhisattva.* SUNY, 1987.

McCrindle, J.W. T*he Christian Topography of Cosmas, An Egyptian Monk.* Hakluyt Society, 1897.

McCullough, W.S. *A Short History of Syriac Christianity to the Rise of Islam.* Scholars Press, 1982.

Malek, R. & P. Hofrichter (eds.) *Jingjiao: the Church of the East in China and Central Asia.* Steyler Verlagsbuchhandlung GmbH, 2004.

Mar Abraham *Forgotten East.* Ephrem's Pubns. 2001.

Mathew, C.P. & Thomas, M.M. *The Indian Churches of Saint Thomas.* I.S.P.C.K., 1967.

Menachery, G. (ed.) *The St. Thomas Christian Encyclopaedia of India.* 2 vols. Trichur, STCEI, 1973.

Mingana, A. *The Early Spread of Christianity in Central Asia and the Far East. Bulletin of John Rylands* Library, 9(2) 297-371, 1925.

_____. *The Early Spread of Christianity in India.* BJRL 10(2) 435-495, 1926..

Moffett, S.H. *A History of Christianity in Asia* (vol.1). Harper Collins, 1992.

Moule, A.C. *Christians in China before the Year 1550.* S.P.C.K., 1930.

Muir, W. (ed.) *Apology of al-Kindy* (9th cent.?). S.P.C.K., 1887.

Mundadan, A.M. *Sixteenth Century Traditions of St Thomas Christians.* Dharmaram College, 1970.

_____. *History of Christianity in India (I). From the Beginning up to the Middle of the Sixteenth Century.* Bangalore Theological Publications, 1984.

Murray, R. *Symbols of Church and Kingdom - A Study in Early Syriac Tradition.* Cambridge University Press, 1975.

Muskens, M.P. *Partner in Nation Building : The Catholic Church in Indonesia.* Mission Aktuell Verlag, 1979.

Nau, F. *L'Expansion Nestorienne en Asie.*: S.P.C.K., 1914.

Neale, J.M. *History of the Holy Eastern Church.* 5 vols. J. Masters, 1847.

Neusner, J. *Judaism, Christianity and Zoroastrianism in Talmudic Babylonia.* University Press of America, 1986.

Norris, R.A. *Manhood and Christ.* Oxford, 1963
O'Leary, De L. *How Greek science passed to the Arabs.* Routledge and K. Paul, 1949.
Outerbridge, L.M. *The Lost Churches of China.* Westminster Press, 1952.
Palmer, M. *The Jesus Sutras.* Ballantyne, 2001.
Pelliot, P. 'Chrétiens d'Asie Centrale et d'Extreme Orient'. *T'oung Pao* 15: 623-644, 1914.
_____. 'Christianity in Central Asia in the Middle Ages'. *Journal of the Central Asian Society* 17(3) 301-312, 1930.
_____. *Recherches sur les Chrétiens d'Asie Central et d'Extrème Orient.* Imprimerie Nationale, 2006.
Parry, K. *The Blackwell Companion to Eastern Christianity,* Wiley-Blackwell, 2008.
Perrier, P. & X. Walter *Thomas fonde l'Eglise en Chine 65-68 après Jésus-Christ.* Sarment Éditions du Jubilé,, 2012.
_____. *L'évangélisation de la Chine de 64 à 87 .* Sarment Editions du Jubilé , 2015.
_____. *L'Évangile de la miséricorde: Avec les chrétiens d'Orient.* L'évangile au Cœur. Books on Demand, 2015.
Philip, T.V *East of the Euphrates. Early Christianity in Asia.* CSS & ISPCK, 1998.
Pieris, A. *An Asian Theology of Liberation.* Orbis Books, 1988.
_____. *Love Meets Wisdom: A Christian Experience of Buddhism.* Orbis,1988.
Quérè, M. 'Christianity in Sri Lanka Before the Coming of the Portugese'. *Aquinas Journal* (Sri Lanka) 4(2) 127-153, 1987.
Renaudet, E. (tr.) *Ancient Accounts of India and China by Two Mohammedan Travellers.* S. Harding, 1733
Rossabi, M. *Voyager from Xanadu: Rabban Sauma and the First Journey from China to the West.* Kodansha, 1992.
Saeki, P.Y. *The 'Nestorian' Monument.* Waseda University; S.P.C.K., 1916.
_____. *The 'Nestorian' Documents and Relics in China.* Maruzen & Co., 1951.
Samir, S.K. & Nielsen, J.S. (eds.) *Christian Arabic Apologetics 750-1258.* Brill, 1994.
Sims-Williams, N. 'Sogdian and Turkish Christians in the Turfan and TunHuang Manuscripts', in Cadonna, A. (ed), *Turfan and Tun-Huang: The Texts,* 2007.
_____. *Biblical and other Christian Sogdian texts from the Turfan Collection.* Brepols Publishers, 2014.
Starr, S. F. *Lost Enlightenment. Central Asia's Golden Age.* Princeton, 2013.
Sungshil Univeristy *Korean Christian Museum at Sungshil University.* Sungshil , 1988.
Stewart, J. *'Nestorian' Missionary Enterprise: The Story of a Church on Fire.* T. & T. Clark; Christian Literature Society, 1928.
Suh, D. Kwang-sun *Theology, Ideology and Culture.* WSCF Asia, 1983.
The Book of Ser Marco Polo the Venetian Concerning the Marvels and the Kingdoms of the East. Revised by H. Cordier. 2 vols. Gyan Books, 2018 (1903).

Tibbetts, G.R. 'Early Muslim Traders in South-East Asia'. *Journal of the Malayan Branch of the Royal Asiatic Society* 30(1) 1-45, 1957.

———. *A Study of the Arabic Texts Containing Material on Southeast Asia*. Royal Asiatic Society & Brill, 1979.

van der Ploeg, J.P.M. *The Syriac Manuscripts of St Thomas Christians*. Dharmaram Publications, 1983.

Vermander, B. "The Impact of Nestorianism in Contemporary Chinese Theology" in Malek & Hofrichter *2006*.

Vine, R.A. *An Approach to Christology*. Independent Press,1948.

von le Coq, A. *Buried Treasures of Chinese Turkestan*. Oxford University Press, 1985 (1928).

Vine, A.R. *The 'Nestorian' Churches*. Independent Press, 1937.

Vööbus, A. *A History of Asceticism in the Syrian Orient*. Secretariat du orpusco, *1958*.

———. *History of the School of Nisibis*, Louvain, 1965.

Wallace-Hadrill, D.S. *Christian Antioch- Early Christian Thought in the East*. Cambridge,1982;

Wang Wei Fan 'Christianity in China – 1st Century'. *China News Update*, January,2003.

Weatherford, J. *The Secret History of the Mongol Queens: How the Daughters of Genghis Khan Rescued His Empire's Crown*. Broadway, 2010.

Wensinck, A. *Bar Hebraeus's Book of the Dove*. Leiden, 1919.

Whitfield, R. (ed.) *The Arts of Central Asia : The Stein Collection in the British Museum - Paintings from Dunhuang*. 3 vols. British Museum & Kodansha, 1982.

Wilkinson, J. *Egeria's Travels*. Aris & Phillips, 2006.

Wilmshurst, D. *The Martyred Church: A History of the Church of the East*. East & West Publishing, 2011.

Winkler, D.W. (ed.) *Syriac Churches Encountering Islam*. Gorgias, 2010.

Wolters, D.W. *Early Indonesian Commerce : A Study of the Origins of Srivijaya*. Cornell University Press, 1967.

Wright, W. *A Short History of Syriac Literature*. A. & C. Black, 1894.

Young, J.M.L. *By Foot to China : The Mission of the Church of the East to 1400*. Radio Press, 1984.

Young, W.G. *A Handbook of Source Materials for Students of Church History*. C.L.S. & Lutterworth, 1969.

Yule, H. & H. Cordier *Cathay and the Way Thither*. Revised by H. Cordier. 4 vols. John Murray, 1921 (1913-16).

Zacharia, P. 'The Surprisingly early History of Christianity in India'. *Smithsonian Journeys Quarterly*, February 19, 2016.

Chapter - 2

Ecumenical Movements in Asia since the 3rd Century

There can be few developments more significant in recent decades for our understanding and knowledge of Christian History and theology, than the recovery for the whole church of 'the other half" of our Christian story. This is the record and witness, the writings and thought, of Asian Christians and churches before the year 1500; before, that is, the wide-spread arrival of western traders, missionaries and colonizers.

The pre-colonial history of Christianity in the region is now much more widely known[1], although serious study of its present applications, for education, theology and mission, has barely begun. This *'other half'* (or more) of the history of world-wide Christianity, is still largely ignored - not least in its ecumenical dimensions - not only by western Church historians but by many colleagues in Asia, Australasia and Oceania. That history however is now well established.

To recapitulate most briefly: Christian presence in our region – of west, central, east, southeast and south Asia – is now known to date from at least the 2nd century; was found in at least a dozen countries east of Persia by the 8th century; and throughout all Asian regions by the 16th century, from Afghanistan eastwards to Turkestan, Tibet, China, Mongolia, Korea and Japan; and southwards to India, Sri Lanka, Burma,

Siam, Indochina and the East Indies.² There are whole libraries of its histories, literatures and archives which reveal not only the persistence of ancient, and often culture-confined traditions, but also of dynamic movements in mission and ecumenical action, of community service and theology. From these I believe, we can learn, and live, much of faith and 'following the Way' today.

It cannot be overstated that records for these people and places represent the wide spread of *non-Western* Christian traditions, which developed, as early as the second century, in conscious distinction from Greek and Latin thought-forms and standards – not least in liturgies and statements of faith. It is significant also that in some areas of both the Roman and Persian Empires, 'Nestorian' and 'Orthodox' Christianity fostered, in the fifth and sixth centuries for example, the beginnings of conscious local identity and 'nationalism'.

I. World-oriented and Ecumenical mission: the first ten Centuries

In this period there were many features of church life which can be recognized as already ecumenical; that is, not just in limited inter-church relationships – which were often subject to changes in local, dynastic or national power structures – but centred upon Christian concern, with others, *for the whole world and for the everyday life and faith of all people in their own place*. This is despite the protracted and often bitter debates, or the rivalries of some imperialist theologians concerning particular aspects of denominational belief or of church polity. Through being the focus of many 'official' church histories these debates have unfortunately often seemed to dominate many studies of early church history. Far more important for ongoing Christian and worldly mission was the courageous witness and missionary endeavour, carried out by countless women and men in their local and most diverse contexts.

The *roots* for ecumenical concern and action in early eastern traditions can be seen in the different emphases held in their theology, liturgical practice and missional presence. To mention just a few seminal features here: the work of Jesus Christ is seldom pictured by early Syriac writers in the legal terms of making persons just, nor as a payment of ransom, but rather as the self-emptying demonstration of God's love for all creation; the restoration of harmony and of full humanity, and the healing of life's bodily and mental wounds with medical care and the 'medicine of the Gospel'.[3] The Holy Spirit, as in some Semitic traditions, was often portrayed – up to about 400 at least – as Mother, as was the Church itself of course. For this, both Mary the mother of Jesus and Mary Magdalene appear as symbols. Bisexual imagery was also used for God the Father and Mother in some writings. The focus in the Eucharist (of for example, the widely used *Addai and Mari* liturgy) is similarly not upon beliefs concerning the Trinity, the centrality of 'Body and Blood', nor even upon the passion and resurrection of Jesus per se. Instead it is the *presence* of Christ that is central in the Eucharist, for in this is the power to re-create the world, to establish the Kingdom of God and to transform and fulfil all things.[4]

The outworking of such a theology is seen in many prophetic and monastic movements, along with long traditions of education, medical care and state service, and carried out by generations of Persians and Arabs, Turks, Syrians, Indians and Chinese. Included among them there was the widest diversity of life-style and occupation: merchants and camel-drivers; scholars, linguists and teachers; women and men religious; women and men as prophets, priests and confessors; soldiers and traders; physicians and chancellors; tribal chiefs and khans; mothers and chieftainesses; preachers and writers. The large majority of these were in 'secular' occupations, often carried out with little regard (if at all) for either religious or denominational limitations.

A 'common religiosity' for many of these communions included stress on Christians being the 'new people' (replacing the Hebrew 'chosen people'); upon the humanity and the physical body of Jesus Christ; upon 'spiritual marriage', emphasizing the Holy Spirit as 'Mother'; and on the Church as a pilgrim group on the way to the fulfilled Kingdom.[5] In the earliest period, for which records from West, South and Central Asia are the most plentiful, there are therefore numberless examples of 'ecumenical' engagement, mission and writing, spread *far beyond their own communion or nationality*. A small selection of these follows.

In the 2nd century: *Tatian of Adiabene* (northern Iraq) produced the first *Harmony of the Gospels*, and vigorously advocated localized (*non*-Greek) witness and theology.[6] His writing and witness became widely influential throughout West and Central Asia. In the same century, Bardaisan compiled his *Book of the Laws of the Lands* which chronicles the presence of Christians (of various communions) as far east as Afghanistan and as far south as India. In Bactria – part of present-day Turkmenistan, Afghanistan, Uzbekistan, and Tajikistan – he writes (c.180 CE) of Christian women who showed in their daily lives the qualities of public and private life that linked them with Christian communities throughout the region.[7]

In South India, where there had been Christian churches since the 1st century, it is clear from many sources that Christians were 'Hindu in culture, Christian in faith and Oriental in worship'[8], community-oriented, and partners with Hindu neighbours in many ways. They were often, for example, 'trustees of the temple' as Hindu colleagues were of the church. They included local religious festivals and observances in their liturgy; and often shared articles used in festivals, from drums to elephants! Hindu customs regarding bathing, lamp-lighting or sleeping were shared by Christians, although given Christian interpretation.[9] So in many ways it can be said that the life of St Thomas Christians 'was strikingly similar', and in sympathy with, their Hindu neighbours. Here were certainly strong elements of an ecumenical awareness, albeit seldom articulated at that time.

Christian colleges in Syria at Antioch and in Persia, at Nisibis and Edessa (Urfa), from the late 3rd century on, trained many who, whether lay people or religious, became merchants or physicians, interpreters, counsellors or administrators along any part of the 'silk routes', from Persia to Japan in the east or Java in the south.[10] There is evidence that the medical school (or at the least 'teaching hospital') at *Gondishapur* (Beth Lapat) from the late 3rd century (and still now fully active), trained physicians who later, and ecumenically, served shahs and caliphs, khans and chieftains across the region.[11] Many cities, throughout Asia were therefore also centres for Christian worship and training, not only in the Christian faith but also in medical knowledge and practice, and in the skills of translation, clerkship and administration. Evidence for these could be found, for example, from Antioch in the west to Quilon in south India; from Samarqand in central Asia to *Chang An* (Xian) in China, and further to Mongolia and Japan.[12] And this would continue in some localities until as late as the 14th or 15th centuries.

In the next few centuries many Eastern theologians, such as *Theodore of Mopsuestia* (d.428) *Nestorius* (d.452), and later, *A-Lo-Pen* (early 7th century China) and *Timothy I* (Patriarch 780-823), taught and wrote on the similarity of Jesus Christ's life struggles to ours, and of the likeness of Christ's humanity to ours, so that we find him in our everyday world.[13] This is certainly a 'worldly' (i.e. for the *oikumene*) focus for theology which was also *embodied* in the lives of many of our Asian forebears of those centuries. By the ninth century something of this focus can be seen in the work of other leaders of the Church of the East such as *'Ammar al-Basri* (d.c.845), as they entered fully into dialogue with Islam (See further below). In this they often even adopted the methods and terminology of Muslim scholars.[14] Although the purpose here was most often apologetic, there was clearly also a willingness to engage in public debate on issues of community life and relationships.

Then too there are many other records of the commitment of our Christian forebears to the concrete needs of surrounding communities. A neat summary of this appears near the end of the so-called 'Nestorian' or *'Sian-fu'* Monument (c.780 C.E.) of China, where 'reverent service and proper worship' are defined as:

'The hungry came and were fed.
The naked came and they were clothed,
The sick were cured and raised to health,
The dead were buried and laid to rest.'
And to make clear that this was not only for those within the churches,

the scribe declares:
'The people enjoyed happiness and peace…
While all creatures were exempt from calamity and distress…
And all the kingdoms enjoyed a state of peace…'[15]

The same spread of occupations and life-styles for Christians as noted earlier, can be seen in other lands to the east of Persia. Here too there were many other ethnic groups to be found with active Christian communities now, including Syrian, Chinese, Indian, Malay, Tai, Tibeto-Burman, Korean, Japanese, Mongol, along with diverse Tribal groupings. Recent historical research has shown that by the 9th-11th centuries these communities numbered more than those of the Latin and Byzantine traditions combined. This was a remarkable extension of Christian presence, mission and service across the whole Asian region. Along with the varying responses of state rulers or religious leaders this was the setting for individual and group commitment to 'ecumenical mission' for the 'world'. Some examples taken from many follow.

Social teachings of such early eastern (west Asian) Fathers and Mothers as Sts. *Gregory Nazianzen, Basil, (Ms.)Macrina* and *John Chrysostum* (4th century), are well known, for their strong criticism of the wealthy and of usury, their defence of the poor and famine-stricken, and their extension of the Kingdom of God to eventually include *all* humankind. For this the Cappadocian community led by (Mother) Macrina became a clear earthly model. There are however many lesser known figures to be recalled: a few of many possible examples follow. [16]

Amongst these *Euphemia,* the Christian prophetic widow of Kurdistan (6th century), adopted the simplest life-style which yet united both contemplation and social action. She befriended destitute families, regularly visited and helped the sick, homeless and disabled, and welcomed refugees. As Basil had, Euphemia also directly challenged rich citizens – in her case standing at their gates (!) – to provide food, shelter and justice for their poor, saying to them 'What mighty thing are you going to do for Christ, he to whom all your wealth belongs?'[17] An ecumenical witness indeed!

In following centuries Christian and Buddhist scholars of Central and East Asia, were co-operating in research and translation. An outstanding example is the collaboration between the Chinese Christian monk *Ching-ching* (Adam) and the Indian Buddhist monk *Prajna* (of Kabul), in translating the Buddhist *Satparamitra* Sutra into Chinese.[18] In the same period (late 8th century) the Taoist 'Immortal' Lü Yan (Lü Dongbin) along with other Taoist and Buddhist monks helped Christian monks from Persia to translate their texts from Syriac to Chinese. Here were preludes to the ecumenical exchanges and mutual borrowing that are reflected in many Christian Sutras from the 9th-12th centuries which have been discovered in Central and East Asia.[19] (see below).

In the same period Syriac culture was flourishing in Persia and this was the setting for many examples of co-operation between those of different communions and faiths. In Merv, Baghdad and Bukhara of the 8th to 11th centuries in particular, there was much creative and intensive encounter between cultures, faiths, and languages. Many Christian scholars such as *Hunayn ibn-Ishaq* (Arab Christian), his son, his nephew and colleagues, co-operated with Muslim colleagues in the shared endeavour of translating Greek and Syriac classics into Arabic. Similarly the *Bukhtishu* family of Gondishapur were for generations writers, translators and physicians sometimes serving the Caliph himself. *Hunayn* , who is described as one of the greatest scholars and translators of the age, in Greek, Persian, Arabic, also became private physician to the Caliph *al-Mutawakki*, despite refusing to supply him with poisons.[20]

Hunayn is but one of the many Christian physicians recorded across the region, many of whom were also active in the tasks of retrieving, translating and editing classical writings. It is often not understood that these were to be the chief sources in the medieval period through which European scholars would later discover the world of Greek learning.[21] Again, a major ecumenical undertaking.

Then there were the series of amicable debates in those years (despite many others less amicable!), between Christian and Muslim leaders;

for example those between Patriarch *Timothy I* and the Caliph *Mahdi* (c.780);[22] and in the 10th century, debates between *Yahyaibn Adi* and *Theodore Abu Qurra* and Muslim guests of the Caliph *al Mamun*.[22] There are preludes here also, to the dialogues that were held much later at the courts of the Mongol Khans (see below). Although in these debates it was seldom an 'open-minded acceptance of truth wherever that may be found', at their best there was at least willingness in these debates – urged or accepted by the Caliph or Khan of course – to listen to each other, to discuss together, and sometimes to recognize also the differing traditions within one's own communion.

It should be remembered here that from 325 to 869 CE, eight 'Ecumenical' Councils[24] were held, some achieving less consensus and reconciliation than others (!) Supposedly including Christians from the 'whole inhabited earth' (*oikumene*), they were also supposedly accepted by all churches in both the East and the West. But this was so only in the case of the first two councils at most, for others – and sometimes all – were rejected by various eastern communions. References to participants then from south, central or east Asia are in any case also extremely rare. Despite major and sometimes bitter controversies, the overall aim of each was however to establish, or restore, unity for the whole church, in order to both recognise and enlarge 'the mission of God' in the world. We can only surmise at the fuller ecumenical experience that would have been known if the extensive development of churches throughout the East by the 8th century had been recognized by such councils.

There is surprisingly contemporary ecumenical relevance for us however, from many countries in these centuries: in for example, the mobility and diversity of congregational life in the Churches of the East; in their passion for world-wide mission along with a close identification with local peoples; in the emphasis made by their theologians upon the human life of Jesus and the inter-connectedness of all in the created world; in the work of their scholars in humane letters, arts and sciences; in their blend of cultural and religious openness with a clear Christian identity; in the integration, in life and witness, of worship and secular life, and of spirituality with education and medicine, agriculture and administration.[25] This is despite both the context of recurring persecution, migration or violent conflict in which they lived and the many weaknesses also discernible in much of the history of many Asian churches of that time.

2. World-centred mission and Ecumenical Encounter: the 10th to 15th Centuries

In this period ecumenical 'presence' and 'mission' take even more diverse forms. This can be seen first in the collections of the important Christian manuscripts discovered in East Turkestan – Turfan and Dunhuang especially – from the 9th-12th centuries. These are found in more than a score of languages and include more than a dozen subject areas in historical and scientific, medical and astrological, theological and liturgical categories. Manuscripts of important Christian teachings often retell lengthy sections from the Gospels, or re-shape earlier creeds and canticles, while using *local* language and idiom, religious image and metaphor.[26] Context and locality are here taken most seriously as is the involvement in the *worldly* service of health care, community building, scientific discovery or government administration.

During the centuries when the Church of the East was most widely present in the Asian region, (7th-12th centuries), these extant records show that Christian communities in many countries were open to, and also were nourished by, ecumenical experiences in their own context. Not only did they co-exist peacefully with those of other faiths, but they also happily exchanged, and grew, in their understanding of religious faith and life through this encounter. Note for example, that the most significant writings we still have from them take the form of *sutras* (the name for Buddhist discourses), and freely use Buddhist or Taoist terms and imagery to present New Testament teaching. Terms chosen for 'salvation', 'the holy Spirit', 'kingdom of God' are also vividly contextual, reflecting the landscape and life-condition of Christians widely scattered across deserts, mountains, steppes and coastlands.[27]

Judging from the paintings and manuscripts discovered at Dunhuang for example, the Christian community there include, by the 8th century and until the 14th century in some territories, scholars, merchants and scribes, along with skilled artists and craftsmen. This was similar to records found in the wider Turfan and Dunhuang districts and to those recorded in large cemeteries at Tokmak and Pishkek (Kyrgyzstan), where many hundreds of scholars and merchants, priests, soldiers and ecclesiastics, with their families, were buried, whether Chinese or Persian, Uighur (Turk) or Indian, Syrian or Mongol.[28] In a return exchange, scholars have found evidence of major Christian influence in such Mahayana teachings as those concerning the nature and work of *Bodhisattvas;* in Pure Land teachings regarding 'faith in the Name' *(Nembutsu)*; and in some of the beliefs that developed for the *Prajnaparamita* (the Lady 'Wisdom beyond Wisdom'), sometimes termed the 'Mother of all Buddhas'.[29]

But the wider dimensions of ecumenism are also present here. From the earliest period, in Persia (pre-400 C.E.), until the later history of Mongol ascendancy (14th century), the role of Christians in key professions, and their commitment to all that promoted peoples' welfare, is widely recorded. In medical care and education in particular, the universities and medical schools they had founded by the 4th century were later spread in many countries east of Persia. Libraries in their colleges, monasteries and churches – in locations such as Pamapkuda or Cochin (South India), Shui-pang or Dunhuang (Turkestan), Da Quin or Chang-an (North China) – included a wide range of medical, agricultural and historical writings, in addition to Biblical, inter-faith, liturgical and ecclesiastical materials.

From at least the 8th century on also, significant numbers in the major Mongol clans (in east, central and west Asia) were already Christian, as were members of many Khan families. Prominent among these were the mothers and wives of at least *nine* Khans (See further below). Most notable was *Sorghagtani Beki,* mother of *Khubilai Khan* (13th century). She ensured that her tribes stood out as being free of abuses of power, moderated *Khubilai Khan's* policies, and was widely lauded - by European missionaries, Persian historians and Syrian physicians alike - as 'towering above all the women of the world'.³⁰ Although her back-ground was in the Church of the East, her life and ministry were clearly 'ecumenical'.

But just as remarkable were the family dynasties of physicians, counsellors and in particular, chief administrative officers, upon whom Shahs, Caliphs and Khans were dependent over many centuries. Names and in some cases, bio-data have survived for some of these. The roles of significant women are also to be found there. The position of 'Chancellor' or 'Vizier' was sometimes hereditary in families (as with *Hunayn* or the *Bukhtishu* clan earlier) such as that of the Christian *Ai Hsieh* from the 12th century. Pre-eminent amongst *Kublai Khan's* officials as Chancellor and Director of the Offices of Astronomy and Medicine, *Ai Hsieh* yet rejected all bribes and astrological speculations. He is also reported to have curbed a number of major injustices, even persuading Kublai Khan to forego planned oppressive military campaigns.³¹ Here was not only inter-faith encounter, dialogue and social concern but also the exercise of appropriate power in vastly scattered, polyglot and multi-cultural communities.

The larger framework within which Christians could take such roles was that established by Genghis Khan himself. On the basis of 'more tolerant' Shamanist tradition Genghis (*Temujin*) had been willing to welcome – for the vast range of his multi-racial and polyglot tribal groupings – a similar range of religious practitioners and faiths. All became welcome at his courts. Each of his followers were to 'abide by his own religion and follow his own creed' he declared.³² That the founding and often merciless Khan of all the Mongols should declare that the 'call to prayer' was permitted for all faiths in his dominions was a paradoxically ecumenical phenomenon. At the same time we must note that Mongol Christians themselves were often notably 'flexible' in relating to those of other faiths; persecuted by no one they persecuted none; living by basic Christian beliefs they assisted their Khans as secretaries, translators, healers and military leaders; accepting some *Shamanist* practices they yet rejected some of the key aspects of contemporary *European* Christian practice.³³

As with earlier Khans in 13th century Karakorum also, the Khan *Mangu* convened inter-faith debates between representatives of the Christian (jointly Nestorian and Roman Catholic), Muslim and *'Tuin'* (i.e. Buddhist, Manichaean and Shamanist) communities. Later Il-khans such as *Hulagu* (in 'Persia'), were reported to be influenced towards partly moderating the use of armed conflict, by such inter-religious encounters, as they were also by their Christian wives. (Scholars who have examined all the records now available affirm that in the century until 1294 every Khan had either a Christian mother and/or a Christian wife!) The lives and aspirations of Mongol khans and their families therefore are greatly more diverse and tolerant than wide-spread myth would suggest. So it was that as part of the *Pax Mongolica* of the 13th-14th centuries, this setting made possible a measure of religious tolerance and exchange in many areas of Eurasia.

3. The 16th-19th centuries

This period presents a very wide spectrum of ecumenical examples in the life of Christian communities. In the more limited sense of church and inter-faith ecumenical relations these range from a tentative recognition of diversity within one's own tradition, to Christian affirmation of pristine Hindu beliefs, or from the presentation of the Gospel in Confucian terms, to acceptance of some Buddhist or Shinto practices as the means of preserving faith.³⁴ As well, a number of further inter-faith dialogues are recorded, often in detail, in for example India, China, Vietnam and Japan. These are most interesting as early ecumenical endeavours, even though the aims of each participant are sometimes, at least in part, 'evangelistic' and sometimes also in order to exercise political power.

For the 'larger ecumenism' of inter-faith commitment to the world and its people we have to look in the main for movements apparently outside the mainstream of Asian church history. These would include the struggles of persecuted Christian minorities to survive oppression and to continue caring for their immediate community in for example, Japan, Vietnam, and Ceylon; the work of scholars and others to present the implications of the Christian Gospel for cultural reform or policies of government in for example Korea, China, Vietnam, the Philippines; and in 'subversive' groups or movements which reshaped the style of Christian presence under colonial or totalitarian regimes in for example Japan, Korea, India, the Philippines. The continuing role of liturgy, prayer and Biblical study (however interpreted) remain central for almost all these groups and movements, as does the often over-looked participation and leadership of women. (Refer to volumes of *Asian Christian Theologies* below).

Looking more closely at such movements and individuals we discover many instances of wider inter-church or world-centred aims and endeavours. I will be able to include here only a few representative examples from the numerous cases available. Amongst these, are the inter-faith endeavours in early-17th century China by a number of neo-Confucian literati, to restore and complete Confucianism as a path to national reform. This they found presented in a Christianity which was sensitively grounded also in ancient Chinese tradition. So Christian faith is here an amplification and intensification of neo-Confucian wisdom. But Christian teaching is also modified and enriched in this encounter, just as Confucian teachings are modified in the light of Christian faith.[35] Then from the early -17th century also we can trace the emergence in Vietnam for example, of 'The Three Fathers' (*Ba Cha*) theology, in which God is 'High Father', the king of one's country is 'middle father' and one's blood father is the 'low father'. This merging of Confucian and Christian insights was to form the basis for much later contextual reflection and life. It appears first in Alexandre de Rhodes' book *Phepgiang tam ngay* ('Catechism explained in eight days') of 1651.,[36] and it would become a central tradition in later Catholic thought in Vietnam; often merged with strong nationalism, as in *Danh Duc Tuan* (d.1875), and much later, in scholars such as *Hoang Gia Khanh* (b.1955).[37]

This tradition, along with full engagement in 'worldly' concerns for the human community as a whole, can be seen also in the thought and labours of such activist Vietnamese philosophers as *Nguyen Truong To* (b.1827). A scholar of classical Chinese, he was also a teacher, architect and prolific Christian writer. From 1861, he submitted a stream of memoranda to the Emperor, advocating extensive reforms in the administration of justice, taxation, the army and international affairs. This was to make possible equitable incomes, indigenous production and the elimination of corruption. 'Urgent measures', in which he personally also worked, included the formation of co-operatives, of crèches and hospices and the development of irrigation and land settlement schemes.[38]

In India, in the late 17th, and early 18th centuries, over thirty conferences had been held between Danish missionaries and *'Malabarian* (south Indian) *Brahmins'*. Reports of these encounters were edited by Bartholomeus Ziegenbalg and published in London in 1719.[39] Later in the 18th century Indian Sanskrit scholars and French Jesuits, collaborated to present Sanskrit documents entitled *Pristine Hinduism Vindicated*: in which Christian meaning was discerned in the religious insights of the Hindu texts.[40] The authors clearly believed that the central truths of Hinduism were 'wholly congruent with the Christian faith'. It is thus an early example of contextualizing, but of equal importance to the content for our purpose in these studies is the ecumenical collaboration which produced it.

In 19th century India, amongst many who studied and integrated central insights of Hinduism into Christian faith – including C.Moozoomdar (1840-1905), *Keshub Chandra Sen* (1838-1884), *Krishna Mohan Banerjee* (1813-1885), and *Brahmabandhav Upadhyaya* (1861-1907)[41] – was a remarkable woman, *Pandita Ramabai* (1858-1922). Her Brahmin father had, at the price of being himself excommunicated by his caste, taught his wife and daughters Sanskrit and the classical 'Hindu' scriptures. Later, the Senate of the University of Calcutta uniquely honoured her with the prestigious titles, *Pandita* and *Saraswathi* in acknowledgement of her deep learning. She then joined the *Brahmo*

Samaj (a reformist Hindu association). In 1883 she deepened her knowledge of Christ and Christianity with the assistance of *Nehemiah Goreh*, finally receiving baptism in the Anglican Church. From 1886 to 1888 *Ramabai* lectured and studied social reform in north America and England, also canvassing support for the Houses for Brahmin child-widows which she had founded, the *Sharada Sadan*.

But the *Pandita* also worked on Marathi Bible translation, while her main contribution to what we now term 'ecumenical mission' is the pioneering work that she did for the liberation of Indian women through the *Arya Mahila Samaj* (Arya Women's Society) which she founded to provide refuges and education for discarded child widows. This work together with her writing caused many Indians to rethink their attitudes to, and treatment of, women. In theology she and those with her sought a less dogmatic, less metaphysical Christianity, in tune with Hindu ethos and with more direct 'experience of the Holy Spirit'. She also denounced the denominational divisions within Christianity. Only when Christians overcame divisions, and established one united and indigenous Christian Church, would they be worthy to preach Christ to the Indians she declared. She then challenged believers to go out to serve society as she herself had done.[42]

In the Philippines, *Don Pedro Pelaez* (d. 1863) was the principal leader in the movement of Filipino clergy from 1849 on, to rectify injustices within the church and to establish a church in which Filipino and Spaniard were equally regarded. He became lecturer in both philosophy and theology, secretary to the Archbishop and administrator of the Manila Diocese. But in his teaching and writings he was an eminent advocate for the Filipinization of the church, drawing on a wide knowledge of history, scientific discovery, canon law and theology. There he articulated a theology of national identity and Filipino Christianity in its social and political application and fostered wide Filipino participation in this.[43] The essential features of ecumenical engagement are clearly to be seen in his quite prophetic life.

His famous protégé, *José Apolonio Burgos*, was martyred in 1872 for his learned advocacy for an independent church and people. While remaining loyal to Rome, Burgos had strongly rejected the colonialist policies and abuses of the Friars and worked tirelessly for social justice, for Filipino identity and a contextualized Filipino church. He wrote extensively in the cause of reform and social justice, for the recognition of Filipino clergy, and for the full equality of Filipino and Spaniard. He co-founded the journal *El Eco Filipino* (Madrid) to publish these concerns. There and elsewhere he drew on a wide knowledge of history, scientific discovery, canon law and theology to articulate a theology of national identity and Filipino Christianity in their social and political application. His writings extant include articles, letters, and manifestos.[44] Later, others such as *Isabelo de los Reyes* (d. 1938) would 'Filipinize' Christian faith through a merging of native folk-lore and religion with traditional Catholic beliefs.[45]

For Japan, there is *Takahashi Goro* (1856-1935), born into a Samurai family in Niigata. He became a talented linguist and co-operated in the translation of the Japanese Bible. His particular study however was undertaken widely in Buddhism. He became 'the leading Christian expert' on Buddhism in the 1880s, amongst other prominent Christians like *Ibuka Kajinosuke, Hiraiwa Yoshiyasu, Uemura Masahisa* and *Kozaki Hiromichi* who also showed a deep concern for the understanding of Buddhism. Takahashi himself remained critical of some aspects of Buddhism in many articles of his that appeared in the journal *Rikugo Zasshi*. He also wrote four volumes on Japanese religion, which while having an apologetic purpose, nevertheless argued for an unbiased search for truth in all religious study. 'Leave prejudice,' he wrote in *Rikugo Zasshi*, 'forget the conventional criticism; open your minds and empty your hearts and consider thoroughly what I have written about Buddhism ... and make your own impartial judgment'. Despite rejecting many Buddhist doctrines his work is known as the beginning of serious and comprehensive inter-faith study in Japan.[46]

Ecumenical theology and action was thus to develop in many streams in the 19th century, before the modern' Ecumenical Movement' as usually understood, began. Just to consider inter-denominational conferences of missionaries in the region: these were first held in India from 1825 (although they were first proposed by William Carey in 1806). They became regular events in India in that century and later occurred also in Japan (from 1872) and in China (from 1877). In India they came to include a growing number of nationals, and to consider not only the issues of 'comity' in mission but also the questions of Christian unity and the role of a national 'three-self' Church in each country. Missionary unions and associations were often formed, sometimes in association with local or national movements, in emergency relief, education and publication, social concern and inter-faith activities.[48] All this activity would precede the consultations of the 1890s and early 1900s.

But the pattern for future joint action in mission and theological formulation was largely established in particular by movements of students and teachers within and outside the region: in YMCAs (from 1854) and YWCAs (from 1875), in SCMs (from 1886), and in particular, in activities of the WSCF (World Student Christian Federation, from 1895).The participation and leadership of Asian Christians in these, as in subsequent ecumenical movements and consultations was, and is, extensive. The 20th century was of course to see a greatly expanded development of many diverse ecumenical movements and of participation of Asian Christians within these, but this must await another occasion for treatment.[49]

Conclusion

To recognise in the few examples given above in their very diverse contexts, an 'ecumenical spirit', or even an 'ecumenical purpose', is yet to ignore the central thrust of their histories, which would be much further developed in the 20th century. For that thrust is the move from 'interest' or even 'intention' to the *enactment* of a common faith and vision – that of embodied love for neighbour, community and world. These are to be seen in the qualities of life-in-community; of sensibility, compassion and creativity that are revealed in the restoration or fulfilment of distinctly human life being attempted or hoped for, whatever the details of rite or doctrine or ideology may have been. There are of course innumerable opportunities taken to share – between denominations and between faiths – the creative insights of one's own tradition. But here we see deep concern for the other as the driving force of the *one* faith for *one* humanity: through collaboration in study, in translation or teaching, in joint Church actions, in advocacy for people's welfare, in movements for radical change, and in personal dedication for the everyday life and faith of all people in their own place.

We can see also in the wider ecumenism the witness of other living faiths. As the Hindu Reformer Swami Vivekenanda would call us all to service of humanity in 1910, we are to 'first feel from the heart!'[50] The questions for us therefore are 'what are the present hopes of our people?' 'What qualities of life-in-community, of sensibility, compassion and creativity, are revealed then – or can be validly inferred – in them?' 'What kind of human life was being attempted or hoped for, whatever may have been the details of belief held, liturgy practised or institutional form favoured?'

For the periods outlined, a central conclusion could well be that from a (renewed) experience of the concrete life-situations of our people, in for example, 'live-in' encounters, or situation exposures, there could come a greater freedom to 'live on the fringe' and develop new forms of' non-institutional' Christian presence. Many examples of these forms can be seen across the region, and many more could be developed: authentically rooted both in particular secular worlds and in new patterns of Christian community life, study, and prayer. This also often brings a mutually beneficial co-existence with neighbours of other faiths such as (in particular) Hinduism, Buddhism and Confucianism, Sikhism, Shamanism and Islam. And the concerns include community survival despite repression and persecution; peace-making and the building of just and humane communities; along with creative scriptural interpretation, theology and spirituality. All of these movements offer rich resources for the present life, thought and action of all Christians in company with their colleagues).

And a final question we are left with: How can we therefore enlist 'church leaders', activists, seminary staff directly in such encounter, study and mutual commitment? Practical steps could well be taken to implement fuller ecumenical orientation towards our peoples where they are today: through action-oriented field-education in our seminaries; through studies in the rich history of ecumenical endeavours in Asia; through co-operation in training, action and research programmes with our regional networks of study- and social-action centres (and seminaries); as well as through live-in exposures arranged as the regular prelude to our ecumenical conferences and assemblies. In these and similar ways I believe, we can carry forward the long heritage of people-oriented and ecumenical mission in our region, finding creatively new and prophetic forms for our commitment to the 'oikumene' in coming decades.[51]

Endnotes

[1] See chap. 1 this volume and for example, A.S. Atiya *A History of Eastern Christianity* (Methuen, 1968 and Kraus, 1991); S.H. Moffett *A History of Christianity in Asia* vol.1 (Harper Collins, 1992); J.C. England *Hidden History of Christianity in Asia* (ISPCK, 1998); T.V. Philip *East of the Euphrates. Early Christianity in Asia* (CSS and ISPCK, 1998); I. Gillman and H-J. Klimkeit *Christians in Asia before 1500* (Curzon, 1999); Mar Abraham *Forgotten East.* (Ephrem's Pubns., 2000); W.Baum & D.W. Winkler *The Church of the East.* (Routledge Curzon, 2030); C. Baumer *The Church of the East. An Illustrated History of Assyrian Christianity* (Tauris, 2006).

[2] The communions sometimes collectively termed 'Oriental Orthodox' include Syrian Orthodox/Jacobite/Monophysite, who with the 'Nestorian'/Church of the East/Tachin, rejected Chalcedon doctrines (and a Roman 'Pope'), in contrast to the Chalcedonian/Melkite communions.

[3] Gregory Dix *The Shape of the Liturgy* (Dacre Press, 1949) 183ff.

[4] Refer A.C.Moule *Christians in China before the Year 1550* (SPCK, 1930) 228ff.; Dix op.cit.; R. Murray *Symbols of the Kingdom* (Cambridge, 1975) 21f.145ff.; P. Gregorios 'East Syrian Worship' in *A New Dictionary of Liturgy and Worship* ed. J.G. Davies (SCM Press, 1986) 217; M.K. Kruriakose *History of Christianity in India; Source Materials* (CLS, 1982) 21ff., 73f.; I. Gillman and H-J. Klimkeit Christians in Asia before 1500 (Curzon, 1999).62, 181,

[5] See Gillman and Klimkeit op.cit. 1999, 61ff. ; also Sebastian Brock, and Susan Ashbrook Harvey *Holy Women of the Syrian Orient* (University of California Press, 1987).

[6] Refer *The Diatesseron and Address to the Greeks.* (English translations in The Ante-Nicene Fathers. Vol. 3. Scribner, 1903).

[7] Modern editions of Bardaisan's volume by Cureton 1848 and 1855, Renan 1855, Land 1862, and Wright 1872. Most recent edition H.J.W. Drijvers *The Book of the Laws of Countries: Dialogue on Fate of Bardaisan of Edessa.* (Gorgias Press, 2007). See also Gillman and Klimkeit (op.cit. 1999) 43.

[8] See extended discussion in A.M. Mundadan *History of Christianity in India* vol.1 (Church History Assoc., 1984); c.f. J. Thomas 'The South Indian Tradition of the Apostle Thomas.' *Journal of the Royal Asiatic Society* (New Series 56.S1, 1924) 213-223; Benedict Vadakkekara *Origin of Christianity in India: A Historiographical Critique.* (Media House, 2007) chaps. 1 & 2; Eric Frykenberg *Christianity in India: from Beginnings to the Present* (Oxford University Press, 2008) 101; *The Encyclopedia of Christianity*, Volume 5, (Eerdmans Publishing, 2008) 285.

[9] For the extent of 'cultural exchange and assimilation see L.W.Brown *The Christians of St Thomas* (London, 1956) 75, Gillman and Klimkeit (op.cit. 1999) 169 ff. c.f. A.M. Mundadan (op.cit. 1984) 29ff.,64; J.C. England (op.cit. 1998) 62ff.

[10] Refer to Gillman & Klimkeit (op.cit. 1999), 148f.; England (op.cit. 1998), 46f.,

[11] On this and other early colleges see Arthur Voobus *History of the School of Nisibis*(Louvain, 1965); Mattam (op.cit. 2000) 119ff.; Baumer (op.cit.2006), 81ff. For an outline of the evidence and discussion see also *The Physicians of Jundishapur* Gail Marlow Taylor (University of California Thesis, 2010. www.sasanika.org/wp-content/uploads).

[12] See references under 1 above.

[13] Refer *Asian Christian Theologies. A Research Guide to Authors, Movements, Sources* 3 vols. ed. John C. England et al. (ISPCK, Orbis; Claretian 2001-2004) vol.1, 8ff.; also Baum and Winkler (op.cit. 2003) chap.1.

[14] See Sydney H. Griffith *The Beginnings of Christian Theology in Arabic* (Ashgate, 2002) viif. 155f. and passim.

[15] Yoshiro Saeki *The Nestorian Documents and Relics in China* (Maruzen, 1951) 64ff.

[16] See Julian J. *Corominas Macrina. La Madre.* (Jaca Book Ed., 2005); Carla D. Sunberg *The Cappadocian Mothers* (Pickwick Publications, 2017).

[17] S. Brock & S.A. Harvey (op.cit. 1987) 126ff.

[18] Philip Jenkins *The Lost History of Christianity.* Harper One, 2008), 15-16.

[19] For the Lü Yan reference see Saeki op.cit.(1951) 398. Refer also to Martin Palmer *The Jesus Sutras.* (Ballantyne, 2001), Li Tang, *A Study of the History of Nestorian Christianity in China and Its Literature in Chines* (Lang, 2003), R. Riegert and T. Moore (eds.) *The Lost Sutras of Jesus. Unlocking the Ancient Wisdom of the Xian Monks.*(Souvenir Press, 2004).

[20] K. Hitti *History of the Arabs. From the Earliest Times to the Present*.10th edn.(St Martin's Press, 1974) 312 ff. See also Jim Al-Khalili *Pathfinders; The Golden Age of Arabic Science* (Penguin, 2010) 46, 48, 74-75; A.O. Whipple *The Role of Nestorians and Moslems in the History of Medicine* (Princeton, 1967). For the Bakhtishu family see Peter Francopan *The Silk Roads*. (Bloomsbury, 2015) 97.

[21] See Al-Khalili ibid., J. M. Healey 'The Syriac-speaking Christians and the Translation of Greek Science into Arabic'. (Address, Manchester.2006) www.muslimheritage.com/article/syriac-speaking-Christians. For the wider setting for Christian scholarship in Arab and Persian learning and cultures see J. Lyons *The House of Wisdom* (Bloomsbury, 2009) 62ff.; J. Al-Khalili (op.cit. 2010) chaps. 3, 5; S. F. Starr *Lost Enlightenment. Central Asia's Golden Age* (Princeton, 2013) chaps. 3,9,12.

[22] See Timothy I (Patriarch) 'Apology for Christianity'. *Bulletin of John Rylands Library* 12, 1928.

[23] D. Thomas (ed.) *Christians at the Heart of Islamic Rule. Church Life and Scholarship in 'Abbasid Iraq* (Leiden: Brill, 2003) especially chaps.5,7,8; see also Lyons (op.cit. 2009); D. W. Winkler(ed.) *Syriac Churches Encountering Islam* (Gorgias, 2010), Starr (op.cit. 2013).

[24] The fullest study of these is *Decrees of the Ecumenical Councils From Nicaea I to Vatican II* (ed. by N. Tanner and G. Alberigo et al. (Georgetown Univ. 1990), although it must be noted that this gives Roman Catholic interpretation prominence..

[25] England (op.cit. 1998) chap 2; S.H. Moffett (op.cit. 1992), 77f. Also Gillman and Klimkeit (op.cit.) 143ff.

[26] See for example, Saeki (op.cit. 1951);.England (op.cit. 1998) 124ff.; Gillman and Klimkeit (op.cit.), 275ff.; also Palmer (op.cit. 2001);R. Riegert & T. Moore (op.cit. 2004); Baumer (op.cit. 2006) 187ff..

[27] J. Foster *The Church of the Tang Dynasty* (London: SPCK, 1939) 154ff. For example the Holy Spirit is the 'cool wind'; salvation is 'refreshing dew', 'a raft on a sea of flame', and 'liberation from sorrow'; creation is the 'divine arrow' constantly held in flight by God', who remains the 'unseen archer' within and also beyond this world. See the full collections of scrolls in Saeki Yoshiro (op.cit 1951).

[28] J. Stewart *Nestorian Missionary Enterprise: the Story of a Church on Fire*. (T.& T. Clark; & Christian Literary Society, 1928) 206ff.; Gillman and Klimkeit (op.cit.) 213.

[29] (Ms.) Romila Thaper, *A History of India* - Vol 1. (Penguin, 1966) 131-134; also A.L. Basham, *The Wonder That Was India: Before the Coming of the Muslims* . (Grove Press, 1959); *Buddhism and Christianity in Dialogue*, ed. P. Schmidt-Leukel, (SCM press, 2005) 176-199).

[30] M. Rossabi *Kubilai Khan His Life and Times* (Berkeley: University of California, 1988) 11ff. C. Dawson (ed.) *The Mission to Asia: Narratives and Letters of the Franciscan Missionaries in Mongolia and China in the 13th and 14th Centuries* (Harper, 1966), C. Dawson (ed.) *Missionaries in Mongolia and China* (Sheed and Ward, 1980); also England (op.cit. 1998) 82ff. On the significant roles of Christian women in courts

of the Khans see also Jack Weatherford *The Secret History of the Mongol Queens* (Crown, 2010) 41f., 55 et seq.

[31] A.C. Moule *Christians in China before the Year 1550* (London, SPCK, 1930) 228ff.

[32] Jack Weatherford *Ghenghis Khan and the Quest for God.* (Viking, 2016) 177.

[33] James Muldoon *Popes, Lawyers, and Infidels: The Church and the Non-Christian World, 1250-1550.* (Univ. Pennsylvania, 1979); Richard Foltz *Religions of the Silk Road* (Palgrave Macmillan, 2010); James D. Ryan 'Christian Wives of Mongol Khans: Tartar Queens and Missionary Expectations in Asia' (*Journal of the Royal Asiatic Society* Third Series, 8. 3 (Nov., 1998) 411-421, See also Jack Weatherford (op.cit. 2010) 105ff.

[34] See writings included in *Asian Christian Theologies* (op.cit. 2001-2004, vol.1) 27ff.

[35] See chap. 4 below and e.g. N. Standaert *Yang Ting Yun Confucian and Christian in Late Ming China.*, Brill, 1988.

[36] Outlined in C.Phan *Mission and Catechesis Alexandre de Rhodes and Inculturation in Seventeenth Century Vietnam* (Orbis, 1998) 220ff. See also chaps. 5 & 6 below.

[37] *Asian Christian Theologies* (op.cit.vol. 2), 566f., 633f.

[38] Nguyen Truong To's writings have been collected in *Nguyen Trung To 1830-1871* ed. Ba Can Truong (Institute of Research on Chinese and Vietnamese Culture, 1991). See also *Asian Christian Theologies* op.cit. vol. 2), 567ff.

[39] See B. Ziegenbalg, & J. E. Grundler *Thirty Four Conferences Between the Danish Missionaries and the Malabarian Brahmans in the East Indies, Concerning the Truth of the Christian Religion...*(H. Clements, 1719); this has been most recently published as *Die Malabarische Korrespondenz : tamilischeBriefean deutsche Missionare; eineAuswahl. Fremde Kulturen in altenBerichten* ; Bd. 5, Kurt Liebau, (ed.) Verlag: Sigmaringen : 1998.

[40] A. Amaladas & R.F. Young *The Indian Christiad. A Concise Anthology of Didactic and Devotional Literature in Early Church Sanskrit* (Anand: Gujarat Sahitya Prakash, 1995). Refer chap.4 below.

[41] Full references for these are given in *Asian Christian Theologies* (op.cit. 2001 vol.1).

[42] Amongst many sources by and about Ramabai see *Pandita Ramabai Through Her Own Words: Selected Works.* ed. by Meera Kosambi (Oxford University Press, 2000); Clementina Butler *Pandita Ramabai Sarasvati: Pioneer in the movement for the education of the child-widow of India.* (Fleming H. Revell 1922); Gupta *Pandita Ramabai Saraswati: Her Life and Work* (Asia Publishing House, 1970); Adhav, S.M. *PanditaRamabai* (CISRS; CLS, 1979); Uma Chakravarti *Rewriting history: the life and times of Pandita Ramabai..* (Kali for Women & Book Review Literary Trust, 1998).

[43] See chapter 5 of this volume for both Pelaez and Burgos. Works by Don Padre Pelaez include *Brebesapuntes* (Memoranda, Vatican Archives); *Documentos importantes para la question pendiente sobre la provision de curatos en Filipinas.* (El Clamor Publico, 1863); *Letters* in Archivio Segreto Vaticano (Arch. Nunz Madrid) & Archives of Archdiocese of Manila. *Memorial to Queen of Spain* (opposing Decree of 1861. Manila: 1861).

⁴⁴ Refer J.N. Schumacher *Revolutionary Clergy: The Filipino Clergy and the Nationalist Movement, 1850-1903.* (Ateneo de Manila University Press, 1981); Schumacher *Father Jose Burgos: Priest and Nationalist.* (Ateneo de Manila University Press, 1972); Schumacher *Father Jose Burgos A Documentary History. With Spanish Documents and their Translation.* (Ateneo de Manila University Press, 1999).

⁴⁵ Works by Isabelo de los Reyes include *Ilocanadas: Articulosvariossobre Etnologie, Historias y Costumbres del Pais* (Manila: 1887), *El Folk-lore Filipino.* (Manila: 1889), *La Religion del 'Katipunan', Filipinas: Independencia y Revolucion!* (Madrid: 1899), *Oficiodivino de la Iglesis Filipina Independiente. (*Barcelona, 1906), *Letters* (IFI Archives, St Andrews Theological Seminary, Quezon City).

⁴⁶ N.R.Thelle. *Buddhism and Christianity in Japan: From Conflict to Dialogue 1854-1899* (University of Hawaii Press, 1987) 71.ff.

⁴⁷ For this history see W.R. Hogg *Ecumenical Foundations: A History of The International Missionary Council and its Nineteenth-Century Background* (Wipf and Stock, 2002/1952).

⁴⁸ The pioneer work on this history was H.R. Weber *Asia & the Ecumenical Movement 1895-1961.* (SCM Press, 1966). See also N. Koshy (ed.) *A History of the Ecumenical Movement in Asia.* (WSCF-AP, YMCA-AP, CCA, 2 vols. 2003, 2004).

⁴⁹ For these wider dimensions of ecumenical movements see chap. 6 in this volume. For studies ofAsian ecumenical movements in the 20th century see Weber op.cit.1966, T.V. Philip *Ecumenism in Asia* (ISPCK & CSS, 1994), Koshy op.cit. 2003, 2004.

⁵⁰ The words of Vivekenanda are featured in his *To the Youth of India* (Advaita Ashrama, 1972). See also for example, Rose M. Cecchini *Women's Action for Peace & Justice: Christian, Buddhist & Muslim Women Tell Their Story* (Maryknoll, 1988); Mary R. Battung and others *Religion and Society: Towards a Theology of Struggle.* Book I.(FIDES, 1988); M. G. Augustine, (ed.) *25 Years of ACISCA 1970-1995.* (ACISCA, 1996); C.S. Queen & Sallie B. King *Engaged Buddhism* (SUNY, 1996); Swami Agnivesh Religion, *Spirituality and Social Action* (Hope India, 2003.

⁵¹ For a recent treatment of these and related issues see particularly D. P. Niles (ed.) *Windows into Ecumenism: Essays in Honour of Ahn Jae Woong* (CCA, 2005).

Chapter - 3

The Early Christian Art of Asian Peoples

Early Christian art-forms of Asia, that is in the region from the Ural mountains and the Mediterranean Sea, to Kamchatka in the north, and to India and Indonesia in the south, has been discovered in many countries of the region from the earliest centuries. No full survey of the countless frescoes, carvings, artefacts and paintings has however yet been made. They form part of the evidence for the widespread presence in Asia of Eastern churches over many centuries which is still largely unknown. These included the traditions often named Syrian Orthodox or Jacobite, '"Nestorian" ', Chaldean or Church of the East, sometimes termed collectively the Oriental Orthodox Churches.[1]

The shortest summary for the history of these churches would say that their life and mission developed rapidly in Syria and Persia from the 1st century on, and extended eastwards in that century from Persia to China and India. They were found in west, central, south, east, northeast and southeast Asia by the eighth century at least. In many areas of the region these Christian communities remained vigorous for up to fifteen centuries, and some are still active in India, west and central Asia (and now also north America and Australasia). This is the 'other half' of Christian history which is yet to be fully recognized in our churches, colleges and universities.[2]

For many Asian countries unfortunately, the history is largely unknown, being largely hidden in older volumes not easily accessed or in lesser-known journals. There are however extensive writings and also *art-forms* created by Asian Christians extant, from as early as the first century in some countries. The diverse body of Christian art is found in many different forms and media and show clearly that the Eastern Churches were able to creatively express Christian truth in the art-forms and imagery of west, central, south and east Asian cultures. It is possible here to outline only a small selection from the vast range of those materials which are now available for our study and reception.

The chapter following attempts to outline the ways in which art in Asia has expressed and interpreted – or sometimes challenged – Christian faith; and to present some of the unique forms of that art. Aspects of the relationship between art and faith will be included, along with the varieties of artistic skills and media employed and the historical settings and religious context for particular forms of Christian art. It will be noted that these sometimes present unexpected insights or alternative interpretations for Biblical texts or the doctrinal traditions of other regions.

Imagery of the Cross
Along with the fish (ICTHYS), the chalice and the bread-loaf, one of the most widespread of early art-forms found in many parts of the region between Persia and Japan and south to Sri Lanka and India, is the incised, framed and ornamented (empty) cross. Something of the remarkable spread of eastern Christianity over many centuries can be glimpsed if we trace the spread of images for the cross (below)[3]: from likely origin in Persia (1, 2) to developed forms in India (3,4), Inner Asia (5), Sri Lanka (6) and China (p.2). In all of these images the extremities of cross-members are ornamented or enlarged, either with flames, pearls or petals (these indicating the power, the treasure or the *life* of the Gospel). Over the course of five or six centuries the early 'flowering' cross from Persia becomes placed upon a large (Hindu/Buddhist) lotus in India and Sri Lanka; this being an Asia-wide symbol of purity, spirit,

spontaneous life and compassion. A dove, or a base of columns or steps are sometimes added. In Inner Asia and China this was stood upon forms of the lotus, with sometimes clouds, a dragon or even figures added.[4] Pillars and monoliths that are still to be seen also include large standing granite crosses, and tall or hanging multi-lamp stands. Some of

these, as in the case of the altar crosses, have inscriptions (regarding for example, the death of Jesus, the Resurrection or of Christian sufferings); or carvings (of for example, the Marys standing at the cross). Carvings of birds or floral designs are sometimes included at their base. It will be noted that none of these forms include the figure of a crucifix, which, along with various 'atonement' theologies as its basis, is in any case a later western addition. (See chap. 1 above, n.45).

To understand further developments in Christian art across the region other images from west Asia should be first considered.

I. Syria, Persia and the Byzantine Empire

Christian presence in Syria and Persia has long been known to date from at least the 2nd century and in the Byzantine Empire from the

4th century. Many architectural epigraphical and art-forms from the earliest centuries attest to very wide-spread Christian communities and to many different artistic traditions developed in each of these contexts.[5] These include carvings and mosaics, murals, architecture and icons, often including diverse symbols in Christogram form (HIS, XR or ICHTHYS), or images representing incidents from the gospels such as the nativity, the calling of the disciples, Jesus healing or teaching, Jesus as shepherd, the foot-washing, the 'last supper' or the empty tomb. Amongst these are a remarkable number of the incised, carved or cast crosses also that have been discovered in this region.

It was in Persia that forms of the cross symbol were created which would provide the basic pattern (as above) for countless crosses carved and erected throughout the Asian region. Hence this form has been sometimes named 'the Persian Cross' wherever it has been found. For this the arms are of equal length and have at their ends flowers and/or buds of various patterns – hence sometimes termed the 'budding cross'. These symbols, along with the absence of any figure, are to symbolize new and resurrection life. At the base many have steps or a representation of leaves, and so are termed 'stepped' or 'leaved crosses'. (As at left)

Some of the clearest examples of Persian crosses are actually found in India. (See further below). Examples extant in Persian territories are almost always badly defaced. But the Persian stone crosses in Malankara (Kerala)

are lasting witnesses to the strong Malankara-Persia connection from the earliest centuries. At present, five such Persian crosses exist, two at Kottayam Knanaya, at the Jacobite Valiyapally (greater church), with one each at St. Thomas Mount, Mylapore, at Kadamatom St. George Jacobite Church and Muttuchira Roman Catholic Church.[6] Many other crosses of similar design, spanning over a thousand years, are to be found in over fifty different locations in South India.

Along with diverse forms of the cross, and other frequent symbols such as the fish, grapes (or cup) and bread, a dove, or the Greek letters Chi Ro and Alpha and Omega. The image of the Good Shepherd seems to be one of the earliest representations of Jesus to be found anywhere (as at Dura Europos, right). It is one which would be carried throughout all Asia's region.

It is now well-established that the earliest known Christian church building is that at *Dura Europos,* east Syria, above (230+ CE).[6a] The frescoes that decorated this chapel's baptistery predate almost all those known of in the Roman catacombs and were painted long before the time of Constantine. They are therefore probably the most ancient Christian paintings so far known and include the earliest portrayals of Jesus Christ which we have (above), and the former paralytic now healed and carrying a bed on his back (at left). There are also other scenes in this earliest church, which are obviously based on incidents in the gospels.

Amongst other early forms of Christian art the very frequent subject typical of Christian art of angels holding a shield or medallion with the portrait of the Redeemer is also of Oriental origin. In addition to

Dura Europos, this theme was found in the frescoes of the catacombs of Palmyra which were also painted long before those found in the Latin West'. In these frescoes of Palmyra some 'Victories' along with angels are androgynous (above left).

Byzantine art

To cover the whole of Byzantine art we would have to include icons, murals, paintings and architecture created from the 4th century to the 15th century, not only in West Asia but also in many parts of the Levant and in North Africa. Certain central features can however be seen throughout the region.^{6b} The rich diversity of icons in particular, depicting figures and incidents from all Biblical and doctrinal history, served as channels of access for the faithful to the spiritual world. Similarly mosaics and other images sought to present a transformed earthly realm into which worshippers could enter. (There were also of course images that affirmed the 'holiness' of known leaders or the feudal power of present rulers).

The wealth of Byzantine art cannot be outlined here however except to give some points of entry, considering first the form of Byzantine crosses. These have traditionally been shown with two or three cross beams making them distinctly different from other Christian crosses. They are sometimes superimposed on a budding cross, or have all beams budding (to also represent the coming of new life). The top-most beam is normally taken to represent the plaque bearing Pontius Pilate's inscription "Jesus the Nazorean, King of the Jews". This cross also sometimes has the acronym *IC XC NIKA* added (Greek "He conquers"). The lowest beam represents a foot-support and began appearing in Eastern Christian art in the 6th century.

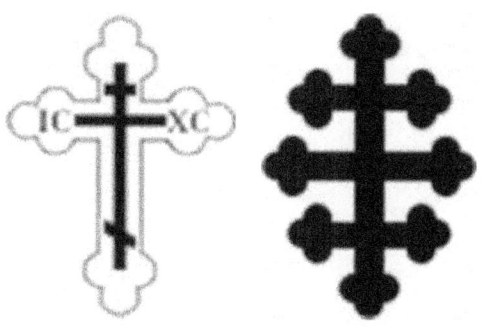

In many churches or basilicas of Byzantine tradition there can be seen many variations of this basic three-armed cross, At right is one of many depictions in a mosaic of the Resurrected Jesus, this from the monastery of *Hosios Loukas,* Greece (11th) century.

Symbolism found in East Asia, in other depictions of Jesus in Byzantine art, such as the labarum and the Trinitarian symbol of first and third fingers joined, are found far across Asia, in Christian art-forms of Turkestan, India and China (See below).

Of quite unusual interest is this giant Candlestick holder with Christian scenes created by Dawud ibn Salama al-Mawsiliin in 1248-1249 in Syria. This example of advanced 13th century skill in metals was recently featured in the major exhibition of Christian Art *Christianity in Asia: Sacred Art and Visual Splendour* (held at the

Asian Civilizations Museum, Singapore, Oct. 2017). Sixteen inlaid me subjects or motifs. Interesting for its glimpse of hidden Christian history, this example which is now held in the Louvre Museum Paris, was created during the Muslim Ayyubid Dynasty, which ruled Egypt, Syria and Palestine, late 12th/early 13th centuries.

The East Byzantine Empire (c. 527 to 1453 CE.) was notable also for its lavish architecture, paintings and mosaics of Roman and Greek artists who created new Eastern Christian images and icons which influenced much later Asian art. Above left, the Transfiguration of Christ, still to be seen at the Church of the Virgin, Monastery of Saint Catherine, Mount Sinai, West Asia and was created ca. 548–65. At right is the earliest known painting of Christ the Pantocrator, also at St Catherine's Monastery Sinai (note the two different facial expressions – to depict the two different 'natures' of Christ).

Parallel to the Byzantine Empire was that of Persia which at its height extended as far eastwards as North India. In Syria, Turkey and Iran there are many remarkable remains of earlier Christian presence, many of which have been greatly damaged even in just the last century. Along with ruined churches or monasteries, standing crosses or tombs, some early or late medieval examples of murals and manuscripts have been however preserved. These are found either in situ, or more often, in ancient manuscripts, held in the museums of Europe or north America.

These are important to note because of their later influence upon art-forms in distant parts of the region.

The next two pictures, chosen here from a very large number, show a less usual understanding of the common ground that is understood to lie between Christianity, Islam and Judaism. On the left is a 12th century mural from the monastery of *Mar Musa*, Syria, showing Moses, Jesus and

Mahomet all held in the bosom of Abraham. The second image comes from Rashid ad-Din's *History of the World*, written in *Tabriz*, Iran.[7] It portrays Nestorius, who at the right gestures his acceptance of Mohammed (anointed by an angel at left), as being the first to recognise him to be a prophet. Here also two major faiths are shown to have areas of common acceptance.

Paintings or mosaics on Christian subjects have also been completed by members of other faiths. Generations of eclectic Muslim artists for example, have left paintings and miniatures which include the portrayals of incidents drawn sometimes from

the Hebrew scriptures but more often from the life of Jesus. At right, disciples try to wake Jesus in the storm on lake Galilee (detail *Mir'at al-Quds manuscript*). Two further examples from a very wide number are given below:

At left is one showing Mary and Jesus (from Safavid dynasty, 16th century). At right, Isa [Jesus] 'brings down heavenly food for his disciples' (Quran 5:111-115, [cf. John, ch. 6]). Many localities across the former Persian empire, especially in India, show examples of such 'Christian' art from Muslim artists. Often created at the behest of the caliph or king, such paintings showed a recognition of Jesus as being also a great prophet.

II. In Armenia, which is known to have had the earliest 'state church' anywhere in the world (ca. 301 CE)[8] there was a similar and rich development both in church architecture and in art-forms for the cross. Many of these took the form of stones erected for

the deceased. These *Khachkars* or memorial stones were free-standing and up to 10 m. in height.

They were also empty of any figure superimposed, thus also symbolizing resurrection and new life. They were however to gather much elaborate decoration in following centuries, especially where created as tomb-stones at cemeteries such as that of *Gegharkunik*. On some can be seen lotus-like or global images also (see below).

Traumatic experiences in the history of Armenian Christianity in the 4th to 7th centuries had led to development of various alternative methods by which to communicate the Gospel and this was especially seen in the skills used by craftsmen in their wood and stone carvings. From their arts the early simple unadorned cross later became 'the cross as a fruit-bearing tree' which was elaborately carved with vegetal or geometric motifs. Behind this symbolism lay the Biblical concept of the 'world as a garden in which all blessings would finally be found'. The (two photos above and at left are from the *Gegharkunik* cemetery of Armnenia. Calligraphic arts in medieval West Asia also became highly skillful and sophisticated in illuminated Syriac and Armenian Bibles; Armenian manuscript sources being particularly rich. At right, from

a Syriac parchment codex, is a page from the Armenian Bible copied in 1317 by the scribe Astuacatur and deposited at Karbi (British Library Or. 2680).[9] The central figures have been identified as portraying Bishop Abba standing before Jesus. These pages are one fold of seven fully painted scenes from the life of Jesus Christ.

III. India

There is now scholarly consensus that the apostle Thomas founded churches in south India and possibly also in the north of India.[10] Amongst the carvings and remains from the centuries following, are over fifty crosses and monuments, many of which are believed to be, along with neighbouring churches, from the earliest centuries.

Most of these crosses which are the most ancient of Indian Christian artforms, have been found in Kerala and along the Malabar coast of south-west India. There are however also examples found in Goa to the north and in Tamil Nadu to the east, as well as in such northern localities as *Takht-i-Bahi* (near Peshawar) and Taxila (now in Pakistan).

A strong tradition holds that one of the earliest carved 'Cross of Christians' was placed by St. Thomas the Apostle at *Cranganore*, and that this cross acted as the early model for all the other crosses erected in different parts of India and beyond. Inscriptions on many of these crosses could support a very early date, being in Syriac and Pahlavi scripts, both of which are derived from Aramaic and date from the earliest centuries. Similar Pahlavi writings have also been discovered in caves near Mumbai, along with many Aramaic inscriptions elsewhere in northern India. These crosses are characteristically of Persian style in which the cross is shown rising from a lotus blossom which symbolizes a purity that grows spontaneously from earth and water. It has similar symbolism throughout Asia but here it is also the national flower of India.[11]

One of the oldest of the Indian crosses, named *Kottakkavu Sliba*  (left below), is now at Kottakkavu, *North Paravur*. The church at *North Paravur* is reputed to be the 'first church in India', dating from 52 C.E. and the cross is preserved in the Mar Thoma Syro-Malabar Pilgrim Centre there. Familiar images found in ancient Persian crosses are placed here within a surrounding circle., similar to Indian images of 'the Wheel of Dharma'. Compared to other Indian crosses so far discovered it appears to be of more ancient provenance, but as yet no more exact dating has been possible.

Many carved figures of Jesus and Mary are extant from later periods, in wood and in ivory, from both India and Sri Lanka. At right, this dates from 16th century Ceylon at the time of widespread Dutch presence but also at the time of extensive missions there of Fr Joseph Vaz and his colleagues.

Much more elaborate carving from early Indian churches is preserved upon large fonts (as below) for adult baptismal immersion (here *Kaduthurithi, Kerala*) still used in some south Indian churches, but dating from well before the pre-Portuguese period. The imagery here is freely borrowed from Hindu cultural motifs, often including figures in relief which are clearly Indian.

In such artefacts, dated between the fourth and fifteenth centuries, the cultural 'symbiosis' that has often been noted in the earliest Indian Christian traditions is further illustrated. Hindu, Jain, Buddhist, Jewish, Christian and Islamic communities coexisted, mutually borrowing custom and symbol, yet also retaining their own identity in creed and way of life.[12] The characterization of these early churches as 'Hindu in culture, Christian in faith and Oriental in worship' only partly conveys the integration of worship, life-style and witness which research is now uncovering.

Much of the ancient heritage of India in its Christian churches has however been tragically destroyed. "To the great loss of Christian archaeology" writes Matthew Lederle, "most of those ancient churches have either been ruined or have been demolished to be replaced by churches in Portuguese style". What we do have does nevertheless show that same integration of faith and culture which is observable in India from the earliest centuries. "Yet we can find today some examples of the Indian Christian art of the ancient Church of Malabar" continues Lederle. And he draws attention to the large monolithic cross behind the old Church of *Kaduthurithi*, where "the pedestal is beautifully decorated with lotuses, elephants and other motifs which are usually found on the walls of ancient Hindu temples."[13]

In India also, traditions of Persian artists were preserved by the Mughal artists of the 16th to 18th centuries.[14] Many of these readily included Biblical themes, especially that of the infant Jesus with his mother, in their work.

At left below, the focus in a less well-known painting is again on Jesus and his mother or here on the Holy Family, painted by an anonymous Mughal artist. At right is one of many paintings that emerged following

renewed Christian mission in 17th century India. Jesuit priests Acquaviva and Monserrat (in black) participate in interfaith debates at *Fatehpur Sikri* (with Emperor Akbar seated at right). Such dialogues were often arranged by Akbar in his search for toleration amongst major religions in India.[15]

IV. China

In China it has long been known that the early history for Christianity there from the 7th century was recorded a century later upon the *Sian-fu* (so-called "Nestorian") monument[16] (see below). Additional research has recently shown that there were Christians present there in the previous century.

But now more recent discoveries have shown that Christian presence almost certainly began many centuries earlier still. Through the research of Prof. Wong Wei Fan in *Xuzhou*[17] we now know of Chinese steles and an urn, at right above, which have been identified as belonging to the first century (Han Dynasty).

The urn is precisely dated, as with so many ancient Chinese artefacts, and here the engraved date is verified as being 86 C.E. This example is most important, as it depicts what can be seen to be five loaves and two fishes, making a Christian identification virtually certain. With the carving of loaves and fishes there is also added the character "Yi"(in Chinese 'one', 'one people', 'together').

In the *Book of Records* – one of the Five Classics which are considered part of the sacred scriptures of China – it was said that 'the offering is to God', where the *yi* is used for offering by the Emperor. The word *Yi* also means "sharing" as this was so used in the *Book of Poetry* (another of the five classics). It is therefore thought possible by scholars studying the urn in careful laboratory-standard detail, that in the Eastern Han period such an urn, was used in the context of Christian worship for celebration of the 'Eucharist' or similar 'agape'-type meals.[18]

Other carvings discovered by Wong Wei Fan include a manger scene which clearly shows the baby held on the lap of his mother, along with celestial beings above the roof and 'Wise ones' coming to pay homage. Other panels are interpreted as depicting incidents from Genesis or the Prophets as well as from the Gospels. Although some scholars have been skeptical of the claims for these artefacts, a full study and favourable assessment of similar discoveries of such early examples has been recently published by two French scholars. Later volumes also explore aspects of a greatly revised chronology now necessary for Christian history in China.[19]

Perhaps most well-known of all engravings in the history of Asian Christianity however is the so-called '"Nestorian"' (that is the *Church of the East*) Monument.

It was discovered near *Sian-fu* (near *Xian*) in 1623, but was created in 781 CE. Extensive research on the stele has been continued by many Jesuit and Protestant missionary scholars, and more recently by Chinese experts in Tang history and epigraphy[20].

Measuring over three metres high by one metre wide and 30 centimetres deep, the stele is inscribed with almost two thousand Chinese characters along with seventy words in Syriac. It records the early history of the Church of the East in China during the Tang dynasty (7th-10th centuries). At the head of the stele however is a Persian cross, standing within a lotus blossom and edged with flame, flowers and cloud formations. Flanking the cross and head inscription are two magnificent dragons, symbolic in Chinese tradition of heavenly order and of earthly peace.

The monument text takes the form of a Eulogy commemorating the spread of the 'Ta'chin Luminous Religion'

(Christianity) in 'the Central Kingdom' and begins with an ascription of praise to 'the only unoriginated Lord of the Universe'. The main inscription ends by picturing the 'reverent service and proper worship' which the monks of twelve monasteries performed: "The hungry came and were fed; The cold came and they were clothed; The sick were healed and raised up. The dead were buried and laid to rest."

Similar Christian steles can be seen at other locations such as *Fangshan* (at right above) north of Beijing, as well as in Inner Mongolia (see further below).

V. Inner Asia, Turkestan

Many examples of Christian art have been uncovered across the steppes and deserts of Inner Asia and Turkestan, in territories formerly part of Russia (Kazakhstan, Kyrgyzstan, Tajikistan, Uzbekistan, Turkmenistan), or in China (Xinjiang), and Tibet. The early work of Saeki Yoshiro[21] has been especially important in the study of these remains but many later scholars have added to our knowledge.[22]

Possibly the fullest development of some of these traditions is illustrated in the paintings discovered early last century by Stein, Pelliot, le Coq and others, in the churches and cave-temples of east Turkestan (now west China).[23] Often found in sealed caves or ruined churches, these had been preserved over a thousand years by the dry desert conditions. They are now held and being studied in almost twenty museums world-wide. It is possible here to introduce only a selection of some of the more striking examples so far identified from the holdings for the Churches of the East.

This contemplative figure (left) of a youth in flowing robes comes from ruins of the Church of the East at *Khocho*, *(Karakhoja, Turfan)* discovered by Albert von Le Coq in

1913. The reddish-brown over- garment has very full sleeves hiding the hands and the white under- garment hides all but the toes of the shoes. This painting of a young Uighur Turk (9th century), who may be a priest assistant, is markedly different from Buddhist and Manichaean art found nearby.[24]

The cross at right comes from *Herat* in present-day Afghanistan, which was for many centuries the seat for a Metropolitan of the Church of the East (A Metropolitan was usually responsible for at least six bishoprics). The inscription on this processional cross is in the Middle Persian language with some Syriac words in Pahlavi script, similar to the inscribed crosses of south India. Here the inscriptions speak of a person named 'Mare', of the Church of Herat who entrusts the community to 'Saint (or Holy) Karisise'. There is also a statement that there are not three Gods but only One; along with a wish that the church will prosper, and 'be the hosts to the Church of my good teaching'.

From East Turkestan also comes the Christian fresco discovered by A. Le Coq in 1905, which has been identified as depicting a baptismal service being celebrated on Palm Sunday. The priest (left) shows some Byzantine characteristics, holding a thurible and vessel of holy water or wine. The three figures before him – which likely include women – carry bunches of green leaves, most likely willow, in place of palms. The festival and sacrament are vividly depicted, giving a glimpse

of church life in ninth century Turkestan.[25] (Ignore the horse's hoof of a later artist!)

One of the most remarkable of the paintings discovered by Aurel Stein in the *Dunhuang* library in 1907-8 is that he named "Le Bon Pasteur".[26] Dating from the tenth century, and surviving centuries of drought, the image clearly depicts a Buddha-like image of Jesus.[27] Also shown here is a reconstruction by the Japanese artist, Furuyama, which gives the colours of the original painting. The painting is of silk and has been preserved for almost a millennium in the driest desert conditions of a sealed ancient room at Dunhuang. Crosses of Church of the East style adorn the coronet, the necklace and the labarum. These, together with the hairstyle and the hand-gesture (linking the *third* and first fingers to indicate the "Three-in-one") distinguish the figure as being clearly Christian. It is noteworthy that the early art of Turkestan which has been unearthed most often features Jesus himself, often with congregational members but unlike contemporary art further west, omitting Jesus' mother Mary. Here indeed is a striking presentation of a Christ-like Asian figure, with some Byzantine features, although close in form to paintings of the Buddha or of Bodhisattvas which are so widespread in the region.

The examples above graphically show both how Christianity in 'early medieval' Asia was deeply rooted in local cultures, and how its art and other forms yet maintained distinctive Christian features, some of which were modelled on Byzantine images. There was clearly no hesitation in utilizing Buddhist imagery for the portrayal of Christian art forms.

Another art-form spread most widely throughout this region is the carved tomb-stone, sometimes found in extensive 'medieval' Christian cemeteries.[28] Those from west Turkestan, of which there are many hundreds in various localities, often show a simplified "Nestorian" cross, with lotus base, and with angelic or sometimes memorial figures added.

First rediscovered in the late 19th century, examples continue to be found in the course of construction or excavation in Inner Asia or China.

Many carvings in relief which have been found in ruined churches or cemeteries also include both figures – in the case below of three donors – with the 'Persian' cross upon lotus of the Church of the East (at far left). This scene in relief from the 7th-8th centuries, comes from *Semirice*, west Turkestan and is held in the State Hermitage Museum, St Petersburg. The border of pearls for

the cross at left is a Sasanian motif from Persia. Figures similar to these are to be seen in supposedly Manichaean carvings of the same period and in adjacent localities.[29] The Hermitage museum was opened again to scholars in 1994 and has revealed many artefacts drawn originally from history of the Church of the East in Russia's 'far east'.

Of quite a different character, and here of practical use, are the household artefacts that have been discovered in many settlements along the old 'Silk Routes'.

This large blue iron corn-measure from *Lhasa*, Tibet, shows clearly in silver engravings the four-armed cross of the eastern churches.[30] The design bears similarities to some simpler Persian crosses that have been found in Ladakh and other parts of Inner Asia. There is evidence of Persian contacts and trade between Persia and Tibet also from at least as early as the 5th century. Christian communities must have developed soon after for we know they were numerous enough to require the appointment of metropolitans and bishops for Tibet by Patriarch Timothy in the 8th century. (Refer chapter 1 above).

Particularly interesting are other examples of early Christian art from the region which are emerging from newly opened archives in Russian museums. Outstanding amongst these are the engraved silver dishes with carvings in relief, recently displayed also in the Hermitage Museum of St. Petersburg.[31] These show a merging of Persian, Central and east Asian influences

The one illustrated below comes from Kyrgyzstan, although it was discovered farther west in the Ural mountains. It depicts Jesus' crucifixion, burial and resurrection in separate panels. The surrounding images are of soldiers, Peter's denial and Daniel. Mary does not appear in the resurrection scene, in accord with the eastern rejection of some western traditions.

In form, the series of panels follows the style used in contemporary Buddhist *Jataka* artefacts which would also portray incidents in the Buddha's life. The technique and artistry employed reveals that Turco-Sogdian artists produced this in the ninth or tenth centuries, thus linking Persia, central Russia, and Kyrgyzstan (and eventually St Petersburg) in the extensive range of practice and influence of the churches of the East. Such artefacts also reveal the acceptance and exchange of images and art-forms that followed from the encounter and dialogue between major religious traditions, in this case with Buddhism.

VI. Mongolia

The Mongol Empire (1162-1368) at its highest point extended in Asia from the Black sea in the west to Burma in the south and to the sea of Japan in the east. For that period some of the art-forms found over many centuries have been already mentioned above. Here the focus will be only upon the 'Mongol heartland' in northeast Asia, including Manchuria and the two Mongolias of today. Here we have many examples of Christian art in stone as well as metal artefacts

and graphic art. Such gravestones as these (above) at Olon Sumé are found today in many localities across this northeast region as well as in other regions under Mongol rule. Many still remain in situ.

The early Mongol khans followed shamanistic traditions which being without formal 'scriptures', 'clergy' or institutions was well able to tolerate the practice of other faith traditions. They had however come to interpret the 'Eternal Heaven' of some Shamanist traditions in monotheistic terms (the Lord *Tengri, T`aŋgiri* or *Tenger*). This still made possible a tolerance of diverse faiths and even the encouragement of religious freedom.[32] This meant that throughout the Mongol Empire from East Asia to far West Asia, and under successive khans, Christian communities were accorded toleration and often even protection. The Church of the East was also at times invited to share in dialogues between spokesmen for the various religious communities, including Muslim Manichaean, Shaman, and Buddhist. However such a Shamanism would also later, as in other monotheist traditions, justify extremities of violence in the imposition of imperial rule in the name of the 'One God' throughout Asia and beyond.

These Nativity scenes are one series of a number found on many groups of tombs in *Chien-shan*, Manchuria. Dating from the 13th century, they depict the holy family and the wise ones, while others nearby show household or travel scenes. Costumes and forms of architecture or transport have been identified as being clearly local to the region.[33]

From the same period come countless seals and crosses of Mongol crafting that have been discovered across the whole region. These date from the 11th to the 14th centuries. Particularly large collections of these are held in Hong Kong, China and North America. At right below is one example that shows a copper amulet worn by '"Nestorian" ' Ongut Mongols.[34] Here also there is a blend of traditions which join the ringed cross with a central (eastern) swastika, the ancient symbol which here likely represents the mind of the Buddha. Tibetan Buddhism had increased its influence in Mongolia during the ascendancy of the Yuan or Mongol dynasty, retaining there however some features of earlier shamanist traditions.

The equal-length and almost triangular arms of the cross in many such seals retain the basic form of a Persian cross. Amongst the whole body of imperial, personal, commercial and religious seals which have emerged there are many which as here, clearly contain variations upon other Christian symbolism.

The selection at right is seen on a poster advertising an exhibition held by the Museum and Art Gallery of the University of Hong Kong.

The Bronze section there includes the largest collection of seal crosses from the Yuan Dynasty now held anywhere in the world. They have been assembled from the wide extent of the Mongol empire demonstrating very extensive distribution of (amongst other symbols) clearly Christian

emblems.

Paintings also from that period and region have been assembled. Among the many portraits of the Khans are some which record the most outstanding woman leader in Mongol history. This was Sorgaqthani Beki, a princess of the largely Christian Kerait tribes (from 'Kherees' meaning 'cross', the most dominant of the five tribal confederations of the Mongols). She was daughter-in-law of Chinggis Khan and is depicted here with her husband Tolui by a Persian artist.

As Khatun (Empress), and Beki ('Chieftainess'), Sorghaghtani was then called the "wisest woman of the world"[35] and the "directing spirit of the house of Tolui". She was a member of the Church of the East who was however tolerant and supportive of other religious traditions. Her sons, including Khubilai (Kubla) Khan, all became known for their religious tolerance and sometimes moderate imperial policies.

Another son of Sorghaghtani, Hülegü, became Khan of Persia and West Asia where he established a semi-independent Khanate. He also showed tolerance for peoples belonging to the Church of the East and is alleged to have assisted the construction of churches and even to have been himself Christian. (As with similar allegations regarding other Khans the evidence for this is uncertain). Above left, is a portrayal of 'Saint Hülegü' and his wife Doguz Khatun, who is known certainly to have been a Christian. They are holding a triple-beamed Byzantine cross (see above), and are here depicted as being the new "Constantine and Helen" (from a contemporary illustrated Syriac Bible). Note that in the 13th century every Khan had either a Christian mother and/or a Christian wife!

Much Christian art in this context can be seen on tombs still remaining in situ. Typically the tomb carving above combines a small cross with the lotus, along with angel and cloud images that are found on many Church of the East crosses. This one has been identified as celebrating a Christian leader of the Kubilai dynasty period.[36]

The Church of the East village of *Olun Sume* (northeast Inner Mongolia) and nearby *Shizhuziliang* are amongst the localities which have yielded very extensive remains of Christian presence. Apart from many such cemeteries, other articles such as the

baptismal font at right have been later found in the 'cultural yards' of such Cities as Hohhot or Zaohe. (This from Hohhot).

Conclusion

Much more work must of course be done to assemble and identify the art-forms of 'late antique', 'medieval' and 'early modern' Christian communities in Asia (and of course of later periods also when Christian artists have been astoundingly prolific). This will require much more research both in each country of the region and in major museum collections world-wide.

But equally important is the full recognition we must accord to this largely unknown history of creativity in expressing the Christian Gospel from within Asian cultures. For Christians everywhere this is the art of the 'other half of Christian history'. For all Asian Christians this offers not only new sources for lively art and symbol but also a great enrichment in our own *Asian* Christian identity. The examples given, only a small selection from many, show a Christian identity quite independent of western art forms. They also show clearly a strong allegiance to central Christian truths, expressed as these are experienced and discerned within the life and thought-forms of particular cultures and peoples of the Asian region. Their insights and images offer rich resources for Christian art in both the East and the West today.

NOTE: For sources for Asian Christian Art in following centuries see, along with references above, and the quarterly Image (Asian Christian Art Assoc. since 1975) works by: Masao Takenaka & Ron O'Grady *Christian Art in Asia*. (Kwo Bun Kwan, CCA, 1975, *The Bible Through Asian Eyes* (Pace, for ACAA, 1991), *The Place Where God Dwells* (Pace, for CCA/ACAA, 1995); Pongracz, Patricia et al. *The Christian Story: Five Asian Artists Today* (Museum of Biblical Art, New York, 2007). Amongst the Christian artists in particular countries for whom we have published vols. see: He Qui (China), Alfred Thomas, Frank Wesley (India), Sadao Watanabe (Japan), Carlos V. Francisco (Philippines), Nalini Jayasuriya (Sri Lanka), Sawai Chinnawong (Thailand).

Endnotes

[1] See chap. 1 in this volume.

[2] Amongst many works on this history see chapter 1 above, and for example, A.S. Atiya *A History of Eastern Christianity* (Methuen, 1968, & Kraus, 1991); S.H. Moffett *A History of Christianity in Asia* vol.1 (Harper Collins, 1992); Mahmoud Zibawi *Eastern Christian Worlds* (Liturgical Press, 1995), J.C. England *Hidden History of Christianity in Asia* (ISPCK, 1998); T.V. Philip *East of the Euphrates. Early Christianity in Asia* (CSS & ISPCK, 1998); I. Gillman & H-J. Klimkeit *Christians in Asia before 1500*

(Curzon, 1999); Mar Abraham *Forgotten East*.(Ephrem's Pubns., 2000); W. Baum & D.W. Winkler *The Church of the East*. (Routledge Curzon, 2003); C. Baumer *The Church of the East. An Illustrated History of Assyrian Christianity* (Tauris, 2006), Li Tang & Dietmar W. Winkler (eds.) *From the Oxus River to the Chinese Shores*. (LIT, 2013).

[3] See Elisabeth Goldsmith *Ancient Pagan Symbols* (G.P. Putman, 1929); D.J. Fleming *Christian symbols in a world community* (Friendship Press, 1940).

[4] Refer Ian Gilman, & Hans-Joachim Klimkeit, (*op.cit.*) 86 ff..

[5] ibid.; see also Hassan Dehgani- Tafti, *Christ and Christianity Among the Iranians*. 3 vols. (Sohrab Books, 1992); Z.C. Pakizegi *History of the Christians in Iran*. (Sooner, 1992); M. Bradley *Iran and Christianity : Historical Identity and Present Relevance* (Broché, 2011).

[6] Refer *M. Lederle*, "Art India, Christian Paintings in Indian Style"..*Jeevadhara*, 1971; J.F.Butler, *Christian Art in India*. (CLS, 1986).

[6a] For Dura Europos see K. Weitzmann *The Frescoes of the Dura Synagogue and Christian Art* (Geneological Press, 1990); M. Peard *The World's Oldest Church: Bible, Art, and Ritual at Dura-Europos, Syria* (Yale 2016); T. Mathews *The Dawn of Christian Art in Panel Paintings and Icons* (Getty, 2017).

[6b] See Rice, D. Talbot Byzantine Art Penguin Books, 1954; Grabar, A. *Greek Mosaics of the Byzantine Period* (A Mentor-Unesco Art Book), New American Library and Unesco, 1964; Kitzinger, Ernst *Byzantine Art in the Making: Main Lines of Stylistic Development in Mediterranean Art, Third to Seventh Centuries.* Faber, 1987; Cormack, Robin *Byzantine Art* Oxford University Press, 2018.

[7] *Jami al-tawarikh* ("Collector of Chronicles" 1314); see B. Gray, *The 'World history' of Rashid al-Din: A study of the Royal Asiatic Society manuscript* (Faber, 1978); R. Blair, *A compendium of chronicles : Rashid al-Din's illustrated History of the World* (Khalili, 1995). C.f. L. Xavier López-Farjeat *Cross Veneration in the Medieval Islamic World: Christian Identity and Practice under Muslim Rule.* (Tauris, 1917). For a full treatment of Christian art-forms in west Asia see also M. Zibawi *Eastern Christian Worlds*. (Liturgical Press, 1995).

[8] See G. Vigen. "Armenia." In *The Encyclopedia of Christianity*, ed. E. Fahlbusch & G.W. Bromiley (Eerdmans, 1999); K. Barsamian *Conversion of Armenia to Christianity: A Retelling of Agathangelos' History.* (Armenian Church of America, 2001).

[9] S. Whitfield *The Silk Road* (British Library, 2004) 123; Refer also S.Der Nersessian *Armenia and the Byzantine empire;: A brief study of Armenian Art and Civilization*. (Harvard, 1945); Der Nersessian *Armenian Art* (Thames & Hudson, 1978). Valerie Goekjian, *The Christian Literature and Fine Arts of the Armenians*. (Armenian Church of America, 1973).

[10] G. Menachery, (ed.) *St. Thomas Christian Encyclopaedia of India* (STCEI, 1973). Robert Eric Frykenberg *Christianity in India: From Beginnings to the Present* (Oxford, 2010) chap.4.

[11] Refer Menachery, op.cit. Vol. 2; A.M. Mundadan *History of Christianity in India*

2 vols. (Theological Publications in India, 1982-84); R.E. *Christianity in India Oxford History of the Christian Church* (Oxford, 2016); G. Burke *The Apostle of India* https://ocoy.org/original-apostle-of-india (2018).

[12] H. Zimmer, *Myths and Symbols in Indian Art and Civilization* (Harper & Row, 1962); S.G. Pothan, *The Syrian Christians of Kerala*. (Asia Publishing House, 1963); A.M. Mundadan *Sixteenth Century Traditions of St Thomas Christians* (Dharmaram College, 1970); 'St Thomas Cross' //en.wikipedia.org/wiki/Saint Thomas Christian Cross.

[13] Lederle op.cit.1971.

[14] Refer S.P. Verma *Crossing Cultural Frontiers : Biblical Themes in Mughal Painting*. (Aryan Book,2011); A. Amaladass, & G. Lowner *Christian Themes in Indian Art: From the Mogul Times till Today* (Manohar Publishers, 2012).

[15] See e.g. P.Du Jarric, & C. H. Payne *Akbar and the Jesuits*. (Routledge, 1926); P.M. Carvalho *Mir at Al-Quds* (Mirror of Holiness): *A Life of Christ for Emperor Akbar*. (Cleveland 2011).

[16] Standard works include A. C. Moule *Christians in China before the year 1550*. (SPCK, 1930); Aubrey Vine *The "Nestorian" Churches: A Concise History*. (Independent Press, 1937); J. Foster, *The Church in T'ang Dynasty*. (SPCK, 1939); Lee S. K. *The Cross and the Lotus* (Christian Study Centre on Chinese Religion and Culture, 1971).N. Standaert.) *Handbook of Christianity in China. Vol. I: 635-1800*. (Leiden, Brill, 2001); Li Tang *A Study of the History of "Nestorian" Christianity in China*. (Peter Lang, 2001).

[17] Wong W.F. "Christianity in China – 1st Century". (*China News Update*, January 2003). See also *Christianity in Asia: Sacred Art and Visual Splendour Exhibition* (Asian Civilisations Museum, Singapore, May - Sep 2016).

[18] P. Perrier & X. Walter *Thomas fonde l'Eglise en Chine 65-68 après Jésus-Christ*. (Sarment Edns. 2008) Fig.19.2, c.f. Figs 1.1 – 13.1

[19] See also Perrier, *L'apôtre Thomas et le prince Ying Kong Wang Shan: —L'évangélisation de la Chine de 64 à 87* (Sarment Edns. 2012), C.f. Wong W.F. (op.cit. 2005).

[20] See especially J. Legge *The"Nestorian" Monument of Hsi-an Fu in Shen-hsi China*, (Trübner, 1888, repr. Paragon Book, 1966); Saeki Y. *The "Nestorian" Monument in China*. (SPCK, 1928); D. Wang "Remnants of Christianity from Chinese Central Asia in Medieval ages" in Roman Malek & Peter Hofrichter (eds.) *Jingjiao: the Church of the East in China and Central Asia*. (Verlagsbuchhandlung, 2006); M. Keevak *The Story of a Stele: China's "Nestorian" Monument and its Reception in the West 1625-1916*. (Hong Kong University Press, 2008).

[21] Saeki Y. op.cit 1951.

[22] See Gilman & Klimkeit (*op. cit.* 1999) 186ff.; M. Palmer *The Jesus Sutras* (Ballantyne, 2001); Baumer (op.cit 2006); T.H.F. Halbertsma *Early Christian Remains of Inner Mongolia* (Brill, 2008).

[23] See for example A. Stein *On Ancient Central-Asian Tracks* (University of Chicago

Press, 1964); A.Von Le Coq *Buried Treasures Of Chinese Turkestan* (G. Allen & Unwin ltd., 1928); P. Pelliot *Kao-Tch'ang, Qoco, Houo- Tcheou et Qarâ-Khodja*, (ReInk Books, 2017).

[24] Tamara T. Rice *Ancient Arts of Central Asia*. (Thames & Hudson, 1965).Wall painting of young worshipper, from "Nestorian" Church in Khocho, 9th century. (Berlin State Museum);

[25] von le Coq (*op.cit.* 1985).

[26] A. Stein, *Ruins of Desert Cathay: Personal Narrative*. 2 vols. (Dover, 1987).

[27] Frontispiece for Saeki (op.cit. 1951).

[28] As at Tokmak and Bishbek, Kyrgizstan. See J. Stewart, *"Nestorian" Missionary Enterprise: the Story of a Church on Fire*. (Madras, C.L.S., 1928).

[29] Gilman, & Klimkeit, (op. cit. 1999)

[30] G. Tucci *Transhimalaya*. (Barrie & Jenkins, 1973).

[31] Gilman & Klimkeit, (*op. cit.* 1999).

[32] See especially J. Weatherford *Genghis Khan and the Quest for God*. (Viking, 2016).

[33] One of eight carved panels of Nativity scenes, on tombstones in Chien-shan, north China. 12th/13th century. (Saeki,1951).

[34] See Baumer (op.cit. 2006) chap.IX; Halbertsma (op.cit. 2008).

[35] R. al D. Hamadani declared this in his *Jâmi≥ al-tawârîkh* (op.cit.1314), Cited M. Rossabi *Voyager from Xanadu: Rabban Sauma and the First Journey from China to the West*. (Kodansha, 1992).

[36] The fullest treatment of these and similar remains are found in Halbertsma (op.cit.)

Chapter - 4

Bamboo Groves in Winds from the West:

Indigenous Faith and Western Influence in Asian Christian Writings of 16th-18th Centuries

Entering the Grove

There are so many preliminary questions regarding the cultural and intellectual context and content of Asian Christian writings in the 16th to the 18th centuries to note – so many critical qualifications to make – that I can refer to them only briefly, as if to an agenda for any future study, and as a brief framework for considering particular writings. These, in turn, can be only a very small sampling from the extant literatures.[1]

i) The most fundamental issue is of course the widespread neglect of extensive writings by Asian Christians in the period, and the unwarranted assumptions which allow this to continue. As in other studies of Asian cultures and histories, we have to accept that many of our usual critical categories or methodologies do not function easily here. Presuppositions regarding the paucity, insignificance and possible 'heresy' of such writings must also be rejected in the course of developing the hermeneutic and criteria which will be adequate to the vast and diverse range of material available. We are in fact in the 'excavatory phase' for a study of these materials, in order to unearth, recognise and name both the writings and traditions themselves, along with the characteristics of Asian thought and literature which largely shape them.

ii) Then come the questions as to what terms and periodization are to be employed, what genres of writing are to be recognized, and what methodologies used for their interpretation. Cross-cultural and Asia-regional categories and criteria must now be utilized for these.[2] Regarding the period itself, it has been customary to refer to it as the 'early modern', the 'colonial' or 'early mission' period, or even the 'period of first acceptance', all of course being the obvious imposition of western categories. Looked at from the 'other end', many Asian (and other) scholars view this time as one part of a long history of cultural encounter in which the East has often been the major contributor and in which also contextualizing Christian theology has had a continuing history.[3] Unfortunately it is possible to recognise the partial theological retreat in this period, from earlier more creative Asian theologies, as found in for example, the major theologians in Syriac of the 2nd to 5th centuries and the Turfan and Dunhuang collections of the 9th to 11th centuries. (Refer to chap.1).

iii) The sheer diversity of contexts, agents and partners in the encounters between 'natives' and 'foreigners' in the period requires extensive study and explication. Theologies which are either transplanted/colonizing *or* incarnational/ liberating are found in the work of both local Christians and missionary teachers. The integrity of native tradition may be affirmed and western interventions criticized or rejected; or creative aspects of each may be blended in a new articulation of tradition. Cultural-political assumptions regarding the host culture, rather than nationality or ethnicity, are primary here, and we will see that either nationals or expatriates may perform either contextualizing *or* colonizing functions.

iv) The anonymous and cooperative character of Asian intellectual life, art, architecture and writing in the period, with its purpose of 'collective moral edification' also requires much more careful study and reception by us.[4] For it contrasts strongly with our western fixation on individual authorship or skill, or on recognizably 'new' texts of a particular genre, and with procedures often adopted for precise dating and classification. The tradition of anonymity has also led to many writings being wrongly attributed to known missionary authors as well as leading to the neglect of local scholars whose close collaboration was in any case always necessary for any writings in the vernacular languages.

v) The determining role of indigenous socio-cultural concerns (rather than purely 'religious' responses) is a particularly important feature of major Asian writings and is yet to receive full recognition. In country after country, careful study of major writings reveals that urgent issues of national reform, people's welfare and social reconstruction, rather than questions of doctrine or declared religious allegiance, shape the indigenous response in clearly contextualizing writings.[5] Here faith is expressed in a deep commitment to the building of just and humane communities rather than firstly to a confession of orthodox belief.

vi) The larger setting for Asian Christian writings in this (religiously) 'post-classical' period (fourteenth to nineteenth centuries) is that of abundant and creative interpretations within Buddhism, Confucianism, Islam and Christianity alike. And these reshaped and indigenized each 'classical' tradition. Yet this was strangely at the very time when *missionary* agents absolutized their own (and other) thought forms and practice. There was also a rich diversity which we must note, of other sources of thought and creativity available, in native humanist traditions, indigenous art and literary forms, and in contemporary socio-political movements and structures.[6]

These and other contextual issues require from us, I would suggest, a reorientation of research and interpretation in order to recognise 'the other half of the world' in Asian Christian literature and history. We must also more completely reject colonial and neo- colonial assumptions in both literary criticism and theological evaluation. Such a reorientation would involve as well a 'counter-appropriation' (to earlier western appropriations), of indigenous traditions and idioms and a reclaiming of Asian resources for doing Christian theology. Resources for these tasks are currently multiplying: in the continuing debate on orientalism and post-colonial discourse[7], the burgeoning literature regarding the rights and contributions of indigenous peoples[8] as well as in recent studies of Asian moral thought and of pre-/post-colonial Christian traditions.[9]

A particular field of resources which urgently needs to be reclaimed is that of theological reflection and writing by women in this period. Some references for such women of this period in the countries mentioned appear below and in *Asian Christian Theologies Vol. 1*. These include, to mention only a few representative examples, such outstanding figures as Hosokawa Tama Gracia (Japan), Ota Julia (Korea), Anna Satthianandhan (India), Catherine Bauzem (Ceylon), Candida Hsu (China) and Jeronima de la Asuncion (Philippines).

Sources and functions[10]

An overview of the 'types of discourse' represented in literary or art forms however - from the hands of 'local' clergy, lay women and men, and from 'foreign' laymen and clergy -- could be summarized as follows:

i) Local friends/converts, interpret and collaborate with westerners (in almost every country) - in for example, catechisms, grammars, liturgies, manuals ...

ii) Local Christians encounter, modify, and even reject, western teaching (in e.g. India, China, Korea, Japan) - in commentaries, treatises, narratives ...

iii) Indigenous verse, drama and art forms express and reshape Christian thought (in e.g. Ceylon, Indo-China, China, Japan, Philippines).

iv) Indigenous religious tradition is restored and reconciled with Christian teaching in dialogues or treatises (in India, China, Malaya).

v) A complete integration of vocation, lifestyle and writing can be observed in the works of some authors/artists, and is especially notable in the lives of a number of women.

vi) Chronicle, testimony, apologetic, biography, also appear in letters, diaries, confessions and narratives across the region.

vii) Exceptional forms extant from some countries include *memre*, encyclopaedia, *babad*, *pasyon*, and *Maria-Kannon* ...

The Bamboo Stands - Selected case-studies from four countries.

1. Japan

The so-called "Christian century" following Xavier's arrival in 1549, saw the emergence of Christian writings in many forms, written both by Japanese converts, and through their collaboration with Jesuit scholars - in translation, interpreting, teaching, printing and writing.[11] These include a flood of devotional and catechetical literature from the Jesuit presses (1585-1600); the plays and other writings of Paulo Yoho-ken (1510-1596) and Vincente Hoin (b. 1538); the fables of Takai Gosme (fl. 1590); and extensive correspondence, biographical writings, poetry and meditations largely by unknown authors. The letters, poems and life-witness of Tama Gracia (1563-1600, wife of Hosokawa Tadaoki) are notable amongst these. Also the later collections of *Kakure Kirishitan* documents and artefacts (seventeenth and eighteenth centuries) forms a body of materials 'from the underground', which is unique in Christian history.[12]

Where lies genuine Apologetic? In Japanese Christian literature of the period the writings of Fucan Fabian (1565-1621) have a special, and controversial, place. His *Myotei Mondo* (Dialogue between Myoshi and Yutei, 1605) is the earliest known work of Christian apologetic by a Japanese.[13] In this each major religious tradition is judged by the criterion: 'what brings true salvation?'; that is, what belief ensures peace in this world and happiness in the world beyond for the people of Japan? Fucan answers: only Christianity.

The intrinsic value of this work has often been neglected because of Fucan's later booklet *Hadeus* (Deus Refuted, 1620) which in turn, refutes each Christian teaching point by point.[14] But this again is because he judges it to have brought more conflict not less, and to have brought no significant social reforms nor any recognition of Japanese identity and tradition.[15] He has also remarkably come to reject such teachings as Biblical inerrancy, original sin, and eternal punishment for *any* people; for he asks, "how can the 'universal religion of salvation' restrict salvation?"[16]

Until recently most references to Fucan have taken his 'apostasy' as the determining criterion in assessing his writings, with some scholars making *Hadeus* a key entry-point to the literature of anti-Christian polemic.[17] But amongst the clear rejections here of many Christian dogmas, there are remarkable insights which reflect more wide-ranging Christian concerns. Stable peace, humane community, mutuality in relationships, individual choice and 'the ways of nature' remain the criteria by which he judges religious practice.[18]

His earlier scorn for indigenous religious traditions changes to a recognition of their contribution to these goals in for example, Jodo Buddhism's linking of Amida Buddha with the natural order, or the five-fold Way of Mutuality, of Confucianism.[19] Against the dominant role of expatriate priests he asserts the rights of nationals, and some of his sharpest condemnations of the missionaries are made in the name of indigenous custom and national identity, which are being undermined by western colonialism and arrogant proselytism - surprisingly contemporary concerns.[20]

However much *Hadeus* may be shaped by personal resentments, it is still apparent that this writing and the earlier *Myotei Mondo* are both expressions of Fucan's continuing search for peace, human community and social order in this world,[21] by which the Japanese people may find their full identity in union with nature and with the (inexpressible) ultimate reality. This, he still maintains, is salvation.

Despite his ambiguous position in Asian Christian literature, Fucan provides a sharp example of critical but creative indigenous response to the particular forms of western missionary presence. Many of his central concerns are yet to be interpreted in the context of a comprehensive and holistic theology.

2. India

From here we have probably the oldest extant corpus of Christian writing and art, east of Persia - from the fourth century on – now held in, amongst others, eleven libraries of south-west India. The later contextualizing materials from the sixteenth to eighteenth centuries show a transition from early welcome and friendship for western Christianity to a fierce rejection of any intervention and coercion (from west Asia also), in areas of liturgy, doctrine, church polity and priestly training.[22] In addition Indian authorship and/or extensive collaboration is well established for a wide range of catechisms, treatises, hagiographies, letters, poems, verse epics, and dialogues, in the Tamil, Marathi, Konkarni, Telegu, Bengali, Persian, Syriac and Malayalam languages.

Pristine Hinduism vindicated. "Early Church Sanskrit" is a body of didactic and devotional writings in classical Sanskrit, from the 17th to 19th centuries, in which Christian meaning was discerned in the religious insights of the ancient Hindu texts.[23] It is thus an early example of contextualizing Christian writing. Any precise dating for origins are impossible, but the earliest examples may come from the mid-17th century, being known also in Europe early in the following century, in both Sanskrit and French.[24] The anonymous authors seem to have included Indian Sanskrit scholars along with French Jesuits, from both north and south India, as the Sanskrit reflects both Bengali and Tamil influence.

Two of the earliest and most notable of the manuscripts are the dialogues *Ezour Vedam* (Jesus Veda) and *Chamo Beda* (Final Rest [?] Veda) in which named Vedic sages present on the one hand the monotheistic beliefs of pristine (proto)-Hinduism, in contrast to the corruptions of contemporary Hinduism on the other.[25] The texts are wholly in Hindu language and idiom; in particular in the terms used for God (Deva, Prabhu), in choice of the divine attributes (*sat, cit, ananda*) and in the literary form of the dialogues themselves.[26]

The authors clearly believed, on the basis both of classical Hindu insights and a 'Thomist harmony' of nature and grace, that the central truths of Hinduism were "wholly congruent with the Christian faith".[27] To them the Veda presented the Sanskrit equivalent of Mosaic teachings, showing that uncorrupted 'Hinduism' already contained the basis for Christian faith. But reading some of the verses in *Chamo Beda*, for example, verses praising "the most high God", go further. Placed in the mouths of historical figures who are depicted as recovering the knowledge of early sages, the One God is addressed as "creator", "sustainer", "pure spirit". "source of all knowledge", "merciful deliverer", and "the only source of salvation".[28] This is to claim that distinctively Biblical and Christian truths are embedded in ancient proto-Hindu beliefs and this was a major reshaping of the missionary teaching from the west.

Other expatriate writers such as Jean Calmette (1693-1740), William Carey (1761-1837), W.H. Mill (1792-1853) and John Muir (1810-1882) continued the tradition of Church Sanskrit in many forms including prayers, Biblical paraphrases and meditations. But a number of important contextualizations of belief, for example the uses of *sat, cit, and ananda* for divine attributes and even for the Trinity itself, became central to the work of such nineteenth century Indian theologians as Keshub Chunder Sen, Brahmabandhav Upadhyay and their successors.[29]

3. China

The very extensive writings from the early seventeenth century in China, from Li Ma Tou (Matteo Ricci) and his colleagues are well known, but only in recent decades have full studies appeared of some of the most prolific Chinese colleagues and followers of Ricci, such as Yang Tingjun (1557-1627), Zhang Xingyao (1633- 1725) or Yan Mo (d. c.1720).[30] Many other Chinese authors for our period have yet to be fully studied, yet their collaboration in translation, defending, interpreting, teaching and recording Christian teaching, both made possible, and also reshaped, the theological ventures of Ricci and his European colleagues.

Any full treatment of their work would have to include the expression of Christian insight and belief within the forms and imagery of traditional art and poetry by for example, Wu Yushan (1632-1718) and Wei I-chieh (1616-1686); the encyclopaedic writings of Xu Guanggi (Hsu Kuang-chi d. 1633); the compilations and apologetics of Li Zhi-zao (Li Chih Tsao c.1540-1630), Li Jiubiao and Li Jingong (fl. 1630) and Lo Wenzao (Gregory Lopez, 1615-1690), as well as the 'hermeneutic' of life, letters and conversation of such women as Xu Candida (1607-1680).

We now know however of bodies of writing by a number of neo-Confucian literati, who sought the restoration and completion of Confucianism as a path to national reform. And this they found presented in a Christianity which was sensitively grounded also in ancient Chinese tradition. The writings of Yang Tingyun and Zhang Xingyao are of particular interest.

Neo-Confucian-Christian Orthodoxy. Yang Tingyun's writings are found in a series of treatises and commentaries, in which recent research has revealed his understanding of, and allegiance to, Christian faith as an amplification and intensification of neo-Confucian wisdom. But Christian teaching is also modified and enriched in this encounter as Yang reshapes Confucian teachings in the light of Christian faith.

If neo-Confucian 'heaven and earth' – the source of all – themselves require an intelligent Creator, as Yang came to acknowledge, He/She is the source wholly of illustrious virtue. Human nature is therefore originally all good, for the mind tends to good as its original nature.

The Adam-and-Eve tradition is therefore rejected but the teaching of the sages, Mencius and Confucius, is honoured.[31] If the compassion for truly good actions is now given by the Master of Heaven, who is the great Father and Mother (!) of us all (*da-fu-mu*), this "teaching by grace" naturally works as the fulfilment of the earlier teaching by nature and the written teaching of the sages.[32] Christianity has thus an internal consistency with the ethical humanism of Confucian tradition.[33]

To 'venerate (as Christians) the Master of Heaven' *is* to 'brightly serve the lord-on-high', declares Yang. To 'love one's neighbour as oneself *is* to treat 'all people as brothers and sisters'. To overcome oneself *is* the concreteness of loving people. To love people – to feed, clothe, house, cure, deliver them – is the truth of revering heaven. To act out these beliefs Yang, once he accepted Christianity, established benevolent societies for the poor, as well as churches and a school.[34]

The process Yang exemplifies here is 'incarnational' rather than 'indigenizing'; a way of animating the practical wisdom of Chinese culture rather than 'accommodating' Christianity to it. And in this Yang goes beyond Ricci's method. His major concern remains the practicality, which is a *real* learning he declares, of moral value and active compassion in both personal and political life. Devotion to a personal 'Tien' (Heaven) *is* the practical morality and government given by the God known in Jesus Christ, who offers a national reconstruction and salvation. Here too we find a dynamic indigenous response to the Gospel which is authentically Chinese, deeply humane and fully Christian. Yet aspects of (western) accepted Christian belief have been rejected where they oppose the best of indigenous traditions.

4. Philippines

The crucial role of nationals in collaboration with European missionaries noted above is no less notable in the Philippines: in translation and interpreting, in engraving and printing, and also in writing. This remains true throughout the period. Amongst the many notable engravers and printers who came to incorporate Filipino perceptions and folk elements in their art are Juan de Vera (d. c.1607), Thomas Pinpin (d. c.1680), and Juan Correa and his son Geronimo (active 1710-1752). Pinpin also authored a book on Castilian which incorporated songs and other distinctively Filipino features.

Many of the earliest Christian writings by Filipinos are in verse form: in the epic poetry of Pedro Bukaneg (1590-1626) and the poems of Ladino writers like Bagongbanta (fl. 1605) and Ossorio (fl. 1625), whose work is strongly influenced by folk poetry.[35] By the late seventeenth century many doctrinal, apologetic and medical writings appeared from Indio (Filipino) or mestizo authors such as Ignacio Mercado (1648-1698), Gregorio Manesay (1675-1732) and Bartolome Saguinsin (1694-1772).[36]

Missionary colonialism subverted: The Pasyon. This unique category of Filipino writing, as a poetic narrative on the events of Holy Week for public recitation and dramatic performance, emerged by the late 17th century. A printer and poet who was working for the Jesuits, Aquino de Belen (fl. 1700-1720), wrote the classical version of the Pasyon, *Ang Mahal no Pasion*, in 1703.[37] It is likely that a major purpose in writing this was to provide a form of canticle, which could be used in pastoral care for the sick and dying by 'magpapahesus', that is by prayer leaders who acted as native 'priests'.[38]

Although using a Spanish form, de Belen's *Pasyon* is an original Filipino work displaying "sensuous visual imagination and unfaltering psychological penetration".[39] Stanzaic pattern and imagery are clearly in Tagalog idiom although all stereotypes are avoided. More importantly, the characters are distinctly Filipinos, created as if for the first time: so 'they behave like Indios!' was the surprised response. The humanity of Jesus in personal relationships as well as in brutal suffering is stressed and Peter for example, uses 'Indio' curses, being pursued with condemnation for his denial, for 32 stanzas![40] Judas is confronted not with 'God's love and saving purpose', but with his betrayal of Mary's hospitality to him as "one of the family".[41]

By 1760, this work had been printed five times, was widely used in non-church settings and found in many folk versions by the end of the century. A standard collation of these (1814) extends from the Creation to the Last Judgement, and has become a universal history with elements also of a social epic. The Pharisees come to represent the wealthy and educated 'aristocrats' of Filipino society who are strongly condemned.[42] Mary protests to God at the injustice of elevating such sinful men while they want Jesus killed. Jesus is portrayed as a subversive who attracts the lowly, divides families and forms a '*Katipunan*' (brotherhood) of those who like himself are poor, and have no fame or rank, and whom he calls to work for a new world.

In the narratives of Christ's suffering, death and resurrection thus had been found "powerful images of transition from ... despair to hope, misery to salvation, death to life ... from the dishonourable age of Spanish rule to a glorious era of freedom (*Kalayaan*)".[43] The departure of Jesus from Mary "to suffer and die in order to save mankind" had now become an image which the Indio could act out by leaving home to join a rebel nationalist leader. Certainly this was to be done, and celebrated in the *Pasyon,* by countless Filipinos in the next two centuries.[44] And late in the 19th century the Revolutionary Brotherhood which played a central role in securing eviction of the Spanish rulers, would be named the *Katipunan*.

Conclusion

The conclusion cannot be avoided that here also, as in other works we have reviewed, the response of local Christians is not shaped primarily by their assessment of particular missionary teachings or practices. It is rather their aspirations for a quality of human life in community – shaped both by the classical and folk traditions of their people and by the present socio-political context – which determines the questions they address to the western Christianity of their time and which also determines the creative response they make to it. An obsession with questions of orthodoxy, church growth or influence have, I believe, hidden the incarnational dimensions in such writings, and in the praxis which they nurtured, whether of this period or in the centuries preceding and following it.[45] The concern of this paper has therefore chiefly been to present sympathetically the intention and (in brief) the substance of selected writings by Asian Christians which may reveal such dimensions. But this has necessarily meant that many issues of interpretation, and of comparative significance, have been omitted. These, along with such questions as those summarized in the introductory paragraphs above, have received as yet little careful study but they suggest many fruitful lines of research. Such research however must also recognise, as the above outlines have sought to do, the autonomy and continuing validity of creative Asian Christian traditions. There is a rich diversity of contextualizing theologies which they make possible along with at least some of the wide-ranging implications such theologies have for our own contemporary tasks.

Endnotes

[1] For a study of the role of the bamboo in Asian (Christian) culture see M. Takenaka *When the Bamboo Bends* (WCC, 2002), especially 39ff. For an annotated selection of Asian Christian writings (until 2000) see John C. *England et al. Asian Christian Theologies. A Research Guide to Authors, Movements, Sources 3 Vols.* (ISPCK, Claretian, Orbis 2002, 1.27-77); and for later publications, such vols. as Chung Meehyun *Breaking Silence. Theology from Asian Women.* (ISPCK/EATWOT, 2006); P.S. Chung *Constructing Irregular Theology. Bamboo & Minjung in East Asian Perspective.* (Brill, 2009); H.Y. Kim et al. (eds.) *Asian & Oceanic Christianities in Conversation.* (Rodopi, 2011); H. Chhungi et al. (eds.) *Doing Indigenous Theology in Asia. Towards New Frontiers* (NCC/SCEPTRE/GTC, 2012); D.P. Niles *The Lotus & the Sun.* (Barton Books, 2013); P. Jesudason & R. Rajkumar (eds.) *Asian Theology on the Way. Christianity, Culture & Context.* (SPCK, 2012); S.W. Ariarajah *Strangers or Co-Pilgrims?: The Impact of Interfaith Dialogue on Christian Faith and Practice* (Fortress Press, 2017). See also Appendix Chap. Ten.

[2] Refer H. Nakamura *Ways of Thinking of Eastern Peoples: India-China-Tibet-Japan.* (University of Hawaii, 1964); J.B. Chethimattam *Patterns of Indian Thought: Indian Religions and Philosophy.* (Chapman, 1971); E. C. Eoyang *The Transparent Eye* (University of Hawaii, 1993); J.J. Clarke *Oriental Enlightenment. Encounter: Between Western and Asian Thought.* (Routledge, 1997); J.C. England (op.cit.1998) 154-161; R.E. Nisbet *The Geography of Thought.* Free Press, 2003.

[3] See especially D.F. Lach *Asia in the Making of Europe* (Chicago, 1971) vol.1; The most recent work to outline this long history is P. Francopan *The Silk Roads* (Bloomsbury, 2015) xiii-xix, 27-62.

[4] See D. WYATT & A. WOODSIDE (Eds.), *Moral Order and the Question of Change. Essays on Southeast Asia Thought* (Yale Univ.Univ.1982), 5ff.

[5] In addition to the case-studies below, and those in chaps. 5 & 6 following, see for example. the work of Syrhak-Catholic writers in Korea of the late 18th cent. such as Chong, Yak-jong and Chong, Yak-yong, (J.C. England et al. (2002) vol. 3, 59ff.).

[6] A few of the key works would include R. Ghose (ed.) *Protest Movements in South and South-East Asia:* (Univ. Hong Kong, 1987); E. Van Erven, *The Playful Revolution: Theatre and Liberation in Asia.* (Bloomington, 1992); D. Smyth (ed.) *The Canon in SEA Literatures* (Routledge, 2000); H.K. Bhabha, *The Location of Culture* (Routledge, 2007 (1994); See also e.g. C. CALDAROLA (ed.), *Religions and Societies: Asia and the Middle East* (Mouton, 1982); T. EAGLETON et al. *Nationalism, Colonialism and Literature* (Univ. Minnesota, 1990) 4ff. & passim.

[7] See e.g. R.S. Sugirtharajah *Asian Biblical Hermeneutics & Postcolonialism: Contesting the Interpretations* (Sheffield, 1999); (Ms.) Kwok, Pui-lan *Postcolonial Imagination and Feminist Theology.* (WJK, 2005); A. W. Longchar, *Returning to Mother Earth: An Indigenous Perspective* (SCEPTRE, 2012); the series of volumes of *Subaltern Studies* and especially V. DAS "Subaltern as Perspective" in G. Ranjit (Ed.), *Subaltern Studies 6* (Delhi 1989), 310-323; D. Landry & G. McLean (eds.), *The Spivak Reader.* Selected Works of Gayatri Chakraverty Spivak (Free Press, 1996), 5ff., 24-28, 202-235; .

[8] The most complete recent volumes for the region are. A. Gray, & B. Kingsbury (eds.) *Indigenous Peoples of Asia.* (Ann Arbor, 1995); G. Harvey (ed.) *Indigenous Religions.* (Cassell, 2000). C. Erni (ed.) *The Concept of Indigenous Peoples in Asia. A Resource Book.* (Taschenbuch, 2008). Cf. A.L. Becker & A.A. Yengoyan (ed.), *The Imagination of Reality. Essays in Southeast Asia Coherence Systems* (Ablex, 1979); and D. M. Lewis, *Millenium, Tribal Wisdom and the Modern World* (Viking, 1992).

[9] See e.g. works of J.C. Scott, such as *The Moral Economy of the Peasant: Rebellion and Subsistence in Southeast Asia* (Yale, 1976); A. Reid & D. Marr (eds.), *Perceptions of the Past in Southeast Asia* (Heinemann, 1979); D. Wyatt & A. Woodside *Moral Order and the Question of Change* (Yale Univ., 1982); (Ms.) C. Keller et al. (eds.) *Post-Colonial Theologies Divinity and Empire* (WJK, 2004).

[10] See the full though not exhaustive listing of sources in England et al. (2002, 27-77).

[11] The most complete bibliography of these is J. LAURES *Kirishitan Bunko . A Manual of Books and Documents on the Early Christian Mission of Japan* (Sophia Univ.,1957).

[12] England et al. 2002 op.cit. vol.3, pp.22-28.

[13] French translation by P.R. Humbertclaude "Myotei Mondo. Une apologetique chrétienne japonaise de 1605" (*Monumenta Nipponica* 1, 1938, 515-525, and 2, 1939, 237-267). See also LAURES, (op.cit.)106-107.

[14] English version by (Ms.) E.L. Hibberd & Hiraishi Yoshimori *Refutation of Deus by Fabian* (Sophia, 1962). Cf. critical edition in Japanese by A. Ebisawa in *Toyo Bunko* 14 (Tokyo 1964, 273-333). See also "Fabian Fucan Pro and Contra" in *Sources of Japanese Tradition Volume 2, 1600 to 2000*, ed. Wm. Theodore de Bary, (Ms.) C. Gluck, and A. E. Tiedemann (Columbia Univ., 2nd ed. 2005).

[15] I draw here on the work of O. MAYER ("Fukansai Fabian and Kirishitan - A Paradigm of Modern Awareness" *(Japanese Religions* 19. (1994) 1-2, 23-43), in bringing together the interpretations of contemporary Japanese scholars such as S.Yamamoto, I. Katsuymi, and H. Noriaki.

[16] Fucan's criticisms are summarized in J. Jennes *A History of the Catholic Church in Japan. From its Beginnings to the Early Meiji Era (1549-1873).* (Tuttle, Revd. edn. 1973). See also (Ms.) M. Schrimpf "The Pro- and Anti-Christian Writings of Fukan Fabian (1565-1621)" *(Japanese Religions* 33.1 & 2, 2006).

[17] See e.g. G. Elison, *Deus Destroyed. The Image of Christianity in early Modern Japan* (Cambridge, 1973). Also J. Gernet's treatment of Fucan in *China and the Christian Impact* (Cambridge 1985).

[18] Yamamoto Shichikei *Kinben no tetsugaku* (Philosophy of Diligence) (Univ. Kyoto 1979), and *Ben-Dasan Nihonkyoto* (The Adherents of Japanism) (Univ. Tokyo 1975), 153. Cited MAYER, *Fukansai* 32, 36.

[19] Ibid. and Mayer (op.cit. 1995).

[20] Jennes (op.cit. 1973) 176, & Mayer (op.cit 1995) 33, 36.

[21] Ibid., 27f.,32.

[22] See J.P.M.Van der Ploeg, *The Syriac Manuscripts of St. Thomas Christians.* (Dharmaram, 1983). Refer England et al. 2002, 41ff.

[23] Refer A. Amaladas & R. F. Young *The Indian Christiad. A Concise Anthology of Didactic and Devotional Literature in early Church Sanskrit* (Gujarat Sahitya Prakash, 1995). This is the fullest recent collection of such writings and provides a full bibliography. See also L. Rocher (ed.) *Ezourvedam: A French Veda of the Eighteenth Century* (John Benjamin, 1984); and *Bibliography of Original Christian Writings in India in Sanskrit*, compiled by Bhaskar Jadhav and others (UTC Bangalore 1994).

[24] For the fullest account of the possible origins of one MS, see L.Rocher, op.cit. 1984).

[25] Eight early Sanskrit MSS were discovered by F. Ellis in 1816, and published by him in "Account of a Discovery of a modern imitation of the Vedas, with Remarks on the Genuine Works" (*Asiatic Researches* 14, 1822, 1-59), cited in *Amaladas & Fox Young* (op.cit. 1995).

[26] Ibid., 11f.

[27] Ibid., 9.

[28] Ibid., 12-14.

²⁹ See amongst other volumes of the *Library of Christian Theology D. Scott* (ed.) *K. C. Sen* (CLS, 1979) 227f.; J. Lipner & G. Gisbert-Sauch (eds.) *The Writings of Brahmabandhab Upadhyay* (Dharmaram, 1991).

³⁰ Refer works of e.g. N. Standaert *Yang Ting Yun. Confucian and Christian in Late Ming China* (Brill, 1988); *The Fascinating God. A Challenge to Modern Chinese Theology* .(Pontifical Gregorian University, 1995); and *Methodology in View of Contact Between Cultures: The China Case in the 17th Century* (Hong Kong: 2002). Also D.E. Mungello *The Forgotten Christians of Hangzhou* (Univ. Hawaii, 1994); G.R.Tiedeman (ed.) *Handbook of Christianity in China: Volume 2*, 1800-2000 (Brill, 2010).

³¹ Standaert *(op.cit. 1988)* 144ff..

³² Ibid. 150f.

³³ Ibid.. 218f.

³⁴ Yang Ting Yun, preface to work of Oike, (cited Standaert 1988) 120f.

³⁵ See particularly B.L. Lumbera *Tagalog Poetry 1570-1898. Tradition and Influences in its Development* (Ateneo Univ.,1986).

³⁶ See L. Santiago *The Hidden Light* . The First Filipino Priests (Ateneo Univ., 1987), 77f., 148ff.

³⁷ Refer Lumbera (op.cit.) 57-66, R.B. Mojares *Tagalog Poetry 1570-1898.* (Ateneo Univ., 1983) 51ff. and R.B. Javellana (ed.) *Casaysayan nang Pasiong Mahal ni Jesucristong Panginoon Natin.* (Ateneo Univ., 1988), 11ff.

³⁸ Javellana (op.cit. 1988) 12; Javellana introduces and translates the full text of the Pasyon published in 1814, which collated many 18th century traditions.

³⁹ Lumbera, (op.cit.), 61.

⁴⁰ Javellana (ibid.) 194f. Earlier version of de Belen is given in Lumbera, (op.cit. 1986) 154-162.

⁴¹ op. cit. 189; cf. de Belen's version in Lumbera, (op.cit. 1986) 63f.

⁴² op. cit. 198. This thrust of the Pasyon is analysed by R.C. Ileto *Pasyon and Revolution.* Popular Movements in the Philippines, 1840-1910 (Ateneo Univ., 1979), 19-23.

⁴³ Ileto (op.cit. 1979) 18f. See J. Perkinson & (Ms.) S. L. Mendoza "Indigenous Filipino Pasyon Defying Colonial Euro-Reason". *Journal of Third World Studies* (Spring 2004); Mellie Leandicho Lopez *A Handbook of Philippine Folklore* (Univ. Philippines, 2006), 265ff.

⁴⁴ For the role of Pasyon tradition in the 19th and 20th centuries see Lopez. ibid., and J.M.C. Francisco in e.g. "The Christ Story as the Subversive Memory of Tradition. Tagalog Texts and Politics around the Turn of the Century" in D.M. Roskies (ed.) *Text and Politics in Island South East Asia* (Univ. Ohio, 1993) 82-110. Recent studies include R. E. Aligan *Pasyon.* (Univ. San Tomas, Manila, 2001),

J. D. Blanco *Frontier Constitutions. Christianity & Colonial Empire in the Nineteenth Century Philippines* (Univ. of California, 2009) espec. Chap.7; P. J. Bräunlein *Passion Pasyon (*Paderborn, 2010).

[45] For an outline of Asian Christian writings prior to the 16th century see England et al. (op.cit. 2001) vol.1, 3-26.

Chapter - 5

Cranes Ever Flying:
Creativity and Continuity in Contextual Asian Theologies

Introduction

The vast extent and diversity of Asian Christian theologies has been increasingly recognised in the last 20 years, but they have seldom been studied as historical movements, with their own autonomy and long continuity, in particular cultural contexts. Many partial approaches to their study and teaching have been taken, to present for example: 'Patterns of Christian Acceptance;' 'Asian responses to western theology;' 'Asian voices in global debates;' or an 'only-now-emerging Asian theology.'

All of these designations reflect an obviously western orientation in both methodology and interpretation. There are however 'pre-colonial' traditions in Asia's autonomous theologies dating from at least as early as the second century, and 'post-colonial traditions' in the modern period from the sixteenth century. Then dating from at least the 1850s there is a history of sharp critiques of colonial, westernizing or neo-colonial theologies. These, along with their parallels to the mid-20th century, are part of the many creative sources now emerging more clearly for present critique and construction in Asian theology, as well as for the necessary inter-cultural hermeneutic these involve. Apart from precursors in Syria and Persia (3rd-9th centuries), and Turkestan (9ᵗʰ–14ᵗʰ cents.), we have many examples from India or China, in particular in the 17ᵗʰ–18ᵗʰ centuries (see above, chapters), and from across the region in the period 1800-1950. Many have been rediscovered during preparation by an Asia-wide team for the Research Guide to *Asian Christian Theologies*.[1]

To briefly summarize: these are represented in literary or art forms from the hands of 'local' clergy, lay women and men, and from 'foreign' laymen and clergy, and demonstrate theologies other than simple acceptance or the imitation of introduced forms. They include the following:

i) Local Christians encounter, but also modify, or even reject, western teachings or doctrinal formulations

ii) Indigenous verse, drama and art forms express and reshape Christian thought as brought by western missionaries

iii) Indigenous religious tradition is restored and reconciled with Christian teaching , in dialogues, verse-forms and treatises, etc.

iv) A complete integration of vocation, lifestyle and writing, seen in the works of some authors/artists, and especially in the lives of a number of women.

A Case-study to Sharpen the Issues

In my previous paper on 'indigenous' Christian writings (refer chap. 4), the case of Fucan Fabian SJ (1565–1621) was presented in order to highlight the question *Where lies genuine Apologetic?* (Here I briefly recapitulate). Despite the widespread dismissal of Fucan as being merely an 'apostate', fuller study of his writings in their context reveals that his refutation of then major Roman Catholic doctrines arose from more wide-ranging humane concerns such as: have such doctrines brought a measure of reconciliation and peace? Have they brought any significant social reforms or any recognition of Japanese identity and tradition?[2]

Fucan here applies surprisingly contemporary criteria to 'Christian' doctrine and practice, and in his writing – both in the earlier *Myotei Mundo* and the controversial *Hadeus* – expresses his continuing search for peace, human community and social order in this world. It is through this that the Japanese people may find their full identity in union with nature and with (the inexpressible) ultimate reality. This, he still maintains, is salvation. He therefore provides a sharp example of indigenous theological response, both creative and critical, to particular forms of western theology.[3]

I. What Is Specifically 'Theological'?

So it is not just the early existence of 'indigenous' critical reflection, its quantity or continuity, that is most significant, but the surprising transformations we discover in our forebears' motivation, their theological stance and in their formulations. Much discussion of Asian theologies assumes, not only for the pre-20th century period but in our own period, that the primary issues in Christian mission and Christian presence – and therefore of theological reflection upon these—are those of outwardly expressed Christian belief and allegiance. This being often understood to include acceptance of certain (western) doctrinal formulations and allegiance to certain (western) institutions and devotional practices. Behind this are of course a series of assumptions regarding the central Gospel truths: that these require firstly if not only a specifically devotional experience, along with an 'orthodox' affirmation of faith.

If the Gospel however is that 'God's realm is upon us', the first, if not the only requirement is a *hope-in-action* for God's coming commonwealth of peace, justice and communion. This active love, rather than orthodox belief, is clearly central in the Gospel records of the 'life-of-Jesus-with-others'.[4] Assumptions are also made that theological reflection has as its primary task the explication of existing doctrines, or of the life of the institutional Church, or the building of new systems of belief. But surely theological reflection is fundamentally the discernment, acceptance and following of the signs in one's society and world through which God's reign comes.[5]

The history of Asian theology provides us with many examples of reflection shaped by all or any of these assumptions, but study and research have very often resulted in the application of doctrinal or ecclesial criteria, rather than the exposition of localized insights and the clarification of contextualizing processes. This is plainly seen too in the widespread neglect of many writers and movements—not only in recent decades but also in earlier centuries—whose theological articulations have arisen from controversial movements in their society, or nation, or whose primary concerns have been judged to be 'secular', 'syncretistic', or 'subversive'. Then too the primary concern has often been to apply contemporary (western) theories of literary, historical or philosophical interpretation to reflection and writing which have their own such resources and genesis.

Perhaps most to be deplored are the assumptions made by some of our theological colleagues that the philosophies, terminology and Christian experience of Graeco-Latin cultures—both past and present—are somehow normative for the discernment and articulation of theologies in a region which has millennia of its *own* Reformations, its *own* Renaissances, Revolutions and Rebirths, and its *own* Enlightenments.[6]

It must be recognized therefore that the thought patterns, the terminology and the interpretive principles used in contextual Asian theologies are often markedly different from those which are usually assumed to be normative in some other regions. The systematic metaphysical construction that emerged in the post-medieval West, for example, has seldom been an indispensable—or even recognized—element in contextual Asian theologies. Asian Christians have long possessed different models—of insight and wisdom, discernment and truth-seeing, of heart-knowledge and life-shaping—by which they 'do theology' in reflecting upon and living the faith. Over some centuries creative theologies have emerged in our Asian cultures, shaped primarily not first by doctrinal or philosophical concerns but by the urgent challenges for national liberation and reconstruction, for self-hood and social reform, and for the restoration of living cultural symbols.[7] (Refer to chap. 3 above). Such a shaping, along with their sharp vision and motivation, means that we may not find in these theologies many of the terminologies, the theoretical issues or textual forms we often expect: so we may in fact not initially recognise them as specifically 'theological'.

For here we often have theological reflections that are completely integral to work, and art, style of life and action; forms of writing dictated by the present demands of cultural situation, of hope and struggle. The methodology moves through steps such as identification and solidarity, social analysis, study of tradition, inductive reflection, and communicable response; to use our later terminologies.[8] Theologians will have at hand, along with any western concepts of methodologies – and as alternatives to *'theos logoi'* – concepts for their reflection and writing drawn from their own intellectual and wisdom traditions and images, often re-interpreted in co-operative and communitarian ways. To briefly characterize these, for 'theology' there are different terms such as *anubhava* ('direct experience/insight'); or *dhyana* ('meditation, contemplation'); for 'interpretation', images such as *ngelmu* ('seeking knowledge of harmony'); or *yang chi'i* ('fostering the spirit of life'); and for the goal of theological endeavour, *manana* (the critical vision of reality); *darsana* ('fullest seeing, meeting'); or dharma (the universal law and teaching) and the *dao* (the 'way of communion with all things').[9]

To explore the descriptions or conclusions often found in these reflections we very often have here a quest and a communion rather than a declared doctrine or definition. The endeavour is contemplative, intuitive, or experiential, nurturing, convivial, evocative, or celebratory: offering different knowings ... 'usings' ... ends. It is more personal story in form and intuitive rather than analytical; with informal 'jottings' or poems, proposals rather than theoretical syntheses. We find there a merging of imagination, seeing, and autobiography; a dialogue of life and therefore of author and reader; of quest and reflection within the struggle; not proof or defence but a heightening, a treasuring, a sustaining and transformation of experience. And in such a re-shaping and restoration of theology's central functions the role of the insight and wisdom of women is obviously a crucial component.[10]

II. Brief Case-studies

The following examples may serve to unpack and demonstrate the living-out of such theologies. All show to a greater or lesser extent the vital unity of reflection with life, of vision and action, which is presented in the creative elements of our own cultural and intellectual traditions, and which emerges again in sharp contemporary struggles for identity, social justice and peace. This will be something of a rapid tour, to uncover people and their thought-in-context, so that discussion of many issues raised by their alternative life-theologies will necessarily have to be left for another time. It is hoped that enough of their intentions and affirmations will however be introduced, to uncover lesser-known resources and their challenge for coming Asian theologies. I give first brief cameos of selected writer-activists, and later outline the theological approaches which can be here recognized. It is to be noted in particular that all these present the encounter of 'good news of the Commonwealth' with the historical situation and urgent needs of women and men.

1. Vietnam

Radical leaders in Vietnam offer revolutionary theologies of nationalism, social justice and reconstruction, human rights and community culture.

i)   Dang Duc Tuan Joachim (1806–1874)

Dang was trained and ordained at the then College General (Seminary) of Penang but after six years as priest he was imprisoned during the prohibition of Catholicism in Vietnam from 1862. He had become deeply concerned both at the King's edicts which allowed severe persecution of Christians as well as at the oppressive actions of French military forces as they imposed control on particular districts. The suffering which resulted for priests and people affected him greatly. Already a celebrated poet, he now addressed a series of petitions to the Emperor

To Duc, denouncing French oppression and advocating the mobilization of all cultural and military resources in order to end this. He continued writing after his release, both poetry and extensive petitions, which foreshadowed many later nationalist writings.

In his 'Policy regarding Western Repression ... by 'a writer living in a thatched hut,' Dang Duc Tuan draws on both Christian and traditional Vietnamese resources to reject colonization and the theft of people's livelihood. He also calls directly on the wealthy and privileged to greater discipline and simpler styles of life. Mandarins especially are to cease their fine feasts and are to welcome poor writers who sleep 'on bare boards and eat the bread of hardship'.[11] In other documents he condemns the abuse of religion in justifying aggression and insists that to thus betray the people is to sin against God. 'The French may be our co-religionists but culturally [and politically] they are strangers to us,' he wrote.

His poetry takes up many related themes and becomes an alternative vehicle for 'socio-theology'. His *Confession to the King* clearly links worship of God with loyalty to the king and piety to one's father (drawing on the 'Three Fathers' of earlier Vietnamese theology: refer chapter 2 above). The faith he presents draws on natural religion, scriptural insight and 'present obedience to the law of heaven'. This faith he declares, drawing on both Christian and indigenous insights, is not brought from the west but is the religion of the Lord and creator of the universe.[12] Such affirmations were for Dang Duc Tuan far from merely 'theological' statements but were instead both spiritual and bodily commitments made at the cost often of his health and well-being.

ii) Nguyen Truong To (1827–1871)

A Chinese classical scholar who also studied in Europe, Nguyen Truong To was a teacher, architect and prolific Catholic writer. Returning to Saigon in 1861, he submitted a stream of memoranda to Emperor Tu Duc, advocating extensive reforms in the administration of justice, taxation, the army and international affairs. These reforms were to make possible equitable incomes, indigenous production and the elimination of corruption. 'Natural forces and the elements', he declared, 'must be studied first, for they were created by God for 'the betterment of humanity.' So for him scientific study and economic production come before literature, or conventional laws and customs. He also, therefore, proposed mass education and the inclusion of western studies in schools and colleges. 'Urgent measures' in which he personally also worked, included the formation of co-operatives, of crèches and hospices, and the development of irrigation and land settlement schemes.[13]

Such proposals by a passionate Roman Catholic patriot constituted an assault on almost every vested interest in Vietnamese society and even on established policies of the Roman Catholic Church. He was actually proposing for Vietnam 'more ambitious reforms than any others, between the 1880s and 1945'. They also contain the basis of a theology of society, which places people's welfare and an egalitarian society above established institutions and authority. He carefully presented interpretations of God as Creator, of the nature of humanity and of religious freedom, along with the importance of the 'middle father' (Emperor), of filial piety within Vietnamese culture, and of the relationship of 'earthly' well-being to 'spiritual' blessing.

His writings have been often republished and are extensively used by Catholic reformers in Vietnam today.[14] For Truong To there could be no separation between the best of Vietnamese cultural tradition, democratic freedoms and progressive Christian belief and action. His writings remain challenges to both the institutional preoccupations of the Roman Catholic hierarchy and to economic and political policies of the Vietnamese party and government.

iii)   Mai Lao Bang ('Gia Chau') (d. 1945)

Mai Lao Bang studied in the major seminary of Xa Drai. Leaving after two years with six others to become members of *La Societé du Modernisme* (an anti-colonial association for radical reform), he became a close associate of Phan Boi Chau, the later colleague of Ho Chi Minh. As part of his attempt to draw on insights from a recently 'arrived' Asian nation, in 1908 he also led a delegation of Roman Catholic students to Japan for study.

His writings at this time included the poems *Conseils de Lao Bang* and *Exhortation a L'unaminité*, addressed to fellow Catholics in Vietnam. In them he advocates people's unity and solidarity beyond personal interest, in the cause of a revolution against colonial overlords. Poems such as these were widely used amongst nationalist and Christian groups. Mai's prose writings were also influential and have been included in national collections.[15]

From 1913 to 1917 he was imprisoned along with Phan Boi Chau and three other Catholic priests, and was afterwards exiled until 1933. He continued to write poetry which was widely used by nationalist and revolutionary groups. 'Khuyen Dong Tam' for example, calls for an end to all animosities within Vietnamese society, and for their unity in struggle, citing as a model Le Loi and his followers opposing the Ming Chinese 400 years earlier. In later years he maintained a pharmacy, 'for the life of the nation', but avoided further involvement with the increasingly violent (though disintegrating) revolutionary movement. He is today included in recent studies of nationalist Catholic writers and respected as a Christian patriot. He is also regarded more widely in the region as an early revolutionary and nationalist leader.[16]

2. The Philippines

In the Philippines we have theologies of nationalism, of struggle for independence, of revolution, cultural renewal, and social reform.

i) Don Pedro Pelaez (d. 1863) and José Apolonio Burgos (1836–1872)

Born of Filipino-Spanish parents, Pelaez was the principal leader from 1849 in the movement of Filipino clergy to rectify injustices within the church and to establish a church in which Filipino and Spaniard were equally regarded. He became lecturer in both philosophy and theology, secretary to the Archbishop and administrator of the Manila Diocese.

In his teaching and writings he was an eminent advocate for the Filipinization of the church along with Frs. Mariano Gomez, Agustin Mendoza, and José Guevarra, as well as being a senior mentor to all Filipino priests. He opposed injustices done to Filipino clergy, especially regarding the deprivation of parishes and their relegation to inferior positions, reprinting Abp. Sancho de Santa Justa's statements on their behalf. He was deeply concerned and tireless in advocating Church reform, although remaining strict concerning the requirements of canon law. Pelaez founded, with Francisco Gainza, the *El Catolico Filipino* newspaper in 1862, and also wrote a series of articles on behalf of Filipino Clergy, published in *La Generacion* (Madrid).[17]

The protégé and successor of Pelaez was José Burgos, Rector of Manila Cathedral, a brilliant scholar and theologian, and a leader in the *Comité de Reformadores*. He remained loyal to Rome while rejecting the exploitative policies and theology of the friars and remained faithful also in advocating the Filipinization of the Church. He wrote extensively in the cause of reform and social justice, for the recognition of Filipino clergy, and for the equality of Filipino and Spaniard. All these advocacies brought him into direct conflict with Spanish authorities who increased their harassment of him and his colleagues.

With Joachim Pardo de Tavera, he founded the journal *El Eco Filipino* (Madrid) to publish these concerns. There and elsewhere he proved himself a polymath, drawing on a wide knowledge of history, scientific discovery, canon law and theology to articulate a theology of national identity and Filipino Christianity in their social and political application. His continuing role in movements for Filipino identity and equality was fiercely opposed by Spanish Friars and the military, leading finally to his imprisonment and finally his martyrdom in 1872 (with Mariano Gomez and Jacinto Zamorra). His extant writings have been recently again republished and include articles, letters, and manifestos, with many collections and studies of his work and thought being published.[18]

ii) Gregorio Aglipay (1860–1940) and Isabello de los Reyes Sr. (1864–1938)

Gregorio Aglipay became active in supporting the campaigns for the Filipino clergy by the 1890s, as priest in Manila and later in Cavite. He remained in contact with nationalist groups and leaders in the later revolution against Spain. As the ('Revolutionary') Vicar General, Aglipay issued 'semi-schismatic' manifestos (Oct. 1898) and was excommunicated by the Spanish hierarchy in 1899. His augmented role in Filipino churches had flowed directly from concern that there should be continuing pastoral and training provision for them in the wake of Spanish departures. Following attempts to form a national Roman Catholic Church, he joined Isobelo de los Reyes in the establishment of the *Iglesia Filipina Independiente* (IFI, 1902). In the same year de los Reyes had founded the first labor union in Philippines: *Union Obrera Democratica* (Democratic Labor Union). The IFI quickly became a mass movement enlisting Filipino Catholics who also espoused Filipino independence and came to represent especially the concerns of labourers, share-croppers and other exploited Filipino groups.[19]

In theology, his early orthodoxy was modified by the movements for religious liberty, for nationalism and for Filipinization. He came to believe that only by revolution would the friars be forced to relinquish lands and their controlling power and only thus would the Spanish hierarchy be replaced by Filipino bishops. Following the reluctant break with Rome, he was influenced by Unitarianism in belief and, with de los Reyes, by Filipino traditions and aspects of ancient Filipino religious beliefs. These markedly diluted the Roman Catholic character of the new church's theology. These elements were themselves later diluted and following the end of the Pacific War a full concordat between the IFI and the Filipino Episcopal Church was signed in 1948. Careful study reveals that IFI theology however remained clearly liberalizing and nationalist in its direction, while retaining much of the structure of Catholic doctrine.[20]

Isabello de los Reyes was an ardent nationalist and Filipinologist, and has been termed the 'father of Philippine folk-lore.' He was also a vigorous labour leader and the founder and/or editor of six papers and journals including *Filipinas ante Europa* and *La Iglesia Filipinas Independiente: Revista Catolica*. Through founding the *Union Obrera Democratica*, he was a prominent leader in movements of workers and was jailed for agitation on behalf of poor labourers. He campaigned for the rights of Filipino clergy, was firmly anti-American and a close associate of Aglipay and Mabini. He then became the key organizer, liturgist and theologian for the IFI. In later years he was to be co-founder of the Republican Party of the Philippines.

In doctrinal and liturgical formulations, de los Reyes combined elements of ancient Filipino belief in the nature deity *Bathala*, with Christian beliefs and scientific thought. In the *Oficio Divina* (1906) he rewrote a revised Roman Missal to express Filipino devotion and cultural heritage and in this he departed from many traditional Christian concepts. His liturgies and prayers however have been judged to be 'deeply sensitive' and 'keenly ethical'. He retained belief in the Incarnation but not in the Trinity as traditionally understood, nor in a sacrificial atonement. Throughout all his writings, the central concern is for a faith, and life of worship, which expresses Filipino self-hood and is liberative for the Filipino people.[21] Here again there was a dynamic link between the immediate (and long-term) needs of Filipino people and the development of Christian understanding which responded to and supported activity within both and society.

3. China

Here there are contextual theologies of nationalism, reconstruction, indigenous leadership, social reform, and mission practice.

i) Ma Xiangbo (c. 1840–1939)

Scholar and priest, educator and ardent nationalist, human rights advocate and theologian, Ma Xiangbo is chiefly remembered as the founder of *Zhendan daxue* (Aurora University, merged in 1952 with East China Normal University and Fudan University). He also contributed later to the establishment of the *Fudan daxue* (University of Shanghai which is now one of the C9 group of most prestigious Chinese universities). His hopes for an overall body for Chinese academic learning were later realized in the Academia Sinica which was established by his close friend Cai Yuanpei in 1928.[22]

Ma came in fact to be called 'the most influential Chinese Catholic thinker of the modern period.' Although becoming a Jesuit (1862), he later left the order (1874), not being able to accept the wholly European framework for the life of a Religious, nor the increasing aggressive actions of France toward China. He was also later unable to accept the overly French orientation which developed in the *Zhendan daxue*. Instead he worked with his close colleague Ling Lianzhi for the establishment of a Catholic University of Peking, later renamed *Fu Jen* Catholic University, and other schools. The university eventually expanded to include all faculties as well as to publish Sinological research.

In 1886/87 he had married and also travelled to France. For a period he also served as a diplomat to Europe and the United States. Although he was at times placed under surveillance by warlord regimes for his political activities, he was nonetheless able to make significant contributions to religious, and political movements in China, both through his pioneer educational activities and through his prolific writings. After long illness he died in Vietnam in 1939 while en route with many colleagues to Kunming, West China as a result of the Japanese invasion. In that year also a Republic of China Commemorative Coin was struck in his name

In his extensive writings Ma Xiangbo explored, as a committed Christian, the issues of Chinese modernization, educational reform and the role of democratic political parties. He also wrote and advocated for the Church's role within the state, for constitutional and political responsibility, for educational and professional innovation, for the relationship of religion to society and the indigenization of Christianity. A four-volume collection of his works – religious, political and educational – is now being prepared.

Along with his major contributions to the shaping of China's tertiary education institutions, Ma Xiangbo contributed to the development of Chinese Catholic theology, by his application of classical Confucian thought along with Christian insights, to the major social and political questions of a Chinese society in transition. This is yet to be fully recognised, studied and received in the present context of China's universities and churches.

ii)   Frédéric Vincent Lebbe (1877–1940)

Frédéric Vincent Lebbe (*Lei Mingyuan*) was priest, activator and advocate for the autonomy of the Catholic Church in China and for the development of its native clergy. He was a strong critic of the liaison between colonial power and missions in China and of the arrogance and Eurocentric mind-set of most missionaries there. He therefore worked for many years to limit and end the French Protectorate in China. Almost from his arrival in China (1901), and working first among intellectuals in Tientsin, he began to identify himself closely with Chinese colleagues and with their lifestyle. He took Chinese nationality, observed many Chinese customs and refused the privileges normally accepted by foreign missionaries. He worked closely with Chinese colleagues and devoted himself especially to the study of Chinese language and writing, culture and history. On this basis he was to become a unique leader in missiological reform, in the recognition and formation of Chinese leadership and indigenous clergy, and in the articulation of Chinese Christian self-hood.

Lebbe quickly developed his own reshaped catechism, the so-called 'method of Tientsin,' in order to 'inculturate the Christian message in the Chinese context'. He then undertook an intensive programme of lecturing on these issues and upon Christian social doctrine. With Chinese colleagues and his confrère Anthony Cotta he formed Catholic lay associations and founded the first Catholic weekly newspaper in China, *Yi shi bao* ('the public well-being') (1915). This was established in a district outside the French controlled 'concession' territory and became one of the 'Four Great Newspapers' of the Republican period. He was also involved in relief work and ecumenical charities.

In this and other periodicals he wrote regular 'religious' columns. But because of his increasing influence amongst younger Chinese intellectuals, as well as for his outspoken criticisms of French mission practices he was transferred to Ningpo from Tientsin (1917). He nonetheless prepared the *Memoir on the Catholic Mission in China*[23] which led directly to the promulgation of Pope Benedict XV's encyclical *Maximum Illud*. This and the later *Rerum ecclesiae* of Pius XI (1926) marked a radical change in mission practice, and through his work with Cardinal Constantini effective moves to form an indigenous Catholic church were made. Political control of mission by the French was ended, six Chinese bishops were consecrated (1926) and increasing numbers of Chinese were ordained priests.

Lebbe had long worked to organize lay movements as well as to mobilize auxiliary associations for the Chinese Church. He assisted also in the formation of two Chinese religious orders and following the outbreak of the 2nd Sino-Japanese War he organized and led a Catholic 'battlefield rescue and relief team' which assisted wounded soldiers and refugees. He had continued also to write, both on behalf of indigenous Chinese leadership and in opposition to Japanese imperialism. Many of his theological contributions are recognised to be seminal for today's contextual reflection, and groups have been formed to continue his work, in particular those such as the 'Vincent Lebbe Centres' established in both China and Belgium.[24]

4. Japan

In Japan in this period we have theologies of protest and reform, indigenous history, ecology, feminism, and socialism.

i) Tanaka Shozo (1842–1913)

Tanaka Shozo (1841-1913) was son of a village Headman in Tochigi Prefecture and was later Headman himself. He was also a social activist opposing industrial pollution and supporting local autonomy and he has been called Japan's 'first conservationist'. Although falsely imprisoned four times for exposing corruption and opposing high officials, Tanaka dedicated his life to the championing and protection of oppressed rural people and their environments. From boyhood on he had studied Confucian ethics and the life of the Buddha, becoming Christian later in life under the influence of Arai Osui when in prison (1902).[25] He became a member of the regional parliament (1880–1884) and of the National Diet in Japan's first General Election (1890).

More importantly he became 'one of the pioneers of the people's movement in modern Japan.' Throughout his life he worked to sustain the livelihood and safety, the land and villages of peasant farmers, especially as these were being destroyed by mining, heavy pollution and land confiscation in the Yanaka district. He has been, and is being, acknowledged as the pioneer in struggles for conservation and community development.[26]

Tanaka's ethics were based on the joy and responsibility inherent in nature and the land, and in neighbourhood and community. In each of these contexts he discerned the presence of the living God. "God is working among us" he wrote in his diary, "opening our eyes to see the things around us we acknowledge the presence of God ... If we search nearby we can find him... God exists not only... in the pure place, but also in the 'bad place' and the 'dirty place.'" He also recognised human responsibility to the state and to political process, declaring that despite Japan being now a constitutional monarchy it was also a robber state in the way trade was conducted, the ways that land was owned, and the systems by which ordinary people were exploited. Somehow Japan is to become again 'a family', he challenged.

Though not a member of any church, Tanaka was deeply Christian and found in the Bible 'the Heavenly way' of love and justice, peace and disarmament, as well as care of nature and for neighbour. He found in Jesus Christ a full humanity 'without losing the quality of holiness,' and with the courage also to stand unwaveringly for truth. As Arai had done, he also found there "the reality of resurrection continuously occurring in the midst of cosmic life."[27] From this came the strength to continue his campaigns, identifying fully with the cause and living conditions of Yanaka peasants, and also recognizing their wisdom. 'Learning from the people of the bottom fits in the heavenly way,' he declared.

One year before his death he testified at the local court that: "The hope of Shozo Tanaka, a resident of Yanaka, is the resurrection of self-government of the people." There remained for him always, hope for 'the Heavenly way' being known again in the life of Japan.[28] In Tanaka's work surely there is a life-centred unity of critical reflection and action, of theology and ecology, that offers resource for our living theologies and action today.

ii)   Yamada Waka (1879–1957)

A former migrant and prostitute in San Francisco, Yamada Waka was 'rescued' by Donaldina Cameron, who directed a women's refuge there. She became Christian in 1904 and was soon literate, quite remarkably becoming educated to a very high standard. Upon her return to Japan she began, with her former tutor and now husband Yamada Kakichi, a language and literature school in Tokyo in 1905. This soon became a centre for students, socialist-minded workers, intellectuals and informed women. She soon became a regular contributor to *Seito Magazine*, published by the 'Bluestocking Women's Literature Club', which had been founded in 1914 to raise the consciousness of women. Yamada also wrote for other journals and became a skillful translator of such authors on women's concerns as Olive Shriner, Lester Ward and Ellen

Kaye. The Yamadas maintained a frugal life-style, but developed a large library of Japanese and western books. Their house became also a shelter and a hostel as well as a well-attended educational salon.[29]

Through discussion groups, seminars and writings —especially in the magazine she founded (*Women and the New Society*) —Yamada Waka came to play a central role in emerging women's movements and in expressing a practical theology in their activities and concerns. As with Ellen Kaye 'her central interest was in protecting and elevating women's roles as wife and mother.' This approach differed from that of some other Japanese feminists who were more critical of women's domestic roles. Yet her writings, which also appeared regularly in the prominent newspaper *Asahi Shimbun* (from 1931) and in the magazine *Shufunotomo*, address many social issues from specifically a 'liberated' Japanese woman's point of view. Her subjects in articles, translations and books included women's education, labour unions, free love, abortion, voting rights, love and marriage, and new trends in women's thinking.

Yamada's collected essays were published in 1920, including the widely-read articles 'Love and Society,' 'Society and Family' and 'Women Bow Down to Society' (on women's working conditions, labour unions, voting rights and women's new understandings). Although strongly critical of aspects of Japanese society, Yamada Waka persistently advocated social co-operation and volunteer service at every level of national life. Her approach to the dilemmas of women in particular, was most simple and personal and her writings had wide impact. This was because for her, Christian faith, practical service and social criticism were one united cause and calling and not to be fragmented.[30] She had become such a popular social critic that she was invited to lecture in a tour of the U.S.A., to promote international understanding. She also established Japan's first refuge for women and children who were victims of domestic violence, and later, a 'Girls' School' for training in vocational and life skills.

Here also we see a different unity of lived theology and prophetic life. The close parallels in the lives of Nakajima Shigaru (d.1946) and Kagawa Toyohiko (d.1960), to mention only two near contemporaries of Yamada, are clearly to be seen. Her earlier experiences remained clear to her but she would also publicly affirm that she had been 'reborn… Because I have been resurrected from hell, I have plenty to tell you.' Whether Yamada herself saw her work in women's human concerns as 'doing' or 'living' theology, there is obvious unity in her life of animation and writing (along with her husband), between a deep social concern and the application of Christian faith to urgent human issues. This clearly qualifies to be what we now term 'applied', 'practical' or 'interdisciplinary' theology. Needless to say her writings and life are yet to be fully studied as such 'practical theology'. There is however an extensive archive of her writings held in Waseda University Tokyo, and reprints of her volumes have been issued in 1982, 1986, 1992 and 2018.

5. What Is Happening Here Theologically?

When considering the case-studies outlined above it is not possible to overlook, in these patterns of action-reflection-writing, the essential aims and functions of what we term 'contextualizing/incarnational theology.' In these examples, the response of localizing theology is not shaped primarily by doctrinal or devotional beliefs or practices. It is rather their aspirations for a quality of human life in community—shaped both by the classical and folk traditions of their people and by the present socio-political context—which determines the questions they address to the Gospel. It is this also which determines the creative response they make to it in presenting the 'coming Commonwealth of justice and peace'.

By the mid-20th century they would have many successors (to mention only a few examples from many) like Kim Jai-joon (Korea), Wu Lei-chuan (China) and Amir Sjarifoeddin (Indonesia); and amongst them women like Michi Kawai (Japan), Sophia Blackmore (Malaya) and Wang Li-ming (China). Those who later stand in this tradition are too numerous to list but include such comparatively unknown but pioneering theologians like Inoue Yoji (Japan), Khin Maung Din (Burma), D. S. Amalorpavadass (India) and Paul Caspersz (Sri Lanka). [These and many others are covered fully in the research guide to *Asian Christian Theologies* cited above].

Few of these however have yet been studied adequately nor accorded the role in theological interpretation—Asian or western—which they obviously merit. An obsession with systematic and philosophic forms in the doing of theology, especially as these have developed in the post-medieval west, have, I believe, displaced earlier patterns for the doing of 'theology', and hidden the incarnational and transformative dimensions of much Asian reflection and writing. These have often been so embedded in the life of their people, grounded in their intellectual, social and religious life, and so organically related to 'living as if God rules in the midst,' that it has been all too easy to assume that something less than 'theology' is here. This is of course to disregard not only the Biblical patterns for doing theology, but also the many other dimensions of authentic theology; other models of discernment, response and reflection; other images and visions for human life which live in the best of our cultural traditions. It also fails to recognise the 'alternative hermeneutic' of *lived* faith in community; the shared action and conviviality which is itself our 'text' for contextual interpretation.[30]

So what are the genuinely 'theological' ingredients, and processes in the examples given above? An *interim reflection* would include the following:

1. Obviously there is a dynamic theological understanding present that envisions a coming 'peaceable commonwealth'—the reign of God which is now at hand and which is the central 'Gospel' we have been given. There is also the most important context of an internalized experience of creative traditions within one's own culture. But there is also in many the fruits of wider religious, humanist or political studies, along with a fearlessness in tapping

these. The vision of God's realm has developed to become an intention and life-style which is shaped by living faith and living culture.

2. There is a particular commitment to and identification with the aspirations of one's own people, which leads on to situational analysis of, and involvement in, their most urgent human and societal issues. Theological obedience has therefore included both engagement and critical reflection; both co-operative action and synthesizing formulation. This includes a certain identity and selfhood, careful attention to place and environment and a measure of both 'nationalism' and communitarianism. But the fundamental commitment is to the core activities of compassion, social justice, creativity and community-building.

3. But note that these reflections-in-life are directly applied to particular localities and histories. The intention is to discern the challenge for 'peace, justice and the integrity of creation' and to respond within a present and concrete situation or struggle; to work through social and political action explicitly for the common good and reflection upon that; to take the 'next step in (God's) mission' by understanding the dilemmas and aspirations of our peoples and our response in life and thought to those.

Collaborative communication therefore possesses here a priority over construction; just as theological mobilizing and alliance-building has priority over theological debating. The sequence here is not normally to move from study to reflection, to theoretical-debate and to writing, but rather to first set in place a fuller seeing-hearing-acting, *along with* reflecting. This is a gathering of resources *within* a committed involvement, which is first communicated and with partners mobilized. Only after further 'being-and-doing-together,' is it revised for publication![32]

4. From, and only because of, the above commitments, comes fuller engagement in the living out of 'theology'; more ample

resource-gathering; along with critical reflection and action. Only later again come the national and inter-national discussion and exchange; the publishing beyond the immediate needs for communication and collaboration; and wider, deeper action, networking and research, with consequent wider responses.

Postscript

Many issues of interpretation, and of comparative significance, have been omitted in this outline, and the examples given are only a few from the extensive number now available for our study. They do illustrate however, the autonomy and continuing validity of creative Asian Christian traditions, the rich diversity of contextualizing theologies they make possible and (at least some of) the wide-ranging implications such theologies and their processes have for our own contemporary tasks.

Great diversity of written forms is not the least feature of such 'contextualizing theologies' (or *'theodaodharmas'*). These reflections-in-life have resulted in a series of volumes, or collections of articles for only some of those studied. The thought and explication are sometimes extant only in fragmentary writings, letters, biographies or poetry. Some are emerging from present historical study but more await the fuller research that will restore to us more of our own story, and more of the resources we will need for coming 'theologies.' They have had strong influence upon their people's life and aspirations in their times and form the often unacknowledged sources for some of our most creative socio-theological movements today. For the spirit of the One Living God still brings her Common-wealth amongst us in peace, justice and love. And we 'would-be-theologians' in our region discern, join with, and reflect on those comings, as our creative forebears have, in on-going thought and life. …The cranes are ever flying.

Endnotes

[1] *Asian Christian Theologies. Research Guide to Authors, Movements, Sources.* (3 vols. ed. John C. England et al. ISPCK; Claretian; Orbis Books, 2002-2004). See also chap. 1, 4, & 6 in this volume

[2] I draw here on the work of Oskar Mayer (most recently in Mayer 1994, 23–43), in bringing together the interpretations of contemporary Japanese scholars such as Yamamoto Shichihei (aka Isaiah Ben-Dasan), Ide Katsuymi, and Hakamaya Noriaki. See also Mayer (1985).

[3] Jennes (1973) particularly emphasizes this..

[4] Such active and outgoing love is clearly the heart of that Life. And even a cursory study of the synoptic gospels shows that Jesus seldom if ever required statements of belief whether from disciples, followers or those helped or healed, before accepting, healing, counselling or calling them to assist him.

[5] A small selection of sources which show this clear emphasis could include: Paulos Mar Gregorios (1968); Carlos Abesamis (1983); Park Soon Kyung (1983); (Ms) Elizabeth Dominguez (1984); Tissa Balasuriya (1990); (Ms) Kim Sung Hae (1996); V. Devasahayam (1997); K.H. Ting (2000); Nguyen Y Doan (2004); Felix Wilfred (2008); Levi Oracion (2010). See also Joseph, M.P. et al. (2018).

[6] Refer to M.G. Hodgson (1993); J.J. Clarke (1997) (especially chaps. 1 & 12); D.F. Lach (1970, 1977); Brian Carr & Indira Mahalingam (1997).

[7] Refer to J.C. England (1981) passim and ACTS (op.cit.) (2001) vol. 1, 3-77.

[8] Among many sources for these unities see e.g. Coomaraswamy, (1956); Ching (1976); Pieris (2000).

[9] For a fuller outline of these terms see my article "Moving Beyond, Returning from Theology" (forthcoming)

[10] For an earlier collection of such 'doing of theology' see my *Living Theology in Asia* (SCM Press 1981, Orbis Books 1982). Refer also to 'Doing Theology in Asian Ways', chap.7 in this volume.

[11] For this and following quotations see Đang Đúc Tuâ (1970); and Phan et al. (1988). For further on Dang Duc Tuan see *Asian Christian Theologies*, vol. 2, 566f.

[12] Hoàng Gia Khánh (2000).

[13] Hoang Thanh Da (2000); *Nguyên Trường Tô* (1992); Truong Buu Lâm (1907). [Includes translations of 20 key documents of Nguyên Trường Tô].

[14] Nguyen Truong To's writings have been collected in Truong 1991. Vol. 1 Study of Nguyen Truong To's life and work; volumes II and III give his writings. See also Hoang (2001); Vo Đúc Hanh (1969); *Asian Christian Theologies* , vol. 2, 567ff.

[15] See Vu Dinh Lien et al. (1985 [1963]), Dang Thai Mai (1964).

[16] Mai Lao Bang. 1964; Vu Đình Liên et al. 1963; David Marr (1971); Phan Huy Lê, et al. (1988).

[17] Schumacher 1981, 7-14; see also de la Costa and Schumacher 1980.

[18] Schumacher (1972, 1999, 2009) (chap. 5); See *Asian Christian Theologies* vol. 2, 344f., 46f.

[19] Teodoro Agoncillo (1960) 283.

[20] Schumacher (1981) (chap. 6); Salanga 1982; *Asian Christian Theologies* vol. 2, 350ff.

[21] Scott (1982), 245–299; *Asian Christian Theologies* vol. 2, 352f.

[22] The fullest treatment of Ma in English is still (Ms.) Ruth Hayhoe & Lu Yongling (1996). See in particular Lu Yongling "Statesman and Centenarian: Ma Xiangbo as Witness of China's Early Modernity" ibid. See also J-P. Wiest (2010) 41-60.

[23] Refer *Memoria sullo stato dell'evangelizzazione in Cina e sulla formazione del Clero indigeno,* (Ponente, Rome 1922); Lebbe (1925). See Soetens (1982); Leclercq (1965); *J-P. Wiest (1999);* also *Archives Vincent Lebbe; and Asian Christian Theologies* vol. 3, 50ff.

[24] See Soetens (1982); Leclercq (1965); *J-P. Wiest (1999);* also *Archives Vincent Lebbe; Asian Christian Theologies* vol. 3, 50ff.

[25] For Arai Osui see Arai, 1941; Arai Assoc. (2000).

[26] Tanaka's Complete Works have been published in 19 vols. (Iwanami Shoten, 1979-80), with single volumes being published in 1989, 2009, 2013.

[27] Takenaka (1984) 202.

[28] Refer Strong (1977); Stolz (2013); *Asian Christian Theologies* vol. 3, 340f.

[29] The full biography is given by Tomoko Yamazaki (1985). See also *Asian Christian Theologies* vol. 3.349 for sources. The full archives of Yamada Waka are held in Waseda University, Tokyo. See also Linda Johnson (2002)

[30] For examples see Yamada (1920, 1935, 1986). Refer Tomoko (1985), chap. 11-14. For background to women's magazines in Japan in this period see recent comments by C. Harding (2018) 82-84.

[31] Refer here to such works as Ananda K. Coomaraswamym (1956), Chen 1993, Ching (1976); Pieris (2000). For further on methodological assumptions see chap. p. 7 in this volume.

[32] Concrete examples of such process can be seen in the series of *Theology in Action* workshops held in various parts of the region in the 1970s/1980s.

Selected Bibliography and works cited

Abesamis, Carlos *Where are we going: Heaven or a New World?* (Foundation Books, 1983);

Agoncillo, Teodoro *A Short History of the Filipino People* (Univ. of Philippines, 1960).

Arai, Osui *Inward Prayer and Fragments* (Horii Printing House, 1941).

Arai Osui Memorial Association, *The unknown lives of thinkers: Rediscovering Arai Osui.* (Shumpusha, 2000).

Blanco, Roberto Andrés "Pedro Peláez, Leader of the Filipino Clergy". (*Philippine Studies* vol. 58 nos. 1 & 2 (2010): 3–43.

Carr, Brian & Indira Mahalingam (eds.) *Companion Encyclopedia of Asian Philosophy* (Routledge, 1997).

Chen Eoyang E. *The Transparent Eye* (Univ. of Hawaii Press, 1993).

Ching, Julia (ed). To *Acquire Wisdom: The Way of Wang Yang-ming* (Columbia Univ. Press, 1976).

Clarke, J.J. *Oriental Enlightenment* (Routledge, 1997), especially chap.ps 1 & 12; Coomaraswamy, Ananda K. *The Christian and Oriental Philosophy of Art* (Dover, 1956).

Đang Đúc Tuân. *Tinh Hoa Công giáo Ái quôc Viêt Nam* [The Genius of Catholic Patriotism in Vietnam] (Tác Gia Tu Xuat Ban, 1970, Reprint).

Dang, Thai Mai. *Van Tho Cach Mang Vietnam Dau The KyXX* [Vietnam's Revolutionary Prose & Poetry in Early Twentieth Century] (NXB van Hoc, 1964).

de la Costa, Horatio and John N. Schumacher. *The Filipino Clergy: Historical Studies and Future Perspectives. Loyola Papers* 12. (Loyola School of Theology, 1980).

Devasahayam, V. *Doing Dalit Theology in Biblical Key* (Gurukul College 1997).

Dominguez, Elizabeth (Ms) "Signs and Counter-signs of the Kingdom of God in Asia Today" (*Voices from the Third World* 7.2 1984)

Elison, George. *Deus Destroyed: The Image of Christianity in Early Modern Japan.* Harvard Univ. Press, 1973.

England John C. *Living Theology in Asia* (SCM Press 1981, 2012).

England, John C. et al. (eds.) *Asian Christian Theologies, A Research Guide to Authors, Movements, Sources*. 3 vols. (ISPCK; Claretian, Orbis Books, 2001-2004).

Gernet, Jacques. *China and the Christian Impact.* (Cambridge Univ. Press, 1985).

Gregorios, Paulos Mar *The Gospel of the Kingdom* (CLS, 1968).

Harding, Christopher *Japan Story: In Search of a Nation 1850 to the Present* (Allan Lane, 2018).

Hayhoe, Ruth and Lu Yongling, (eds.) *Ma Xiang Bo and the Mind of Modern China 1840–1939.* (M. E. Sharpe, 1996).

"Hero of the Philippine Revolution". (MSC Publishing, 14 April 1998).
http://www.msc.edu.ph/centennial/burgos.html

Hoàng Gia Khánh. "Filial Piety Against the Background of the Doctrine of Tam Phu - Triple Fatherhood." In *Filial Piety and Christian Faith in Vietnam, Papers from the Seminar at Huê, 1999* (Institute for the Study of Religion, 2000).

Hoang, Thanh Dam. *Nguyen Truong To. Thoi Tu Duy Cai Cach* [Nguyen Truong To His Time and Reformist Thinking]. (Nab Van Nghe, 2001).

Hodgson, M.G. *Rethinking World History* (Univ. Cambridge Press, 1993).

Humbertclaude, Myotei Mondo. Une apologetique chrétienne japonaise de 1605. (*Monumenta Nipponica* I: 515-525, 1938; *Monumenta Nipponica* II: 237-267, 1939).

"Isabelo de los Reyes" National Historical Commission of the Philippines http://nhcgov.ph/isabelo-de-los-reyes/

Jennes, Joseph *A History of the Catholic Church in Japan from its beginnings to the early Meiji Era.* (Oriens Institute for Religious Research, 1973).

Johnson, Linda L.. "Yamada Waka". Women in World History, Vol. 17: Y-Z. (Yorkin Publications, 2002) pp. 16–17.

Joseph, M.P. et al (eds.) *Wrestling With God in Context* (Fortress, 2018).

Kim Sung Hae (Ms) "The Kingdom of God as the Christian Image of Harmony"(*Inter-Religio* 29 (1996);

Lach, D.F. *Asia and the Making of Europe.* 2 vols. (Chicago Univ.Press, 1970, 1977).

Langlet, Philippe *Point de Vue sur Nguyet Truong To et le Réformisme Vietnamien au Milieu du XIXe Siècle.* (Etudes Interdisciplinaires sur le Vietnam, 1974).

Lebbe, Vincent *Que sera la Chine demain?* (Xaveriana,1925); *Recueil des Archives Vincent Lebbe. Pour l'Eglise Chinoise.* Introduction et notes par Cl. Soetens (Louvain Faculté de Theologie, *1982/83).*

Leclercq, Jaques *Vincent Lebbe. Der Apostel des modernen China* (Herder, 1965).

Marr, David. *Vietnamese Anti-colonialism 1885-1925 (*Univ. of California Press, 1971).

Martinez, Salvador & Alan Torrance (eds.). *Doing Theology in Asian Ways.* (ATESEA Occasional Papers 12, 1993).

Mayer, Oskar. 1994. "Fukansai Fabian and Kirishitan - A Paradigm of Modern Awareness". *(Japanese Religions* 19 [1-2]): 23-43.

Ming Ben She Yi *Patriotic elderly Ma Xiangbo. (1840-1939)* (Zhenjiang historical material) (Danyang Cultural and Historical Data Series, 2015).

Nguyen, Van Trung et al. 1993. *Ve Sach Bao cua Tac Gia Cong Ciao: The Ky XVII-XIX* [Books and Articles by Catholic Authors, 17th-19th Centuries]. (Univ. of Ho Chi Minh Ville, 1993).

Nguyen Khac Vien & Huu Ngoc. *Vietnamese Literature: Historical Background and Texts. (*Red River Foreign Lnguages Press, n.d.)

Nguyên Truòng Tô and the Country's Reforms: Symposium on Nguyên Truòng Tô, a Great Reformer of the Nation. (Centre for Chinese and Nom Languages, 1992).

Nguyen Y Doan, *People's Theology in Vietnam* (ISPCK, 2004).

Oracion, Levi *Rumours of a Divine-Human Synergy in our Midst* (New Day, 2010).

Park Soon Kyung *The Kingdom of God and the Future of the Nation.* (Korean Christian Books, 1983).

Phan Huy Le et al. *La canonization des martyrs dans le contexte historique du Vietnam.* (Selection of presentations at the National Symposium 8-10 June 1988). (National Committee for Social Sciences in Vietnam. 1988).

Pieris, Aloysius *Mysticism of Service.* (Tulana Centre, 2000).

Ramsay, Jacob *Mandarins & Martyrs: The Church & the Nguyen Dynasty in Early Nineteenth- Century Vietnam.* (Stanford Univ. Press, 2008).

Recueil des Archives Vincent Lebbe, 5 vols. (Louvain 1982–86).

Rodriguez, Isacio R .*Gregorio Aglipay y los Origenes de la Iglesia Filipina Independiente.* (Departamento de Misionologia Espanola, 1960).

Salanga, Alfredo Navarro. *The Aglipay Question. Literary and Historical Studies on the Life and Times of Gregorio Aglipay.* (Research Institute for Social and Ideological Studies, 1982).

Schumacher, John N. *Father Jose Burgos. Priest and Nationalist* (Ateneo de Manila Univ. Press, 1972).

Schumacher, John N. *Revolutionary Clergy: The Filipino Clergy and the Nationalist Movement, 1850–1903* (Ateneo de Manila Univ. Press, 1981).

Schumacher, John N. *Father Jose Burgos: A Documentary History with Spanish Documents and Their Translation* (Ateneo de Manila Univ. Press, 1999).

Schumacher, John N. *Growth and Decline: Essays on Philippine Church History* (Ateneo de Manila Univ. Press, 2009).

Scott, William Henry. *Cracks in the Parchment Curtain and Other Essays in Philippine History.* (New Day, 1982).

Schrimpf, Monika "The Pro- and Anti-Christian Writings of Fukan Fabian (1565-1621)" *(Japanese Religions* 33 [1 & 2] 2008).

Soetens, Claude. *Inventaire des Archives Vincent Lebbe* (La-Neuve, 1982).

Stolz, Robert. 'Remake Politics, Not Nature: Tanaka Shozo's Philosophies of 'Poison' and 'Flow' and Japan's Environment' *(The Asia-Pacific Journal.* Nov. 8, 2013).

Strong, Kenneth. *Ox Against the Storm. A Biography of Tanaka Shozo, Japan's Conservationist Pioneer* (Paul Norbury, 1977).

Takenaka Masao "Ethics of Betweenness – from a Case Study of Shozo Tanaka (1841-1913)" in (*East Asia Journal of Theology* 2.2 1984).

Tanaka Shozo *Shozo Tanaka Zenshu.* (Collected Works – 19 vols.)(Tokyo 1979-1980).

Ting K.H. (Ding Guangxun) *Love Never Ends* (ed. Janice Wickeri (Yilin Press, 2000).

Tomoko, Yamazaki. *The Story of Yamada Waka: From Prostitute to Feminist Pioneer.* (Kodansha International, 1985).

Truong, Ba Can, ed. *Nguyen Truong To 1830–1871.* Tap I [Vol. I]. *Con Nguoi* [The Man].[Institute of Research on Chinese and Vietnamese Culture, 1991].

Truong Buu Lâm. *Patterns of Vietnamese Response to Foreign Intervention 1858- 1900.* (Yale Univ., 1907). (Includes 20 key documents of Nguyên Truòng Tô).

Truong Buu Lâm *Colonialism Experienced: Vietnamese Writings on Colonialism, 1900-1931* (Univ. of Michigan Press, 2000).

Vo Đúc Hanh, E. *La place du catholicisme dans les relations entre la France et le Vietnam de 1851 à 1870.* 2 vols. Part 2, Les Documents (Brill, 1969).

Vu Đình Liên et al.(eds.) *Hop Tuyên Tho Van Viêt Nam 1858-1930* (A Collection of Vietnamese Poetry and Prose 1858-1930). (Nxb van Hoc, 1985 [1963]).

Weber, Hans-Ruedi. *Asia & The Ecumenical Movement 1895–1961* (SCM Press, 1966).

Wiest, Jean-Paul, "The Legacy of Vincent Lebbe" (*International Bulletin Missionary Research.* 1999.01). ww.bu.edu/missiology/missionary-biography/l-m/Lebbe

Wiest, Jean-Paul "Ma Xiangbo: Pioneer of Educational Reform". In Carol Lee Hamrin. *Salt and Light*, Volume 2 (Wipf and Stock, 2010).

Wilfred, Felix *Margins the Site of Asian Theologies* (ISPCK, 2008).

Yamada Waka *Fujin no kaiho to seiteki kyoiku* (Collected essays). (Toyo Shuppansha, 1920).

Yamada Waka *The Social Status of Japanese women.* (Kokusai Bunka Shinkokai [The Society for International Cultural Relations], 1935).

Yamada Waka *On'na Hito Haha* [Women, Human Flower] (Fuji Shuppan, 1986).

Chapter - 6

Within our Movements and Histories: The Crane is Ever Flying

Abstract

Our studies of 'Church History', especially in the 'Global South', regularly ignore the history of thought and theology which shape the historical identity and action of Christian communities. Defining these as peoples who, of whatever ethnicity, belief or tradition, discern and replicate the life-of-Jesus-with-others radically changes our conceptions of 'church', 'mission' and 'church history'. This then becomes the story of 'Jesus-like presence', wherever and by whomever – under whatever label – this presence is enacted in the community at large. For Christian communities the story of their reflective thought and engagement becomes then central to their 'Church History'. In each case this is necessarily a dynamic *movement*, seen in infinite diversity within and beyond particular countries. The thought which shapes and is shaped by such people movements for human community, justice and concord is the substantial basis for any 'church history', or 'history of Jesus-like community'. The 'theology' of creative movements in India, Sri Lanka and the Philippines, as they discern and join the 'work of God' in our world, are presented in illustration. Reference is confined to intra-Asian discussions rather than to those outside the region. I will first consider possible new directions for such historiography (1); then outline the contexts which require us to explore these (2). This will be followed by notes on earlier critical responses to non-Asian theologies-in-history (3), and selected case-studies from three countries of contextualizing theological movements of the early 20th Century (4). Some working conclusions conclude the paper.

Prelude

It is not always accepted that our histories of the church necessarily include the history of the *thought and intention* which is shaping those histories: that is, our theological (and ideological) assumptions and affirmations, whether these are acknowledged or unacknowledged. For these necessarily form alike the inner life of historical action, and the foundations of our historiography, both being modified as in all our histories, according to period, place and a particular people's culture. In any case we know that we never possess objective nor 'unbiased' truth in our historiography, and that no philosophical or scientific pattern of thought is free of the shaping by assumptions or context. Our methods in Christian historiography and hermeneutic are normally formed by (western) presuppositions as to the nature of 'church' and 'mission', of 'liturgy', 'ethics' and even 'faith'. As example: our treatment of incident, church, movement or individual person will of course greatly differ, whether we see church history as being the story of institutional expansion or of continuity in form, leadership or doctrine, *or* understand it rather as the story of our discernment and joining (or rejecting) God's presence and work in our world.[1]

'Discerning the work of God in our world' is of course the heart not only of doing theology, and of church history, but of the Gospel itself – the recognition of the work amongst us through which the 'just and peaceable Commonwealth of God' indeed comes (Mark 1.14). So I wish here to explore the linkage between 'Gospel', 'discernment' and 'work', by way of theology's role in shaping the ongoing history of Asian churches. And this will necessarily refer us to the hermeneutical assumptions which lie behind the 'how', 'why' and 'what' in the writing of those histories.

1. Taking a look behind or within the history?

A major question that is only sometimes asked in our research into 'Church History' concerns the terms 'Christianity', or 'Church' themselves, To what extent are our studies understood as the history of 'Jesus-like (or 'the Spirit's') presence' ? That is, 'the history of the movement connected directly or indirectly with the name of Christ... which is rightly conceived, a *universal* history'? I echo Kaj Baago's claim here[2] for a much wider recognition of 'Christian presence': not so much the measurable numbers or influence, nor patterns of leadership, worship or fellowship and their continuity in history, *but* what in a people's life together cooperates with the (cosmic) work of God on earth, whether this be institutionalized or fully documented or not. A number of writers in both 'north' and 'south' have for some decades been questioning the conventional usage of the terms 'church', 'mission', or 'Christianity', as these have been interpreted in 'western' or 'west-oriented' traditions (see below). They have emphasized that deep-down we all know that the Great Spirit's call is not necessarily to *this or that* 'church', *this or that* 'mission' or even *this or that* 'Christianity', but rather to God's New World being formed through Jesus Christ in our amidst.

We do know that any reference to 'mission' (for the Christian church) begins with *God's mission* in God's world, and consequently our talk of Church history must begin also with the story of *God's activity* in our world: that is, how and where the Commonwealth (the 'Kingdom', not the 'church') is coming to be. So how broad can be our conception of God's 'activity' or 'mission', to and within all humanity? This of course raises further questions as to 'what would be the marks of such activity or presence'? 'How do we recognise these in the life of our Christian communities?' I would claim that the Gospel that God's rule comes requires for 'would-be Christians' that we recognise the signs to it in *following* (living by, *not* primarily 'worshipping') *the life-of-Jesus-with-others*: that is the Jesus-like actions in history, to befriend and share meals with, to champion, rescue and restore, to teach and heal, to protest and resist injustice or inhumanity.

The range of human situations and contexts within which this inter-acting nexus of compassion, resistance and restoration may be discerned stretches of course across our region (and the globe), and is found as a part in the activities of countless religious, and humanitarian, educational, service and emergency agencies. The church, where it is faithful to the life-of-Jesus-with-others, becomes part of that 'community', and high-lights it as being the coming of God's Commonwealth: the church being 'signpost to' not 'container of' the Kingdom . But note that we historians of Christianity in Asian lands have a share too in critiquing those 'Christian' narratives and histories which do not relate to either 'God's New World of justice, creativity and peace', nor to 'the concrete histories and lived realities of the people'.

Such questions immediately make more theological assumptions of course. But this means that in assembling our 'church history' we do have for our 'principles of interpretation' additional sources over and above the accepted methodologies of 'history' or 'philosophy', of 'sociology' or 'anthropology'. To see our histories as 'the story' of human response to the Spirit's movement' – 'the discernment of God's Presence in history' – straightway broadens our focus to recognize the dynamic of such a movement wherever the marks of *Jesus'-life-with-others* may be discerned.[3] It focuses too upon the particular lives of individuals and movements, and upon the sources for our understanding of these in manuscript, the arts, or other media, and in epigraphy, architecture or archaeology.

So the underlying questions which church historians may have are:

a) 'What, *on earth, is* God doing?' Do we conclude (or in our methodology assume) that this is primarily 'gathering women and men into the church, which is a fore-runner of the 'Kingdom', *or* that it is God nurturing and sustaining *all* living beings?... creating, nurturing, inspiring, rescuing, transforming *all* human (and cosmic) life? ...and is therefore to be found in *all* that makes possible full human community, justice, peace?

b) *Where* do we see the-life-of-Jesus-with-others in this or that historical process? ...that is, if the marks of that life are befriending, accepting, walking-with, championing, protesting, healing, rescuing, resisting, and doing so *in the market-place, amidst the suffering* (whether this is appropriately labelled, acceptable, in church-related form or not)?

c) *What thought,* writings and artefacts provide an entry to some of the inner drive and intention not only of Christian presence and mission – and also movements and endeavours which arise from those – but of those actions and movements in supposedly 'secular' society which in reality do justice, make peace, heal and reconcile? in this revealing marks of *the-life-of-Jesus-with-others*? Does this not lead us into a form of 'church' history which takes shape as a 'social history' of Jesus-like praxis'?

2. For historians there may be no excitement in research that quite matches coming suddenly across an old artefact or an ancient manuscript that extends the existing evidence or throws quite new light upon a period, a movement or a particular person. I think here for example, of items in the St Thomas Museum in Chennai, or in the Shimabara Castle Museum in Kyushu, or of the Forest of Steles in Xian. It may too be a rare book, or an unpublished article or report which recovers the work of a forgotten scholar or activist, with the alternative history he or she supplies. Yet rather than the record itself, is not the *heart* of such a discovery for our *Christ-like* histories, the thrust and direction of mind and heart which it reveals?... the aspiration, insight or wisdom, the Jesus-like action, which is enacted or miscarried; the 'movement of the just and compassionate Spirit' that is discernible there? We are then not so much identifying a development in institutional activity, or a specifically devotional experience, nor the more-or-less 'orthodox' affirmation of faith, but firstly discerning a life or movement of *hope-in-action* (or Pascal's 'wager') for God's coming Common-wealth of peace, justice and creativity. This surely is the central Gospel which Jesus declared and lived.

And here we seem to be firmly within the dynamic of contextualizing theology. But I would affirm that such a wider, deeper conception of 'church' history is required, not just by many contemporary (and earlier), critical and 'de-colonized' Asian theologies[4] (not to mention similar critical approaches in other living faiths[5]), but by the actual nature of Christian movements and contexts themselves in the region. Required too by the specific nature of our historical sources and the methodologies for understanding these. Here I only need to mention some of the features in these that require of us quite diverse and new methodologies, and with which we may all be already familiar in our research and writing. These would include:

- the almost infinite diversity in the materials, texts and sources which we now have – and within most diverse cultures and societies – for two millennia of Christian history 'east of Antioch'; in epigraphy and relic, ruined churches and shrines, steles and statuary, manuscripts and paintings, scrolls and books, plaques and crosses, gravestones, way-stones and seals (See chaps. 1 and 3 above).

- the anonymity, collective authorship, or folk-traditional nature of many Christian sources; the indigenous socio-cultural concerns shaping these; and the consequently great diversity of signifiers to be interpreted there.

- the immense challenges presented by continuing and extensive upheavals in our region in the last century: the major political transitions for hundreds of millions of people; the tangled processes of de-colonization; the massive rural-to-urban migration; the presence of sharp ethnic and religious divisions; and the eruption of wide-spread social unrest, now greatly exacerbated by the destructive forces of economic globalization.

- the distortions that have resulted from still inadequate research into the pre-colonial, and post-colonial fields of evidence for Christic presence in specific localities; and of course the distortions often imposed through uncritical transference of non-Asian philosophical assumptions and historical methods. This brings about the ensuing need for critical assessment of interpretations proposed for us in inherited/traditional, colonial/pre-fabricated or post-colonial/'hybrid' hermeneutics.

- then the gaps in methodologies we yet have for interpreting the sources for such major features of Christic presence in our histories as:

- the characteristic life of Christian communities in a dozen countries east of Persia by the 8th century, which by a century later out-numbered the Greek and Latin churches together;

- life in the vastly scattered communities of expatriates and indigenes in our history – and our present-day – of the most diverse doctrinal or ecclesial identity;

- the long-persisting life of persecuted or hidden Christian communities of West or Central Asia, of China, Vietnam or Japan and elsewhere;

- the people-movements throughout our region in recent history – often ecumenical and inter-religious – which have drawn on creative tradition and contemporary analysis to establish the rights and powers of victimized, oppressed and destitute communities.

- and all this in a region which has millennia of its own seldom-interpreted 'Reformations' and 'Renaissances' (e.g. in Indian, Thai or Japanese religious history); its own 'Revolutions' (in China or Indonesia, Vietnam or the Philippines…), its own philosophical wisdoms and 'Enlightenments' (in almost every country).[6]

3. Such a world of diverse histories, cultures and human experience requires then, more than the tools of rational criticism or traditional historiography; more than customary concepts of 'church', 'Christian' or even of 'evidence'. I am here proposing that many of these other tools are available to us placing the study of the history of Asian Christian theologies and spiritualities, within their social context, in tandem with our study of 'Church History' as such. For the story of our Asian theologies draws on cross-textual, cross-cultural and inter-religious methodologies along with Biblical, literary and socio-political sources. They often arise from particular social endeavours and struggles, and are also open to collective, prophetic and mystical insights as these arise within new, Jesus-like movements for survival or justice, for peace, livelihood or identity.[7.]

So if the inner life and force for Asian Christian presence, over 20 centuries may be found in Asian theologies, as they seek to discern the presence and activity of God in our midst, then the vast extent and diversity of Asian Christian theologies, along with their great diversity of form, language and context, must be explored much further. And this becomes significant in revealing the 'inner drive' – indeed the very Spirit – of our Christian history. But then these theologies must themselves be evaluated by that same *'life-of-Jesus-with-others'*, within particular cross-textual, cross-cultural and inter-religious contexts.

In the history of Asian theologies however we often see similar limitations in presupposition and methodology to those found in many Asian church histories. The main concern often seems to interpret only inherited or 'pre-fabricated' formulations or terms, and for this to employ only doctrinal, statistical or ecclesial criteria. Neither the exposition of localized or cultural insights nor a clarification of social-political context or of contextualizing processes are included. Nor is there explication or discussion of 'Christian history in the light of the Commonwealth of God at hand and upon us'. We therefore see a widespread neglect, in the history of both church and of theology, of those writers and movements whose 'theological' articulations have arisen from and nurtured, 'controversial' but clearly humanitarian or 'Jesus-like' movements in their society, their Christian community or nation.

These purposive groupings have seldom been studied as historical *movements*, with their own autonomy, inner development and long continuity, in particular cultural contexts. Yet we do in fact have long 'pre-colonial' traditions in Asia's autonomous theologies dating from at least the third century, along with 'post-colonial traditions' in the 'modern' period from the seventeenth century. Then dating from at least the 1850s there is a history of sharp critiques or revisions of colonial, westernizing or neo-colonial theologies, particularly in India, Sri Lanka and Indonesia, in China, Vietnam, and Burma, in the Philippines, Japan and Korea.[8] Precursors for these critiques can be found in Turkestan (9th–14th centuries), and in many examples from India or China, Japan or the Philippines in the 16th–18th centuries.[9] They continue in countries across the region into the 21st century. In this historical-theological praxis:

- Local Christians encounter, but also modify, or even reject, western teachings or doctrinal formulations, in the light of 'wisdom' found in their own social and cultural experience;

- Indigenous verse, drama and art forms express and reshape Christian thought as brought by western missionaries or confessional tradition;

- Indigenous religious tradition is restored, critiqued and reconciled with re-interpreted Christian teaching in dialogues and verse-forms, meditations and treatises.

- A complete integration of vocation, lifestyle and writing can be observed in the works of some authors/artists, and is especially notable in the lives of a number of women.

- 'Contemporary' and indigenous theological reflection, within concrete situations, has led to ecumenical and inter-religious encounter and collaborative response to urgent social or political issues.

In other chapters of this volume I have written on some of the lesser-known 'incidents', people, and writings, that are significant for earlier periods of Asian church history, especially as providing entries to key movements.[10] It is however some of the more recent examples which I wish to consider here, through a selection of theologians-in-praxis who in their work with others exemplify the 'inner life', along with the outer forms, of Christian history in our region. In each case basic assumptions found in much Asian church historical writing and theology are questioned, sometimes even rejected, in theologies of nationalism and revolution, of inter-faith understanding, of social justice and reconstruction, of ecology and feminism, as well as of indigenous leadership, cultural renewal and human rights.

It is therefore the significance of theological *movements* in the life of churches and the development of missional and social movements – as these shape our 'church history – that is to be noted in the case-studies following. Since the Asia-Pacific war ended there have been, for example, a growing number of local and regional ecumenical movements in particular, which have enriched and re-formed the life of Asian-Pacific churches. These include notably the EACC/Christian Conference of Asia (CCA) and its related movements, along with (and often now collaborating with) the Federation of Asian Bishops' Conferences (FABC) and its related movements. Together these include (to mention a few only): the National Christian Councils in almost every country, the student movements of the WSCF Asia-Pacific and the IMCS, the Association of Christian Institutes for Social Concern (ACISCA), the SVD Asian Pacific Association for Mission Research (ASPAMIR), the Asia-Pacific Interfaith Network, the Asian Christian Art Association (ACAA), the Programme for Theology and Cultures in Asia (PTCA), Inter-Religio, the Congress of Asian Theologians (CAT), the Ecclesia of Women in Asia, and the Asian Movement for Christian Unity (AMCU). All of these, as well as their contributory groups or movements, have historically been shaped by specifically contextual, theological and social concerns throughout the region.

Please note that in the theologies themselves introduced below, and in their persisting influence, can be seen a dynamic movement in both thought and commitment into which succeeding generations enter. This is the *historical sequence* of discernment and study, of vision and hope, of action and reflection, which have largely shaped the life of churches in their societies and on their Asian frontiers.

4. **To illustrate: just a few examples of such Theological Movements of the early 20th Century.**
I draw here in part upon relevant sections of the Research Guide to *Asian Christian Theologies* (vols. I and II, note 1, above). Similar cases of theology-in-movement could be outlined for other countries of the region.

i) **In India**, K. T. Paul (1876-1931) was one of the founders of the National Missionary Society of India at Serampore (1905), for the Indian propagation of the Gospel and the Indigenization of the Church. Together with Bishop V.S. Azariah he also instituted the monthly journal *National Missionary Intelligencer* (later *National Christian Council Review*). He later became the national general secretary of the YMCA in 1916, and a leader in the South India United Church movement.

Paul coined the phrases 'Christian Nationalism' and a 'New Dharma of Citizenship', and many colleagues later considered him to be the first Christian statesman of India. He sowed the seeds for a theology of the Church and her mission in the context of the developing nationalism of a religiously pluralistic country. He developed also a theological interpretation of the Indian national movement in which God works out God's plan through history. So for him and those following him, the British-Indian experience and the national self-awakening can both be seen as falling within the framework of Divine Providence.[11]

Earlier in the 19th century Keshub Chandra Sen (1838-1884) had worked to indigenize Christianity in pluralistic India, and to synthesize Hindu and Christian elements in belief and practice.[11a] In his many lectures and writings he portrayed the 'Divine humanity' of Christ as the centre for the harmony of all religions. While making a distinction between the universal Christ and fragmented Christianity, he presented the Trinity as '*sat-cit-ananda*' ('being, consciousness and bliss') drawing on the rich traditions of Hindu scriptures. This was soon to strongly influence Upadhyaya Brahmabandab and others like K.T. Paul.

For Paul, Christ is present in the historical process as the agent of both creativity and of redemption. The Christian mission is to discover what is of God and what is not of God in society in the light of Christ who is the norm, and so to proceed in building up a creative and humane society. For this Paul insisted that Christians should enter the mainstream of society and give up the narrow ideas of communal self-protectionism. The indigenized Church is instead to transcend denominational, caste, ethnic and racial divisions to become a true fellowship in Christ, called to be the servant of the nation through its struggle for creating a just and peaceful community.

The thought and work of K.T. Paul would in turn provide foundation for that of Paul D. Devanandan (1901-1962) and the *Christian Institute for the Study of Religion and Society* (CISRS) which was founded by the National Christian Council of India in 1957. Of this Devanandan was the first Director, both urging the churches to 'journey towards the realization of the New Creation' in Christ, and urging the recognition of God being at work within other religious and secular movements.[12]

These thrusts, along with the CISRS journal *Religion and Society*, were to be further developed by Devanandan's co-worker and successor, M.M. Thomas, in a significant enlargement of the institute's scope and influence. Thomas's courageous writing, advocacy and statesmanship – both in pioneering the role of theology within struggles for identity and justice, and especially through the period of national emergency declared by Indira Gandhi – has greatly contributed both to Asian theologies and to social and theological movements throughout Asia. It is not too much to say that the impact of Thomas's thought and activism in both these histories, is second to none across the region (and in many areas beyond).[13]

Quite numerous individual scholars of many traditions in India and throughout Asia have been inspired and enriched by this creative tradition, as a perusal of the Research Guide to *Asian Christian Theologies* (see note 1, above) will reveal. Other movements and centres in India alone, which have been largely shaped by these theologies include: (amongst many seminaries): *United Theological College* (Bangalore), *Bishop's College* (Calcutta), *Gurukul Lutheran Theological College* (Chennai), *Kerala United Theological Seminary* (Kannammoola) and *Tamilnadu Theological Seminary* (Madurai). Amongst many other such centres, are the *Ecumenical Social and Industrial Institute* (W. Bengal), the *Bombay Urban-Industrial League for Development* (BUILD), the *Ecumenical Christian Centre* (Bangalore), the *Association for the Rural Poor*, the *Institute for Development Education* (Chennai), the *Vellore Institute of Development Studies* (Vellore) and the *Yuhanon Mar Thoma Study Centre* (Trivandrum).

Clearly here the history of the Christian communities – and therefore of the Church –in India and Asia has been widely molded by particular and outstanding Asian theologians, and by the (socio-) theological insights and struggles of this tradition of scholars and activists, of centres, colleges and movements. We can see here an inner movement of mind and spirit which shapes and energizes new forms of Christian life and new shapes for the church and for peoples' movements

ii) In Sri Lanka, James de Alwis (1823-1878) was a Christian and a lawyer, well qualified in English, Sinhala and in Pali, He became recognised as a prominent student of Buddhism, was Secretary of the Ceylon League, and a Member of the Legislative Council. His greatest desire was for the re-creation of Ceylonese society through principles of Buddhist tolerance and Christian equality. He opposed caste, favoured the education of women and advocated social reform and the recovery of Ceylon's highest traditions. Active as a public lecturer on Buddhist literature, he recognised the high morality and inspiration of Buddhism while still declaring the superiority of Christianity rightly understood. He was however critical of many aspects of Christian mission and writing along with much of western philosophy. Concerning urgent human issues in Ceylon's society, he sought to apply in his work in legal advocacy, in national government, popular education, and in the Ceylonese renaissance, a practical and localized Christian faith and social concern.

His writings, many of which have been recently republished, include volumes on Buddhist and Sinhala language and literature, series of articles in the *Ceylon Magazine*, the *Observer* and the *Examiner*, and poetry that freely utilizes Biblical imagery. de Alwis' *Contributions to Oriental Literature for Leisure Hours* (1863) remains as a primary source for linguistic study in Lanka, while his study and teaching of Buddhism and its relation to Christian faith pioneered much of the later inter-faith understanding found in Sri Lanka.[14]

Many of his concerns are seen also in the work of Isaac Tambyah (1860-1940), a theologian and a lawyer, and later Vice-Principal of the Divinity School, Colombo. He also founded and edited the *Ceylon Law Review*, and *Tambyah's Reports*. Tambyah also pioneered work for inter-faith understanding, the end of communalism and the re-direction of Christian mission. Studies in Hinduism and Buddhism, and in Ceylonese literature, led him to reconstruct Christian understanding along with the acceptance also of other faiths. He strongly affirmed the Jesus of the Gospels, but was critical of many forms of Christian evangelism, proposing radical changes in Christian practice. His chief concern was for a 'self-supporting, self-propagating, self-expressive and self-reliant indigenous Church in Sri Lanka'[15].

In these concerns he worked closely with Lakdasa de Mel, G.B. Ekanayake, R.V. Becket de Silva and James Wirasinha, all leading figures in the Sri Lankan church. Both his and de Alwis' work have been taken further in the last sixty years, by the Ecumenical Institute for Study and Dialogue. Since 1951 leading staff members there have been Graeme Jackson, Lynn de Silva, (Mrs) Langanee Mendis, Kenneth Fernando and Marshal Fernando. Amongst those who have greatly extended this movement of dialogue and social concern in the last half century, must be included D.T. Niles (central founding figure of the EACC), the CISRS institute (Jaffna), Lakshman Wickremasingha (in new centres), Jeffry and Anna Abayasekera, (Ms.)Pauline Hensman, (Ms.)Audrey Rebera (SCM), and Wesley Ariarajah. To these must be added those who have founded and led particular centres or ashrams, such as Yohan Devananda (*Ibbagamuwa Devasarana Aramaya*), Tissa Balasuriya (*Centre for Religion and Society*), Aloysius Pieris (*Tulana Research Centre*), Michael Rodrigo (*Suba Seth Gedera*) and Paul Caspersz (*Satyodaya*).[14]

Other movements and centres in Lanka which have related a contextual theology to the life-issues of local communities and churches include the *National Christian Council* (since 1923), *Theological College of Sri Lanka* (Pilimatalawa, since 1963), *Jaffna College* (since 1867), *Christaseva Ashram* (Chunnakan, since 1939), *Christian Workers' Fellowship* (since 1958), the *Sarvodaya Shramadana* and the *Udu-Gira Aramaya* (Galgamuwa),

iii) **In the Philippines,** Joseph A. Mulry SJ (1889-1945) along with his students and his colleagues at Ateneo University, were leaders in the Philippine movement of *Catholic Action*. For this they brought the social teaching of the encyclicals *Rerum Novarrum* and *Quadragesimo Anno* to bear on the social issues of Philippine society. In literature classes, round-tables with citizens, and the Bellarmine Evidence Guild, Mulry inculcated the principles of social justice and compassion. This was often seen to provide alternatives to communism as then understood. This was especially to guide the work of graduates (largely from land-owning gentry families though they were), as they returned to the land to work with landless farmers. The guild lectured in Manila plazas and sat down with town workers and farmers to share their social problems in light of the social doctrine of the Church.

Mulry himself wrote prolifically for newspapers and journals such as *Cultura Social*, and became the mentor of national leaders such as Raul Manglapus and Manuel Quezon. His work would be extended by the radio dramas and publications of the 'Catholic Hour'. It would be continued in the influential *Institute of Social Order* (ISO, from 1947), the *Federation of Free Workers* (1950) and the *Federation of Free Farmers* (from 1953), as well as through the work of John Patrick Delaney, Walter Hogan and Horacio de la Costa.[17]

De la Costa in particular would articulate the history, principles for research, communication and action upon which this social apostolate would be based. Much of his thought therefore concerned the sources of Filipino identity; the unity of evangelism, human development, Christian work for justice and liberation; and a liberating theology of the local church. He finds the central marks of Filipino identity in such deeply human values as *pakikisama* (willingness to share burdens and rewards), *pagkakaisa* (the building of community by people themselves), and *pagkabayani* (putting common good above private interest).[18] Hogan meanwhile had worked with labour unions from the late 1940s to implement the church's social teachings. He too was a key organizer of both the ISO and the FFW. He believed in the 'natural rights of workers' to fair reward and to good conditions and well-being, and campaigned vigorously for these despite opposition from government officials as well as from the Catholic hierarchy of the time.

By the 1960s many of these policies and practices had become adopted widely by the Philippine churches. Leading theological colleges such as the *Loyola School of Theology*, the *Maryhill School of Theology*, *St Andrew's Theological College* and the *Divinity School of Silliman University* developed further these traditions of prophetic teaching and leadership in the Filipino churches. This tradition also led to the formation of many other networks and movements seeking to lead the church in its encounter with massive injustices in Philippine society. Many similar movements were growing from the work – in theology and social animation – of such theologian/activists as Fidel P. Galang, Frank C. Laubach, Dennis Murphy (ISO), Henry Aguilan and Richard Poethig (National Christian Council of the Philippines), Frank Ambayan and Jose Cunanan (UCCP), Nael and Ruth Cortez of the *Institute for*

Religion and Culture (IRC), and Edicio de la Torre in movements of students, farmers and urban poor; along with the staffs of such centres as the *Kapatiran Kaunlaran Foundation* (KKF) and the *Socio-Pastoral Institute*.[19]

One can see here the later development of a rich tradition in social and religious concern and action, of such pre-revolutionary church leaders as Don Pedro Pelaez (d.1863 – leader of movement of Filipino clergy against injustices and of a campaign for the secularization, in effect the Filipinization, of parishes); José Apolonio Burgos (1836-1872 - brilliant scholar and theologian, and successor of Pelaez, who articulated, and died for, a theology of national identity and Filipino Christianity in their social and political application); and Isabelo de los Reyes (1864-1938 – ardent nationalist and Filipinologist, founder of labour unions and movements, and the founder and/or editor of six different papers and journals). The tradition of theologically-inspired social concern and action would be furthered by post-revolutionary churches such as the *Iglesia Filipina Independiente* (IFI - from 1902), the *United Church of Christ* (from 1929), as well as by other radical movements within the Roman Catholic Church. (Refer chapter 5 above).

The theology and practice of nationalism, self-support and social justice would be central to the work of all these bodies and associated movements.[20] Within these and through the often most costly commitment of individual, priests, ministers, social workers and community organizers, has flowed a spirit that maintains the vision and endeavours for a just and peaceful society. These have clearly been inspired and nourished by working theologies of Christ-like service, of social justice and civic freedom, of Liberation or Struggle, of Filipino identity, solidarity or creative culture.[21] And these diverse movements have of course initiated and shaped Christ-like forms of the Filipino church despite formidable political, economic and sometimes ecclesiastical forces that have attempted to destroy them.

Conclusion

In recent decades there has indeed been a rapid growth in studying, and publishing, the Christian social history of Asia. There has also been growth in related inter-disciplinary exchanges and collaboration, along with the wider development of area-specializations. There have been consequent changes also in our understanding of sources, agencies and periodization for all our work in Asian historiography. And similarly there has been exponential growth in our knowledge of the history of Christianity of the region: in its ancient extent, its present diversity and its contemporary relevance.

For our church histories there are too, the new insights of re-constructed theologies and missiologies in 'the South and East', with the maturing of, for example, 'story', 'narrative', 'people's', 'women's' and 'action-reflection' theologies. Unlike many other theologies these have arisen from within particular contexts; of people-movements, church reform, religious and political changes and of local struggles and creativity. There has also developed a fuller solidarity between colleagues in various disciplines across the region. Then there is the larger context and stimulus, for our emerging theologies and histories, of the post-colonial, post-modern and pluralist interpretations of realities in our 21st century worlds.

For the histories of the churches of India, Sri Lanka and the Philippines (and similar examples are possible from other Asian countries), this has meant a much fuller recognition of rich traditions already within our history. These include in particular, reflection and writing upon the dynamics of movements within church, society and peoples. In these traditions can be seen also a fuller integration of thought and life, theology and action, of history and present experience; a different awareness of people's concrete lives, their hopes and struggles. To place central the 'good news' Jesus brought, is to see that the 'inner life' and Spirit of our peoples' histories necessarily moves towards fulfillment in the New World that God brings.

So present ways of doing theology in the Asian region – as can be seen in the case-studies of movements above – offer here different visions of 'God's Commonwealth', which is both amongst us and beyond us, both individually and societally transforming. And of course they offer too an entry to understanding the forces that drive and shape all our church histories and 'secular' history itself. For here there are dynamic movements of theological discernment, and action, that have continued and developed throughout two centuries. There are here too different portrayals of what it means to follow 'the-life-of-Jesus-with-others', and therefore quite different working definitions of 'church', of 'mission' and of 'Christianity'. In this wider, but also deeper, church historiography, the lives of churches themselves become conscious *parts* of the Spirit's wide, and sometimes incognito, movement in all the world; joining with many to serve, support and witness...'finding each other on the way to God's New World'.

This paper is intended then to ask whether such a methodology in our study and writing of 'church' history – which centres upon 'Discerning the work of God and therefore of 'Christic', (not necessarily church) presence in our world' – might vitally reshape and stimulate our endeavours. It is because the inner life of all church history is necessarily the-life-of-Jesus-with-others, that the unavoidable call to us is to discern the unique quality of that life: a life lived with and for the whole human community in all its suffering and creativity. Clearly it is central for this approach that we trace the theological movements which both arise from, and become the inner life of social and religious, cultural and political movements in our communities, societies and cultures.

We could then make a primary focus upon the marks of Jesus-like activity in our peoples' lives – in befriending, including and championing, rescuing and restoring, in teaching and healing, in protesting and resisting – that is, *wherever* and in *whatever* movements, these can be recognised. We might then be able to discern the Spirit of that life-with-others, as She is moving within our histories; within all the toils and visions, the sufferings and the hopes of the 'People of God'. We may discern too those who *by their lives* are working with the Human One, whether within the 'church' as we know it or outside (and sometimes despite) it. Church history then would become the story of movements which signpost and model, but do not contain, the Common-wealth of God.

End-notes (with expanded references for study)

[1] I here refer you to a few of the many recent volumes which provide instances of this latter approach, or which take these issues further: A. Pieris *An Asian Theology of Liberation* (Orbis, 1988); C.S.Song *Jesus, The Crucified People*. (Crossroad, 1990); J. C. England and Yeow Choo Lak (eds.); *Doing Theology with God's Purpose in Asia*. (ATESEA Paper No.10, 1991) and *Doing Theology with the Spirit's Movement in Asia*. (ATESEA Paper No.11, 1992); P. L. Wickeri (ed.) and *The People of God Among All God's People: Frontiers in Christian Mission*. (CCA & CWM, 2000); D. P. Niles (ed.) *Windows into Ecumenism; Essays in Honour of Ahn Jae Woong*. (CCA, 2005); Felix Wilfred *Margins: Site of Asian Theologies* (ISPCK, 2008). For the larger context of interdisciplinary studies see the *Journal of Interdisciplinary History* and Harry R Ritter & T.C.R. Horn, 'Interdisciplinary History: A Historiographical Review' (1986). History Paper 77. http://cedar.wwu.edu/history_facpubs/77.

[2] See K. Baago 'Indigenization and Church History' (*Bulletin of the Church History Association of India* 1962) 27. J. Webster in his *Historiography of Christianity in India* (Oxford, 2012) describes the changes from 'church history' as the history of missions or institutions to become the 'socio-cultural history of Christian people' – in their ecumenical, regional, and national reality. F. Wilfred declares that *The Oxford Handbook of Christianity in Asia* (Oxford, 2014) which he has edited 'Views Christianity as a socio-religious movement in constant interplay with the history, tradition, culture of Asia'. An earlier and extensive discussion of the necessary 'secularity of church history' is found in Bernad Meland's *Fallible Forms and Symbols* (Fortress Press, 1976) especially chap. Ten.

[3] For history being 'exploration of the human spirit', by which one is to 'discern the thought of its agent', and as being a more universal 'memory' and 'biography', see Collingwood, *The Idea of History* (Oxford, 1961) p.213; Reinhold Niebuhr *Faith and History* (Nisbet, 1949) chap. 12; H. Butterfield *Christianity and History* (fontana, 1957) pp.171ff.; J. B. Metz *Faith in History and Society* (Burns and Oates, 1980) chaps. 11 and 13. For examples of the theology referred to see Oh Jae Shik and J.C. England (eds.) *Theology in Action* (EACC-UIM. 1973); *Spirituality for Combat* (CCA-URM. 1983); G. Ninan, (ed.) *Theology and Ideology in Asian People's Struggle*. (CCA-URM 1985); *On Being Human in the Changing Realities of Asia* (FABC Papers 133, March 201); Takenaka Masao *When the Bamboo Bends* (WCC, 2002) 32f.; P. L. Wickeri op.cit.. especially concluding chapter: 'Politics and the Reign of God'.

[4] See e.g. R.S. Sugirtharajah *Asian Biblical Hermeneutics and Postcolonialism* (1998), J.B.Banawiratma. & J. Muller. 'Contextual Social Theology' (Special volume *EAPR*

1999); Catherine Keller et al. *Post-Colonial Theologies: Divinity and Empire* (Chalice, 2004); Kwok Pui Lan *Postcolonial Imagination & Feminist Theology* (2005).

[5] See amongst others the works of R. Panikkar, and Swami Agnivesh [for Hinduism]; Buddhadasa Bhikku and James Shields [for Buddhism]; R. Henricks, P. Rawson, and L. Legeza [for Taoism]; Lionel Jensen & Jesus Sole-Farras [for Confucianism]; Jonathan Lyons & Zachery Karabell [for Islam]. C.f. Kwok Pui Lan *Discovering the Bible in the Non-Biblical World* (Orbis, 1995); D. S. Thiangarajah & A.W. Longchar (eds.) *Visioning New Life Together Among Asian Religions* (CCA, 2002).

[6] For other 'Renaissances', 'Reformations' and 'Enlightenments' see for example chap.2; Margaret Smith *Rabi'a the Mystic and Her Fellow-Saints* (Llanerch, 1994);. Natalia Isayeva *Shankara and Indian Philosophy* (SUNY, 1993); J. Lyons *The House of Wisdom* (Bloomsbury, 2009); A. Bloom & R. Habito *The Essential Shinran*: (World Wisdom, 2000); S. F. Starr *Lost Enlightenment: Central Asia's Golden Age* (Princeton, 2013); S.A. Wolpert, *Gandhi's Passion*. (Oxford, 2001); R. M. Davidson *Tibetan Renaissance: Tantric Buddhism & the Rebirth of Tibetan Culture* (Columbia, 2005); C. S. Queen & Sallie B. King (eds.) *Engaged Buddhism: Buddhist Liberation Movements in Asia*. (SUNY, 1996); F. Godemet *The New Asian Renaissance: From Colonialism to the Post-Cold War.* (Routledge, 1997); J.J. Clarke *Oriental Enlightenment* (Routledge, 1997).

[7] Amongst others: Rose M. Cecchini *Women's Action for Peace & Justice: Christian, Buddhist & Muslim Women Tell Their Story* (Maryknoll, 1988); Mary R. Battung and others *Religion and Society: Towards a Theology of Struggle. Book I.*(FIDES, 1988); R. Traer *Faith in Human Rights: Support in Religious Traditions for a Global Struggle* (Georgetown, 1991); C.S. Queen & Sallie B. King (op.cit. 1996); Swami Agnivesh Religion, *Spirituality and Social Action* (Hope India, 2003); Peggy Morgan & C. A. Lawton (eds.) *Ethical Issues in Six Religious Traditions* (Edinburgh, 2009).

[8] Refer e.g. Wu Yao Tsung *No Man Has Seen God.* (Association, 1940); Philip L. Wickeri (op. cit. 2000); Catherine Keller, et al. (op.cit. 2004); Muriel Orevillo-Montenegro *The Jesus of Asian Women* (Orbis, 2006); M. E. Brinkman The Non-Western Jesus (Equinox, 2007); F. Wilfred *Margins: Site of Asian Theologies.*(2008), Kwon Jin Kwan *Theology of Subjects. Towards a New Minjung Theology* (PTCA, 2011); D. P. Niles *The Lotus & the Sun.* (Barton, 2013.).

[9] See chaps. 4 & 7 this vol.; c.f. Saeki Yoshiro *The Nestorian Documents and Relics in China.* (Maruzen, 1951); T.V. Philip *East of the Euphrates.* (ISPCK, 1998); I. Gilman & H-J. Klimkeit, *Christians in Asia before 1500* (Curzon, 1999); Mattam, Mar Ab. *Forgotten East.* (Ephrem 2000); C. Baumer, *The Church of the East. An Illustrated History of Assyrian Christianity.* (Tauris, 2006); N. Sims-Williams Biblical and Other Christian Sogdian Texts From the Turfan Collection (Brepols, 2014), J. Jennes *A History of the Catholic Church in Japan* (1549-1873). (Maruzen, 1973). John N. Schumacher *Readings in Philippine Church History.* (2nd ed. Loyola, 1987).

[10] See preceding chapters. For later periods see such works as; A. Suggate *Japanese Christians and Society.* (Peter Lang, 1996); Ng Lee- Ming *Christianity and Social*

152   Part One: Within our Movements and Histories

Change in China. (CSCCR, 1976); W. Fabros *The Church and its Social Involvements in the Philippines, 1930-1972.* (Ateneo, 1988); Shiri, Godwin *Christian Social Thought in India: 1962-1977.* (CISRS/CLS, 1982) chap. 5; P. Digan *Churches in Contestation: Asian Christian Social Protest.* (Orbis Books, 1984); A. Rogers (ed.) *The Prophetic Path to the New Millennium through Social Advocacy.* (F.A.B.C. 2000); M. Nai-Chiu Poon (ed.) *Pilgrims and Citizens: Christian Social Engagement in East Asia Today* (ATF, 2006).

[11] See K.T. Paul *Can Christianity be Nationalised in India?* (SCM, 1921); *How Missions Denationalize Indians* (SCM, 1921); *Responsibility of Indian Citizenship in India* (SCM, 1923). See also Vengal Chakkarai et al. *Rethinking Christianity in India* (A.N. Sudarisanam, 1938); C.E. Abraham *The Founders of National Missionary Society of India* (CLS, 1947); H.A. Popley, *K.T. Paul: Christian Leader* (YMCA, 1938; CLS, 1987); K. Baago *Pioneers of Indigenous Christianity.* (CISRS & CLS, 1969).

For recent volumes on Sen see Keshub Chunder Sen's Lectures in India (Hard Press Publishing (2012), Keshub Chunder Sen's Lectures in India (Wentworth Press, 2016), Ram Chandra Bose, *Brahmoism; or History of reformed Hinduism from its origin in 1830* (Gyan Books Pvt. Ltd., 2013); T. Ebenezer Slater, *Keshab Chandra Sen and the Brahma Samaj: Being a Brief Review of Indian Theism from 1830 to 1884* (Wentworth Press, 2019).

[12] For P. Devanandan see especially *The Concept of Maya* (Lutterworth, 1950); *Our Task Today: Revision of Evangelistic Concern* (CISRS, 1959); *The Gospel and Renascent Hinduism* (SCM Press, 1959); *Christian Concern in Hinduism* (Madras: CLS for CISRS, 1961); *Christian Issues in Southern Asia* (Friendship Press, 1963). See also R.H.S Boyd, *An Introduction to Indian Christian Theology* (CLS, 1969); S.A. Morton, "P.D. Devanandan, M.M. Thomas and the Task of Indigenous Theology" (Ph.D., Thesis, Nottingham University, 1981).

[13] For M.M. Thomas see e.g. *The Christian Response to the Asian Revolution.* (SCM, 1966); *The Acknowledged Christ of the Indian Renaissance.* (SCM 1969); *The Secular Ideologies of India and the Secular Meaning of Christ.* (CLS, 1976). See also T.V. Philip *The Encounter Between Theology and Ideology: An Exploration into the Communicative Theology of M.M. Thomas.* (CLS, 1986), P.T. Thomas (ed.) *A list of the published writings of M.M. Thomas 1936-1987* (Kottayam. 1988); K.C. Abraham (ed.) *Christian Witness in Society: A Tribute to M.M. Thomas.* (BTE SSC, 1998); A. Bird *M.M. Thomas and Dalit Theology* (BTESSC/ 2008).

[14] See J. de Alwis: *Jems da Alvis prabandha saha lipi* (Compilation of his writings, Samskrtika Katayutu, 1996); *Survey of Sinhala Literature:* (National Museum, 1966 /1852); *Buddhism: Its Origin, History and Doctrines; Its Scriptures, and their Language Pali.* (Colombo, 1962). Refer also M.Y. Gooneratne. 'English Literature in Ceylon 1815-1878.' *Ceylon Historical Journal 14* (Tisara Prakasakayo, 1968).

[15] *For* I. Tambyah see *Foregleams of God: A comparative study of Hinduism, Buddhism and Christianity.* (Luzac & CLS, 1925, Indian Book Gallery, 1983); *A Garland of*

Ceylon Verse 1837-1897. (Luzac, 1897); 'The Gate Beautiful: A Plea for the Siddhanta in Christian Missionary Enterprise.' (*East and West,* 1915); *Psalms of a Saiva Saint and a 'Tamil Mystic' being selections from the writings of Tayumanaswamy.* (Asian Educational Services, 1985/ 1921); *Christian Evangelism* (Colombo, 1940).

[16] For Lynn de Silva see e.g. T. B. De Alwis, *Christian-Buddhist Dialogue in the Writings of L. A. de Silva* (Andrews University MI, 1982); for D.T. Niles see e.g. Christopher L Furtado *The Contribution of Dr. D.T. Niles to the Church Universal and Local* (CLS, 1978); for T. Balasuriya see *e.g. Rainbows on a Crying Planet: Essays in Honour of Tissa Balasuriya* (CSS, 2004); for P. Casperzs see e.g. *A New Culture for a New Society* (Satyodaya, 2006); for C.L. Wickremesinghe. see e.g. M. Fernando (ed.) *Visionary Wisdom of a People's Bishop* (EISD, 2009); for Y. Devananda see e.g. *Living Dialogue: Devasarana: Thirty Years Alongside People.* (IDA, 1987); for A. Pieris see e.g. Gloria Patmury *Church in Asia : amidst the many poor and the many religions : a study of Aloysius Pieris' writings.* (Asian Trading Corp., c2008). For these & related theologians see N. Abeyasingha *The Radical Tradition: The Changing Shape of Theological Reflection in Sri Lanka* (EISD 1985); U. Dornberg,. *Searching Through the Crisis: Christians, Contextual Theology and Social Change in Sri Lanka...* (*Logos 31. 3 & 4* 1992).

[17] A collection of Mulry's *Letters and Articles is* held in the Lauinger Library, Georgetown University (USA). See also H. de la Costa, *Asia and the Philippines.* (Solidaridad, 1967); Sr Deolindis 'The Role of Religious Mission Sisters in Church Renewal Today through the Federation of Free Farmers' (*Verbum* 12.4 (1971); Schumacher (op.cit. 1987); A. A. Weiss 'Jesuit Social Apostolate 1859-1956'. (*Philippine Studies* 4.2, 1956).

[18] For H. de la Costa see *e.g. The Background of Nationalism and Other Essays* (Solidaridad , 1965); *Readings in Philippine History* (Bookmark, 1965); *Liberation of all Men : Our Common Objective.* (Progressio Supplement 2, 1973); *An Ignatian Witness.* (Progressio Supplement 10, 1977); 'Church-State Relationships: A Theological Perspective' (*Philippine Priests' Forum* 2.4 1970); 'Faith Justice and Human Development' In *On Faith and Justice,* (Loyola, 1976); *On Faith and Justice II: Faith, Ideologies and Christian Options.* (Loyola Papers 7/8, 1976); *'In Memorium: Horacio de la Costa, S.J.'* (*Philippine Studies, vol. 26, 1978),* and S.S. Reyes (ed.) *Reading Horacio de la Costa. Views from the 21st century.* (Ateneo, 2017). Refer chap. 8.5 below.

[19] Refer W. Fabros,.*The Church and its Social Involvements in the Philippines, 1930-1972.* (Ateneo, 1988); H. de la Costa 'The Filipino National Tradition.' In *Challenges for the Filipino* (Ateneo, 1971); F. C. Laubach, *Teacher. Selected Writings.* (Literacy Laubach, 1990); R. Poethig *Philippine Social Issues from a Christian Perspective.* (UCCP, 1963). R.L. Deats *Nationalism and Christianity in the Philippines* (Southern Methodist Univ. 1967); F. F. Claver *Social Discernment and Theological Reflection.* (HD Research, 1988); Mary J. Mananzan (ed.) *Woman and Religion: A Collection of Essays.* (St. Scholastica, 1998); M. Apilado *The Dream Need Not Die. Revolutionary*

Spirituality 2 (New Day 2000); V. Gorospe *Forming the Filipino Social Conscience. Social Theology from a Filipino Christian Perspective.* (Bookmark, 2000).

[20] See R.L. Deats (op.cit. 1967); J.N. Schumacher *Revolutionary Clergy: The Filipino Clergy and the Nationalist Movement, 1850-1903.* (Ateneo, 1981); Schumacher *Father Jose Burgos: a Documentary History* (Ateneo,1999); W. Fabros (op.cit. 1988).

[21] For a small selection of the relevant literature here see Battung op.cit.; C. Avila, *Peasant Theology: Reflections by the Filipino Peasants* (WSCF Asia, 1976); F.V. Carino (ed.) *Church, State and People* (CCA, 1981); E. de la Torre *Touching Ground, Taking Root: Theological and Political Reflections on the Philippine Struggle* (CIIR & BCC, 1986); Anne Harris, *The Theology of Struggle* (Kasarinlan 21 (2)2006) 83-107; L. G. Hechanova, T*he Gospel and the Struggle* (CIIR, 1986); Victoria Narciso-Apuan et al. (eds.) *Witness and Hope amid Struggle: Towards a Theology and Spirituality of Struggle.* Book II (SPI, 1991); J. Labayan, *Revolution and the Church of the Poor* (SPI/Claretian, 1995); C.H. Abesamis *A Third Look at Jesus* (Claretian, 1999); S. Ruth J. Ruiz-Duremdes, (ed.) *Unleashing the Power within Us* (NCCP, 2001); Kathleen M. Nadeau *Liberation Theology in the Philippines. Faith in a Revolution* (Praeger ,2002); L. Oracion, *Rumors of a Divine-Human Synergy in our Midst* (New day & UCC, 2010).

Chapter - 7

Doing Theology in Asian Ways

A Study of the approaches and methods being used by colleagues in doing and living contextualizing theologies in the Asian region today.

Introducing 'Distances'

Any introduction to the 'doing of theology' in the Asian region must of necessity be highly selective because of the vast extent of models and sources to be noted. It can be only done briefly therefore, as if 'packing for a journey' (as perhaps all theology must be).[1] Three notes are therefore required as a preface:

i) Note first the distances between the 'methods' outlined below and our usual (more westernized) understanding of ways that 'theology is done'. This may be a distance from our place, our culture, and our experience of theology (or from the western philosophical tradition) itself.[2] For many of our theological terms and assumptions do not apply here. Nor does our customary cultural orientation fit easily in a region that has its own many 'Reformations' and 'Renaissances', 'Revolutions' and 'Enlightenments' during over two millennia. There is a very large range of diverse contexts, theologies and resources that must be recognised and received as we consider the ways in which theology has been done in the region. It will be seen that we do not have here merely contributions to the debates in other regions, nor are they raw materials for a later 'more sophisticated' construction.

It should also be noted that the awareness of these 'distances' is no recent development. Asian theological traditions which question or reject the assumptions, terms or processes common to theology in western contexts have a long history. This can be found in writings and records we have from the earliest centuries of Christian presence in Asian lands to early and late modern encounters between missionaries from the west and indigenous movements and interpretation in the Asian region. There are especially sharp examples of this in such countries as China, Japan, India, Indonesia and the Philippines.[3] (See chapters 4, 5 & 6 above).

ii) The larger framework for such theological discernment in our region remains the inescapable diversity of peoples, contexts and histories; the multi-faceted experience of many faiths; countless cultural traditions; and the unending struggles for identity, peace and people-justice across more than half the world. The 'other' which lies around and even beyond these frameworks is of course the pervasive recognition in all Asian traditions and experience of the presence of the Divine in human life; the many dimensions of the Other, in the worlds of nature, art and story and in every aspect of community and individual life.

We must therefore place on our screen a recognition of 'the Other' in the theologies of Asian countries: in history, and in religious experience, in language, thought-forms and intention, and in societal or cultural 'watershed' periods which have shaped their peoples. Then there is also the 'other' which is discernible in the 'inner episodes' of self-understanding: the sense of cosmos or of creation, of community and of symbol in which the age-long experience of a people has been epitomized. In almost all Asian cultures this is originally most often holistic and intuitive, both more experiential and more contemplative; sapiential and even poetic; and centred upon both the community as a whole and the land which has always nourished that.[4] This has been termed by our colleagues of many eastern traditions the 'measureless mystery of God'.

iii) As parts of the context for 'doing theology' in Asia we must also add the successive waves of religious and cultural exchange, including the genesis and development of all the world's major religious traditions. The setting for Christian theology in Asia has always been one of living faiths, of many patterns of religious life and many scriptures, and these have again and again been inter-relating and interacting since the earliest centuries, even though the extensive resources now available are yet to be fully studied. More recently movements for inter-faith encounter and dialogue have been especially fruitful in the period since the Pacific War, fostered by ecumenical councils and networks throughout the region.

These factors mean therefore that Asian Christian theologies which are 'lived, living and contextual', are normally more open to the deepest truths experienced in partnership with their communities, whether ethnic or religious. So they are more often dialogical while still centred on Jesus Christ; cross-cultural while still also being counter-cultural; and even cross-textual in mutually interpreting scriptures while yet holding the uniqueness of the *life-of-Jesus-with-others* as recorded in the gospels.

iv) Then too the waves of cultural and ethnic encounter, along with centuries of colonial domination and exploitation have often caused a *running fire* of violence across the region that greatly sharpens the struggle for identity, for livelihood and even for human survival. It must be stressed that these struggles have been, and are, particularly sharp when undertaken for the dignity, self-hood, and just equality of women and girls in almost every country. Along with ongoing post-colonial struggles for identity, cultural restoration and people-justice there are now the increasing levels of exploitation and inequity resulting from globalized economic deregulation and monopolization.

It is therefore true that for countless women and men in the Asian-Pacific region the recovery or preservation of human and humane life with others must continue in 'a state of emergency', and within the running fire of violence caused by the corruption or greed of foreign corporations or of indigenous elites. In situations of both 'post-colonial' depredation and global neo-colonial exploitation whole communities throughout the region continue to be dislocated or demolished, personal and family life shattered, natural eco-systems to be destroyed.

v) Theology is therefore done here (as in Biblical traditions) on the frontiers of people's suffering and hope, of accelerating cultural and social change, and of the agonies of struggle, and survival.[5] It may also be done on the cusp of joys of celebration or fellowship, as well as in community achievements or in venturing encounters with those of other living faiths. At its best it is a fully collaborative task of all the people of God in particular places. For a 'leap from Israel to Asia'[6] has been made which in theological study and reflection, moves from the history and scriptures of ancient Israel and the earliest Christian communities, not via Bonn, Edinburgh or Chicago, but directly to the heritage, context and experience of particular peoples of Asian. This is to recognise Yahweh's covenant and controversy with *each* of our peoples in the region, always measured by, and fulfilled in the challenge and call of the life-of-Jesus-with-others to each, as recorded in the synoptic Gospels in particular.

It must be recognised that this 'theological' work of women and men, includes teacher or craftsperson, labourer or farmer, home-maker, student, professional, minister and priest. It is communitarian work and concerns the whole of life. In ashram or seminary, house-group or people's movement, 'all are subjects in the doing of theology.'[7] So just as we find in scripture, so also as 'food for the road', such reflection and praxis is found in a great diversity of forms: in story and prayer, in letter or manifesto, poetry or meditation, in art, song or dance, in manifesto or declaration, or the shape of a community's inter-active life.

vi) For far too few of our people is the context one of sustained movements for mutual harmony and just-dealing. In these settings, the first 'theological act' is a commitment to the Common-wealth of God; to discerning and joining, as in 'the life-of-Jesus-with-others', the signs of a new heaven, and new earth dawning. This is to say, as colleagues have claimed, that living Asian theologies are oriented toward wisdom in social transformation. This is a commitment too, to the lives of destitute and marginalized people; to hearing their stories and joining their struggles. Theology here finds the living God of major Biblical traditions in all deeds of compassion, truth, peace and justice, by whomever and wherever these are done.[8]

Theology is therefore sometimes described as a 'living' or 'transformative' theodao/dharma;[9] as centred upon the Way rather than upon the Logos; upon Life as a whole rather than upon only works of reason. This becomes a 'reflection-in-the-doing', as discerning and embracing the 'Asian face of Christ' in the agonies and aspirations of our sisters and brothers; as a 'praxis-oriented reflection leading to transformation'. We will see then that it is a dialogical, multi-topical endeavour, that dynamically relates diverse cultural or ethnic identities, different creative religious 'texts' or traditions, and a complexity of challenging socio-political experiences.

Accordingly the established bodies of Asian Christian theologies over many centuries display most diverse approaches and methods in the doing of genuinely Asian/local theology. Although we must say immediately that all too little of this abundance has yet been tapped by our churches, seminaries and centres. Recovering and tapping this abundance must be taken much further *before* entering into dialogue with methodologies (or theological and philosophical critiques) that have evolved outside the region. For living the faith, and critically reflecting upon it, is very wide-spread in Christian communities of the region and has been discovered in the writings from some countries of Asian from the second century on.[10]

The work of the Programme for theology and Cultures in Asia (since 1983),[11] and of related programmes over many years, has been devoted to rediscovering and reclaiming these very extensive resources – theological historical, social and cultural – which we have as Asian Christians. And this is not just because we recognise this as our story and our context, but also because the story of God's dealings with all the peoples of Asia forms a most significant, if neglected, section of Christian and religious history: 'the other half of Christian history' which in addition, leads to some major reconstructions in these histories as a whole.[12]

A Large Heritage

A full study of the ways and methods in which these resources have been used, integrated and interpreted in the doing of Asian Christian theologies would have to include a very wide range of formats, contents and methodologies. Their diversity can be illustrated by studying such widely scattered examples as the 'Pattu (songs) and hymns of the earliest centuries in south-west India; the contemplative poetry and prose of Ephrem in 4th century Edessa; the prophetic ministry and preaching of Euphemia in 6th century Anatolia; in the so-called 'Nestorian' documents of Bp. Al-op-en and Adam Ching Ching, and the Sogdian and Uighur documents, which express the Gospels and early creeds in the thought forms of Turkestan Buddhism of the 8th-11th centuries; the interpretive art-forms in China and in Turkestan in that same period, or in 12th century Syria or 16th century India; or the historical, Biblical, scientific and philosophical works of Bar Hebraeus in 13th century Syria. (See chap. 3 above).

In studying the extensive materials from the life and thought of the Church of the East in particular (mis-named 'Nestorian'), it is impossible to overlook their differing interpretations of many accepted (western) beliefs. 'Salvation' is interpreted to be full 'Life' rather than a 'delivering' or 'protection'; the presence of Christ in the Eucharist is seen to re-create the world, establish the Kingdom and fulfil all things rather than firstly an individual sanctification; stress upon the humanity of Jesus, upon 'Gospel' as the coming of the Kingdom and a rejection of original sin, quite change the understanding of 'good news'. There is also their openness to and dialogue with those of other living faiths which grounds expression of Christian faith in local and historical context. (Refer chaps. 1 and 2 above).

In a later period the diversity can be seen in the early 17th century, in the Tamil prose of Robert de Nobili who held that much in the Vedas of India was compatible with the Christian faith; or in devotional letters of Tama Gracia (Ms.) in Japan as she faced martyrdom; in theologies of Yang Ting-Yun and Hsu Kuang-Chi, shaped in the encounter between Roman Catholicism and neo-Confucian thought and practice in 17th century China; in classical Church Sanskrit of the 18th century discerning Christian meaning in the religious insights of the ancient Hindu texts; the subversive 'theologies' of 'Pasyon' groups in the Philippines in the 18th and 19th centuries; the seminal re-interpretations of such groupings as *Kakure Kirishitan* authors of (underground) 'Christian Notebooks' and 'Doctrines'; or in India's *Rethinking Group* – including V. Chakkarai and P. Chenchiah – in pre-independence Madras State of the 1930s. This list could of course be greatly extended even for the period prior to A.D. 1800.[13]

In more recent decades we could not overlook the approaches of such colleagues as Wu Yao-Tsung - developing a programme of social revolution for China, in his reflection upon salvation as necessarily being a salvation from selfishness; the seminal work of D.T. Niles in uncovering both the self-hood, and the secular engagement' of the Asian churches; P.D. Devanandan's interpretation of the Resurrection of Christ as including personal and social transformation in Indian history and culture; and Kim Jae Jun's influential work to depict and apply the inner truth of scripture, within the struggles and suffering of Korea's people; and perhaps most importantly the contextualizing theology of Shoki Coe, which has reshaped theologies across the world. (For these see further in chapter 8). And this is without mentioning the very significant Asian ways for doing theology, of other early watershed figures such as M.M. Thomas, Horatio de la Costa, Ahn Byung Mu, Kosuke Koyama, (Ms.) Park Sun Ae, D.S. Amalorpavadass, Sister Vandana, U Khin Maung Din, Peter Latuihamallo, (Ms.) M. Rosario Battung, and many others.[14]

It will be possible in this outline to concentrate upon only a small selection from the large number of Asian methodologies available in the region's contemporary theologies, although in those chosen it will be possible to trace the contribution of much earlier work mentioned above. And in those selected I wish to focus especially upon the element which has become central in the approaches of many of our colleagues, and which I believe presents the key issue for theological method and interpretation. Namely:

By what steps or processes do we move – whether by reflection within daily encounters or in more sustained theological reflection – from historical or relational experience to critical reflection and interpretation? Faced with a particular life-story or struggle, a conserved tradition, ancient symbolism or newly created art-form, how do we discern within and about it, the dimensions of 'God's presence and purpose' which theology then attempts to articulate? These are the questions constantly facing us in Christian life and in the doing of theology and theological education. They may not, of course, be always recognized or *consciously* answered, but certainly they *are* answered, well or not so well, in all our reflection, our teaching, our living.[15]

It must be emphasized that these questions are not posed in order to begin the construction of a theological method which may *in the future* lead to formulation of an 'Asian theology', as if there could be one method or one theology for all Asian peoples, or even for all those of one culture or society. Rather they are used as an entry point into some of the widely-used approaches which *have* long been used in established bodies of Asian *theologies*. Nor are we to ask 'what contribution to theological discussion outside the region can be seen in Asian Christian thought'. The question is rather 'How are our sisters and brothers *already* critically reflecting, and living out Christian theology in Asian contexts, in Asian ways?' And further, 'what methods, patterns and sources are already well established in Asian theologies?'[16]

Pre-understanding

Obviously there are, in all our ways of doing theology ('theodao/dharma') – pre-understandings which shape our procedure and hermeneutic. Some of the *assumptions* which form these for many Asian theologians can be expressed in this way:

i) The one living Spirit is already present and active in every people, place, and time; in every culture and religious tradition. And we can recognize that presence wherever the central actions of Jesus' life are being done in our history to serve or signpost the Commonwealth of God.

ii) The central Gospel (according to many passages in Mark and Luke) is not primarily about 'man or woman as sinner requiring justification or atonement', but that 'God's Reign is upon us and is coming; the Commonwealth of justice and peace is upon us'.

iii) 'Theology', in discerning, responding to and interpreting the activity of God's Spirit, is done (as in Biblical prophetic traditions) on the frontiers of people's suffering and hope, of cultural and social change, of struggle and celebration.

iv) 'Theology', just like ministry and mission, is a fully co-operative task of all the People of God: including artist and labourer, farmer or home-maker, teacher, student, or craftsperson, professional and priest (and needless to say, women as well as men).

v) 'Theology', as reflection, interpretation, 'food for the road', is found (as in Biblical scripture) in numberless forms, and in almost every imaginable genre, whether oral or written, reflective or enacted, declared or demonstrated, published, circulated or performed...

vi) In such theologies, the first steps have been found in a fundamental reorientation:

- to ask first "How are people surviving?"...and "What *on earth* is God doing now?".

- to relate the-life-of-Jesus-with-others directly to a people's present life;

- to fully employ Asian experience and resources in doing theology.

I. Pictures of 'Asian Ways' in theodao/dharma

Rather than discussing further the theological bases or framework for theological methods within the region (a secondary task),[17] the following three sections provide summary descriptions of theological processes already widely used by representative theologians, activists and groups. A number of analyses of these processes have been made, one of the more useful being that of Nihal Abeyasingha of Sri Lanka[18], who distinguishes various approaches depending on which of the following elements is chosen to be central (and therefore the norm) in interpreting others.

i. Study of the Bible - a "Biblical theology".

ii. Receiving Christian tradition – institutional or "orthodox" theology.

iii. Shaping a system of belief - "coherence" and "logic" are central.

iv. Living and communicating the faith - a lived reality in context.

v. Action to fashion history - a liberating theology and praxis.

This is only part of Abeyasingha's analysis, which offers many fruitful insights for the comparative study of Asian theological processes. But this summary illustrates how our first task is rather to see and describe the main thrusts of particular colleagues' work, recognizing that whatever convergences there may be, each Asian way in doing theology has its own identity and its own unique context. It must be added that in studying the forms of 'living theology' which abound in the region we will often find Abeyasingha's elements to be of priority in reverse ordering to his listing: a liberative and lived theodao/dharma being of first concern for many of our colleagues in each country. The following grouping is therefore shaped in order to receive the lived insights of our sisters and brothers by asking the questions:

a) what are the key elements included in the process?

b) what are the basic questions being asked?

c) what are the approaches taken to

- human experience

- the Christian (and other) scriptures

- the theological movement between these?

I. Key Elements

What then are the key elements being included? (Note that these are sometimes pictured as steps to take in a process.) In each case the steps are given as they are found in the texts cited, and to these I have added explanatory comments based on related writings of the author(s).

a) From groups of *Filipino theologians and lay people* working in the years before and during Martial law, partly shaped by the Jesuit Social Apostolate in the Philippines, by the approaches of Peasant theologies[19], and the reflection-in-struggle of many peoples' movements, the elements are:

   i) Direct experience and commitment in a particular life situation ... (this means involvement or exchange with local activists).

   ii) Critical analysis of personal, social and historical factors ... (to clarify the socio- economic structures of poverty, exploitation and conflict).

   iii) Bible-study which situates 'the present in a history of salvation' ... (from the major Hebrew prophets to Mark's Gospel and today's new world).

   iv) Interpretation/reflection on Jesus in our situation ... (discerning the resources and directions for personal and social transformation).[20]

b) Emerging from the *networks of women theologians* in the region, which have become more widely known since the 1970s, come similar elements. They are found in the approaches which are being used by many national associations of women theologians and women's movements and are fostered by the *Asian Women's Resource Centre for Culture and Theology*.[21]

   i) See the reality of Asian women in society and church....(what are the multiplied oppressions under which Asian sisters suffer, and die?)

   ii) Analyze socio-economic structures and the encounter of traditional and western cultural values: what causes severe exploitation and which cultural values enforce or oppose this?

   iii) Study the liberating message of Jesus' attitudes to women ... uncover the transformed role of women brought by Jesus in his life, and now.

   iv) Theological reflection on Jesus in our situation ... how to concretize in all society the eschatological values of Jesus' life already promised in women's lived experience.[22]

This methodology has been further detailed by Asian women theologians to take fuller account of popular literature, oral histories being gathered, post-colonial insights, women's bodily experiences, and issues of sexuality.[23]

c) From the experience and study of *Buddhist monastic and wisdom traditions*, in the context of severe poverty and dedicated spiritual quest comes a somewhat different pattern. The integration of such poverty and quest provides for Aloysius Pieris the 'Asian sense' in doing theology:

   i) Understand our people's struggles for spiritual and social emancipation in their own idiom and history (this is to be a deep sensitivity and listening).

ii) Recognise the meeting of religion and poverty, word and silence, wisdom and love, God-experience and concern-for-humanity (i.e. in the major religious traditions).

iii) Authority will come from the Church's humility, immersion and participation beyond the Church, where concern-for-humanity testifies to God-experience ... (leading to a losing oneself for the human community).

iv) The Asian face of Christ is found in Asian's own search and praxis of personal and social liberation ... (Christian theologies are to reveal the liberating experiences of all Asian's peoples in their own traditions).[24]

d) An *experience-reflection programme* used in the teaching of theology in Indonesian seminaries reveals similar elements to those of a. and b. above. It is similar to the earlier *Hidup Bertheologia* course organized by the S.T.T. seminary in Jakarta which was one of the EACC 'Theology in Action' programmes of the '70s (see below). It now joins 'live-in' experience along with theologies of salvation and hope, and also with study of the Eucharist, of social ethics and of Christology. This includes :

i) Exposure to concrete life situations of local people (days spent living/working in a particular work-place or neighbourhood).

ii) Analysis of the principal problems there in the light of one's faith concern ...

iii) Dialogue and communication with Christian traditions.

.. (studying the past and present, of Bible, theology, church history).

iv) Formulating a theological synthesis ... (both theoretical and practical).

v) Consequent proposals for pastoral commitment and action.

In a *circular* diagram the process moves through these 'moments' from Life Situation to Pastoral action and on to Analysis, Dialogue, and Synthesis.[25]

II. In the Interaction of Life, Bible and theology

We need now to uncover the methods by which elements such as those outlined above, and in particular, human experience and Biblical resources, interact and mutually shape one another in our theological processes.

1. Asian Approaches to Human Experience

The classic statement concerning the response of many of our contemporary colleagues to the realities of their people's experience is that of M.M. Thomas, interpreting early documents prepared by E.A.C.C. groups in the 1960s. For generations of Asian Christians, "basic to the theological participation and dialogue of the Christian and the Church in [its] situation", he writes, has been the "belief in the creating, judging and saving work of God and his Christ in every situation, and the underlying assumption that the dialogue between God and man in Christ through the work of the Holy spirit is previous to the presence and words of the Christian".[26]

This affirms clearly that the delivering and transforming activity of God is already to be found in every human 'secular', worldly situation, in the life of all peoples, in the best of their religious traditions, and in their suffering, aspirations and hope. For Thomas and many colleagues throughout Asian countries the One Spirit of justice and love has always been present, recognised or not, in every people, every place, every time

A. *The Divine within the Human*

Such assumptions were basic to the earlier series of (CCA) *Theology-in-Action* programmes in various countries, in which the following theological process emerged to depict theology in the life of the people and their co-workers. One of the diagrams created showed that theology in the life of our people *begins in*:

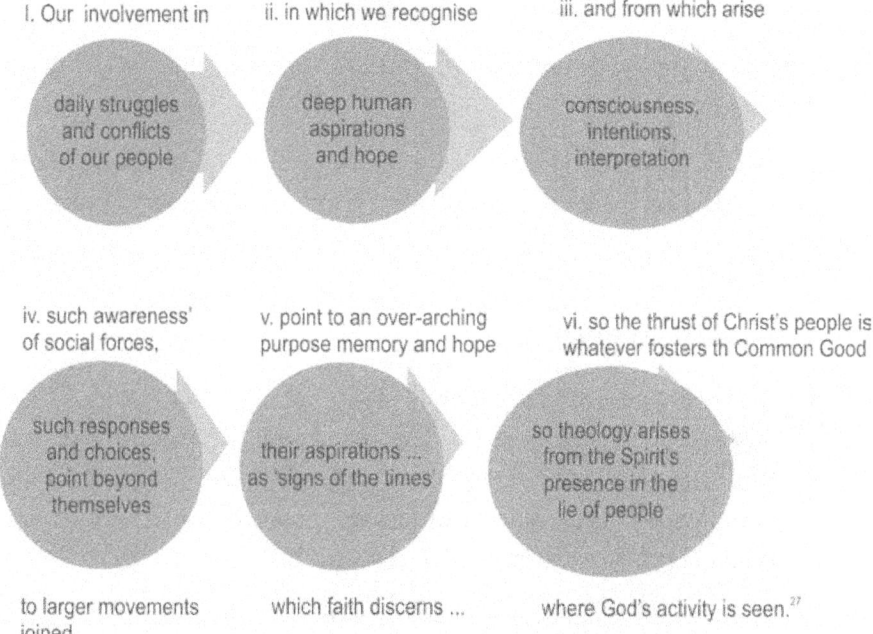

This model therefore finds within the struggles and hopes of our communities (that is, 'the signs of the times', which we must directly experience) those insights and hopes which point beyond themselves in theological interpretation, to the Spirit's work in our world. These are those 'seeds' and 'fore-gleams' within the present which promise God's future.

B. *Story-telling*

In seeking to understand and respond to the realities of our peoples' experience, nothing has been more important in recent decades than the recognition of story-telling as a theological process -- stories in folk-literature or scriptures, from people-movements, tribal groups or urban communities, and especially the stories of women in all these.

The two following examples give different procedures, now widely used, in which story-telling provides the basic theological resource for grappling with human life and struggle:

a) Story-Telling as developed in *PTCA's* former *annual Seminar-Workshops:*

   i) Locate a liberating event (or events), or a renewing movement, in our people's life (in 'secular' or religious history and culture).

   ii) Find a 'story' or stories of women, men and children in their struggles to be fully human ... (in folk-literature, art, Christian mission, social history...).

   iii) Ask how these stories interact with our understanding of God who creates, sustains and restores; our understanding of the life of Jesus as centre and criterion of the Biblical story (the compassion, hope, peace, suffering or restoration of our people being the historical reality of Jesus today).

   iv) Then what insight and direction are given for our present life and struggles? (How can we draw on these wider resources of God's presence and grace?).[28]

b) *Minjung Story-telling* - from the work of Minjung theologians in Korea.[29]

   i) Retell the stories of people's struggles and hopes... (From one's own listening and participation).

   ii) What are the roots and forms of these stories? (Why and how have they emerged?).

   iii) What do they express of aspiration, identity, and acceptance? (Identify the hopes and human values within them).

   iv) Where are the stories of Jesus found in the stories of Minjung? (Recognise the deeds and promises of Jesus there).

v) Explore the counter-theology where 'sinners' and rebels enter the Kingdom first and dominance is not righteousness.[30]

With particular reference to *theological education*, Moon Dong-Whan outlines a similar process in this way:

i) First participate in and reflect on the people's struggles;

ii) Commune with the Minjung, perceiving their world, their 'han';[31]

iii) Recognise the encounter with the living God in that experience;

iv) Reflect upon the above three steps, using Biblical and cultural resources;

v) Communicate the experience and reflection by story.[32]

2. Asian Approaches to the Bible

How can we clarify further the movement between human life and scripture (or tradition)? A simple drawing of parallels or the assembling of related texts will of course not be adequate. Nor is it acceptable to straightway search for particular passages which may directly support assumptions already made or actions already taken. Both the concrete situations and cross-sections of scripture are to be studied on their own terms, and only then viewed and mutually explored so that each of situation and scripture challenges each. We must also come to recognise the framework and assumptions being held for our use of scripture, so that we can critique any self-serving, imperialist or patriarchal interpretations, and come to discern the prophetic and Gospel story within our stories. All of scripture itself is of course to be measured and judged always by the life-of-Jesus-with-others.

a) Present – to Past – to Future

An early diagram used widely in urban mission work within and beyond Asian, shows for example the movement between present, past and future in response to particular events or circumstances. This provides part of a basic framework for finding resources in the Biblical material for present action.

From the Present, via the Past, To God's Future

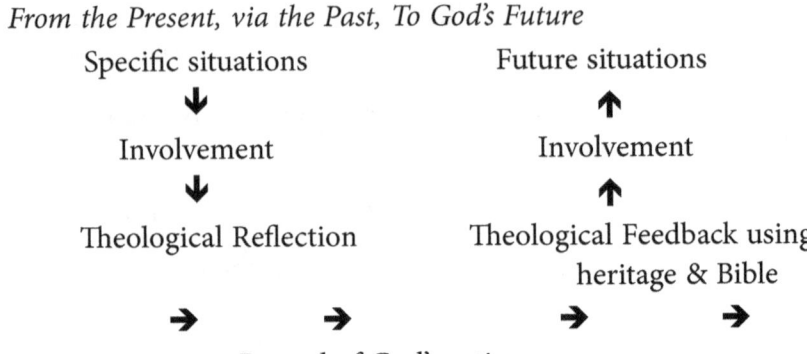

Concrete involvement in a particular situation leads, upon reflection, to a study of God's activity for women and men in the past. This leads to further theological reflection centred on Jesus, which is fed into continuing involvement, to work for a changed future.

b) *Committed Praxis*

Such a framework requires however further hermeneutic detail. A fuller outline of the process by which the Bible and the human context interact in the construction of living theology, has emerged in EATWOT's Asian consultations. This begins in a shared engagement and moves from 'memory', refreshed and questioned, along with cultural and social analysis, on to new vision and praxis, where specific context and received Gospel are joined.

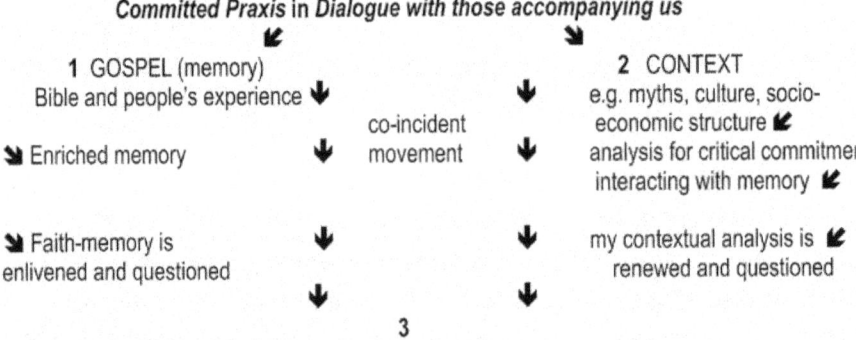

Here the crucial interaction is that between faith-memory and contextual analysis, but the movements to enrich the faith-memory and to deepen the analysis proceed *in tandem*, forming a partnership-in-action to a renewed hope, awareness and action.

3. Asian Approaches to Theological Reflection

It can be seen in the examples thus far given that there are *underlying* questions being addressed which provide direction to both the experience and reflection. They could be phrased in this way:

i) What is happening to people – how are they surviving?

ii) How are they responding as community– what life stories do they tell?

iii) How can we interpret these stories – what resources can be used?

iv) Where do we recognise here the presence of God's Spirit?

v) How then does this become 'food for the road ahead', personally, communally?

In the examples given, the movement between concrete situations – life-story, symbolism, or struggle – and theological reflection and interpretation, has been illustrated and to some extent clarified. Clearly too, many elements, questions and processes outlined above raise further issues for reflection and application. One issue to which we must return again and again however concerns the hermeneutic steps which in our fundamental move, take us from theological (and human) experience to 'theological' (and critical) reflection. How do we recognise on the Way we travel the presence of the One in whom we live?

"*A Doing theology Code*", which has emerged from the work of many colleagues and groups in different countries of the region, does focus on these steps a little more fully and also provides a synopsis of the process found in many 'Asian ways'.

'*Theodao/dharma*' is to be carried out on the basis of:

i) Pre-understanding – that the One Living Spirit of all, bears with, allows, suffers with, delivers and transforms our peoples today;

ii) Direct experience – both of a concrete situation of human struggle and of personal and community hope;

iii) Critical questioning – as to "What is happening to (unprivileged and suffering) people?" and "How do they respond?" (What are the causes of their suffering? How are they surviving as fully human beings?)

With a focus then upon the central *theological* questions:

iv) What experiences or commitments, stories, traditions or symbols, *point beyond themselves* to the Great Spirit who builds all just and creative community? ... What human experiences appear to faith to be 'signs of the times'; 'seeds for later fulfilment' or marks of a fuller humanity? And which of these challenge accepted interpretations of Bible or church or theology?

v) So where can the central actions of Jesus – befriending, challenging, offering, suffering, transforming – be found in our societies and cultures? Where does human love, people-justice, reconciliation, and peace-making become the Asian face of Jesus Christ?.

vi) What are our sources in Bible, culture and history for understanding the process of reflection, 'theological' insight and criteria? ... How do (prophetic) Biblical traditions and the sufferings and hopes of our people mutually challenge and enrich each other?.

vii) How then are we now given 'food for the road', for all God's people? In the models outlined above this is always the bottom-line question: In what way does our theology – our holding together of the three experiences of present history, of Gospel, and of culture / society – provide hope and food for today's labour or struggle?³⁵

To Conclude

It is by further reflecting upon and applying such questions as these last four, I believe, that we will build on the work of forebears and friends, and develop more genuinely Asian and localized ways for the doing of Christian theology, along with the critical reflection which undergirds and resources our 'living of theology'. We will then be able to enter fuller dialogue and mutual learning with colleagues in contextualizing theological endeavours in other regions and contexts.

For most of us the first step may be to pause and listen to the rice-roots voices about us: telling their own story, sharing their struggle, showing us their pain, or alienation, their creativity or hope. We might then spend some days (or at least a frequent day) living and working with deprived or exploited sisters and brothers or with concerned blue-collar or white-collar workers; a concrete sharing of their actual life, with sensitivity and friendship; or it may be a direct involvement in a social movement, community group or Centre.³⁶ For those of us who have known this privilege, our theological teaching and reflecting will then require a weekly or monthly time of listening and sharing with colleagues also working in such situations, to ensure that reflection and theologizing remain in its full context. These are patterns that many of our colleagues share, some even giving up leave time to spend months with villagers or down-towners. Whether in week-ends, odd days or for a 'sabbatical', it is upon such lived experience and sensitivity that all living theology depends. There are in each of our contexts partners and movements where such commitment and concern is shared, and with whom we can deepen both experience and critical reflection.

Along with such exposure and partnership, the other most important but often neglected practice is the ongoing study of our colleagues' and our forebears' writing, teaching and acting in living out *their* theology. Selecting only the more creative of contextual resources that are available to us from our region, we find there is a flood of vivid and accessible insights, encounters and inspiration. And these come not only from recent centuries but, for many of our most pressing engagements there are now many more 'Asian resources' to hand from the earliest periods of Christian history in this half of the world.[37]

The examples given are only a few of the rich resources which we have in our Asian theologies to assist us in responding to the struggles, histories and traditions of our peoples, where living theology is born. They clearly all begin with the prior concern for the life of our peoples in their historical and contemporary milieus and for the fuller realization of God's rule on earth, in people-justice, holistic peace and creative community. It is from this, our colleagues affirm, that theo(-dao/dharma) as reflection-in-action – utilizing traditional, prophetic and creative resources – arises. They require our study, our critique and, from our own and our colleagues' work, amplification and development.

Endnotes

[1] The discussion here has been extensive. One of the Journals where much of this has appeared is the *Bulletin of the CTC* (CCA Commission for Theological Concerns). Notable articles from the last 20 years would include those by T.B. Simatupang (3.2, 1982); (Ms) Padma Gallup (4.3, 1983); Suh Nam-dong, and Hyun Yong-hak (5.3-6.1, 1984-1985); Aloysius Pieris (6.2and3, 1986); Levi Oracion (9.2and3, 1990); Luna L. Dingayan (10.1, 1991); Rienzi Perera (11.2and3, 1992); (Ms) Wong Wai Ching (Supp.1, Nov. 1997); Kim Heup Young (15.1, 1998); James Massey (17.2, 2001); (Ms)Limatula Longkumer (22.1, 2006); James Haire (23.3, 2007); (Ms) Aye New (26.1, 2010).

Other journals (in English) of similar Asia-wide interest include *The Asia Journal of Theology* (ATESEA & SEASGT), *Vidyajyoti* (India), *Madang* (Korea), *Chinese Theological Review*, *East Asia Pastoral Review* (Philippines) & *Pacifica* (Australia). For these & other references in this paper see the Research Guide *Asian Christian Theologies* 3 vols. Ed. by John C. England et al. (ISPCK, Claretian, Orbis, 2001-2004) & papers of this volume.

[2] On specifically Asian views of Christian faith see for example R.S. Sugirtharajah *Frontiers in Asian Christian Theology* (Orbis, 1994), F.J. Balasundaram, *Contemporary Asian Christian Theology* (UTC, Bangalore, 1995), Michael Amaladoss *The Asian Jesus* (Orbis, 2006), Muriel Orevillo_Montenegro *The Jesus of Asian Women* (Orbis, 2006), Martien E. Brinkman *The Non-Western Jesus* (Equinox, 2009), Peniel Jesudason &

Rufus Rajkumar (eds.) *Asian Theology on the Way* (SPCK, 2012). See further on this in the writings of theologians outlined in chapter 9 below. On use of the terms 'East', 'West', 'Eastern' 'Western' in what follows and on the larger issues concerning their inter-action, also the role of 'the other' and varieties of 'orientalism' or 'occidentalism' we now have, see especially Ananda Coomaraswamy *Christian and Oriental Philosophy of Art* (Manoharal, 1974) chap.2; J.J. Clarke *Oriental Enlightenment* (Routledge, 1997) chaps. 1, 11, 12; also B.S. Turner, *Orientalism, Post-modernism, Globalism* (Routledge, 1994); and Ian Buruma,& Avishai Margalit *Occidentalism* (Atlantic Books, 2004). On differences between 'Eastern' and 'Western' ways of thought see Richard E. Nisbett *The Geography of Thought: How Asians and Westerners Think Differently... and Why.* (Free Press, 2004). But beyond such debate there can be no doubt that there *are* recognizably Asian /Eastern resources – historical, cultural, religious and Christian – which are not as yet recognised in most 'western' theologies. It will become clear that I do not consider here the possibilities of a 'fusion of horizons' (Gadamer), nor specifically the 'hybridities' (Bhabha) which are always present in cultural (or theological) encounters. My emphasis is rather upon the diverse approaches to a 'theology-in-life' which are *already established* using Asian resources in these regions and on which any wider encounters or dialogue must be based.

[3] For the early period see I. Gilman and H-J.Klimkeit *Christians in Asia Before 1500.* (Curzon, 1999); Mar Ab. Mattam, *Forgotten East.* (Ephrem's Pubns., 2000); J.C. England *The Hidden History of Christianity in Asia* (ISPCK, 2002); C. Baumer, *The Church of the East. An Illustrated History of Assyrian Christianity.* (Tauris, 2006). For examples of 'resistance and rejection' in the early modern period see chaps. 4, 5 & 6 this volume.

[4] See for example Hajime Nakamura *The Ways of Thinking of Eastern Peoples: India-China-Tibet-Japan* (Univ. of Hawaii Press, 1964); Joseph M. Kitagawa, (ed.) *The Religious Traditions of Asia. Religion, History, and Culture.* (Macmillan & Collins, 1987/89); also Nisbett (op.cit. 2004).

[5] Amongst recent treatments of this see Felix Wilfred *Margins - Site of Asian Theologies.* (ISPCK, 2008); & Gemma Tulud Cruz "Between a rock and a hard place: an Asian Theology of Survival", in Jesudason & Rajkumar.(2012) 75ff. For larger issues of human survival under increasing pressures C.f. Teotonio R. De Souza (ed.) *Discoveries, Missionary Expansion and Asian Cultures* (Concept Publishing, 1994); Feroza Jussawalla *Emerging South Asian Women Writers : Essays and Interviews.* (Peter Lang, 2015); Tom Cliff *The Living Politics of Self-Help Movements in East Asia* (Springer-Verlag, 2017).

[6] The phrase is Song Choan Seng's and is presented in, for example, his "From Israel to Asia: a Theological Leap" (*The Ecumenical Review,* 28.3, July 1976) 252ff. The concept became central in the annual courses of the Programme for Theologies and Culture in Asia (PTCA), since 1983. See *Doing Theology with Asian Resources*, ed. by John C. England and Archie C.C.Lee (PTCA and Pace Publishing, 1993).

⁷ The work of some theologians in Korea provide some of the fuller treatments of this theme: see Kim Yong Bock *Minjung Theology: People as the Subject of History* (CCA-CTC, 1981), Kwon Jin Kwan *Theology of Subjects. Towards a New Minjung Theology.* (PTCA , 2011).

⁸ For responses of indigenous theology to such situations see Wati longchar *Returning to Mother Earth*, (PTCA and SCEPTRE, 2012) 83ff. See also Hrangthan Chhungi et al. (eds.) *Doing Indigenous Theology in Asia* (NCCI /SCEPTRE / GTC, 2012).

⁹ That is, using the key terms which function in eastern cultures as the Greek term 'logos' often has done in the west: the *dao* (in briefest definition, the 'way of communion with all things') and *dharma* (most briefly, 'the universal law and teaching'). On the move from theo-logy to theo-dao/dharma see e.g. Kim Heup Young *Christ and the Tao* (CCA, 2003), and *Theology of the Tao II*, (Orbis,2012); "Life, Ecology, and Theo-tao: Towards a Life Theology of Theanthropocosmic Tao " (*Madang: Journal of Contextual Theology*, 11, 2009), 75-94; Somen Das *Dharma of the Twenty-First Century* (Calcutta, Punthi Pustak, 1996), George M. Soares-Prabhu *The Dharma of Jesus*. (Orbis Books, 2003).

¹⁰ See for example, T.V. Philip *East of the Euphrates*. (ISPCK, 1998); I. Gilman and H-J.Klimkeit *(1999); Mar Ab. Mattam, (2000);* C. Baumer, *The Church of the East.* (Tauris, 2006). Also chaps. 4,5,6, above.

¹¹ For an outline of the movements associated with this Programme see http://ptcaweb.blogspot.co.nz/2011/12/doing-theologies-in-asian-ways-and-with.html. For related programmes see 'Guidelines for Doing theologies in Asia' of the Association for Theological Education in South East Asia (International Bulletin of Missionary Research, April 2008, 77ff.; also in http://www.internationalbulletin.org/issues/2008-02/2008-02-077-asia.pdf.; and those based on Michael Amaladoss' premise that faith is "commitment seeking transformation through understanding and empowerment", see http://sjapc.net/content/asian-way-doing-theology

¹² In what follows, the attempt is made to use language which reflects non-specialist usage, as the relationship between faith-discernment and everyday experience has been central to the 'doing of theology' in Asian contexts since the earliest centuries.

¹³ C.f. James Massey & T.K. John (eds.) *Rethinking Theology in India. Christianity in the Twenty- first century.* (Manohar, 2013). See further in chaps. 1,2,3 of this volume.

¹⁴ For these and many other examples refer to England et al. *Asian Christian Theologies* (2001-2004).

¹⁵ On the 'hermeneutic circle' which is often referred to see Juan Luis Segundo: "The continuing change in our interpretation of the Bible which is dictated by the continuing changes in our present-day reality, both individual and societal... each new reality obliges us to interpret the word of God afresh, to change reality accordingly, and then to go back and reinterpret the word of God again, and so on." *The Liberation of Theology*, Orbis, 1975. See *PTCA Bulletin* 2.1, 1989. Recent

publications talk rather of a 'hermeneutic spiral' but often, as in Grant R. Osborne *The Hermeneutical Spiral: A Comprehensive Introduction to Biblical Interpretation*. IVP, 2006 (1991) this is without Segundo's strong focus upon the shaping of interpretation by the context of suffering or struggle. It is important to note here the long witness of Eastern Orthodox tradition in which there is "awareness of the primacy of life and experience over systematic reflection and interpretation"; A.M. Allchin in *Kingdom of Love and Peace* (D.L.T., 1979) 19.

[16] See Introduction to my earlier *Living Theology in Asia* (SCM & Orbis, 1981). It will be seen in the case-studies below that criticisms made of much 'Asian Theology' by scholars such as Joas Adiprasetya in his "Towards an Asian Multitextual Theology" (*Exchange* 43. 2, 2014) 119, are not wholly justified. For here many different texts and contexts and many diverse resources and processes are clearly reflected and utilized. Regarding the priority of 'text' alleged by Adiprasetya to be always present, I have outlined the presuppositions that may be often chosen but it must be recognised that amidst the concrete struggles of our peoples these are often sharply summarised in such a question as "What on earth is God doing, here, now?" – and surely this is the minimal presupposition in 'doing theology'. We can in any case agree that there are many simultaneous processes of reflecting and acting, engaging and rejecting, or hybridizing and discerning'. But no attempt will be made here to relate these to discussions of hermeneutic or methodology outside the region although convergences, contrasts and influences can of course be later identified.

[17] Refer to chap.1 of this volume. It will be noted that in some of the examples given below a similar procedure is followed to that outlined by Joe Holland and Peter J. Henriot in their *Social Analysis: Linking Faith and Justice*, . (Orbis Books, 1983). Similarities to the 'circle of praxis' of Paulo Freire and the 'hermeneutic spiral' of Juan Luis Segundo will also be noted.

[18] *The Radical Tradition: The Changing Shape of Theological Reflection in Sri Lanka*. (Colombo, Ecumenical Institute, 1985) 91-103..

[19] See Charles Avila Peasant Theology. (WSCFAsia, 1976); c.f. Clemena Reynaldo Ileto, *Pasyon and Revolution: Popular Movements in the Philippines, 1840-1910*. (Ateneo de Manila Univ. Press, 1979); Benigno P. Beltran *The Christology of the Inarticulate: An Enquiry into the Filipino Understanding of Jesus Christ*.(Divine Word Publications, 1987); and *Faith and Struggle on Smokey Mountain*. (Orbis Bks, 2012); Mary Rosario Battung et al. *Religion and Society: Towards a Theology of Struggle*. Book I. (FIDES, 1988).

[20] Carlos H. Abesamis "Doing Theological Reflection in a Philippine Context" in *The Emergent Gospel: theology from the Underside of History* ed. by S. Torres and (Ms.) Virginia Fabella. (Orbis, 1976) 112-123. c.f. M. Radel (pseud.) "The Theologian at Work in the Philippines 1970s-1980s: a Suggestion" (*Philippine Studies* 19.3, 1971).

[21] See their quarterly *In God's Image* (since 1985), and the collective work in 4 vols. *Introduction to Asian Feminist Theologies* (AWRCCT, 2005-2009). For an over-view

see Wong Wai Ching Angela "Women Dong Theology with the Asian Ecumenical Movement" in *Hope Abundant : Third World and Indigenous Women's Theology* ed. (Ms.) Kwok Pui Lan (Orbis, 2010).

[22] (Ms.) Park Sun-Ae "Asian Women's Theological Reflection" (*East Asia Journal of Theology* 3.2, 1985).

[23] See for example (Ms.) Myrna Francia et al. "Asian Women Doing theology" in *Women in Religion*. (Women's Studies Series 2) ed. by (Ms.)Mary John Mananzan (St Scholastica's College, 1988); (Ms.) Aruna Gnanadason "Feminist theology: An Indian Perspective" (*In God's Image* December 1988) 44-51; (Ms.)Kwok Pui-lan "Post-colonial Asian feminist theologies". P. Jesudason & R. Rajkumar, (op.cit. 2012).

[24] A. Pieris "Towards an Asian theology of Liberation: Some Religio-Cultural Guidelines" in *Varieties of Witness* ed. by D. Preman Niles and T.K. Thomas. (CCA, 1980) 21-42,and *An Asian Theology of Liberation*. (Maryknoll, N.Y., Orbis Books, 1988). See also for example, Buddhadasa Bhikkhu "No Religion" in *Me and Mine* (Selected Essays of Bhikkhu Buddhadasa) ed. by D. Swearer. (Sri Satguru, 1991); Sulak Sivaraksa *A Socially Engaged Buddhism*. (TIRCD, 1988); c.f. (Ms.) Wai-ching Angela Wong *The Poor Woman* (Peter Lang, 2002) 136ff.

[25] J.B. Banawiratma and J. Muller. "Contextual Social Theology". *East Asia Pastoral Review* 36, 1-2, 1999. On the 'Theology in Action' see Oh Jae Shik & J.C. England (eds.) *Theology in Action* (EACC, 1973).

[26] M.M. Thomas *The Acknowledged Christ of the Indian Renaissance*. (CLS/CISRS, 1970) 315f.

[27] England J.C. & Oh Jae Shik (op.cit. 1973).

[28] C.S. Song in *ATESEA Occasional Papers* (No. 6, ATESEA 1988). See also D.P. Niles "Story and theology - A Proposal". (*CTC Bulletin* 5.3/6.1, 1984/85) 79-91; (& *East Asia Journal of theology* 3.1, 1985) 112-126.

[29] 'Minjung' refers to the mass of ordinary people, especially those oppressed or ostracised. See Kim Yong Bock *Minjung Theology: People as the Subject of History*. (CCA-CTC, 198); Suh Kwang-sun *The Korean Minjung in Christ*. (CCA-CTC, 1991); Yim Taesoo *Minjung Theology Towards a Second Reformation*. (CCA, 2006); Kwon Jin Kwan *Theology of Subjects . Towards a New Minjung Theology*. (PTCA , 2011).

[30] Suh Nam Dong *"Theology as Story-telling: A Counter-Theology" (CTC Bulletin 5.3-6.1, 1985/85).*

[31] 'Han' is the sense of suppression or agony in serious oppression, victimization or isolation. See e.g. CCA Women's Concerns *Han Theology in a Divided World*. (CCA, 1991); Lee, Jae Hoon *The Exploration of the Inner Wounds - Han*. AARA Academy Series 86.(Scholars Press, 1994).

[32] Moon Dong Whan "Doing Theology in Korea...from a Minjung Theological Perspective" (*East Asia Journal of Theology* 4.2, 1986).

[33] P. Loffler *Secular Man and Christian Mission* (WCC, 1968).

[34] C. Duraisingh et al. EATWOT Consultation, Hong Kong, 1986.

[35] For further sources here (pre-2000) see Thomas, M.M. "Epilogue: Criteria of an Indian Christian theology" in M.M. Thomas *The Acknowledged Christ of the Indian Renaissance* (SCM Press, 1969); M.E. Prabhakar. (ed.) *Towards a Dalit Theology.* (ISPCK and CISRS, 1989) Part I, chapters 4-7; G. Soares-Prabhu, "The Prophet as Theologian - Biblical Prophetism as a Paradigm for Doing theology Today". (*Asia Journal of Theology* 2.1, 1988) 3-11; Wang Hsien Chih "Some Perspectives on Theological Education in the Light of Homeland theology in the Taiwanese Context". (*CTC Bulletin* 6.2-3, 1986) 13-21; Takayanagi Shunishi "Toward a Japanese Christian theology" (on *Japan and the Face of Jesus* by Inoue, Yoji). (*Japan Missionary Bulletin* 10, 1976); A.A. Yewangoe, *Theologia Crucis in Asia*. Amsterdam (Rodopi, 1987), 271-324; Shen Yi Fan "How New China Helps Christians Think Anew Theologically" in *A New Beginning* ed. by (Ms.) Theresa Chu and C. Lind. (Canadian Council of Churches, 1983) 53-56; Ting K.H. *No Longer Strangers: Selected Writings of K.H.Ting* ed. by Raymond L. Whitehead. (Orbis, 1989) chaps 1,9,12; P.L. Wickeri *Reconstructing Christianity in China. K.H.Ting and the Chinese Church.* (Orbis Books, 2007).

[36] This will be recognised as the 'enquentro' (meeting, encounter, exposure) experience which has been extensively used in ecumenical conferences, workshops or courses since the 1960s. It is also of course the daily experience for work of urban-industrial or rural ministries, centres and movements of social concern, and a wide range of social or community workers..

[37] Refer to chap.1 of this volume.

Chapter - 8

Watershed Theologians

Note: This series of studies considers Asian theologians whom I judge to have played a central and 'watershed' role in 20th century (and beyond) Asian theologies. They form a selection of those whose work in the early 20th century broke new paths in theological reflection which would distinguish all subsequent work in theology both in their own county and in the region as a whole.

The other 'Watershed' theologians that could be selected for these studies (apart from the number of significant authors still living) include: Paul Devanandan (1901-1962) and K.T. Paul (1876-1931) India; Nicolaus Driyakara sj (1913-1967) and Tahi Bonar Simatupang (1920-1990) Indonesia; Zhao Zichen (T.C. Chao 1898-1979) and Ding Guangxun (K.H. Ting 1915-2012) China, Takizawa Katsumi (1906-1984) and (Ms.) Kiyoko Takeda Cho (1917-2018) Japan; Daniel Chi Hak Soon (1921-1993) and Ahn Byung-Mu (1921-1997) Korea; Lynn A. de Silva (1919-1982) and Tissa Balasuriya (1924-2013) Sri Lanka; (Ms.) Prakai Nontawasee (1926-2013) Thailand; Bảo Tịnh Vương Đình Bích (1928-2015) Vietnam; and U Khin Maung Din (1931-1987) Myanmar.

The examples below are included here because they are still amongst the lesser known and most underestimated of Asian Theologians of the last century. They have however played particularly significant roles in major theological movements both in Asia and beyond in the past seventy years. Although concentrating here on their individual contributions, each stands within a group of colleagues and represents the work of a larger movement.

1. **Wu Yao Zong (Y. T. Woo) (China: 1893-1979)** *Love as Practice for Change*

There are few national histories in the first half of the 20th century which for massive social and political upheavals parallel that of China. Prostration before the western powers following the imposition of 'unequal treaties' and then suppression of the Boxer revolts, gave place after the 1911 Revolution and its betrayal, to the militant nationalism and cultural revival of the New Thought (1917) and May 4th (from 1919) Movements. At that time the traditional fabric of Chinese society steadily weakened as western science and philosophy was displacing much of Confucian tradition and culture. The struggles between reform movements and the ambitions of war-lords in many provinces since 1911 escalated by the late 1920s into wider civil war between *Kuo Min Tang* and Communist forces. Along with these conflicts, mounting social and economic disorder, major famines and epidemics and the deepening war against Japan made the 27 years following the first World War a period of extreme social and political disruption.

But it was also a period of intense intellectual ferment, of national cultural awakening and of recurring attempts at national reconstruction. it was a time also when despite strong anti-Christian (and anti-western) movements, Chinese Christians gave prominent leadership in almost all aspects of educational and social reform. They were prominent also in international missionary and ecumenical movements and not least in theological teaching and construction. In all these their witness was to a tradition and practice of emphatically Chinese faith amidst the turbulent history of their nation and church.[1]

In the year 1918 a young customs officer, while attending a Bible Study group, discovered the Sermon on the Mount as recorded in

Matthew's Gospel chapters 5-7. He became a confessed Christian that same year. 'These three chapters' he later wrote, "had clearly revealed to me what I had been earnestly seeking in more than ten years…I could also vaguely see between the lines the person who had said these words…and I could not hold back my tears after such an encounter with his personality".[2] This encounter would fully shape Wu's inner and outer life in after years, proving always a source of vision, courage and active hope. From the following year he began his writings on his developing faith and social vision.

These were soon influenced not only by his work in the YMCA and SCM with students from many parts of China, along with theological studies in North America, but by the turmoil of political and military events across the country. In his work with students he became aware of the dreams and struggles of young people as they confronted wide-spread corruption, injustice and civil conflict. With the help of the YMCA he studied in 1924-27 for his M.A. at Union Theological Seminary, gaining his M.A. with a thesis on "William James' Doctrine of Religious Belief". His concern for a 'liberal' faith was nourished at Union Seminary but he soon came to see that this must be indigenized and embodied in practice as a specifically Chinese theology-in-action. This was to be strengthened through his attendance at the International Missionary Conference at Tambaram in 1938. His continuing work with influential student movements to provide the spiritual basis for social reconstruction would later give place to advocacy for the further steps of social revolution. Throughout 1936 he had been speaker at over 40 American universities depicting the Japanese invasion of China and the necessity for international sanctions, as well as being active in negotiations for peace. However his earlier strongly pacifist convictions, influenced by Gandhi whose autobiography he translated, moved under the pressures of civil war and the violence of Japanese invasion from non-cooperation in conflict to support for military action. He would later argue that the use of force, where the over-riding purpose was a larger love for humanity did not violate the spirit of reconciliation.

Few figures in the story of Chinese Christian theology – for which the sources date from at least the 8th century – have been more significant (or controversial) than the young government servant *Wu Yao Zong* (Y.T. Wu) who had been captured by the words and deeds of Jesus. He was advocating more democratic processes when China was still ruled by the *Kuo Min Tang*; nurturing student and YMCA groups in progressive Christian activities and thought; and founding the journal *Tian Feng* (1945). He was however later forced to resign from being editor because of an article which criticized Chinese Christianity for close links with capitalist development and practice in China. He would however continue to write extensively throughout his life in the causes of social reform and an indigenous church: in English in the *Chinese Recorder* and the *China Christian Yearbook,* in Chinese in *Tian Feng* and many other church publications such as *Truth and Life, Xiaoxi, Reconciliation, Zhongguo xueyun* and *Jidujiao congkan.*

In all these ways he was dedicated to building with colleagues a movement which would recover 'three -self' identity for the church and later, sufficient space for church life to continue under communist rule. This would embody the principles of self-support, self-government, and self-propagation, for which Wu introduced the slogan *ai quo ai jiao* (love country, love church). Not least, and throughout his life, came his careful development of a Chinese theology which was fully contextual and liberative within contemporary China.[3] His starting-point here was not that of conventional Christianity, nor of Chinese tradition as such but rather the vision he and others held for a future China which had been transformed by a Christian faith which was lived out in all the areas of common and personal life. For this Wu's principal resource was always the Hebrew prophetic tradition as realized in the life and teaching of Jesus.

The Truth of the Universe, Prayer, Action
Study of his writings reveals that throughout more than half a century of active public life, Wu would not cease from reflecting upon the nature of salvation, sin and repentance, in both personal and political life. And

this he placed in the larger context of struggle for autonomy, truth and self-identity in both Christian theology and social reform. He was also regularly reflecting upon the God who is revealed in Jesus Christ to be "the Spirit, the heart, the power, and the Lord of the universe".[4] Such a faith was also discovered in Bible study and prayer, which he defined as first being a *longing* for God, and for truth. This is an 'awareness in silence' which leads to decision and leads on to 'the road we must follow' in active life.[5] "Prayer integrates and harmonizes everything in life under the will of God" Wu wrote, "the greatest prayer is not asking for this or that either for oneself or for others, but asking to know the truth, to know the will of God in order that it may be accomplished.... The incessant prayer of one who knows how to pray ought to be 'May thy will be done". Writing on Wu's prayer life, K.H. Ting affirms that his emphasis was on the selflessness of genuine prayer, for prayer is for Wu open to God's whole will for all God's people, and is a spirituality of the most exalted kind for it does not centre upon one's self at all but reaches out continually to espouse the common good.[6]

For the purposes of analyzing and describing the measures by which such a *common* good might be found he accepted part only of Marxist theory, because in that a careful analysis of the human condition along with ideals of a just and equitable society were provided.[7] (See further on the CCP below). Developments in the theological understanding of many of Y.T Wu's contemporaries reveal similar elements and conclusions: amongst others this was seen in the work of Wu Lai-chuan, Chao Tsu-chen (Zhao Zichen), P.C. Hsu (Hsu Pao-Ch'ien), Andrew C.Y. Ch'eng (Cheng Jingyi), and T. Lew. (Liu Tingfang).[8] Yet it is clear from Wu's many writings that the controlling belief for all his thought and work remained centred in Jesus Christ and the God revealed in his life and work.

As the 'objective truth of the universe'[9] God is yet clearly manifest in the real flesh and blood of Jesus Christ, declares Y. T. Wu. "The force which penetrates and sustains all existence and all forms of life finds its first and only expression in Christ' as truth, love and freedom".[10] These are for Wu clearly historical realities, and so they are to be realized in concrete situations, no less for society as a whole than for the individual believer. In every area of thought and activity he maintains the necessary interdependence of faith and action, of the individual and the community and of theology and politics. For these unities he finds grounded in an experience of God in which transcendence and immanence are inseparable. The love which moves and unifies the universe is also within each person, Wu affirms, moving us to serve and love our people. Love for Christ, who is present in our history, is therefore fused with loving concern for the well-being of all people.

Such affirmations are remarkable enough in their historic setting, even though we can recognise parallels in such figures as D.T. Niles, Kim Jae Joon, Paul Devanandan and other creative theologians contemporary with him. But their thoroughgoing application to Christian faith and practice which Wu Worked out in both his life and his writing make them all the more remarkable. Looking even briefly at the way in which he maintained such interdependence of thought and action -- throughout many decades of work amongst students, in church leadership and political negotiations – reveals unchanging affirmations. And in these we can see that his greatest concern was always for China's suffering women and men and children who desperately needed relief, liberation and restoration.

The Practice of Love for Change
Wu's theology is rooted then in an understanding of God's will for all people, which is embodied in the life of Jesus and empowered by the Holy Spirit. God's transcendent will and purpose in the universe, Wu believes, is simply a love which we are called to both adore and practise.

God's will is known in prayer, where the "light of God dispels our darkness, melts our stubbornness and unites our words and deed with God's nature."[11] Through the Holy Spirit we are there "face to face with objective truth."[12] Yet we can also know the will of God by observing the objective realities of the universe where God's laws are bringing about the ideal society and environment of the Kingdom. And here the Christian community is to provide the spiritual basis for a national reconstruction.

To believe in God therefore, and in the final realization of God's will, brings enthusiasm for truth and justice and for its realization in both human relationships and the life of society. This is because to be 'saved' is to allow God's truth to change us so that we act disinterestedly for such truth amidst our people. In a most significant theological affirmation Wu declares that salvation, *by definition*, cannot be limited to personal salvation, for it is salvation *from* selfishness, greed and pride and this means release from self-centred or church-centred concern so that we give ourselves for a social salvation which will include all. The spiritual and the material, thought and action, are not to be separated for life is to be seen as a totality of love and service.

Similarly the love of God is not a possession we have or can claim, but a principle of action; it is the will of God within the human context, God within us moving us to love in selfless service, in non-violence and in movements for social revolution. Love as exemplified by Jesus is a direction we must follow: both a principle of action and the concrete actions by which the manifesto of Jesus in Luke 4 is carried out in personal and social life. Life according to the Spirit is precisely this active love working for the renewal of all society and all human life. It is 'siding with the Holy Spirit', who is the bestower of all value and all good, in his unstoppable work for spiritual and material salvation.[13]

So the coming of God's Realm includes basic socio-economic changes, freedom from capitalist imperialism, along with the struggle for people's welfare, healing and release. It includes social service *and* social change; change of heart *and* so also change in material conditions. It was this deep concern which led Wu to respect many of the policies and practices of Communist regimes which he saw putting love into practice. He was therefore willing to endorse socialism because of the widespread social benefit that was promised and the close relation he saw between the earnest pursuit of justice and human welfare inspired by

God and the just society sought in the name of 'dialectical materialism'. Yet the Kingdom cannot be equated with any socio-political changes or reforms, nor with a 'new China', even though the Reign of God may be related to these as ultimate to penultimate. It was therefore a hope within yet beyond history.

Controversy and Suffering
Wu's relationships with both the Communist Party of China and with other Christian leaders were therefore often difficult and problematic, despite the apparently mutual acceptance of the *Christian Manifesto* (for which Wu was partly responsible) on their relationships (1950). To some more conservative colleagues in the churches he sometimes appeared to be only concerned for society and its reform, and his theology likewise only interested in the social implications of the Gospel. Yet leaving aside the issue of the church's long neglect of such concerns, study of Wu's writings reveals a much more comprehensive theology is being built. With theologians and activists across the region Wu also insists that 'God's will on earth' necessarily involves social and not only individual change. The Gospel of Jesus that the 'Kingdom is upon us' applies to the whole of human life. And this relates to similar holistic theologies that were then being forged in India and Ceylon, and in Korea and Japan (see below).

So Wu often pleads for a recovery of the prophetic tension between the temporal and the eternal, between what is and what ought to be. "We do not cherish the utopian vision that society after a period of radical change will become ideal. From the standpoint of Christianity we are positive in standing for a total reconstruction of the present economic order. But we believe that economic change is only the first step wards a complete revolution. A society which would put the value of personality in the central place would require a many-sided and continual revolution. In this regard we believe that the Gospel of Jesus is an eternal challenge to this world". Here too for Wu and his colleagues "reconciliation (in Chinese *Wei Ai*, the way of love or non-violence) and revolution cannot be separated".[14]

These are positions which he constantly refined in the midst of political involvement and of even civil or military conflict, but they are also rooted in his deep understanding of sin and evil. Wu declares that only One is holy, God, and though the value of each person is absolute this comes not from any human perfection but rather from God's love.[15] All things human can be sinful and tend to evil, so that persons and societies must be reborn through the actions of the Holy Spirit. Yet the sin and evil of human lives and institutions is not an a priori assumption that prevents us from acting wherever there are ambiguities in, for example, the political choices to be made. Striving for people's full welfare will always itself have most significant value. In Wu's praxis any spiritual and any material reconstruction requires that both church and society are to undergo a 'genuine repentance' which is expressed in actual commitment and concrete change. And for the church this will result in the reclaiming of her prophetic spirit and prophetic action.

For despite all the contradictions we encounter, God is still with us, Wu affirms, especially where suffering is faced in "a sacrificial spirit of active struggle and forging ahead".[16] The cross is for him the supreme demonstration of such a spirit and Luke 9:24 is one of the two sayings which most strengthened Wu's faith at this point. But here again he stresses the historical causes and outcomes of Jesus Christ's passion. While being the culmination of long centuries of longing for the salvation of all people, Jesus was yet killed because his revolutionary teachings and ministry opposed so much in existing society and religion. The cross is the supreme pledge of God's love yet it also reveals the cost to be met in bringing any liberation of men and women from personal and social evil. Along with Jesus' life the cross initiates the Reign of God, but it must be directly related to the events of our age as the path to all human reconstruction.[17]

Conclusion

Throughout all such theological reflection it is possible to discern Wu's continuing debate with reformers and revolutionaries and also his frank acknowledgement of the truth they hold. Equally clear is his insistence on the careful distinctions in both thought and action for the Kingdom now and to come which the Gospel requires. Distinctions which necessarily lead to choices and actions for the good life of people in their concrete situation as well as to the affirmation of hope that reaches beyond such conditions.

K.H. Ting believes that these and other aspects of Y.T. Wu's legacy show clearly what it means to overcome any divorce between nature and grace, between the Kingdom inaugurated on earth and that which is to come. Any complete gulf between Jesus Christ's nature and our human nature is also overcome for it "was through his endeavour in the way of love and in his moral struggle that Jesus came to find a living God".[18] Writing of the 'Biblical grounds' upon which Wu and his colleagues drew, Ting describes them as "making the whole creation and not just redemption the subject of theology, the whole of humanity and not just the Church the object of [God's] concern; and the whole cosmos and not just religion the domain of Christ's lordship and the Holy Spirit's work of sanctification".[19]

Here then are some of the bases upon which Y.T. Wu, his colleagues and K.H. Ting following him, built a new self-understanding for the Chinese church and a 'co-operative' relationship with the communist government of New China. These principles were embodied in the Three-Self Patriotic movement which, despite sharp controversy enabled the Chinese churches to preserve many public activities in subsequent years (except during the destructive period of the Cultural Revolution of 1966-1978). Since 1978 this working compromise has made it possible to restore and extend congregational life, societal work, ministerial training and the extensive publishing of Bibles in particular.

But the movement as shaped by Wu was far more than the application of a century-old discussion of the 'Three Selfs', or the necessary expedient to ensure the church's public survival. It was the exercise of self-hood by being Chinese in theology, worship and devotion, and in what became a mass movement for the love of God and of the Motherland.[20] "If we really want to achieve the goal of self-propagation", Wu wrote, "we must first free ourselves from the restrictions of the theological systems of the West and their tendency to run away from reality. We must discover anew the central teachings of Jesus Christ in the Bible and build up a theological system for the Chinese people themselves."[21] In this endeavour to build a re-oriented pattern of theology Wu was anticipating the work and life of many colleagues throughout the region in coming decades.

Endnotes

[1] See entries in J.C.England et al. (eds.) 2004), vol.3, chap.3, sections 5.1, 5.2, 5.3, especially pp.116-125, 138-153. See also Ng Lee Ming (1971-1977), and Lam Wing Hung (1983), on Y.T. Wu, Wang Ming Dao, Hsu Po Chien, Wu Lei Chuen; Hayhoe & Lu Yongling (1996); Chu Sin-Jan (1995); Daniel H. Bays. (1999) section 4, and Bays (2011) chap.7.

[2] Refer Y.T.Wu (1929) in *Da Xue Yue Kan* (July 1947), cited by Ng (1972) 8.

[3] K.H. Ting (1990) 159. See also Zhao Xiaoyang (2014) 138f.

[4] Ng Lee Ming (1972) 9.

[5] See 'On Self-cultivation', in an early issue of *Tian Feng*, December 6, 1945; and 'Christianity and Materialism' *Da Xue Yue Kan,* (1947); for further on Y.T. Wu's views on prayer see Wickeri (2007) 253, where Wu stresses that in prayer 'we abandon our own selfishness...seek harmony with God's truth...consecrate to God the potentiality within our own being that it ...may be brought to a higher level [so] we may be partakers in God's work...'.

[6] K.H.Ting (op.cit.1990); Refer Wu *No One Has Seen God,* 1940). For Wu's 'deep and lasting' influence on K.H.Ting and others see Wickeri (2007) 37ff., 41f., 137, 370.

[7] See 'How The Communist Party has Educated Me' (*Tien Feng*, July 1951).

[8] Ng Lee Ming (1973 et seq.), J.C.England et al. (op.cit. 2004) .

[9] Y.T.Wu (1985) 109

[10] ibid. 13

[11] K.H. Ting (1981) 15.

[12] Y.T.Wu (1985) 110

[13] Ng Lee Ming (1972) 17, 13f.

[14] Y.T.Wu *Christianity and China's Reconstructiion* 211, and 'Reconciliation and Revolution' (Chinese recorder 1934) 300, cited by Ng 37 and 40. For a full discussion of Wu's understanding of Jesus' teaching and practice of the way of love and non-violence see Ng 38-45. For Wu's relations with the CPP see Ng 31-37, 45-51, also Wickeri (2007) 36f., 79f., 97.

[15] Y.T. Wu (1985)117.

[16] ibid. 114.

[17] M.A.Endicott (1979) 445.

[18] Y.T.Wu 'My View of the Universe and of Life' 86, cited by Ng (1972) 13.

[19] K.H.Ting (1981) 12

[20] Refer Wickeri (2007). Yu, Kwok-hung (1997)

[21] Y.T. Wu 'New Stage of the Christian Reform Movement' *Hsin Hua Daily*, Feb. 15, 1951

Select Bibliography and Works cited

Primary (English Titles)

Wu Yao Tsung (ed.) *The Jesus I Know*. (Association Press, 1929).

_____. *The Social Gospel* (Association Press, 1934)

_____. *Religious Faith in Troubled Times* (Association Press, 1938).

_____. *No Man Has Seen God*. (Association Press, 1940 – seven editions by 1948).

_____. *Darkness and Light* (Association Press, 1949).

_____. *Lectures on Christianity* (Association Press, 1950)

_____. 'The Significance of Christian Faith in these Critical Times'. *(Chinese Theological Review*, 1985).

Wu, Y.T.. *Three-Self Patriotic Movement* (In Chinese, 1982);

Secondary

Bays, Daniel H. *Christianity in China: From the Eighteenth Century to the Present* (Stanford University Press, 1999) section 4.

Bays, Daniel H. *A New History of Christianity in China* (Wiley-Blackwell, 2011).

Chow, A. (2014). 'Protestant Ecumenism and Theology in China Since Edinburgh 1910'. (Missiology 10.2009).

Chu Sin-Jan *Wu Leichuan: A Confucian-Christian in Republican China* (Peter Lang, 1995).

Documents of the Three-Self Movement: Source Materials for the Study of the Protestant Church in Communist China (NCCCUSA, 1963).

Dunch, Ryan 'Worshiping under the Communist eye'. (*Christian History & Biography* 98, Spring 2008) 14–18.

Endicott, Mary A. 'In Memoriam Y.T. Wu'. (*Canadian Far Eastern Newsletter*, 305, Nov. 1979).

England, John C. et al. (eds.) *Asian Christian Theologies* (ISPCK, Claretian, Orbis, 2004) 3. 34-215.

'Forerunner Y.T. Wu' and 'The Ever-renewing Mr Y.T. Wu' in Janice Wickeri (ed.) *Love Never Ends* (Amity, 2000) 72-85 & 365-371. 'Forerunner Y.T.Wu' also appears in *A Chinese Contribution to Ecumenical Theology* ed. Janice and Philip Wickeri, (WCC, 2002).

Gao Wangzhi 'Y. T. Wu: A Christian Leader Under Communism'. In Daniel H. Bays, *Christianity in China: From the Eighteenth Century to the Present.* (Stanford University Press, 1999) 338–352.

Hayhoe, Ruth & Lu Yongling (eds.) *Ma Xiang Bo and the Mind of Modern China 1840-1939.* (M.E.Sharpe, 1996).

Jones, Francis P. *Theological Thinking in the Chinese Protestant Church under Communism.* (Abingdon Press, 1963).

Kwok Pui-lan 'Theological Counterpoints: Transnationalism and Political Theology in the Asia Pacific' (*Journal of Race, Ethnicity, and Religion* 3.2.5 January 2012).

Lam Wing-hung *Chinese Theology in Construction.* (William Carey Library, 1983).

Miao, Chester S. (ed.) *Christian Voices in China.* (Friendship Press, 1948).

Ng, Lee-Ming 'A Study of Y. T. Wu'. (*Ching Feng* XV. 1, 1972): 5–54; and 'A Bibliography of T.C. Chao and Y.T. Wu (*Ching Feng* XVI, 3-4, 1973).

Starr, Chloë *Chinese Theology* (Yale Univ. 2016) 168-173.

Ting, K.H. 'What We Can Learn from Y. T. Wu Today' (*International Bulletin of Mission Research.* 14.4, 1990) 158–161.

Tiedemann, R.G. (ed.) *A Handbook of Christianity in China.* Vol. 2: 1800–Present (Brill, 2010).

Wickeri, Philip L. *Seeking the Common Ground: Protestant Christianity. The Three-Self Movement, and China's United Front.* (Orbis Books, 1988).

Wickeri, Philip L. *Reconstructing Christianity in China. K.H.Ting and the Chinese Church.* (OrbisBooks, 2007).

'Wu Yaozong' *Baidu Encyclopedia* (in Chinese, Baidu Campus, 2000).

Yu, Kwok-hung *To save the nation a study of Wu Yao-tsung's (1983-1979) ideas of reform (Shi dai de hui ying : Wu Yaozong de jiu guo guan).* Thesis University of Hong Kong, 1997.

Zhao Xiaoyang "Y.T. Wu: Christian Thinker" (*Chinese Theological Review* 26, 2014).

2. **Kim Jae-Joon (Korea: 1901-1987)** *Human History in the Third day*

For a country whose history has seen intense suffering over long periods, the people's experiences for decades prior to 1945 were particularly tragic in Korea. Movements for independence from Japan, which culminated in 1919 but continued until 1945, led to severe and continuing persecution in which many Christians, along with other nationalists were imprisoned and killed. Yet despite strong opposition from the Japanese authorities to any revival of Korean culture or religion, as well as from the conservative orthodoxy into which earlier liberating theological influences (1890 and on) had hardened, this period was nonetheless one of theological awakening. This was also despite pressure to accept and participate in worship of the Japanese Emperor, and the oppression of a most harsh colonial rule. This was soon followed by the agonies of separated families and communities in a divided Korea, climaxing in the Korean War (1950-1953) and continuing until now.

But for teachers, preachers and theologians there also came the pressures of Assembly trials (1924-53) brought against particular theological teachers and ministers for supposed 'heresy' in Biblical interpretation, social action and ecumenical cooperation. And then there were also the subsequent expulsions of 'suspect' teachers or ministers, which would soon lead in turn to major church renewals.[1]

A Vitally Different Concern
There were however groups of scholars who were laying further foundations for a creative *Korean* theology, among them Yang Ju-Sam, Chon Young Taek, Nam Gyumg-Hyok Chong Kuok-Ok and in particular Kim Jae Joon.[2]

It was in this setting that a group of graduate students, anxious to work for a renewed Korean theology, could be found in 1933 meeting with a young teacher for lectures and discussions under the trees of a central park in Pyongyang. Sometimes there would also be meetings in the teacher's home. The young teacher was Kim Jae-Joon who had been refused official recognition because of his 'critical' and 'liberal' teaching of the Hebrew scriptures. He had earlier returned from studies in Japan and North America, with a deep concern to foster the identity of the Korean Church as part of the one world-wide ecumenical Body of Christ. And this was part of his commitment to nurture the faith of his people who were suffering under a brutal Japanese rule. (It is important to note that Kim had felt forced to leave the then conservative Princeton Seminary, going instead to Western Seminary where he majored in Old Testament Studies 1929-1932).

For this he found much of Korea's existing Christian belief and practice quite inadequate – being largely fundamentalist, highly westernized and church-centred as it was. In the following years Kim and his colleagues would be involved in serious disputes both within and beyond the church, and in both theological and political controversies. These would arise over such issues as their advocacy on behalf of those who had previously been forced to bow at a Japanese Shinto shrine; their use of Biblical criticism in interpreting scriptures; their full participation in activities of the World Council of Churches; and later their opposition to many measures of the Park Chung Hee dictatorship. For all these undertakings Kim maintained concern for theological freedom and ecumenical cooperation, as well as for Korean autonomy in church, theological education and in social or political action.

Kim Jae Joon's own theology is not however easily pigeon-holed. Described by a leading contemporary colleague as expressing a conservative faith through a progressive theology, Kim owed much not only to Karl Barth and the two Niebuhrs (Reinhold and Richard) but also to his careful study of Korean society and culture. "I did not want to choose one theology over another – for theology is not the absolute. Christ's life and deeds are the centre: the image of Christ as he is in our life today", he said when remembering those years.[3]

He had earlier translated Mackintosh's *Types of Modern Theology* and in 1949 introduced Kierkegaard together with Barth and Brunner as leading figures in a new orthodox theological movement.[4] He especially valued Kierkegaard in his critique of 'reason in religion' and said of him that "he was the greatest of modern thinkers, greatest in aesthetics, ethics, philosophy, and theology..."[5] Nonetheless any use by Kim of western theological insights was still placed in the context of eastern cultural and religious tradition, for his studies had been deeply grounded in Confucian philosophy and in Korean history.

Rather than any theological system or philosophy however, it was the living, suffering and risen Jesus who remained the centre of his theological witness throughout the next five decades. This enabled him, with colleagues such as Jeon Gyeong Yeon and Kim Chung Choon, to maintain a prophetic witness through the turmoils of colonial oppression and the church conflicts of the 1930s and 1940s, through the Korean war and subsequent sufferings, as well as under the persecution by authoritarian regimes of the 1960-80s. Kim's brilliant teaching, writing and animating was to bear fruit in the formation of the more 'liberal' Presbyterian Church of the Republic of Korea (PROK);[6] formation of the Chosun Theological Seminary (later Hankuk Theological Seminary);[7] and in the inspiration of 'Third Day', indigenous and Minjung theological movements. He has long provided inspiration for the development of democratic, social and urban mission movements which still continue.

During those fifty years Kim Jae-Joon published a number of significant journals which again and again presented new images of the life of Jesus then and now. These notably included the monthly *Crusader* (1936-63) and the quarterly *Third Day* (1970-1984). He also came to be regarded not only as the 'leading' and 'most creative' Korean theologian in his work over six decades',[8] but was also acknowledged as an eminent writer in Korean literature, both secular and religious, being for example, editorial writer for the *Daihan Daily News* for 10 years (1963-1973). Apart from more than thirty periodical volumes he edited, there are eighteen volumes of his collected books, articles and memoirs which have now been wholly republished.[9] Unfortunately little of this extensive oeuvre is yet widely available in translation. What follows is to be considered as only an outline draft of its significance.

A Living Theology

Kim Jae Joon's theology was shaped firstly by the largest view possible of God's creative rule and place in creation and history, as well as by faith in Jesus Christ who embodies that rule in our midst. *All* things, all peoples, all aspects of human life belong to God alone: the natural and the transcendent, the 'secular' and the 'religious', the personal, the ethical and the political. All these aspects God's plan and purpose – which alone is infallible – are always historical, concerned as much for building the nation as for fostering the church's life, as much for human rights as for a personal encounter with Jesus. For the Kingdom of God comes in history where the life of Jesus was and is being incarnated as a 'history within our history'. This will include personal and daily life, vocation and calling, political and economic choices, commitment to human rights, and cultural creativity in the life of the secular world. The Spirit of God is to be found in every part of Korean life and history, yet history itself is not revelation. It only becomes so through interpretation by faith, when it can then become our internal history.[10]

Regarding history itself Kim declared that "Christianity is putting the redemptive history of God's kingdom *into* history so that human history is transformed into God's kingdom…We have received God's commission to transform Korean history into God's kingdom…Therefore we should endeavour to make the Christian spirit to be the transforming soul in the fields of politics, economics, education, and culture of Korea".[10] The Kingdom of God is both a present and future reality, both transcendent and imminent , and thus is called by Kim a 'paradoxical synergism'.

So the Bible too is to be taken as historical literature, in order to understand its origins, its authors and its original readers. The supreme role of scripture through which the living lord is mediated by the Holy Spirit, was not for Kim any reason to abandon careful scientific analysis of its text, nor was it reason to deny the presence of human error which may also be discovered there. But the Bible remains 'inerrant' in the sense only that it brings testimony to Jesus Christ our Lord and teaches us the way of salvation through and in Him. But there must be 'a free study of all the facts', which doesn't assume inerrancy of the Biblical record but can affirm the Bible's 'infallibility and norm' for God's purpose in our world, holding the centre of faith from 'the Living God and Jesus Christ'.[12] Yet the most important truths are always conveyed through symbols and allusions for they deal with questions of life, faith and spirit. And the response to be made is personal, historical, and spiritual, not conformist, mechanical or pietistic.

The Christian life therefore is participation in Jesus' historical life now, *for* the Kingdom of God, *in* the secular world. [13] It is a pilgrimage in hope, in which witness and life is always moving forward; a Christian humanism of free obedience to God; a personal relationship to Jesus and a sharing in his life for humanity in all secular life.[14] This means watching for the 'signs of the times' to discern the historical providence through which God in Jesus Christ is now acting: through love and service for humanity, especially for the needy, for poor farmers and labourers, and for those in factory, classroom and hospital.[15]

In 1972 Kim's younger colleague Kim Jung-Joon – then principal of Hanshin Theological Seminary – summarized Kim's deepest concerns in theology under the five heads: 'Bible', 'World', 'Faith's Adventure with Christ', 'Man – so loved', and 'Korean Culture'.[16] In Biblical study his greatest concern was to elucidate the teachings of the major Old Testament prophets and of Jesus Christ in the Gospels. These together he regarded as forming the central Biblical tradition, by which all scripture is to be measured. "He was deeply committed" writes Kin Jung-Joon, "to introducing the real world of the Bible to ordinary Christians, so that it becomes, by grace, the Living word Jesus Christ".[17]

In theological study, teaching and preaching this means that the adventure of faith in Jesus Christ requires freedom from any denominational tradition, with a Gospel-given freedom and to evaluate accepted dogma by the life and ministry of Jesus, and to recognise the good work of the Spirit wherever that is found. This is also freedom for innovative mission, for and to the world, with freedom too to collaborate for good with those of any faith.

Talking of the main religious traditions known in Korea Kim sharply rejected the judgement of many earlier missionaries that these were the 'products of demons'!, and declared rather that they are "pieces of God's word being worked out by the Holy Spirit. It is dim and not complete as if one sees it in a moonless night but now it can be made clear and complete in Christ."[18] In 'doing theology' this also means that the adventure of faith in Jesus Christ requires freedom from any denomination's requirements, freedom to measure all teaching and endeavour by Jesus' life, and freedom for mission, for and to the world.

A Movement in the Korean and wider World

Such positions were remarkable and courageous in the setting of an embattled, and missionary-dominated church of the 1930s and 1940s. But they were rendered more so in a Korea under Japanese – or later military – oppressive control, by Kim's insistence that Biblical and theological affirmations were directly relevant to the concrete experience of women and men: to their socio-political history, their culture and their ethical lives. For him there are always clear requirements for the building of Korean democracy, for social justice, peace and human rights. Kim never tired of teaching and writing of these issues in cultured Korean prose, until his death in 1987. His forceful interpretations of Biblical teaching in the light of dynamic Korean traditions have therefore inspired generations of Korean pastors, lay-leaders and theologians.[19]

This is due at least in part, to the close relationship that Kim establishes in his theology between the sovereign grace of God in Jesus Christ and the actual world of human life, its cultural traditions and its political development. The world that God so loved becomes in Kim's teaching the concrete reality where women and men are suffering, hoping and struggling for justice and peace. And this is where they must be met and sustained. Yet despite the painful conditions of so much of

Korean lived experience the world remains within God's rule and under the Lordship of Christ, Kim declares. For him "the vertical dimension is enclosed in the horizontal dimension".[20] Here is an understanding of Christ's humanhood which brings 'the divine' into daily human experience to rescue, release and restore. The potential in men and women for renewal, freedom and the divine life remains unlimited therefore, and justice and love, not grasping power, will outlast all else.

Such justice and love are always required also of the church in any action for deprived and tortured women and men. In this prophetic ministry the Church is also sustained by, and contributes to, the worldwide church, for this real world is also where God is already working within, throughout *and beyond* the Church. But by participation in community and political life for the goals of justice and peace, the Christian community also works to reclaim and develop Korean culture as a significant contribution both to nation-building and to humane world culture. "We are called" he wrote in an article of the *Crusader* in 1956, 'to enact the liberating history of Christ within the history of the nation, so that Korean history itself may be transformed'.[21]

Some of the cultural and political implications of this statement are made clear in an article written some years later in which Kim writes that "The tasks which the church in Korea faces are to understand more deeply the heart, faith and work of Jesus Christ, instead of swallowing western Christianity — which was contaminated by Graeco-Roman culture and power-politics — to reformulate the pattern and life of the Christian Church according to the heart and life of Jesus Christ, while absorbing and fulfilling our own indigenous culture."[22]

The Witness Continued
Later developments in Kim's thought and actions elaborate these concerns. As the image of Jesus' life, death and resurrection is central throughout his teaching, by the early 1970s, when the military dictatorship of Park Chung-Hee had become more brutal, Kim's theology came to centre

more upon Jesus' suffering servanthood.[23] Belief in the Cross was now much more than an important doctrine. It had become again the actual experience of many: "nails in my hands and feet", he would say, thinking also of all who resisted military or industrial oppression.[24] This was contrasted to any pious romanticism for the cross or any 'mysticism of the suffering Jesus', as well as to any reverence given to the cross as a sacred 'monument' by either church or individual believer. By then many of Korea's most able theologians, along with students, teachers and pastors were asking the same question as Kim as they sought a contextual Korean Christianity. "If Christ came personally to Korea what might he do…" he asked, when the people struggle against political lawlessness, economic exploitation and the agonies of torture for asking and demonstrating for such questions.

Younger theologians were also writing in Kim's *Third Day* magazine (banned 1974) that suffering and resurrection, crucifixion and the 'third day' are inseparable, both for our reconciliation in Christ and for the restoration of human life in individual persons and in society.[25] "The cross", he declared, "is not only a death of which we say 'Christ died for me', for this may still remain on a level personal satisfaction. The cross is heavier than that".[26] It is both the sign and the power of resistance to entrenched evil and unrighteousness. It is obedience to God rather than to men; it is the means whereby both body and spirit are transformed.[27] Such theology was to inspire and empower many in the years when the oppressions of exploitation in industry, of military rule and the extremes of wealth and poverty which that enforced became more fierce in the 1970s and 1980s.

We may share the suffering of the cross, writes Kim, "whenever we do the truth, declaring in a Christ-like evangelism both what is good and what is evil". But more than that, for Christ's body the church, committed to justice and love, the cross comes to be a daily experience as it stands with exploited and oppressed women and men. "Life is living with death and death is the start of living – the door to the 3rd day of transformation".[28]

Kim Jae-Joon continued to publish 'the liberating history of Christ' and to work for the restoration of Korean democracy during the years of enforced exile in Canada (1974-1983). By then his pioneering insights were being developed by ministers and students, urban mission teams, rural workers and teachers, many of whom had been associated with the *Third Day* group and were now exploring and applying Korea's *Minjung* theology. During his ten-year exile in Canada Kim also continued to actively support movements for the restoration of democracy in Korea, for the unification of Korea and for other related international movements such as Amnesty International which were acting directly for human rights in Korea.

But Kim's legacy is much wider than this: it is acknowledged in Biblical studies, education and literature, in Korean Ecumenism and church mission, in developing a Korean political theology, in movements for greater democracy and in social ethics. This legacy has slowly become known by theologians, activists and ecumenists through the region and beyond and now more so through English-language introductions to his work now being available.[29] And for these he not only talked, states Kim Chung Choon, but also acted: "his own body was given" for God's purpose of a liberated, renewed Korea.[30]

Endnotes

[1] Daniel Adams (2012) p.97f.

[2] Refer to England, John C. et al. 2004) 3. 502ff.

[3] Conversation with this writer Dec. 1976. Along with references to Ryu Dong Shik, Kim Chung Choon and Hwang Sung Kyu below see further on Kim's theological background and understanding in Adams op cit. 87ff., Park 2003, 81ff.

[4] This was in a public lecture entitled 'The Change in the Trend of Theological Thought before and after the Great War' in the first Presbyterian national convention for youth held in the Seoul Citizen's Hall.

[5] Jon Stewart (2008) 137.

[6] The PROK was founded by Kim Jae Joon and his colleagues in response to the PCK's suppression and eviction of teachers and students who rejected highly conservative interpretations of scripture or dogma. Largely through Kim's own endeavours the church established a more liberal and contextual theology along with a full ecumenical participation in world church relations. It remains the most progressive among the

many Presbyterian churches in Korea, voting in favour of the ordination of women for the ministry and for eldership in 1956, and ordaining women first in 1974. The church places strong emphasis on social and political action and has promoted the *Peace-Reunification Movement* since 1987, and, since 1993, the *Peace-Unity Movement* and the *Restoration of Life Movement*.

[7] Kim Jae Joon had been invited to form Chosun Seminary first in 1940, but this had had to await establishment by Kim, along with Song Chang-geun, and Kim Dae-hyun, until after the Pacific War. The principles upon which it was founded listed the role of the world-wide ecumenical faith community, respect for traditional piety and freedom, the possibility of diverse theologies, acceptance of Biblical criticism, and constructive and ethical ministries for the church. (Adams op.cit.) 88. Teachers and students of Hankuk Seminary would later demonstrate their concern for social and political justice, for human rights, for peaceful reunification of Korea and for ecumenical unity of the church. Many of them also suffered harsh imprisonment for doing so,.

[8] Ryu Dong-Shik (1960) 168

[9] *JeoJak Jeon Jib (Collected Works* (1992) For titles of some of the many articles, dialogues or interviews (in Korean) in which much of Kim's thought was communicated see Park Chung Shin (2003) 281.

[10] Hwang Sung Kyu (2005) 137, 195ff..

[11] *Collected Works of Kim Chai Choon* 4.303f. Cited by Hye Kyung Heo (2015) 17.

[12] Hwang Sung Kyu (op.cit.) 73f. Chaps.1 and 3 are devoted to these issues.

[13] ibid. 211 and chap.11.

[14] ibid. 111

[15] ibid.204

[16] Kim Chung Choon (Nov.1972) included in Kim Chung-Choon (2009) .291-299

[17] ibid.

[18] *Collected Works* 7. 341f. Cited by Hye Kyung Heo.

[19] See especially *Collected Works* 1. (1971), passim.

[20] Adams (op.cit.) 91

[21] Ryu Dong Shik (op.cit.)169.

[22] Harold S. Hong et al. (1966) 36.

[23] In letter to this writer (April 1977).

[24] Suh Nam-Dong 'Theology of the Cross in Recent Journal Articles' *Northeast Asia Journal of Theology* 13, (1974) 23f.

[25] Kim Jae Joon Archive document (1973) ,*Rita Mayne England Collection*, Knox College,Dunedin, ANZ.

[26] Kim Jae Joon Archive document (1974).

[27] Kim Jae Joon Archive document, (1976).
[28] Kim Jae Joon Archive document (1974a).
[29] See e.g. Adams op.cit. chap.6, Hwang Sung Kyu (op.cit. 2005).
[30] Kim Chung Choon (op.cit. 2009).

Select Bibliography and Works cited

Primary

Kim Jae Joon *Introduction to the Bible.* (Seoul n.p., 1960)

———. 'The present Situation and Future Prospect of the Korean Church' in Harold S. Hong et al (eds.) *Korea Struggles for Christ Memorial Symposium for the Eightieth Anniversary of Protestantism in Korea* ed. Harold Hong et al. (C.L.S., 1966).

———. *JeoJak Jeon Jib* (Collected Writings in Korean) 5 vols. ed. Choong Woong Sup (Hankuk Seminary, 1971).

———. 'The Relation Between Suffering and Resurrection' (*Third Day,* April 1973).

———. 'The Logic of the Third Day and the Tomorrow of History' (*Third Day,* Oct. 1974).

———. 'Theology of Resistance' (*Third Day,* April 1976).

———. *Beom Gang Ki* (The Way I See Things: Auto-biographic Essays) 6 vols. (Toronto Independent Newspapers, 1981-1983).

———. *JeoJak Jeon Jib* (Collected Writings*) 18 vols. (Hanshin University, 1992).

———. *Essential Writings (Gil Seon-Ju)* Korean Christian Leaders Series (KIATS Press, 2009)..

Secondary

Ahn Byung-Mu "The Korean Church's Understanding of Jesus: an Historical Review". (*Internat. Review if Mission* 74. 293, Jan. 1985 https://doi.org/10.1111/j.1758-6631.1985.tb03321). Adams, Daniel J. 'Kim Chae Joon and Liberal Theology' in *Korean Theology in Historical Perspective.* (ISPCK, 2012) chap.6. Choi Jong Ho, Karl Barth: *The Theology of the Word of God* (Han Dool Press, 2010), England, John C. et al (eds.) *Asian Christian Theologies: Research Guide.* Vol.3 Northeast Asia. (ISPCK, Claretian, Orbis Books, 2004) 517, 539, 542-544.

Hong Chi-Mo 'Kim Jae Joon as seen from the Perspective of Korean Conservative Theology' (*Chongshin Review* 2.1, Oct. 1997).

Hong, Harold S., Won Yong Ji, & Chung Choon Kim (eds.) *Korea Struggles for Christ: Memorial Symposium for the 18th Anniversary of Protestantism in Korea.* (CLS of Korea, 1966).

Hwang Sung Kyu *The Life and Theology of Changgong, Kim Chai Choon.* (Hanshin University Press, 2005).

Hye Kyung Heo (Han) *The Liberative Cross: Korean-North American Women and the Self-Giving God* (Wipf and Stock, 2015).

Kim Chung-Choon *Essential Writings* (KIATS Press, 2009)

Kim Joshua Jin Woon "Ethics as the command of God in Karl Barth's theology" (www.academia.edu/8087260)

Lee Kee-Young "The Implications of Paul's Understanding of the Corinthian Church for the Unity in Mission and Ministry of the Korean Presbyterian Church" (Dissertation, San Francisco Theological Seminary, 1988).

Min, Kyung-Bae *A History of Christian Churches in Korea*. (Yonsei University Press, 2005).

Park Chung-Shin *Protestantism and Politics in Korea*.(University of Washington, 2003) espec. chap.2.

Ryu Dong Shik (ed.) *Hankuk Eni Kitokkyo Sasang* (Christian Thought of Korea) (Seoul, 1960).

Ryu Dong Shik 'Rough Road to Theological Maturity' in G.H. Anderson (ed.) *Asian Voices in Christian Theology*. (Orbis Books, 1976).

Sang Taek Lee *Religion and Social Formation in Korea-Minjung and Millenarianism*) (De Gruyter, 1996)

Sawa Masahiko. *Nam-Boku Chosen kurisutokyo shiron* [The history of Christianity in South and North Korea]. (Nihon Kirisutokyo-dan Shuppankai, 1982).

Stewart, Jon (ed.) *Kierkegaard's International Reception: The Near East, Asia, Australia and the Americas*. (Ashgate, 2008).

Suh Kwang-sun David *The Korean Minjung in Christ* (CCA CTC, 1991).

Suh Nam-Dong 'Theology of the Cross in Recent Journal Articles' (*Northeast Asia Journal of Theology* 13, 1974).

3. Daniel T. Niles (Sri Lanka: 1908-1970) *Christian Selfhood and Secular Engagement*

To believe is simply to meet the Risen Christ...to know him in the actuality of the life he lived and to accompany him in the life he is living now.[1]

The particular thrust of these words of D.T.Niles may seem to have a deceptive simplicity, but any glimpse of his life in Ceylon, Asia and world-wide – or in his writings in more than 25 volumes – reveals a theological witness to such a meeting with God in Jesus Christ that has extraordinary power as well as presenting us with disturbing implications. Of the theologians I have elsewhere designated 'Watershed', only Devanandan's[2] work was known to him yet he displays many of their principal insights as he does of other colleagues, in what is still one of the more comprehensive of Asian theologies.

The period 1930-1970 in Ceylon (renamed Sri Lanka in 1956) was one of unprecedented social and political change. Nationalist movements achieved the end of colonial rule (1948) but were soon fragmented by violent communal conflicts. Severe socio-economic inequities and the contraction of the plantation economy increased and the division between a western-educated, middle-class elite and the rural peasant majority widened. Following independence the resurgence of Sinhalese culture and Buddhist religious (and political) practice led to reduced privileges for the Hindu, Muslim and Christian minorities, as well as to deep political tension and racial conflict.

In the decades preceding and following 1948 a number of Christians stood out as leaders in both church and community: in legal and labour reform, examples would include K. Ekanayake and James Pieris; in advocacy for social justice, Joachim Pillai, F.O. Tambimuttu and Tissa Balasuriya; in the recovery of national culture, religious reconciliation and theological renewal, Edmund Pieris, Lakdasa de Mel, T. Isaac Tambyah, Charles Wickremanayake, S.S. Selveretnam, Lyn de Silva, Laksman Wickremasinghe and Yohan Devananda.[3]

Encounter with Jesus Christ

D.T. Niles, whose own writing spanned the years from 1937-1970, worked closely with many of these colleagues. But it is probably true that none contributed to his wide-ranging ministry and thought more than his wife Dulcie, herself an author.[4]

"The Gospel of Jesus Christ begins", declares Niles, "with God's incursion into human history. He came...he comes. And when he comes, many if not all of the fixed points of one's life get jolted out of position".[5] This divine initiative of God and the sovereign freedom of God's unavoidable, all-embracing will and activity is, for Niles, the overwhelming reality in the universe and the determining centre for all theology. For God who comes to us in Jesus Christ comes unpredictably, re-ordering our lives and the life of nations. Here is one who is previous to us in our creation, in our 'image-relation' and in Biblical covenants; previous in our family or friends, in Christian church, or neighbours, in nature and in the universe itself. For there the Holy Spirit is always and everywhere at work.

These are not for D.T. merely doctrinal assumptions, whatever relationships to Arminian, neo-orthodox or ecumenical theologies, to his experiences in the Student Christian Movement, at the Tambaram Conference of 1938 or in the Ashram Movement, may be seen. He has come to affirm the 'previousness' of the One God in every dimension of existence primarily through a steadily deepened, intensely personal encounter with Jesus in his human life and passion. However widely the affirmation allows him to interpret the mission of God 'upon the earth', in the movements of 'secular' history or the final consummation of all things, these all unfold from this transforming encounter and the all-encompassing enterprise of love which there grasps us.

Niles is of course always speaking to his beloved churches in Ceylon/Lanka, drawing on their long history and exposing them to the larger currents of ecumenical thought and action, especially of these throughout Asia. But he is also responding at a deeper level to the contemporary history of Sri Lanka and the region as a whole. He is discerning there the wideness of God's grace in the Jesus who meets us both in nature and 'secular' history and in God's mission for a new humanity. We can recognise that although he was leader of a numerically small Christian minority in Ceylon he yet speaks directly to the 'post-Christian' worlds we know.

"Jesus meets us", says Niles, as God-with-man/woman made flesh, and we are not called to analyze the divine and human elements in that mutuality. "We can only know God as God is with us. There we find the surprise of his complete humanity, yet in him God's rule had come within the reach of men and women: the grace of God is known to be reality".[6]

"Have you met him?" he asks. "If you have then you know how you came to recognise and accept his hand upon your shoulder, his yoke upon your neck, his goad behind your feet, his call within your heart. You know yourself as his possession and him as possessor".[7] For here is the authority of a human life as 'carpenter' (i.e. Rabbi) and confessor, lived wholly with and for others in an incognito servanthood. Yet we discover, Niles affirms, that he does for us and for all women and men what we cannot do for ourselves: He meets and claims us, uncovers sin and evil, gives acceptance and forgiveness and changes and fulfills our lives. Whether all our immediate needs are met or not He satisfies us with Himself. And the ways he meets us always point beyond themselves to a larger divine reality.

Into all the (secular) World

For there are other surprises. In Him we discover all the concrete particulars of life made richly meaningful, as God becomes human throughout the whole of Jesus' life; in the womb and human flesh, in friendship and human weakness, by being classed with outcastes and renegades in life and in death. Here we begin to see that the world is already God's, for it is now "the place where the incarnate God lived, and lives, where Jesus was crucified and still suffers, where the Risen Lord is continuously at work and where we work with Him".[8]

Because Jesus is risen and present now through the Holy Spirit, the whole of creation becomes meaningful, *all* things cohere and history itself has a purpose of which he is the climax now and to come. Because Jesus is met only in concrete situations, in church and in Bible-study, in concrete social commitment and in the marginal person, he claims us for his way of life in the world. We are "delivered from religious preoccupations and involved in the secular life, because that is the life in which He, the risen Lord, is involved".[9]

Once possessed by him, declares Niles, the heart of Christianity is not a concern for one's soul but concern for a new world; it is not any concern for a 'systematic theology' (!) but for peace on earth. We have been invited to share in this new creation which begins on earth and will also exist beyond this world. Niles insists that it is *human history*, both secular and religious, where God is working to complete creation, and where the Realm of God is coming in just the same way that future breaks into present. Creation, redemption and consummation form one continuous and interpenetrating movement within, but pointing beyond, history so that even deep tragedy, evil and travail can be interpreted and borne.[10] Personal history, secular history and church history are therefore woven together in one movement to become one richly diverse humanity, embraced by one judgement and one providence.

Yet this has also unfolded precisely in the *personal* encounter with Jesus Christ. "In the talk of Jesus we hear not only the accents of home and the laughter of children but also the hum of the bazaar and the talk of the town; we feel not only the whiff of the wind and see the glory of the sunrise but also catch sight of the rich at their feasting and the religious on their parade; we are introduced not only to the carpenter and the shepherd, the fisherman and the farmer but we are also introduced to the king and the emperor, the servant and his lord".[11] In Him also we discover that the self-emptying presence of God-with-us is also the truth of creation in its entirety: God enters, bears and suffers with, working hiddenly in, all created things. The pressure upon our lives of liberating love which we find in Jesus is the same pressure moving all history and nature towards transformation. We stand, affirms Niles, between the liberty of the people of God and the liberation of the whole cosmos.[12]

Christian Community within the Human Community

Nowhere is the impact of such insights made more clear than in Niles' theology of mission. The urgency of proclaiming and joining God's mission is the controlling motive in all his writing and ministry as well as being the central hermeneutic principle of his theology. We know the teachings of Jesus, Niles affirms, and therefore also know how to understand the will of God, only when we 'accompany him in the life he is living now': to be saved is to participate in God's work for a new world. It is there that the mission of God within and beyond the Church is uncovered: it embraces all women and men in their histories, their life together, 'else it had passed by me', echoes Niles. "There is no one about whom there is *no* truth in Jesus Christ', and no nation – all the groupings in which men and women belong – is outside God's purpose."[13]

In this mission many histories find their place in one history: God is found in Jesus Christ to be in every here and now and through the Holy Spirit to be moving in every renaissance of culture, society or religion. We can therefore find a corporate identity with Buddhist or Hindu colleagues in joint work on social issues and human development, as Niles himself did in many settings and situations. But this for him, as with the recognition of grace known in other faiths, was held together with, and found in, the fullness of Christ's stature – the recapitulation of all things in Christ which begins here and now.[14]

Niles sees one of the proofs of this in the way that the renewal of the Church has frequently come about only because of the pressure of secular events. But the church is not to be equated with the Kingdom of God on earth nor is the Kingdom merely the heavenly abode of 'saved souls'. Church and world are instruments of God's mercy and judgment for each other as are the church and other faiths in encounter and dialogue. So too, church and society form one organic whole and the Christian community is always part of the larger human community where God with man or woman shares pain, bears evil and creates a new humanity. Yet the church can be a 'clearer stream' within this tide, and D.T. describes it as not only the outcome of the mission of God but also the instrument and sign, a pointer to what is coming in every place: a more human world, liberated, reconciled, diverse and interdependent.

In such a mission the Holy Spirit for Niles is no mere fan to 'circulate warm air in the room', as much 'evangelism' is confined to doing (!) She is rather a desert wind which sweeps us into the movement of the Gospel whereby new humanity, judgment and grace explode into all history. She does this by placing signs of God's coming realm in all the secular life of the world – wherever wrongs are righted, selfhood achieved, desperate needs met – and by leading the Church out to join the Risen Christ as he suffers, befriends, challenges and transforms there. So the church finds its selfhood first not in reorganization (even for the 'Three Selfs'[15]), nor in increased numbers, but in discovering itself addressed by God in its own culture and society; its particular place in which it is to share in God's mission.[16] And it will do this, Niles declares, through worship: both the renewed worship of Word and Sacrament and worship in the liturgy of social engagement.

This is because just as it is seen in the New Testament, so also there are now to be *koinonia* which are defined by their location (Corinth) and also those who are defined by, for example, their occupation (Caesar's household). Their function is that of salt and leaven in every secular location, life-situation and occupation. "The essential liturgy is the normal day-to-day work of the people of God in agriculture, justice, industry, politics".[17] And when we are there, "Christ says to us," D.T. told the Inaugural Assembly of the World Council of Churches (1948), "the power you will show is the power of the leaven which I have already hid, the harvest you will reap is the harvest of the seed I have already sown."[18]

Conclusion

If there be any who find in such a portrayal of the claims upon us of the life and work of Jesus any departure from the one Gospel, or find in such an understanding of mission a loss of missionary urgency – something which D.T. Niles' world-wide effectiveness as an evangelist and theologian would easily refute – the claim and the urgency possess us, he says, precisely because the world is already forgiven and saved.[19] God has already acted in the life and death and life again of Jesus and no one remains outside this realm. Nothing less than this is required by the all-embracing, unquenchable Love of the One God. The universe and all it contains is already made, loved and lived in by God; already judged, forgiven and reconciled in the cross; all are within the universal will of God for salvation; all are to be gathered up. Evil is an incursion which, however sharp its destructive force, can thus have no final reality.

But Christ still suffers in all who are tortured, exploited, starved; in all who are divided, or unreconciled; and in those who are yet to consciously respond in knowledge and love. The work of God will continue to its end, accomplishing God's Word, but we are welcomed afar off, to share in the vast work of completing creation; gathered as friends who know the secret, who enjoy and witness to the present fruits of the new humanity; friends who are oppressed with the urgency of joining the work of the Holy Spirit through Christ in all the world; building new signs of that presence, shortening the long pain of women and men and – dare we believe – of God with them.

This was the prophetic teaching of D.T.Niles, lived out in his own home locality, in his own nation's life and in his continuous world-wide commitments. It was seen too in his simple house, in the simplest ashram nearby where he often organized conferences and dialogues, as well as in the incisive and charismatic leadership which he offered with penetrating insight to the Asian and global churches. He was to inspire new ecumenical movements in many areas of life for the Asian churches: in Church music through the EACC Hymnal (1964), in Christian Architecture and Art through the volumes initiated by Masao Takenaka (from 1975) and in the Asian Christian Art Association (from 1978), and in the developing programmes of the EACC (from 1959): for Inter-Church Aid, Church and Society concerns, International Affairs, Life Message and Unity, Youth Work, Cooperation of Men and Women, Witness of the Laity, Christian Literature and Urban-Rural Industrial Mission.[20]

Such a proclamation and living of the Christian faith not only address major issues in the theological traditions of churches in both the east and the west, but provide new visions for our present *living* of the faith in all the complexities, tragedies and delights of our worlds.. Here are significant models of God's purposes for all Asia's peoples and nations;

new forms of both understanding and action in our churches, societies and cultures. Here we can move in hope towards the new humanity, new earth and a new heaven.

Endnotes

[1] Niles (1958) 68

[2] Refer Bibliography for Paul D. Devanandan in 'Towards the New Humanity' (ATESEA Occasional Papers 10, 1990) 52ff., 63ff.; England et al. (2001-2004) 1. 236f.

[3] For these and associated leaders see England et al. 2001) 1. 464-509

[4] See her *The Stranger* (Australian Christian Youth Council, 1965); *The Ascending Way*. (ACYC, 1966); & *My Alabaster Box* (Epworth, 1965).

[5] Niles (1962) 46.

[6] Niles (1972) 68, cf. 27-31.

[7] Niles (1962) 51. The most concise outline of Niles' key affirmations is found in the early compilation by his brother Dayalan Niles *D.T. Niles: A Testament of Faith*. (Epworth Press, 1972).

[8] Niles (1958) 65.

[9] Niles (1962) 52. D.T. much liked to picture Jesus, when standing at the door as in the Holman Hunt painting of 'The Light of the World' as calling us, once we've supped, to leave with Him with His staff and light into the world. After all, Niles would say, the Light is not to be an altar light but a streetlight! C.f. George MacLeod's 'Christ was not crucified in a cathedral altar between two candles but ....on the town garbage heap...'. (*Only One Way Left*. Iona, 1956).

[10] Furtado (1978) 124.

[11] Niles (1949) 260.

[12] Niles (1962) 71.

[13] Furtado (1978) 143.

[14] Kyaw Than (1970) 328f.

[15] Self-government, self-support, self-propagation –See Philip L. Wickeri *Seeking the Common Ground*, (Orbis,1988) 1 & passim..

[16] Niles (1962) 139-169.

[17] Ibid. 146.

[18] Kyaw Than (1970) 324.

[19] Furtado (1978) 176f.

[20] The titles for these programmes would later sometimes change (refer Yap Kim Hao and Ninan Koshy below) but the concerns and programmes would embody the vision and directions that D.T. had originally outlined, see his *Ideas & Services* (1967) below.

Select Bibliography and Works cited

Primary (See also annotations in Ariararajah 2009, 156ff.)

Niles, Daniel Thambyrajah. *That They May Have Life.* (Lutterworth Press, 1952).

_____. *Preaching the Gospel of the Resurrection.* (Westminster Press, 1953).

_____. *Reading the Bible To-Day.* (Lutterworth Press, 1955).

_____. *Living with the Gospel.* (United Society for Christian Literature, 1957).

_____. *The Preacher's Calling to be Servant.* (Lutterworth Press, 1959).

_____. *The Preacher's Task and the Stone of Stumbling.* (Harper, 1958). (Also a digital text).

_____. *Studies in Genesis.* (Westminster Press, 1958).

_____. *As Seeing the Invisible: a study of the book of Revelation.* (SCM Press, 1962).

_____. *For to-day: a series of Daily Bible studies for a Whole Year.* (Lutterworth, 1962).

_____. *Upon the Earth: The Mission of God and the Missionary Enterprise of the Churches. Foundations f the Christian Mission.* (Lutterworth 1962. - also a digital text).

_____. *We Know in Part.* (Westminster Press, 1964).

_____. *Whereof we are Witnesses.* (Epworth Press, 1965).

_____. *This Jesus - Whereof we are Witnesses.* (Westminster Press, 1965).

_____. *The Message and the Messengers: Missions Today and Tomorrow.* (Carey Kingsgate Press, 1967).

_____. *Ideas and Services: a report of the East Asia Christian Conference 1957-67 by the General Secretary.* (NZNCC. 1967).

_____. *The Power at Work Among Us: Meditations for Lent.* (Westminster Press, 1968).

_____. *Who is this Jesus?* (Abingdon Press, 1968).

Niles, Dayalan (comp.) *D.T. Niles: A Testament of Faith.* Epworth Press, 1972.

Secondary

Ariarajah, S. Wesley *We Live by His Gifts: D.T.Niles Preacher, Teacher, and Ecumenist, A Personal Account.* (Ecumenical Institute for Study and Dialogue, 2009).

Arumugam, S. et al. *Dictionary of Biography of the Tamils of Ceylon.* (Tamil National Library, 1996) 124.

Creighton, Lacy, 'D.T. Niles,' in Gerald H. Anderson et al., (eds.) *Mission Legacies* (Orbis, 1994), 362-370.

England, John C. et al. *Asian Christian Theologies.* (ISPCK, Claretian, Orbis, 2001-2004) 3 vols. 1.478 ff.

Fernando, Ransiri J. 'Rev. Dr. D T Niles - Memorable personality'. (*Daily News*, Sri Lanka, June 30, 2004).

Furtado, Christopher L. *The Contribution of Dr. D.T. Niles to the Church Universal and Local.* (CLS, 1978).

Gloede, Günter (ed.) *Anne marie Schäfer: Madeleine Barot; Jean M. Fraser; Gerhard Brennecke, D.T.Niles.* (Heimatdienstverlag, n.d.)

Karoon, DST *D.T. Niles' Theory of Preaching- a Reformation Assessment.* (Ph.D.Thesis North- West University, 2015.

Koshy, Ninan (ed.) *A History of the Ecumenical Movement in Asia.* (WSCF-AP, YMCA-AP, CCA, Vol 1, 2003).

Nelson, J. Robert, 'D. T. Niles: Evangelist and Ecumenist,' (*Ecumenical Trends* 9, no. 7, July- Aug. 1980).

Newbigin, L., W.A. Visser t'Hooft & D.T. Niles. *A Decisive Hour for Christian Mission.* SCM, 1960. Niles, D. Preman *From East and West. Rethinking Christian Mission.* (Challis Press, 2004). Philip, T.V. *Ecumenism in Asia* (ISPCK & CSS, 1994).

Satyaranjan D.S. *The Preaching of Daniel Thambirajah (D. T.) Niles.* ISPCK, 2009). *The Christian Community within the Human Community. Statements for the Bangkok Assembly of the E.A.C.C.* ... 1964. Than, U Kyaw (ed.) *We Live by His Gifts. A* Memorial to Dr and Mrs D. T. Niles. EACC *Asia Focus V,* 1970.
The Common Evangelistic Task of the Churches in East Asia: papers and minutes of the East Asia Christian Conference, Prapat, Indonesia. March 17-26. 1957. WCC, 1957. Weber, Hans-Ruedi *Asia and the Ecumenical Movement 1895-1961.* London, SCM Press, 1966. Yap Kim Hao *Prapat to Colombo.* (CCA, 1994?)

4. Hwang Chiong-Hui (Shoki Coe) (Taiwan: 1914-1988) *Today's Gospel and Context*

Many who knew Hwang Chiong-Hui heard him often refer to the complex issues of identity, name and 'nationality' raised for him by the heritage – and the suffering – of his family and his people in Taiwan, as well as by his later experiences in Asia and Europe. Born a Taiwanese, when Taiwan was part of the Japanese 'empire' yet with strong Chinese traditions, and later studying both in Japan and England, there were many times when he pondered – and also suffered for – that identity. But he also drew on that complex identity for images both of Christian and ethnic self-hood and for those words and actions which faith demands at times of revolutionary change. These would sometimes take the form of a strong denial or rejection ('*m-goan*') of oppression or injustice.¹ At other times they formed the basis for his far-reaching theologies of Christian mission, of the Gospel-in-context and of political responsibility.²

i)   Studies and Life Work

Post-graduate study in Tokyo and Cambridge, along with years of teaching at London University and many other encounters during the years in England, would long enrich and shape his world-wide ecumenical ministries later. He had been introduced to the global ecumenical movement through his attendance at the first World Conference of Christian Youth, in Amsterdam, 1939 and following the war, at the second such conference held in Oslo, 1947. He would come to echo William Temple's words on the world-fellowship of Christian churches, that this 'is the great new fact of our era'.³ All his future ministries would be shaped by, and endeavour to embody and promulgate, that new fact, in its local and Christian contexts, across the region and the world.

So it was that Shoki's own lifelong work for Christian unity, and for theology in its local and global context, that would transform and sustain the theological and ecumenical formation of generations of church leaders around the globe. Groundwork for this was laid during the 16 years when he was principal of the newly-reopened *Tainan Theological College* (1947-1965). In that time the College became a centre of innovative and ecumenical developments in theological education that were recognised throughout the region and beyond, as well as being a strong centre for Formosan/Taiwanese national sentiment and identity. Hwang was twice elected Moderator of the Presbyterian Church in Formosa, in 1957 and 1965 and provided leadership in new forms of joint and local mission which were then commenced, as well as fostering action by the churches upon a wide range of social and human issues.

In 1965, when it became necessary for security reasons to join his family who had left Taiwan in 1959, he joined the W.C.C. *Theological Education Fund* as Assistant Director, later Director, notably during the *T.E.F.'s Third Mandate* from 1970 –77. It was there that he and his colleagues developed the new paradigm for *contextualizing* theology which continues to shape all doing of theology around the world.[4] (See further below.) As T.E.F. Director he provided outstanding leadership in the renewal and diversification of theological education throughout the 'Third World' and became the acknowledged mentor of generations of Asian theologians in particular.

As one concrete expression of Christian contextualizing of the Text in its socio-political context, Shoki also became, in 1973, one of the four initiators of *Formosan Christians For Self Determination*[5], which was to have seminal influence for Taiwan's national consciousness. He was in fact the unofficial leader of *Formosan Christians* for many years. He spelt out fully his profound reasons for such actions in 'My Political Involvement' which was demanded by his 'double wrestle' with being both Taiwanese and Christian.[6]

ii) *Theological Prophet and Pioneer*

It is widely known that Shoki Coe's work and writing has been of pivotal importance for every level of Asian theologies in recent decades, not least for his pioneering explorations in placing the Gospel of God's present and coming reign firmly within the setting of people's neighbourly and national life. These creative insights and practices were however deeply rooted in his own, and his people's, historical experience. For Taiwanese this had included the very long history of its aboriginal peoples, the impacts of colonization by Spain and the Netherlands, China and Japan, and the endurance of continuing martial law for more than half a century.

These were the contexts for his reflection, along with the rapid socio-economic changes brought by industrialization, 'modernization', and urbanization. For Shoki himself there was added the years in both Japan and England, along with exposure to theological movements in Taiwan, Japan, Europe, North America and China. His passion for his own long-suffering Taiwanese people, known to him now in many of their local situations, had grown throughout these years. This was soon being enlarged and deepened by experience with Christian communities throughout Asia, and an increasing involvement in the work of the global ecumenical movement.

In each of these diverse cultural, Christian and political settings Shoki confessed later that he had been forced to recognise the shaping and nurturing power of the concrete context in which people were struggling, suffering, or creating community.[7] Then there was also the larger setting for all peoples in Asia, of the vast social, political and religious revolutions taking place throughout the region. It is in this setting, and in the "living context of nation-building,"[8] of modernization and industrialization, that the guiding principles of the Gospel (the 'Text') are to be followed in new patterns of unity, witness and service, as well as for the building of an authentic missionary community.[9] For this he believed a new *self-identity in context*, and in new hope, would be discovered. "Let us once again be renewed by that mission" he declared, "to go into…the new era, into the new context, seeking our new identity in Him, facing that new context with full self-identification".[10]

But along with this full commitment to understanding the contemporary context of rapid change and revolution Shoki gave as much energy to studying and restating the essential insights of the Gospel – its promises, requirements and experience of present grace. A number of his major articles deal comprehensively with the nature and calling of the Church, the priesthood of all in the Body of Christ, and the unity, confession and renewed humanity of the Spirit-led Christian community. This calling is always for Shoki centred upon the life of Jesus Christ, who is Lord of all life, the good news of God's Kingdom and the vehicle of God's saving grace.[11] Yet simply because of those great truths, the Christian church and the Christian believer are inescapably committed to the world. This is of course because they are rooted in Jesus' life which was and is always 'world-directed' to the actual life-situation of men and women. Both the church and individual Christians exist therefore in two dimensions, in unity with both the presence of God's Spirit and with the diverse worlds of peoples.

Constant social and political change across Asian countries along with church developments and political uncertainty in Taiwan would only underline these insights and callings. They would also demand an awareness "that there is no abiding place which is not subject also to the changes of time". In the church's response to God's presence – the *missio dei* – within these changes, Shoki believed we must recognise, and resist, three infections that have been inherited from Christendom: those of colonialism, denominationalism and pietism.[12] For each of these erect barriers in Christian community and mission: in the 'political disease', between colonizer and colonized; in pride and ignorance, between differing church heritages; and in faith response, between personal discipleship and political involvement.

Following his work from the late 1960s and on it would soon become impossible for theologians or church historians of whatever confession or region to omit the considerations of cultural, social and church context in their teaching or writing. In this world-wide influence his most significant writings come from the period 1962 –77.

iii) *Writings on Faith, World, Church and Ministry, 1962 –1968*

We can discern here at least two major themes:

a) The Life-of-Jesus-with-others

Shoki Coe returns again and again in his teaching and writing to consider the human life of Jesus : his *way* of life, his responses to others, his patterns of friendship and of servanthood ministry. And he would emphasize that in each of these Jesus' *companions* were specifically included. This is Jesus' *human life with others* that Shoki presents as the *first* indigenization or contextualization. This is the humanizing and *making-flesh* which is prior to any mission and prior to any teaching of Christology. And the revolution brought by Jesus Christ is that of "a new life, a life centred in God, open and free for all, a life in *koinonia*".[13] Now as then this is the comprehensive life of Jesus with others which is the presence of God in and for the world. In referring to the life of

Jesus Shoki therefore preferred always to talk of *the-life-of-Jesus-with-others*, thus highlighting both the relational or communitarian and the contextual or embodied dimensions of the Gospel.[14]

It is in this world-directed 'servant' life that both the ministry of the whole Body and the life of the Church itself find their identity and source. Ministry is firstly then the worldly ministry of Christ and only secondarily the ministry of the Church[15] So the full stretch of concern and action in that life is given for ministry both to the faithful community and "by entering deeply into the [revolutionary] world of men (sic.) and nations in which we have been set".[16] In that life too is found the Presence of God fulfilling God's mission in God's world.

The life of Jesus (with his friends) for the world, is now described as the Text, which is not only indigenous to but contemporaneous with *all* places and peoples. All particular worlds and localities – urban, rural, occupational, destitute, institutional – are the diverse contexts for this Text. In this interaction between text and context all genuine mission and ministry are to be found, as both a personal and worldly service. Faithfulness to Text, and creative relevance to Context provide the larger missiological excellence, which must be continually renewed.[17] Shoki would come to describe this interaction as the basis for all renewal of the Church and of theological education. It is found when this is nurtured by the disciplines of the 'first-fruits' community', and when it "leads to a real encounter between the student and the Gospel in terms of his own forms of thought and culture and to a living dialogue between the church and its environment".[18]

b) The Church in its World

For Shoki the Christian church is a servant community directed towards the *world*, finding its local identity and mission in ecumenical, cultural and social encounter with people in all their diverse forms of community. "In adopting this originally secular and political term 'ecclesia' as its name" he declared, "I believe the Church recognised, from the very beginning that it exists between two poles or rather two

Dimensions…a unique relationship with God on the one hand and with the world on the other".[19] Excellence in ministry and theological education – of all in the People of God – and also the catholic fullness of church and ministry, come therefore through meeting and serving the changing demands of particular regions and localities where Christ is *already* present.

"The Gospel is directed to the 'world', that is to persons in society" Coe wrote in 1965, "Therefore populations and the *oikoi* [lit. 'houses'] where they live are a basic concern for the mission of the church".[20] This is because the Divine movement is always outward toward others, in 'a love which seeks not His own'. All engagement in mission is therefore "a decisive test because it involves a moving out of the self. Crossing the frontier then becomes a theological and divine necessity".[21] This is also why Christian response amidst revolutionary ferment in Asian countries must include (indirect) advocacy for liberty and justice in the widest terms, Coe believes. And this will mean participation in the social development which is directed to counter hunger and poverty, even if this will bring danger or suffering for the church.[22]

Coe therefore analyses in a series of articles and books, and in some detail, the revolutionary changes that have come to Asian countries in particular, through political independence, industrialization and urban growth. He considers also the impacts of cultural and religious resurgence, and the rapid changes in medical, media, education and welfare systems.[23] The inadequacies and potential of the Church's response to these changes are also carefully assessed in the light of patterns of church life, ministry and mission which have been imported to Asian contexts. He particularly advocates 'world-directed' mission initiatives, and forms of ministry which are ecumenical and diverse, and others which complement the ministries of those 'set-apart'.[24] His particular concern throughout subsequent endeavours would be the development and renewal of theological education for the new ministries thus now required.

iv) Writings on Text and Context in Theology and Theological Education, 1966 –1975.

In this later period Coe builds on earlier biblical, theological and sociological studies to formulate a theology of contextuality and *contextualizing*, which still awaits full recognition. [25]

a) Here he moves beyond the often past-oriented processes of indigenization to the more dynamic process of *contextualizing*;[26] for Shoki this was always a verb for the on-going work rather than any picture of a completed 'contextualization'. It is often overlooked by those who would criticize Shoki's radical and comprehensive practice in contextualizing, that his over-riding concern was always for the realization and reception of the Gospel's liberation in the concrete lives of his peoples. Because of his own and his people's history, this was always deeply rooted in the diverse and on-going experiences and struggles of particular peoples and communities. For Jesus Christ as the supreme 'contextualization' of the Gospel is present to all women and men in their distinct cultural, religious and socio-political context. And in this lies the catholicity of both God's mission and of the church's theology.

So it is not just the determining power of social or cultural contexts that must be recognised but the nature of the church itself which is found in such diverse settings. For the calling and faith of the one people of one God have "the essential marks of locality and particularity", he would declare,[27] being shaped by the most diverse situations and contexts. The church is both local and 'in pilgrimage', called to be in one place but also called to "frontier-crossing, because it is always *on the way*". For these callings in particular 'contexts', the 'text' of the Gospel is of course supremely important. "...but to think that there might be one pattern suitable for all peoples and times, is what I call the 'cathedral mentality.' God's people, as pilgrims, must be free sometimes to pitch their tents and other times to pull them up and move on; for there is no permanent abiding place between the times".[28]

b) Yet Shoki was concerned to stress that in our faithful Biblical studies also we find that that there is "no pure text without a context (or contexts)."²⁹ There is always the concrete setting of a particular author and of those to whom the text is addressed, as well as historical discoveries and new truths found in the ongoing study and interpretation of the Bible. There are too the prophetic insights called forth by multiple social or political revolutions, which parallel the continuing changes in life-setting and social milieu of local Christian communities.

In any case faith itself is both personal and world-oriented, both an inward and an outward journey for both individual and community. In the light of Jesus' Gospel of the Kingdom it is after all impossible for the faithful community to remain silent when faced with the burning issues of the day for the human community, or when faced with the deep suffering of particular peoples. Mission therefore cannot be separated from 'the structure of social existence in state, industry, economic life and culture'³⁰

He goes on to describe a series of dynamic relationships which are here involved: within the double context of revolutionary or technological change within resurgent Asian cultures and of God's actions in the life and death of Jesus; the 'double wrestle' between the concrete life of our people, as one's own social and cultural realities, and the living Text of Christ's continuing presence. This is the textual-cum-contextual criticism model which he modelled in his *Joint Action for Mission* in Taiwan (1968).³¹ The necessary relationship between such a criticism and the conduct of missions was often spelt out, notably in his lectures at Princeton.³²

Shoki therefore believed that contextualization includes indigenization, but is more dynamic and features openness to change as a key factor, thus going beyond mere indigenization. The full sociological and political mosaic defines and conditions the proclamation of the Gospel and response to it. "Contextualization has to do with how we assess the peculiarity of third world contexts .... (It) takes into account the process of secularity, technology and the struggle for human justice."³³ Here the Gospel provides us with not only the source for all critique of society and culture but also the alternative models that are being brought by the Reign of God.

He would go on to write that this approach presumes "a genuine encounter between God's Word and His world. It seeks to change the socio-economic plight by 'rootedness in ... (the) given historical moment' and by leading the populace out of their plight....[This] assumes that God is doing something redemptive in the target culture: that he is fashioning deliverance from the socio-economic bondage in which the multitudes of the third world find themselves".[34]

c) The steps necessary for such a contextualizing Shoki affirmed, would include, along with critical study of the Text, both a *de-*contextualization and a *re-*contextualization of the context. The forces of colonialism and imperialism, of pietism and denominationalism have again and again imposed false and destructive 'contexts'. So this first requires a criticism and ranking, of both texts and contexts where these have been corrupted or imposed from other histories.[35] Then there must be a critique of resulting institutional forms, along with readiness to re-shape these according to central Gospel measures, and within those the most serious contexts which are strategic for the *Missio Dei*. This will also require of the Christian community repentance, a renewed identity and a willingness to 'go outside the camp' to the new context. It may mean too that new forms of church are to be found precisely in suffering with Jesus and his people.[36]

As for the praxis necessary for re-contextualization, this is simultaneously responsive to God's contextualization in Jesus, and to changing historical situations. In equipping women and men for ministry it comes through a three-fold process of people-formation which reclaims both their actual life experience and the heart of the Gospel. So this process is *Christian/Spiritual* (that is *human* as in the life of Jesus), *theological* (the living truth as known in Jesus), and *ministerial* (equipping each one in the People of God – the Body of Christ – for particular and strategic contexts). [37] In this way Shoki maintains throughout his teaching the recovery of the genuine and concrete context along with the centrality of the-life-of-Jesus-with others as both the hermeneutic measure of scripture and history and also the source of all liberation and larger hope.

v) Conclusion

One of Shoki's latest statements would summarize much of his teaching on the relationship of indigenization to contextualization and of these to both Christian Formation and the reform of the church and of theological education. There he high-lighted again the 'double wrestle' necessary with both text and context; the 'extra-ordinary praxis' of self-emptying involved in theological formation; and the necessity for all theology to be *in loco* and *viatorum* [being pilgrim], as the path to having catholicity.[38]

But he also warns there of the danger of fossilized or alternatively 'chameleon' theology, which may come from an extreme contextualization. True contextuality comes rather from a "conscientization of the contexts in the particular historical moment" which is assessed in the light of participation in the *Missio Dei*. And this requires not only words but actions, for the Gospel is the word incarnate, embodied at whatever cost "for the poor and oppressed, for the prisoners and for the neglected".[39]

Shoki Coe's life, teaching and writing were surely such an embodiment of the Gospel which he knew as God's reign over all of one's human experience and of the particular human worlds. It is impossible anywhere today to work theologically or educationally, without drawing on some part of Coe's writings on Text and Context and much writing and teaching in Asia and further afield demonstrates this. But yet it remains true that in many parts of the region (and of the world) the process and resources which he presents have yet to be fully studied or applied in a *double wrestle* with both the Text of 'Jesus'-life-with-others' and with the concrete particularities of daily life and struggle and joy. The implications of his work for our understanding of today's churches, societies or theologies remain profound and disturbing. Perhaps it is time for us to re-dedicate ourselves anew to building creatively upon his endeavours?

Endnotes

[1] Poon Michael Nai-Chiu (ed.) *Shoki Coe Christian Mission and Test of Discipleship.* The Princeton Lectures 1970. (Trinity Theological College, 2012) 59ff.

[2] Wheeler (IBMR April 2002) p.77; Poon pp.27f.,

[3] William Temple *The Church Looks Forward.* Macmillan (1944), 2.

[4] Reflecting on the development of these concepts in 1978, Coe's close colleague Aharon Sapsezian recalled that long before 1972, when he and Shoki were using these words, "Shoki was famous for using the phrase, 'Text and Context', and he was pleading for contextual criticism as a necessary counterpart of textual criticism. In a sense this is the prehistory of the words 'contextuality' and 'contextualization'. The discussions in the house around these two words were that we should go beyond the older notion of 'indigenization,' in the sense that theology would take into account certain aspects of the culture which had been hitherto neglected, such as the social and economic dimensions". Aharon Sapsezian.in F.Ross Kinsler, 'Mission and Context: The Current Debate About Contextualization.' (*Evangelical Missions Quarterly* 14: I, 1978) 24.

[5] The first issue of the bulletin *Formosan Christians for Self Determination* appeared in March 1973.

[6] *Recollections and Reflections.* Formosan Christians for Self-Determination (1993) 233-262, 267f..

[7] ibid. 118f.

[8] 'Into a New Era Together' (*Theology and Church* IV.1 ,1964) 2.

[9] ibid. 8

[10] Poon op.cit. (2012) 38.

[11] See especially 'The Life and Mission of the Church in the world'. *Southeast Asian Journal of theology ((SEAJOT)* VI.2 1964) 11-36; 'Confessing the Faith in Asia Today' in EACC *Confessing the faith in Asian Today.* Epworth (1966).

[12] ibid. 16f., 30f.

[13] 'God's People in Asia Today' *(SEAJOT* V.2 (1963) 37.

[14] Poon op.cit. (2012)

[15] A Rethinking of Theological Training for the Ministry in the Younger Churches Today'. *(SEAJOT IV.2,* 1962) 10.

[16] 'God's People in Asia Today' *(SEAJOT* V.2 (1963) 9.

[17] *Text and Context in Theological Education.* Tainan Presbyterian Bookroom (1966), also *Northeast Asia Journal of Theology* 1.1,220ff.; *Joint Action for Mission in Formosa - A Call for Advance into a New Era.* (C.W.M.E. 1968), chaps. I and IX.

[18] 'In search of Renewal in Theological Education'. (*Theological Education* 9.4, 1973) 236.

[19] 'The Life and Mission of the Church in the World'. *(SEAJOT* VI.2,1964) 13f.

[20] 'Report of Theological Education in Taiwan Today'. *(SEAJOT* VII.2, 1965) 11.

[21] Poon op.cit. (2012) 42f.

[22] ibid. 55f.

[23] See especially *Joint Action for Mission -* (1968) chaps II –VIII; also'God's People in Asia Today'(1963) 9-13; 'Men in Their Oikoi – Urbanization in Taiwan'. (C.W.M.E., July 1966); Poon op.cit. (2012) chap.3.

[24] 'A Rethinking ....'. *(SEAJOT IV.*2, 1962) 20-25; 'The Life and Mission ...'. *(SEAJOT* VI.2, 1964) 11-38; 'In search of Renewal ...'. (*Theological Education* 9.4, 1973).

[25] Full awareness of particular local contexts of God's world he terms contextuality, while the ongoing wrestling with God's word in such contextuality, is a contextualizing theology, always 'on the way'. T.E.F. Staff Papers in *Ministry in Context* 1972 and *Learning in Context* 1973; Preface to *Christian Mission in Reconstruction* by C.S. Song, 1975; Preface to *The Human and the Holy* edited by Emerito Nacpil and Douglas Elwood, 1978.)

[26] *Recollections* 270ff.

[27] 'God's People in Asia Today'. *Southeast Asia Journal of Theology (SEAJOT* V.2, 1963) 15

[28] Coe (*Theological Education*, Vol.11:1, Autumn 1974) 9.

[29] *Recollections* 119

[30] Poon (op.cit. 2012) 31ff.

[31] ibid. 35; Wheeler 79.

[32] See 'Text and Context in Missions' Poon (op.cit. 2012) 21-38; 'In search of Renewal...'. (*Theological Education* 9.4 1973) 239ff.

[33] *Your Kingdom Come,* World Conference on Mission and Evangelism, n.d. 18.

[34] Writing of Julio de Santa Ana's response to Shoki Richard W. Engle recounts that De Santa Ana says, "The contextualization of theological reflection means opting for a particular social context, that which is low, at the base of the social pyramid. Such an option 'means opposing oppression rather than confirming the powerful in oppressing other social sectors. The contextualizer's task, then, is to enter the culture, discern what God is doing, and work with God to bring about the change which God is (supposedly) fashioning....". 'Contextualization in Missions: A Biblical and Theological Appraisal'. *(Grace Theological Journal,* Feb. 1981) 87ff.

[35] 'Text and Context in Theological Education' *Theological Education and Ministry.*

(Tainan Presbyterian Bookroom 1967), also *Northeast Asia Journal of Theology* (1.1,227, 1967); 'God's People in Asia Today'(1963) 14f.; EACC *Confessing the faith in Asian Today.* (Epworth, 1966) 76f.

[36] *Recollections* 275

[37] 'Text and Context...' *(1967) 232; 239ff.;* 'In Search of Renewal...' *(Theological Education* 9.4, 1973)131ff.

[38] *Recollections* 267-275.

[39] Ibid. 274.

Select Bibliography and works cited

Primary (Works variously authored as C.H. Hwang, Shoki Coe or Ng Chiong Hui)

'A Rethinking of Theological Training for Ministry in the Younger Churches'. *(SEAJOT IV.2.,* (1962).

'God's People in Asia Today.' *(SEAJOT* V.2 (1963).

'Into a New Era Together' *Theology and Church* IV.I (1964).

'The Life and Mission of the Church in the World.' *(SEAJOT* VI.2 (1964).

'Come Creator Spirit for the Calling of the Churches Together' *Ecumenical Review* 16.5, (1964).

'A Report on Theological Education in Taiwan Today'. *(SEAJOT* VII.2 (1965).

'Confessing the Faith in Asia Today'. in EACC Confessing the faith in Asian Today. (1966).

'Men in their Oikoi –Urbanization in Taiwan' *International Review of Mission* 55.219 (1966).

'Text and Context in Theological Education.' In *Theological Education and Ministry – Reports from the North East Asia Theological Educators' Conference, Seoul, 1966.* Tainan: Presbyterian Bookroom (1967).

'Conversion in the Perspective of Three Generations' *Ecumenical Review* 19.3 (1967).

Joint Action for Mission in Formosa; a Call for Advance into a New Era. New York: Commission on World Mission and Evangelism, WCC: Friendship Press (1968).

'In Search of Renewal in Theological Education'. *Theological Education 9.4* (1973).

'Across the Frontiers: Text and Context in Mission.' In *Christian Action in the Asian Struggle,* ed. U Kyaw Than. Singapore: CCA (1973).

'In Search of Renewal in Theological Education'. *Theological Education* 9 (4), 1973).

'Theological Education – A World-wide Perspective'. *Theological Education XI.I* (1974).

'Contextualizing Theology.' In *Mission Trends No. 3,* ed. Gerald Anderson & Thomas Stransky. New York: Paulist Press (1976).

'Contextualizing as the Way Towards Reform.' In *Asian Christian Theology: Emerging Themes*, ed. D.J. Ellwood. Philadelphia: Westminster Press (1980).

Recollections and Reflections. Introduced and edited by Boris Anderson. 2d ed. New York: The Rev. Dr. Shoki Coe's Memorial Fund, for Formosan Christians for Self –Determination, 1993; Tainan: Church Press (1994).

(With TEF Staff). *Ministry in Context. The Third Mandate Programme of the Theological Education Fund (1970 –77)*. Bromley: Theological Education Fund, 1972.

_____. *Learning in Context. The Search for Innovative Patterns in Theological Education*. Bromley: Theological Education Fund, 1973.

_____. *Your Kingdom Come*. World Conference on Mission and Evangelism, n.d.

Note: As unofficial Chairman of 'Formosan Christians for Self Determination' he contributed to their periodical *Self Determination*, from 1973 on.

Secondary

Philip Shen "Concerns with Politics and Culture in Contextual Theology: A Hong Kong Chinese Perception" (*Southeast Asia Journal of Theology* 21no1.1, 1980-81).

C.S. Song *The Compassionate God* (Orbis, 1982).

Kosuke Koyama "Spiritual Mentors: Christ's Homelessness" (*Christian Century*, July 14-21, 1993).

Po Ho Huang Ng Chiong Hui (Shoki Coe, Hwang Chang Hui)" in *A Dictionary of Asian Christianity* ed. S.C. Sundquist (Eerdmans, 2001).

Ray Wheeler 'The Legacy of Shoki Coe'. (*International Bulletin of Missionary Research*, April 2002).

Kwok Pui-lan *Post-colonial Imagination and Feminist Theology* (Westminster John Knox, 2005).

Simon Shui-Man Kwan "From Indigenization to Contextualization: a Change in Discursive Practice rather than a Shift in Paradigm". (*Studies in World Christianity* 2005 11:2, 236-250).

Paul D. Matheny *Contextual Theology: The Drama of our Time* (Wipf & Stock, 2011).

Jonah Chang *Shoki Coe An Ecumenical Life in Context*. Geneva (WCC, 2012).

Michael Nai –Chiu Poon (ed.) *Shoki Coe Christian Mission and Test of Discipleship*. The Princeton Lectures 1970. Singapore, Trinity Theological College (2012).

Wilbert R. Shenk 'Contextual Theology: The Last Frontier'. In Sanneh, Lamin; & Joel A. Carpenter, *The Changing Face of Christianity*. Oxford Univ.. (2015) 191ff.

M.P. Joseph, Huang, Po Ho, Victor Hsu (eds.) *Wrestling With God in Context: Revisiting the Theology and Social Vision of Shoki Coe* (Fortress Press, 2018).

See also thetaiwanese.blogspot.com/2005/11/rev-dr-shoki-coe-and-rev-dr-b-t-huang.html

5. **Madathilparampil Mamen Thomas (1916-1996)** *Living Theology in Action*

"Living theology is the manner in which a church confesses its faith and establishes its historical existence in dialogue with its environment."[1]

This conception and application of 'theology' that was developed by M.M. Thomas by the mid-20th century became central to theologians and activists throughout the Asian region in following decades. For Thomas it was the fruit of decades of wrestling with the faith amidst nationalist and independence movements in India and more widely in conditions of what came to be called 'the Asian Revolution'. To this his Christian heritage in the Mar Thoma Church[2] had contributed, along with Gandhi's socialist programmes that he first knew from his father's activities and his mother's work in education.[3] There was also his experience as a teacher at the *Mar Thoma Ashramam* High School, Perumbavoor, where staff gave part of their own meagre salary to support poorest students, along with his own work in founding an orphanage in Trivandrum. He was also strongly influenced by Marxist analysis which he encountered in the Kerala Youth Christian Council of Action. There were also the theologies he studied in his programmes of dedicated self-education: especially those of the Madras Re-thinking Group,[4] along with Asian leaders such as D.T. Niles and Shoki Coe, and thinkers such as John MacMurray, Reinhold Niebuhr and Nicholas Berdyaev.

He began his life-time of writing, mentoring and activism when in 1945-47 he was the first full-time secretary of the *Yuvajana Sakhyam* (the Youth wing of the Mar Thoma Church).[5] Although rejected for both the *Mar Thoma* ministry and for Communist Party membership, he continued his programmes of self-education in the course of committed encounter with the struggles of the poorest and marginalized, with Gandhian thought and practice, with Communist commitment and ideology and with the endeavours of ecumenical Christian movements. From 1947 to 1953 he was on the staff of the World Student Christian Federation based in Geneva, entering more fully the global ecumenical movement of which he would later become a major architect. But it was in local ecumenical groupings in urban and rural communities that he found spirituality, social action and theological reflection joined in fullest prophetic witness. He thus set himself to participate in the revolutionary and ecumenical, movements that were sweeping though the region in post-war years.[6]

As organizer and/or speaker M.M. soon became a key leader in world student and ecumenical movements, while also being from 1957 based at the Christian Institute for Study of Religion and Society (*CISRS*), Bangalore. There he was first the Assistant to the Director Paul Devanandan and from 1962 as Director himself. In 1953 he had already joined the group preparing social questions for the WCC's second Assembly (in Evanston, 1954) and would later chair the world conference on "Christians in the Technical and Social Revolutions of Our Time" (convened in Geneva in July 1966). From 1957 also he would play a key role in founding, with D.T. Niles, U Kyaw Than and others, the first regional ecumenical agency of churches, the East Asian Christian Conference (now Christian Conference of Asia). There he became secretary of the EACC for Church and Society concerns. Amongst other important documents he drafted with D.T. Niles the crucial Report from the 1964 Assembly, *The Christian Community within the Human Community*.[7] Colleagues later affirmed that he was "a quick and clear drafter, producing in these years a stream of literature on Christian social witness which challenged clergy and laity in the churches of Asia to reflection and action on economic and political goals of nation-building."[8]

It is possible here to mention only part of M.M.'s many-sided thought and activism. But every facet of Christian life that his ideological interest, theological reflection, religious experience or social concern touched, came to display new forms at his hands: *Mar Thoma* ideals included those of strong personal, even pietistic, faith, which in his life-work and thought became a holistic spirituality. Christian witness, Biblical interpretation and theology became transformed in the crucible of faith being lived in the everyday *secular* world. *Mar Thoma* concern for the wholeness of the Christian church, became in his life strong motivation for ecumenical activism.[9] Recognition of the histories and witness of living faiths in India and Asia became for him the wider movements through which humanization is being sought. Concern for full human community in the image of Christ became action in struggles for socially just societies and for the poorest, marginalized communities, as well as the sourcing strength for wider political involvement.

Christ and History

Deeply concerned with interpreting the Christian faith in relation to the social revolutions taking place in Asia, which he recognised to be erupting in many forms throughout the region, his point of entry differed markedly from those of most other scholars or theologians at that time.[10] He did not equate social revolution with the coming of the 'kingdom', nor the 'struggling People' with the 'Messiah', nor did he focus upon the solutions to massive inequities or social conflict being proposed by national or international agencies. He was concerned rather that all people (and particularly Christians) discern the presence of a liberating and reconciling God *within* the processes of human struggles for justice, human rights and for peace. How can one share in the struggles for democratic and secular societies while also challenging unjust models of economic and social development? How both participate in social reform movements yet also protest at many levels of injustice still tolerated even there?

Although arising from M.M.'s careful study of leading reformers in the 19th century Indian Renaissance his first major work[11] was also partly a response to Panikkar's works on Christianity and Hinduism.[12] In that he was able to show that far from being unknown or ignored by prominent Hindu reformers, Christ was in fact regularly acknowledged as a source of insight and wisdom. But Thomas applied here also his theological discernment of God's presence within *all* genuine commitment and work for human renewal. He therefore went further to recognise the Christ-like features found and acknowledged in much of the endeavours of such reformers. Here was a deeper unity in major religious traditions in the shared search for social transformation.

Thus it was always the encounter of religion and church with the most urgent social and political issues that Thomas focussed on and in which he found God's movement towards humanity meeting humanity's journey towards God. It was there too that the spiritual dimension of human life was to be found in the prophetic concern of living faiths for social justice, human rights and a new humanity. There, Thomas believed, God was always at work, and 'divine grace' was always offering sharper understandings of human society and deeper experience of just relationships and peace. It is this which is demonstrated supremely in the life and death of Jesus and it was through reflections on the cross that M.M.'s personal faith and social involvement became integrated. In all his writings and work he never ceased to reflect upon the centrality of Jesus Christ, his life, death and Resurrection, for human history.

The cross in particular shows 'divine solidarity with the suffering': an "identification with the poor and oppressed, the refugee and the disinherited, the negro and the outcaste." [13] Yet it also shows both the judgement of, and the release from, human self-righteousness. We see in the cross a 'messiah' who is clearly 'servant' for the rescue and liberation of all, whose life and death demonstrates God's love in a 'cruciform humanity' and which also portrays humanity's highest development. "The cross", he wrote," reveals God and his purpose for His whole creation as Love. It gives the assurance that the whole universe has at its centre not a chaos, not even a cold calculating mind, but a cross - i.e a heart throbbing for all men (sic) with understanding, suffering and forgiving love."[14]

For Thomas, through the risen Christ, the New Man, a new humanity has been created in the image of God. This new humanity, which is far wider than the Church, is the realm where there is forgiveness and reconciliation, grace and justification, renewal, and eternal life. In fact, in every movement that has as its goal the creation of a genuine community, whether it be religious or secular, theistic or atheistic, there is at least an implicit faith-response to Christ as the bearer of new humanity, and Christ is active there.[15] This offers us a basis for openness to, and cooperation with, all religions and ideologies. The mission of the Church is therefore to cooperate with all the movements working for the liberation of human beings in such a way as to bear witness to Jesus Christ as the true liberator of all. The mission is also to establish different levels of Christo-centric fellowships without obliging people to change from one religion to another and without, at the same time, being opposed to such a change.

Salvation as Humanization
Such a theology of mission not only recognises the salvific values within all living faiths but greatly broadens our understanding of what 'salvation' itself is. For Thomas this can only be found in all the processes by which humanity's true purpose is realised and by which human life is rendered more human and humane.[16] He affirmed that this requires both analysis and interpretation of the forces shaping society and culture along with religious/ theological reflection upon these. Because the human person is always a person-in-community and humanization is an integral part of the Christian message of salvation, the realities that de-humanize or destroy individuals and communities must be critiqued and opposed. In this endeavour the crucial requirement is vigorous interaction between a sociology of religion and a theology of society. In earlier writing Thomas thought that either of these could serve as point of entry. "The question is not where you enter, but whether you reach a point where you are aware of the inter-relatedness of the historical and the eternal."[17] Later he would specify that one starts with the humanity of Christ in the life of the world [18] and so our language must be first anthropological before it is theological.

He would later sharpen this insight when considering inter-religious dialogue by recognising more fully both the destructive levels of evil in human action and the humanising forces within living faiths and social movements. The change from his earlier approval for the modernizing force of science and technology to a more 'post-modern' critique of 'development' served also to focus such insights.[19] The quest for full human community can be found in all these and this should be the place to seek both (spiritual) self-understanding and the resources for social transformation. [20] All struggles for basic human rights, for socio-economic justice and for human identity demonstrate this common concern. This commitment to humanization is what provides both a common medium of communication throughout all human-itarian groupings, movements and agencies but also a criterion by which to assess all claims made to offer 'salvation'. This is because Christ and the Commonwealth he brings are always present within the humanizing quest.[21]

So for M.M. it is necessary to affirm both that the Christ-event is central and that this can only be interpreted within its full context which is the quest for fuller humanity shared by all living faiths and cultural quests. This can no longer be limited to changes in the character of individuals when social and political systems de-humanize and even destroy human communities. In any case the radical teaching and life of Jesus Christ clearly challenge *all* abuses of power, or wealth, of property or privilege, and demonstrate a fully human life far more comprehensively than traditional understandings of 'salvation'. This in turn reveals that the function of theology is to humanize all individual and social life by the pattern of Christ's life. Salvation must always render us more human, on the pattern of Christ's fullest humanity.

Living theology
When Thomas works specifically with the functions of theology it becomes obvious that these also are a part of humanization, and theology itself becomes radically reinterpreted. For "Christian theology is not just the Gospel but the interaction between the Gospel and the self-understanding of humans in every age".[22] He would return again and again to depict the concrete implications of this living interaction. It is the encounter between the Word and the World; the participation of individuals and churches in the divine work on earth; for the subject

matter of theology is the life of people, their struggles, suffering and hopes.

But Thomas is not content to say this in general terms. For theology is both to discern the presence of Christ in life of the secular world and also to resource and enable the decisions of men and women in their secular life. It is to "confront the secular world by the Word in the day-to-day lives of common people…moving away from dogmatic, ritualistic and other-worldly spirituality to spirituality of justice in todays' society."[23] The "stuff of living theology", he often said," is the life and witness of the laity in the lay world". It is the layperson trying to "hear and obey the Word of God in the day-to-day decisions of the secular job",[24] whatever their occupation may be. It is also identifying and confronting the evils of dehumanization and their causes: unjust and unequal distribution of land, water, wealth and power; concentration or privatization of people's resources; denial of full human rights or dignity for reasons of patriarchy, commerce or caste; within the cultures of consumerism, capitalist development and the arms race.

'Living theology' is therefore emphatically contextual, being responsive to surrounding social, cultural, religious and political movements and visions. Because its very function is 'humanization' it is responsive to the struggles and sufferings of discarded women, men and children;[25] as it is to the philosophical and ideological visions presented; to the movements for socio-economic justice; and as to the quests pursued within the 'universe of faiths'. There will therefore be differing 'theologies' and differing images of the Christ as these are discovered through the interaction of the life of Jesus with very diverse contexts.[26] He was therefore able to describe the focus of theology as both a "Christ-centred syncretism"[27] and the daily living-out of "suffering love and forgiveness;"[28] a focus both on the church as a new humanity and on the wider movements in which the quest for a new humanity in justice and dignity can be discerned.

But we are to note particularly that 'living theology' is chiefly exercised not by professional 'theologians' but by lay people in their secular situations and their political engagement. For they stand and work at the sharp point of encounter between living faith and worldly life. And this requires also a spirituality that grows within this historical selfhood and action, is prepared to combat all injustice and inhumanity there and envisions its renewal and transcendence.[29] It must also be a spirituality which sustains people in struggle while avoiding forces of corruption and oppression. It will therefore include the reflective practice of open acceptance, religious quest and active forgiveness, both personally and in structures of the collective and institutional life of all in society. All of these flow for Thomas from dependence upon God's grace fully known in the life and death and life again of Jesus Christ.[30]

Application in Life and Theology

When viewing Thomas's life as a whole we can see many ways in which key concepts of his theology were intimately linked, even arose from, his active participation in ecumenical, social and political movements of his time. They arose too from a methodology by which he brought together a sociology of religion with theology of society, the strivings of secular life with the new humanity lived out by Jesus Christ. Involvement in teaching, animating and organising brought fuller analysis of power structures both in Indian or Asian societies and in ecumenical movements and churches. Support for those struggling to bring dignity and restoration to the poorest and most oppressed enhanced his imagery of humanization, and of the messianic forces within people movements. Biblical concepts of prophetic participation and of the 'cruciform humanity' known in Jesus Christ provided fuller theologies in response to on-going historical struggles and conflicts.

Thomas' many-sided thought and commitment of life continue to inspire theologians, sociologists and activists and Studies of his life and legacy are regularly being published.(See below for a selection of these). One of the most recent and fullest of these studies [31] covers many of the aspects of Thomas' life and work which provide basis for future theology and action. These include his pioneer thought concerning the spiritual and cultural dimensions of the changes from traditional societies to modern technical culture (Jesudas Athyal, chapter 1 and Kim Yong-Bock, chapter 9); the role of aboriginal peoples in such changes (Lois Wilson in chapter 3); the paradigm-shift which he charted for ecumenical movements (Hielke Wolters, chapter 5); M.M.'s contributions to more recent eco-justice theologies (George Zachariah, chapter 6); his role in assisting the organization of people's movements (Gabrielle Dietrich, chapter 10); M.M.'s identification of the prophetic concern of living faiths with values of justice and liberation (Ninan Koshy, chapter 12); the ground he provided for much in contemporary political thought (Y.T. Vinayaraj 9chapter13) and for people-organization, protest and political action (C.T Kurien, chapter 13 and Rajendra Sail, chapter 15); along with major new directions in inter-faith dialogue which he charted (Peniel Jesudason & Rufus Rajkumar, chapter 19).

His speaking and writing of doing theology through practical engagement in people's everyday life was clearly applied in numerous endeavours: through participation in both national and Asia-wide urban-rural mission movements; through regular calls upon the Christian and church to take full part in community- and nation-building activities, all that supports an open democracy; in 'subversive' writings and campaigns for human rights and freedom especially during the Indian Emergency; in committed leadership of both regional and global ecumenical networks, especially for Church and Society concerns; being appointed by the Indian government as Governor of the North-eastern State of Nagaland; and into his final years in hundreds of articles and books, both in English and Malayalam. These provided both a series of Biblical commentaries and volumes which addressed urgent religious and political issues.

It may be as the editors of that last volume claim that the banner under which all Christians should continue Thomas' work and endeavours (and which they choose there for their sub-title) is that of "Only participants earn the right to be prophets."

Endnotes

[1] Boyd, R.H.S. (C.L.S., 1975) v.

[2] The reforming branch of ancient Syrian and Orthodox tradition which had later formed close links with the Church of South India.

[3] Laji Chacko (2014), 142.

[4] This group of largely lay theologians spearheaded movements for adaptation and indigenisation in India in the first decades of the 20th century. . The more prominent members of this group were G.V. Job, P. Chenchiah, V. Chakkarai, D.M. Devasahayam, S. Jesudason, Eddy Asirvatham and A.N. Sudarisanam. (See entries above) . The group gets its name from their best-known work *Rethinking Christianity in India* (1938), which appeared on the eve of the IMC World Conference at Tambaram, Madras, in 1938.

[5] Chacko 143

[6] Speaking at the Birth Centenary Celebration of M.M.Thomas in Tiruvalla (31.8.2015) Hielke Wolter characterised M.M.'s theology as one of " Prophetic Participation in Salvation and the Struggle for Humanisation".

[7] This became a seminal volume for much later EACC, and wider ecumenical, programmes. See also *Asian Christian Theologies* ed. by John C. England et al. (ISPCK, Claretian, Orbis, 2001), vol.1, 86f.

[8] Charles C. West (1997) 208-210.

[9] This deep concern would lead to a life-long commitment to action in (and often leadership of) ecumenical ventures, networks and institution, upon which he also extensively reflected and published. For a full outline of these refer to T. Heilke Wolters (1996). Of Thomas's writings see especially *Man and the Universe of Faiths*. (CISRS & CLS, 1975); *Towards a Theology of Contemporary Ecumenism* (CLS, 1978); *My Ecumenical Journey,* 1947-1975 (1990).

[10] The study on *The Christian in the World Struggle* which he and Davis McCaughey completed for the WSCF in 1951 was the first ecumenical response to these "revolutionary changes". He would later write more fully on these for Asia in *The Christian Response to the Asian Revolution.* (1966).

[11] *The Acknowledged Christ of the Indian Renaissance* (SCM Press, 1969).

[12] Raimundo Panikkar *The Unknown Christ of Hinduism* (Darton, Longman & Todd, 1964).

[13] See Hielke T. Wolters in Athyal et al. (2017) 68f. for a full discussion of M.M.'s thought here.

[14] *New Creation in Christ* (1976) 18. See also M.M.'s *Realization of the Cross* (1972), and "Through the Asian revolution, God is preparing the Asian people to face up to the challenge of deciding for or against Jesus Christ." *The Christian Response to the Asian Revolution* (1966) 66.

[15] The understanding of Christ as being the bearer of New Humanity is found also in other Indian theologians such as K.C.Sen, A.G.Hogg, P.Chenchaiah, V.Chakkarai, and P D Devanandan. On the cross God also identifies himself with oppressed and suffering humanity. See also Chacko (op.cit. 2014) 144.

[16] See particularly *Salvation and Humanisation* (1971), and *Man and the Universe of Faiths.* (1975).

[17] Salvation *and Humanisation:* (1971) 9f.

[18] Athyal in The life, Legacy and Theology…(2017) 10ff.

[19] Refer Wati Longchar *(*2017) 119f.

[20] See preface to *Man and the Universe of Faiths*, (1975); and on p.45 "Our thesis is that the universe of unitive faiths is today being brought into the 'anthropological' and 'theological' circle of messianic faiths in a radical way"

[21] Refer to Chacko op.cit. 144 "Thomas interprets salvation as being glorified in the humanity of Jesus Christ or as being incorporated into the glorified humanity of the risen Christ, and therefore, salvation is closely related to the struggle of the oppressed for a richer and a fuller human life or to the process of humanization".

[22] *Religion and the Revolt of the Oppressed.*(1981) 55.

[23] Longchar (2017) 116.

[24] "Criteria of a Living Theology' in T.Dayanandan Francis & Franklyn J. Balasundaram (1992) 10.

[25] Adrian Bird argues (*Theological Signposts,* 2008) that although M.M. did/could not present a 'theology for Dalits', he did nonetheless offer "significant theological signposts for the emergence and development of Dalit Christian theology." This can be seen in Thomas's treatments of concepts of "salvation, humanisation and justice relevant to the emergence of Dalit Christian theology." Bird then outlines this relevance by analysing the discourse of twelve second generation Dalit theologians. M.M. had in any case been long concerned with the circumstances, government policies and potential of Tribal communities. (See. M.M. & Richard Taylor (1965). It was to be cited by James Massey, (2013).

[26] "There is therefore the need for pluralism in Christology to meet the diverse needs of the situation. We must think in terms of Christologies rather than Christology. Each type will have its own apologetic problems …" Editorial: The Christological Task of India" (*Religion and Society, XI.3* September 1964) 5f.

[27] *Risking Christ for Christ's Sake (*1987).

[28] See *The Realization of the Cross.* (1972) & *The Gospel of Forgiveness and Koinonia.* (1994).

[29] This is the 'spirituality of combat' he often referred to, which had first been described by David Jenkins, the director of the WCC Humanum Studies (1969-1975) in his 'Theological Inquiry Concerning Human Rights' (*The Ecumenical Review,*

XXVII.2, April 1975)103. See also *Spirituality for Combat* (1983).

[30] Refer such passages as that in *New Creation in Christ*, p.20; *Ideological Quest within Christian Commitment 1939-1954* (1983) 131; and by David Paton (1976) 239. See also Paulos Mar Gregorios on Thomas: "…M.M. is a pious liberal Christian, devoutly committed to Jesus Christ, but not to the Christ believed by the Church. It is a Christ about whom he learned much from Marxism and Gandhism, and whose main work is in society rather than in the Church or in the individual soul. Christ is at work in technology, in the Asian Revolution, in all social change everywhere. Christ is also the norm for our participation in all change."www.paulosmargregorios. Work of Mar Gregorios /English%20Articles/Tributes/M.%20M.%20Thomas.htm.

[31] Athyal et al. 2017.

Select Bibliography

Primary

Thomas, M.M. *The Christian Response to the Asian Revolution*. London: SCM, 1966.

—————. *The Acknowledged Christ of the Indian Renaissance*. London: SCM, 1969.

—————. *Salvation and Humanisation: Some Crucial Issues of the Theology of Mission in Contemporary India*. Madras: CLS, 1971.

—————. *The Realization of the Cross*. Madras: CLS, 1972.

—————. *Man and the Universe of Faiths*. Bangalore: CISRS & Madras: CLS, 1975.

—————. *New Creation in Christ*. Delhi: ISPCK, 1976.

—————. *The Secular Ideologies of India and the Secular Meaning of Christ*. Bangalore: CISRS, 1976.

—————. *Some Theological Dialogues*, Madras: CLS, 1977.

—————. *Towards a Theology of Contemporary Ecumenism: A Collection of Addresses to Ecumenical Gatherings (1947-1975)*. Madras: CLS, 1978.

—————. *Response to Tyranny : writings between July 1975 and February 1977*. New Delhi: Forum for Christian Concern for People's Struggle, 1979.

—————. *Religion and the Revolt of the Oppressed*. Delhi: ISPCK, 1981.

—————. *Ideological Quest within Christian Commitment: 1939-54*. Madras: Christian Literature Society, 1983.

—————. *Faith and Ideology in the Struggle for Justice*. Bombay: Bombay Urban Industrial League for Development, 1984.

—————. "Towards an evangelical social gospel; a new look at the reformation of Abraham Malpan." CLS, *Krisht Vidya*, 4.1 March 1985.

—————. *Risking Christ for Christ's Sake: Towards an Ecumenical Theology of Pluralism*. Geneva: WCC, 1987.

—————. *My Ecumenical Journey, 1947-1975*. Trivandrum, India: Ecumenical Publishing Centre, 1990.

_____. *The Gospel of Forgiveness and Koinonia*. Tiruvalla, India: CSS, 1994.

_____. *A Diaconial Approach to Indian Ecclesiology*. Rome: Centre for Indian and Inter-religious Studies & Tiruvalla, India: Christava Sahitya Samitha, 1995.

_____. *The Church's Mission and Post-Modern Humanism: Collection of Essays and Talks, 1992-96*. Delhi: ISPCK, 1996.

_____. *God the Liberator*, trans. T.M. Philip. Tiruvalla, India: CSS, 2004.

_____. *Spiritual Body*, trans. T.M. Philip, Tiruvalla, India: CSS, 2005.

_____. *To the Ends of the Earth*, trans. T.M. Philip, Tiruvalla, India: CSS, 2005.

_____ & Paul E. Converse. *Revolution and Redemption*. Friendship Press, 1955.

_____ & Richard Taylor (eds.) *Tribal Awakening* (CISRS, 1965)

A complete collection of Thomas's published and unpublished writings is in the archives of United Theological College, Bangalore.

Secondary

Abraham, K. C., ed. *Christian Witness in Society: A Tribute to M. M. Thomas*. Bangalore: Board of Theological Education of Senate of Serampore College, 1998.

Athyal, Jesudas M. *M. M. Thomas: The Man and His Legacy*. Thiruvalla Ecumenical Charitable Trust and CSS, 1997.

Athyal, Jesudas M., George Zachariah and Monica Melanchthon (Eds.) *The Life, Legacy and Theology of M. M. Thomas*. Routledge, 2016.

Bird, Adrian. "M.M. Thomas: Theological Signposts for the Emergence of Dalit Theology." PhD dissertation, University of Edinburgh, 2008. Pubd. as *M.M. Thomas & Dalit Theology*. BTE/Sathri, 2008.

Boyd, R.H.S. *An Introduction to Indian Christian Theology*. Rev. ed. CLS, 1975.

Francis, T.Dayanandan & Franklyn J. Balasundaram (eds.) *Asian Expressions of Christian Commitment* (CLS, 1992)

Chacko, Mohan. *Interpreting Society: A Study of the Political Theology of M. M. Thomas and its Implications for Mission*. Dehardun, 2000.

Longchar, Wati *Transforming Cultures and Praxis*. PTCA & YCTS, 2017.

Laji Chacko, *Introduction to Christian Theologies in India* (SCEPTRE, 2014).

Massey, James et al. *Rethinking Theology in India* (Manohar, 2013).

Mitchell, Eric Robin. "M.M. Thomas' View on Church and Society: A Comparison with the Liberation Theology of Gustavo Guttierrez." PhD dissertation. Drew University, 1985.

Miyamoto, Ken Christoph. *God's Mission in Asia: A Comparative and Contextual Study of This-Worldly Holiness and the Theology of Missio Dei in M. M. Thomas and C. S. Song*. Wipf and Stock, 2007.

Morton, Stephan Andrew. *P.D. Devanandan, M. M. Thomas and the Task of Indigenous Theology*" PhD dissertation. University of Nottingham, 1981.

Ninan, M. M. Life, *Legacy and Theology of M. M. Thomas: An Anthology.* Global Publishers, 2009.

Paton, David (ed.), *Breaking Barriers Nairobi 1975* (SPCK/ Eerdmans, 1976).

Philip, T. M. *The Encounter Between Theology and Ideology: An Exploration into the Communicative Theology of M. M. Thomas.* CLS, 1986.

Spirituality for Combat. URM discussion series 1983. Hong Kong. CCA-URM. 1983.

Sumithra, Sunand. *Revolution as Revelation: A Study of M. M. Thomas' Theology.* International Christian Network, 1984.

Thomas, P.T. ed. *A list of the published writings of M.M. Thomas., 1936-1987*.Kottayam. 1988.

Thomas, T. Jacob *Ethics of a world community : contributions of Dr. M.M. Thomas based on Indian reality.* Punthi Pustak, 1993.

Thomas, T. Jacob. *M. M. Thomas Reader: Selected Texts on Theology, Religion and Society.* CSS, 2002.

West, Charles C. "Dr M M Thomas: A Tribute " in *The Princeton Seminary Bulletin,* XVIII. 2 New Series 1997, 2

Wolters, T. Heilke. *Theology of Prophetic Participation: M. M. Thomas's Concept of Salvation and the Collective Struggle for Fuller Humanity in India.* ISPCK, 1996.

6. Horacio de la Costa sj (1916-1977) *Identity and a Liberating Theology*

Horacio de la Costa studied first at the Novaliches seminary (MA 1939), but during the Pacific War he worked with those resisting the Japanese occupation and for this he was imprisoned for some months in fort Santiago. Continuing his studies after the war at Woodstock College and Harvard (PhD 1951), he returned to the Philippines to teach history, philosophy and theology, principally at Ateneo de Manila University. Initially also a playwright and historian, he came to be an eminent theologian and civic leader and later, he became first Filipino provincial Jesuit superior and adviser to the Jesuit Superior General. He also served for a term as editor of the premier journal *Philippine Studies.*

i) An Integrated life

He has been described by many colleagues as being maturely liberal, humanist in basic principle, and a 'Renaissance man' in the breadth of his interests and scholarship. His major work upon the Jesuit history of the Philippines,[1] has long been 'the best overall history of 16th-18th century Philippines'.[2] In 1962, he had become a research associate of the London School of Oriental and African Studies and over these years he received honorary doctorates from universities in Japan, the United States and the Philippines. He was in addition one of the founding members of the Philippine Academy of Science and Humanities, as well as a co-founder of the International Association of Historians of Asia.

Along with heavy teaching and speaking schedules de la Costa long continued writing in many formats: in journals such as *Philippine Priests' Forum, Teaching all Nations (later East Asia Pastoral Review), and Philippine Studies,* as well as *Philippine Social Sciences and Humanities Review, Bulletin of the Philippine Historical Association, Hispanic American Historical Review, Comment, Science Review,* and *Theological Studies*. He also contributed to the series of books published by Ateno de Manila University as *Loyola Papers* and in later years to *Progressio Supplements* of the Christian Life Community.

His many writings include studies of Filipino nationalism and its leaders, of the history of Filipino clergy, and of church-state relationships, as well as studies of faith, justice and human development. We also have from him studies of the 'eastern Christ', and of inculturation and theologies of liberation, of humanization and of the local church.[4] These writings range in content from his early poetry (until 1947), along with works of apologetic such as his book *Light Cavalry*, to detailed historical research on 16th-18th century Philippine history; as well as from early radio plays for a church under many stresses to learned but most readable articles on Asian and Philippine historiography, Philippine culture and society, on the wider issues of social change, the goals of humanist education and the relationship of faith and reason.

But for over 40 years de la Costa also worked to apply the social doctrines of the Church to the contemporary situation and necessities of the Philippine islands: in writings and broadcast plays, and in social action which included spiritual assistance to labourers and labour leaders, in mediation and conciliation, and in the promotion of healthy social organizations and institutions. For Christian social action in particular he would articulate the history, principles for research, communication and action upon which this social apostolate would be based.

In fostering these concerns in his teaching and writing he also worked to apply them in the current social and political realities of the Philippines. In this he cooperated closely with Joseph A. Mulry and Walter Hogan in the influential Institute of Social Order (ISO, which was founded in 1947), the Federation of Free Workers (in 1950) and the Federation of Free Farmers (in 1953).[4] It was for this apostolate amongst workers and farmers that he provided much of the theological basis and groundwork.

Fundamental to his approach in all writing and teaching however is the conviction that human life is to be seen whole and that in particular "religion is not something you think, but something you feel; not a proposition but a yearning; not a logic but poetry".[5]

ii) *The Centrality of Filipino identity*

In his historical research and teaching de la Costa was dedicated to develop an authentic Philippine historiography, to assemble the resources for this and to make them widely available.[6] In this he shared with other scholars in a wider movement in post-war years to research and develop the historical narratives of indigenous people in southeast Asia. For this there was then a new consciousness of identity abroad along with newly-emerging bodies of materials for identification and research. But for de la Costa such studies and teaching were also required by a theology which affirmed that the struggles and hopes of every local community were finally the place where 'divine presence' is to be found in human life. With others like Pedro Arrupe and Catalino Arevalo he assumed and advocated "that every sector of humanity [and] every local church, had its contribution to make to the universal church; that every sector of humanity had to contribute something to this larger church".[7]

Much of de la Costa's thought therefore concerns the sources of Filipino experience, identity and hope. This leads him to research and promote the unity of evangelism, human development and the Christian work for justice and liberation. He therefore dedicated much of his writing and teaching to spell out and foster the implications for Filipino churches of a "liberating theology of the local church".

Beginning with the issues of Filipino identity he finds the central marks of this in such deeply human values as *pakikisama* (willingness to share burdens and rewards), *pagkakaisa* (the building of community by people themselves), and *pagkabayani* (putting common good above private interest).[8] Grounding these in incidents in Philippine history, he believes these elements could be recognised as both the heritage of Filipinos and their future project to be now worked for and eventually fully achieved. But they could also be seen he believed, in the finest aspirations and commitments of men and women in India, China and throughout Asia. These have always been the signs of God's presence in Filipino life, he affirms, and indeed they form "the eastern face of Christ" throughout the region.

Because 'Filipino identity' includes for de la Costa elements of both the 'heritage' of all Filipino people and the 'present task' which is yet to be completed he holds firmly a vision of full and creative unity of Filipino peoples formed from the all diversities that have comprised Filipino history. And this is a story that must be told by Filipinos themselves and not just through the eyes of others who sometimes think that Filipino history began only in the late 19th century, or only in the 16th century.[9] Yet there can be no denial of many foreign influences on Filipino life and history and at various periods these have obviously included strong Chinese, Malay, Muslim, Christian, Spanish and American contributions – both positive and negative – to mention only the most significant. De la Costa recognizes such contributions, although he is thought by some colleagues to have under-estimated the disparities of power that are always present in encounters between various cultural traditions.[10] He does however accept that a Filipino consciousness may only be known once it is more fully achieved.

iii) The Church in Changing Society

An essential factor in all de la Costa's work and writing is the complex of social and political contexts that surrounded his ministries. So his writings as well as his actions can be seen as responses to those settings and events which are therefore much more than mere backgrounds to his thought or teaching. He therefore asks always what is the deeper meaning of the processes and happenings in ongoing Filipino history and cultural change: what is the goal of increasing secularization? and what is the changing role of the Church? How can the conflicts between different socio-economic and political forces be resolved? How can corruption in government be named and countered and also the "disregard of human rights and common welfare" by the wealthy and powerful? Although his earlier responses to systems of injustice and exploitation sometimes portray movements opposing these, but which are 'outside the faith', i.e. 'communist', as being intolerable also, his concern is not such 'dark forces' as such but the societal and personal conditions which give them birth. "More insidious and far more fatal" he writes, "is that corruption in high places, that cynical and heartless disregard for human rights and the common welfare…" in those with wealth and influence: "Let those who cry the loudest against Communism see to it that their injustices towards their servants, their tenants and their laborers do not cry even louder for vengeance".[11]

The thought and writing of de la Costa forms a dynamic body of work which draws on creative elements of Filipino life and culture but also responds to the changing context and events of contemporary Filipino history. Colleagues have therefore been able to trace transitions in his work which display his response to social and political change and the role of religion within these. Earlier writings show his concern to defend and present the genuine teachings of the church in situations where it appears embattled by the forces of secularization, alternative Christianities and communism. In later work and writings de la Costa's underlying concern for the struggles and suffering of Filipino people finds fuller expression and consequently in the 1970s there is more understanding of the goals of rebel 'communist groups' and less sharp criticisms of them.[12] Activities of the Institute of Social Order and its associated movements become more central to his thought; as do ecumenical and global concerns for 'the progress of peoples' following the changes brought by Vatican II.

Regarding the relationship of evangelism to struggles for justice and liberation therefore he makes a serious critique both of Spanish and U.S. practices, as well as of Catholic social action which does not address the causes of massive economic injustice. Liberation from these is primary for him, but it is to be a self-liberation that utilises the rich resources of Filipino civilisation. His later writings focussed especially upon this under-standing which must become a fully grounded conscientization for both individuals and communities. This is the 'unfinished revolution' that he and other colleagues believed (and believe…) is still to be struggled for. [12a]

iv) *A Liberating Theology*

Writing for the World Federation of Christian Life Communities de la Costa presents proposals for their work for the 'liberation of all men (sic)'.[13] Here he draws freely from the encyclicals *Octogesima Adveniens* and *Gaudium et Spes*, from reports from Vatican II and the Synod of Bishops 1971, from documents of SODEPAX[14] by Rubem Alves, Father Land and Charles Elliott, as well as words by Pedro Arrupe and Gustavo Gutiérrez. He is here able to portray both the extent of vast injustices and oppressions prevalent in today's world but also the many different levels of liberation that are urgently needed. The theological grounds for taking co-operative action upon such issues are also outlined. Using a 'methodology of discernment' , for 'the signs of the times'[15] de la Costa analyses such terms as 'dependence' and 'domination', 'development', 'liberation' and 'conscientization', but he also warns against taking too much time before acting together. "Discernment" he affirms," should lead to action, not paralyze it."[16]

A "theology of liberation" for de la Costa therefore, thinks "not so much in terms of timeless truths ... but of concrete happenings ... what men are doing or suffering, creating or destroying within the range of one's experience."[17] This is shaped by our particular landscape and community, by (firstly) Philippine social realities as well as by the Spirit's life within our local church. So this theological method concludes, in the work of the most diverse groups, by asking where in this particular history and place is the Holy Spirit working, and how may we join this work? Quoting the poet Antonio Macha he writes "Wayfarer, there is no way to go; one makes a way by going".

For the actions that are necessary he places a particular responsibility upon lay people for 'the renewal of the temporal order', but in collaboration with religious and the Christian Life Communities, along with other citizens and movements who are working for social justice peace of peoples. The *crucial* path to be taken is that of education for men and women for the reconstruction of society. And this will mean "a radical reform not only of our institutions but of our own ways of thinking and acting"[18] so that all citizens are participating in governing themselves and serving each other.

In speaking to students and staff for the Ateneo Commencement in 1972 de la Costa had outlined such an orientation for Christian and theological reflection; in fact for the central task of relating Christian faith to all daily life and work, struggle and hope. He ended by picturing the places where this could best be done: it could be, he declared , on the verandah of a sari-sari ('all sundries') store in the barrio (village); or around a (rebel) camp-fire in the Sierra Madre (the central mountain range)(!); it could even perhaps (and here he was smiling) be here in these Loyola halls! Here the very human and witty de la Costa was at work, purposely surprising, even shocking both students and venerable staff members with his images of 'living theology'. [19] It was for these qualities as much as for his dedicated work for the most vital human issues facing Filipinos, for Filipino scholarship, and for the Society of Jesus, that de la Costa is celebrated. Many writers and scholars have taken his thought and work further and this has been celebrated and amplified in recent series of lectures organized by Ateneo de Manila University and Loyola House of Studies.[20] His continuing influence can be seen in the thought, research and activism of scores of Filipino centres, faculties and movements.

Endnotes

[1] *The Jesuits in the Philippines 1581-1768.* (Harvard University, 1961). This takes the history of the Society of Jesus in the Philippines from the arrival of the first Jesuits in 1581 to the expulsion of the Order from the islands in 1768. This last because Charles III of Spain was 'determined to control all possible ownership of resources or sources of communication or criticism in the Philippines'. (pp.594ff.)

[2] J.N. Schumacher (1978). For recent accounts of de la Costa's early and later writings see Reyes (2017) chaps. 3-7, especially Reynaldo C. Ileto on de la Costa 'the Filipino Historian,and the unfinished Revolution' (pp.117-142),and Jose Maria C. Francisco sj on 'The Filipino and the 'Other': de la Costa's Notion of Hybridity' (pp.143-156).

[3] Four volumes of his selected writings have been published in R.M. Paterno (2002). See also the complete *Bibliography* ed. by Schumacher & Valera (1978).

[4] A collection of Mulry's Letters and Articles is held in the Lauinger Library, Georgetown University (USA). See also Sr. Deolindis 'The Role of Religious Mission Sisters in Church Renewal Today through the Federation of Free Farmers' (*Verbum* 12.4 (1971); Schumacher (op.cit. 1987); A. A. Weiss 'Jesuit Social Apostolate 1859-1956'. (*Philippine Studies* 4.2, 1956). From the late 1960s de la Costa often referred to the struggles of Filipinos for social justice and civic freedoms as 'the unfinished revolution' - a revolution which began in 1896. See Ileto in Reyes op.cit. 135ff.

[5] Paterno (2002) vol. 4.173.

[6] See for example his *Readings in Philippine History* (1965).

[7] C.G. Arevalo Interview (*National Catholic Reporter,* 47 (12) 2011).

[8] De la Costa 2002, 2.58-69.

[9] (*Philippine Studies* 9 (2) 1961) 346ff.

[10] On these isssues of Filipino identity as both heritage and project in de la Costa, see J.M.C. Francisco in Reyes op.cit. (2017) 151ff.

[11] Sermon 'To Preach the Gospel to the Poor' (1950) in Paterno, (2002) vol. 4.27-82.

[12] Paterno (op.cit. 2002) vol.2: 152ff., 207ff.

[12a] Reynaldo C. ILETo The 'Unfinished Revolution' in Philippine Political Discourse Southeast Asian Studies,Vol. 31, No. I, June 1993 .

[13] (*Progressio Supplement* 2, 1973) 25ff.

[14] The Joint Commission for Society, Development and Peace of the World Council of churches and the R.C. Pontifical Commission Justice and Peace.

[15] Pope John XXIII used this phrase to refer to the world-wide movements of people – especially mentioning women and other workers – struggling for justice and peace.

[16] (*Progressio Supplement* 2, 1973) 26.

[17] Loyola School of Theology, 1976a).

[18] 'The Filipino National Tradition' (1971) in Paterno, (2002) vol.2.79.

[19] Refer *Progressio Supplement 2 (*1973) for de la Costa's notes on what should then follow.

[20] For these full contemporary studies of de la Costas's work see Reyes 2017.

Selected Bibliography and Works Cited

Primary

For a complete Bibliography of works by Horacio de la Costa.see:

Published Writings of Horacio de la Costa, S.J. ed. by J.N. Schumacher and R.S. Valera Philippine Studies vol. 26, nos. 1 and 2 (Ateneo de Manila University, 1978).

The Jesuits in the Philippines 1581-1768. (Harvard University, 1961).

"History and Philippine Culture" (*Philippine Studies* 9 (2) 1961.

The Background of Nationalism and Other Essays (Solidaridad Publishing House, 1965).

Readings in Philippine History: Selected Historical Texts (Bookmark, 1965).

Asia and the Philippines (Solidaridad Publishing House, 1967).

"Church-State Relationships: A Theological Perspective." (*Philippine Priests' Forum* 2.4, 1970).

"The Filipino National Tradition" In *Challenges for the Filipino,* by Horacio de la Costa, Edicio de la Torre and Pacifico A. Ortiz. 1971 (Ateneo Publication Office, 1971.

"Evangelization and Humanization." (*Teaching all Nations* 3, 1973).

Liberation of all Men: Our Common Objective. (Unedited texts) (P*rogressio Supplement* 2, 1973).

Four papers on mission, justice and peace : first presented at the American Jesuit Missions Conference, 1974, August 1974 (American Jesuit Missions. Conference, 1974).

"Faith Justice and Human Development." In *On Faith and Justice,* edited by P.S. de Achutegui. Loyola Papers 5. (Loyola School of Theology, 1976a).

On Faith and Justice II: Faith, Ideologies and Christian Options. (Loyola Papers 7/8, 1976c).

An Ignatian Witness (Unedited texts). *Progressio Supplements* 10 (1977), reprint, n.d.

Five Plays (New Day Publishers, 1982 [1940]).

The Trial of Rizal: W.E. Retana's Transcription of the Official Spanish Documents (Ateneo De Manila Univ., 1997).

De la Costa & and J.N. Schumacher *Church and State: The Philippine Experience.* Loyola Papers 3. (Loyola School of Theology, 1976b).

_____ & J.N. Schumacher John N. *The Filipino Clergy: Historical Studies and Future Perspectives*. Loyola Papers 12 (Loyola School of Theology, 1980).

_____ & A.B. Lambino and C.G. Arevalo. *On Faith and Justice II: Faith, Ideologies and Christian Options*. Loyola Papers 7/8 (Loyola School of Theology, 1976).

_____. *Selected Writings*, 4 vols. R.M. Paterno (ed.) (2B3C Foundation, 2002).

Secondary

"In Memorium: Horacio de la Costa, S.J." (*Philippine Studies*, Special issue vol. 26, 1978).

Joseph Baumgartner "Horatio de la Costa" *Philippine Quarterly of Culture and Society* (Vol. 5, No. 1/2, 1977).

J.N. Schumacher "Horacio de la Costa, Historian" (*Philippine Studies* 26: 1-2, 1978).

Published Writings of Horacio de la Costa, S.J. ed. by J.N. Schumacher and R.S. Valera *Philippine Studies* vol. 26, nos. 1 and 2 (Ateneo de Manila University, 1978).

Angon, Chenlee I. "Horacio de la Costa (1916–1977): Eminent Writer, Scholar and historian". Archived from the original on October 27, 2009.

W. Fabros *The Church and its Social Involvements in the Philippines, 1930-1972*. (Ateneo, de Manila Univ., 1988).

R.L. Deats *Nationalism and Christianity in the Philippines* (Southern Methodist Univ. 1967).

F.F. Claver *Social Discernment and Theological Reflection*. (HD Research, 1988).

R.C. Ileto "The 'Unfinished Revolution' in Philippine Political Discourse". (*Southeast Asian Studies* 31, 1993).

V. Gorospe *Forming the Filipino Social Conscience. Social Theology from a Filipino Christian Perspective* (Bookmark, 2000).

R.M. Paterno "The Young Horacio de la Costa: a Biographical Background" in *Horacio de la Costa, S.J. Selected Writings*, 4 vols. R.M. Paterno (ed.) (2B3C Foundation, 2002).

J.J. Magadia "The Political Landscape of 70s and some Jesuit Responses to the Changing Times" in *Down from the Hill: Ateneo de Manila in the First Ten Years under Martial Law, 1972-1982* ed. by Cristina J. Montiel & Susan Evangelista (Ateneo de Manila Univ., 2005).

J.N. Schumacher "The Rizal Bill of 1956: Horacio ce la Costa and the Bishops" (*Philippine Studies* 59: 4, 2011).

C.G. Arevalo Interview with T.C. Fox "Founding Loyola School of Theology" (*National Catholic Reporter*, 47: 12, 2011).,

Soledad S. Reyes (ed.) *Reading Horacio de la Costa, SJ: Views from the 21st Century*. (Ateneo de Manila Univ., 2017).

7. Lee Park, Sun-Ai (1930-1999) *Women's Story in Future Theologies*

Sun-Ai Lee Park stands as a unique pioneer of women's theology in the Asian region, with a key role in fostering, gathering and publishing the work of Asian women in theological reflection.

i) Biographical Outline

Lee Sun-Ai was born in Korea and later graduated from Yonsei University, Seoul, where she later became Director of the Korean Language Institute 1959-1966. This was followed by periods in Switzerland and the United States where she studied at Candler School of Theology and San Francisco theological Seminary. She developed further her thought and writing while living in Korea, Switzerland and Singapore, concentrating particularly upon women's studies and human rights projects.[1] At Emory University USA she completed post-graduate study in theology and was ordained a minister of the Disciples of Christ. She also taught for one year at McCormick Theological Seminary, Chicago.

Already widely known as a poet and theologian, it was in Singapore that with three colleagues Sun Ai Lee Park founded the journal *In God's Image* in 1982. Since then this has become the major journal for women's theology in the region, and the basis for both national and international initiatives in mobilizing and publishing theological work by women. There are now associations of theologically trained women in many Asian countries, some with their own journals and with a regional *Asian Women's Resource Centre for Culture and Theology*, also co-founded by Sun-Ai.[2]

In numerous articles and poems Lee Park Sun-Ai has presented both the struggles and life-situations of Asian women, and the resources in theology and culture which are available to them. A generation of younger women theologians have been inspired by her, and by the insights of earlier Christian women in Asia which her work has helped them rediscover. And this was achieved before her debilitating illness, in only 13 years of her active ministry: certainly as one of Asia's 'watershed theologians'.

ii)   Primary concerns

For Park Sun-Ai Lee amongst her primary concerns were all movements which fostered equality and mutuality between women and men; all that supported and strengthened the struggle of women for survival and social justice, and for recognition and full respect. As she and her close colleagues declared in their vision for the AWRCCT, this is a new humanity which "is liberating, inclusive and celebrating. ... On the one hand, we strive to be in solidarity with women in struggle who are most oppressed because of class, race and gender. On the other hand, we strive to liberate our churches from the sexist and patriarchal ways" of all its life and activities, its worship and theology.[2a] In following years Sun-Ai would, along with others, lead the AWRCCT in drawing on Biblical, historical and cultural resources to fulfil these aims. Sometimes focusing on the stories of disprivileged women in early Hebrew records, or the historical oppression and violent abuse of women in Asian societies she was able to speak directly to her Korean sisters, as well as increasingly to others throughout the region.

Sun-Ai's deepest concern was for the suffering of women under unjust social structures which most often has been institutionalized by unquestioned cultural traditions, as well as being religiously sanctioned. Along with the pervasive cultural authority which imposes such structures Sun-Ai saw that the churches have themselves also maintained unjust social, cultural and gender discrimination through distorted teaching which 'justifies the subordination of women'. She strongly criticized ways in which the church's pattern of leadership perpetuated male hierarchies, for this is one of the ways in which the 'practice of classism, sexism and racism' continues in the church. Whereas the church should model the equality, mutual respect and full acceptance that belongs to the community of Jesus Christ, women again and again, she could see, were being denied these fruits of the Gospel. And this she could see occurring even within the membership of 'progressive theological movements', where active concern for full mutual recognition and equality should be especially practised. This meant for her both that a number of traditional teachings of the church regarding the role of women must be questioned and that women should explore new forms of ministry and of theology which demonstrate the call and discipleship of women in Jesus Christ's fellowship.

But for Park Sun-Ai there were other levels on which true equality and mutual respect are to be expressed and this she knew from her own experience with her husband and family. These levels start in the ordinary affairs of household and family life and in the daily actions by which life is carried on. And this is not just to provide enhanced living conditions for women but also to provide fuller and more holistic lives for men. These actions to maintain a household, prepare meals and care for children are to be fully shared and valued, she declares, so that "men can attain higher values in life, while women can accumulate the social experience and political skills which they have hitherto been deprived of and which are necessary in order for them to hold leadership positions in the broader society".[3] Bringing together such concerns and the wider issues of oppressive cultural tradition, theological distortion and church practice shows some of the new resources which Sun-Ai was able to raise more clearly for both the structures and theologies of Christian communities in Asian countries. Here was a theologian who embraced the whole life of women and men, from 'rice-roots and kitchen sink' activities to national and international struggles for justice and peace; a pioneer "to really think globally and act locally".[4]

iii) *Biblical Bases*
One of the fullest articles which Park Sun-Ai worked on to present the situations and hopes of Asian women – along with Biblical bases for responding to these – was jointly written with her husband Park

Sang-Jung as an 'Asian Reflection on Man and Women in Community'.[5] The joint writing itself growing from and demonstrating the holistic partnership envisioned by Sun-Ai and the AWRCCT. Beginning with an analysis of the "pseudo-religious ethos of Confucianism in Asia", Sun-Ai joins with her husband in outlining the "sexist practices which have exploited women" in the Northeast Asia which they know directly. There the whole structure of harmony in family and society, nation and even in cosmic order, was to be established on the basis of "the exemplary virtue of the one in authority, namely the father...The mother was not one who shared authority, nor did she have a complementary role to that of the father. She was seen as subordinate" in each of these structures. "This harmony could not be maintained without victimizing and domesticizing women". Examples of similar oppressive structures from east and south Asia are then included to show the pervasiveness of religiously-justified cruelty under which Asian women suffer.

Sun-Ai and Sang-Jung then outline in this article the development of patterns of discrimination in Christian history as well as the misinterpretations of scripture on which these are based, which exalted male leaders over women, and of ordained clergy over unordained laity. This has meant – and still means for much of the Christian church – the continuing sin of excluding women from leadership roles, in particular from that of ordained ministry. Here too is a source of suffering for women as well as being deprivation for the church as a whole. The two authors continue to consider stories from the gospels including that which contrasts the words of Jesus with those of other male critics in response to the gift of costly ointment by an unknown woman who poured it upon the feet of Jesus. This appears in all four gospels (Mt. 26:6-13; Mk. 14:3-9; Lk. 7:36-50; John 12:1-8) with all critics being males who are shown by Jesus to know little of true love and little as well of his coming suffering. Despite being 'unknown' and apparently also unwelcome (even 'unworthy'?) this woman stands out in her understanding and love of the Messiah whom even his disciples seem regularly to misunderstand. This article ends with a call for ecumenical organizations to themselves rectify patterns of injustice within their own membership and leadership, as well as to dialogue and collaborate with those of other faiths in all actions to build just societies.

Park Sun-Ai however had also reflected further on the Biblical images for suffering and had found a close relation between these and both the roles depicted of women there and the historic experience of women in Asian societies. In her theological reflection upon such prophetic passages as Is. 42:2-4 and 53:7, Park Sun-Ai moves freely, as we now expect, between Biblical concepts, events of national history and the concrete details of women's life. In the Biblical symbol of the Lamb she finds the elements of both the innumerable stories of cruelty and suffering inflicted upon women and the equally countless instances of struggle for justice and freedom which show the redemptive activities of even those who are most oppressed. Amongst these are especially women who have been made victims and scapegoats, and can in fact be seen as "the lamb bearing the sins of the world." Yet they can also be instead the redemptive lamb if they create a growing "spiral of scientific analysis, organization, effective action, theorizing, and theologizing in the creation of a new model and new human relationships."[6] Here is a programme for both practical and theological action which follows directly from exposition of a key Biblical symbol which is embedded in women's experience today.

iv) *Theological Approaches*

Her own theological approach which has informed all her work, includes elements that are central to the work of other Asian theologians, such as Suh Nam Dong and other *Minjung* theologians (Korea), Virginia Fabella, Carlos Abesamis and other theologians of *Struggle* (Philippines), Henriette Katoppo and *Double Wrestle* theologians (Indonesia), Aruna Gnanadason, and M.M. Thomas along with *Dalit* theologians (India), C.S. Song and *Homeland* theologians (Taiwan), along with numbers of other colleagues. But she has clearly shaped these and other insights to reflect and address the concrete experiences and hopes of Asian women.

Citing Kwok Pui-Lan's article on Sun-Ai's 'Dream for Asian Feminist Theology', Adams lists three main areas of Sun-Ai's work in theology,[8] and it is possible to trace through her actions and writings, along with the work and writings of colleagues in the AWRCCT and *In God's Image*, the ways in which these areas have been acted upon.[9] The dreams are first for an Asian Feminist Theology that would result in a true community that mirrors the Kingdom of God; secondly, for participation in interfaith dialogue that would discover "the power of female symbolism in Asian tradition" that might "enable Asian Christian women to imagine a different symbolic universe and alternative ways of speaking about the divine";[10] and thirdly, hope for a church which would be itself a sign of the Kingdom of God. This last would require "a faith that is dynamic, not stagnant; a spirituality that is holistic not dualistic; and a religious practice that is daring, not tradition-bound".[11] These visions have continued to inspire the work of AWRCCT and in many places around the region they have also been at least in part fulfilled.

To illustrate further how theological reflection can grow within the ongoing life of women in both society and church, Park Sun-Ai lists the possible steps that move us from the 'present situation' to 'theological reflection and action'.[11] The following outline presents the main features of the theological method she advocates:

i) See the reality of Asian women in society and church ... (what are the multiplied oppressions under which Asian sisters suffer, and die?) Sun-Ai sometimes refers to the 'triple and quadruple oppressions' – from poverty, patriarchy, class and church – under which Korean and other Asian women suffer.

ii) Analyse socio-economic structures and the encounter of traditional and western cultural values ... (what causes severe exploitation and which cultural values enforce or oppose this?) This requires awareness of historical and political processes and oppressions.

iii) Study the liberating message of Jesus' attitudes to women ... (uncover the transformed role of women brought by Jesus in his life, and now).

Here the remarkable story of Jesus-with-women is to be discerned and absorbed anew.

iv) Theological reflection on Jesus *in our situation* ... (how to concretize in all society the eschatological values of Jesus' life already promised in women's lived experiences). Here the vision of God's coming rule and its presence already in Jesus' life and the 'full community of women and men' can provide a "collective power of sisterhood and peoplehood to overcome all our burdens and be free. Our freedom will then transform us into a new creation not only as individuals but also as a people and as church."[12]

Central to this approach is the story of Jesus which for Sun-Ai enables Korean (and other) women to come to see that the power of Christ is "life-giving" for the powerless and oppressed.[13] In the incidents recorded of Jesus' encounters with women in the gospels she finds powerful symbols which can inspire and empower women today. She also found in study of the Hebrew scriptures the examples of Miriam and Deborah, Rebekah and Huldah, who although often by-passed – or portrayed as being inferior or victims – in Biblical interpretation yet in their roles and actions demonstrated the grace and "openness of God" which can be also found in women's experience today.[14]

Similar approaches are being used by many Asian women and by national associations of women theologians. They are also reflected in the recent writings (published by major European and American publishers) of such women theologians as Chung Hyun-kyung , Kwok Pui-lan, Mary-John Manazan, Aruna Gnandason and Marianne Katoppo. They provide growing evidence for the claim that now-and-future theologies in Asia, and in the 'two-thirds world', are being transformed by the experience, and the wisdom, of women. Park Sun-Ai has played a water-shed role in making this possible.[15]

Endnotes

[1] In these years her husband Park Sang Jung was first on the staff of the WCC based in Geneva, and later the Assoc. General Secretary of the Christian Conference of Asia based in Singapore.

[2] The most recent statement of purpose and activities for the AWRCCT reads that it is "an organisation of women and women's organisations in Asia who are engaged in promoting Asian women's theology. It was formed in November 1987 in order to form a regional, community of Asian women engaged in theology and ministry and to encourage them to articulate Asian women's contextual theology". This has been done through regular consultations and international exchanges, as well as through the theological journal, *In God's Image*, and the regular newsletter, *Womenet*.

AWRCCT affirms that :

"It is sinful to justify and maintain the discriminatory social and cultural barriers imposed on women over the centuries. It is also evil to endorse the present model of development that is increasing environmental degradation, poverty and gender inequality. ...It is also our vision that Asian women's theology in action can help transform the church and society...We envision a community of women, men and children who ... relate with one another in mutual respect, care and responsibility. This new humanity is liberating, inclusive and celebrating. ...

[2a] Purpose of AWRCCT included in each issue of *Womenet* newsletter.

[3] "A Theological reflection" in *We Dare to Dream* (1989, 2015) 81.

[4] Adams (2012) 210.

[5] "Woman and Man in Community: An Asian Reflection " (*The Ecumenical Review*, April 1994). In this article Park Sun- Ai & Park Sang-Jung quote from their earlier writings and in particular from *Asian Women Doing Theology : Report from Singapore Conference, November, 1987* (AWRCCT,1989).

[6] "Korean Women as the Lamb Bearing the Sins of the World" (*In God's Image*, June 1988) cited by Orevillo-Montenegro (2007) 32.

[7] Kwok Pui-Lan (*In God's Image* 18.3, 1999) 32ff.

[8] Adams (2012) 209.

[9] Kwok Pui-Lan (1999) 34.

[10] Ibid. 34.

[11] "Asian Women's Theological Reflection" (*East Asian Journal of Theology* 3.2, 1985) 173-182.

[12] "Korean Women as the Lamb Bearing the Sins of the World" (*In God's Image*, June 1988).

[13] Orevillo-Montenegro (2006) 100f. See this vol. for full surveys of 'The Jesus of Asian Women'.

[14] See e.g. "Openness of God: Openness of Human Beings" in Lee Oo Chung at al. (1992) chap.18.

¹⁵ The history of Asian women in ministry and theological reflection that dates from at least the 4th century should be recognised as the larger story of which In God's Image and the AWRCCT is part. (See the research guide vols. of *Asian Christian Theologies*). For a recent outline of the work of Asian women theologians see the articles "18 Asian Female Theologians You Should Know About" and (broadening the coverage) "114 More Asian (and Asian American) Female Theologians You Should Know About" (https://theglobalchurchproject.com/18-asian-female-theologians/)

Reference should also be made here to the later formation of *Ecclesia of Women in Asia* (EWA), a forum of Asian Catholic women theologians and women doing theology in Asia. Since 2002, eight Asia-wide conferences have been held with the ninth to follow in January 2020 in Kuala Lumpur; the theme to be "Displacement and Disqualification: Its Surfaces Silhouettes". A number of volumes and articles have also been published by ISPCK for EWA. See https://ecclesiaofwomen.com/.../01/07/list-of-asian-female-theologians.

Select Bibliography and Works Cited

Primary

Park Sun-Ai Lee "Asian Women's Theological Reflection" (*East Asian Journal of Theology* 3.2, 1985).

_____. "Understanding the Bible from Women's Perspective" (*In God's Image* Dec. 1986).

_____. "Reflections" (*In God's Image*. Sept '87).

_____. "Asian Women's Theological Conference" (*In God's Image*, Nov. 1987) (Section on Christology).

_____. "Behold I Make all Things New" (*In God's Image*, Dec. 1987- Mar.1988).

_____. "Korean Women as the Lamb Bearing the Sins of the World" (*In God's Image*, June 1988).

_____. "Emerging Spirituality of Asian Women" in *With Passion and Compassion: Third World Women Doing Theology. Reflections from the Women's Commission of the Ecumenical Association of Third World Theologians* ed. by Virginia Fabella & Mercy A. Oduyoye (Orbis Books, 1988; Wipf and Stock, 2006).

_____. "Confucianism and Women" (*In God's Image*, June 1989). *Asian Women Doing Theology : Report from Singapore Conference,* November 20-29, 1987 (AWRCCT Hong Kong, 1989).

_____. "Envisioning a Future Church as an Asian Woman" (CCA Osaka, mimeo'd, 1990).

_____. "An Asian Perspective" in Third World Theologies: Commonalities and Divergences ed. K.C. Abraham (Wipf & Stock, 1990, 2004).

_____. "A Theological Reflection" in *We Dare to Dream : Doing theology as Asian women.* (AWRC, 1989; Orbis Books, 1990; Wipf & Stock, 2015).

_____. "The Forbidden Tree and the Year of the Lord" (*In God's Image,* Mar. 1992).

_____. "Openness of God: Openness of Human Beings" in *Women of courage. Asian Women* (AWRCCT, 1992).

_____. "Asian Women in Mission" *International Review of Mission Volume* (April 1992, 81, Issue 322).

_____. *Reading the Bible.* Lee Oo Chung at al. eds.(AWRCCT, 1992).

_____. (ed.) Lee Oo Chung *In Search of Our Foremother's Spirituality* (AWRCCT, 1994). (with Don Luce eds. and trans.) *The Wish. Poems of Contemporary Korea* (Friendship Press, 1983).

_____. (with Virginia Fabella, eds.) *We dare to dream : Doing theology as Asian women.* (AWRC, 1989; Orbis Books, 1990; Wipf & Stock, 2015).

_____. (with Sang Jung Park) "Woman and Man in Community: An Asian Reflection" (*The Ecumenical Review*, April 1994).

Secondary

Chung Hyun Kyung *Struggle to be the Sun Again: Introducing Asian Women's Theology* (Orbis Books, 1990) 18-21,50.

_____. "Han-pu-ri": Doing Theology from Korean Women's Perspective. *Ecumenical Review* Jan. 1988 https://doi.org/10.1111/j.1758-6623.1988.tb01515

Soon-Hwa Sun Women, "Work and Theology in Korea". *Journal of Feminist Studies in Religion* Vol. 3, No. 2 (Fall, 1987).

Choi Man-Ja "The Herstory of the Revd. Sun Ai Lee-Park" (*In God's Image* 18.3, 1999) 2-5.

Kwok Pui-Lan "Asian Feminist Theology: the Dream of Sun Ai Lee-Park (*In God's Image* 18.3, 1999).

Kwok Pui-Lan *Introducing Asian Feminist Theology.* Introductions in Feminist Theology. (Sheffield Academic Press, 2000).

Ahn Byung-Mu *Jesus of Galilee.* (Christian Conference of Asia, 2004) chap.VIII

Muriel Orevillo-Montenegro *The Jesus of Asian Women.* (Orbis Books, 2007) chap.3.

Yong Ting Jin et al. *An Introduction to an Asian Feminist Re-reading of History* (4 vols. AWRCCT, 2007-2008).

Pak, J.S. "The Anguish of the Korean Woman's Soul: Feminist Theologians on a Real-Life Issue". *Pastoral Psychology* 60, 291–303 (2011). https://doi.org/10.1007/s11089-011-0337-8

Daniel J. Adams *Korean Theology in Historical Perspective.* (ISPCK, 2012) 205ff.

8. D.S. Amalorpavadass (India: 1932-1990) *Vision of Universal Salvation*

Because the God we know in Jesus Christ is present in one universal history, the Kingdom is both within and beyond culture, and God's plan for all peoples and histories is wider, older and greater than the Church. This is a foundation premise for all the new directions offered in the teaching and writing, the animating and artistic work of Amalorpavadass.

i) Biographical Outline

D.S. Amalorpavadass studied philosophy and theology at St. Peter's Seminary, Bangalore. On the staff of the Regional Catechetical Centre, Tindivanan from 1959-1962, he spent the next three years studying at the Institut Catholique in Paris, and was able also to attend much of the Second Vatican Council. His graduate theses were 'L'Inde a la rencontre du Seigneur' - a critical examination of the life and history of the Church in India - and 'Destinee de l'Eglise dans L'Inde d'aujourdhui', considering especially the conditions for effective evangelization.

In 1966 the Catholic Bishop's Conference of India appointed him Founder-Director of the National Biblical, Catechetical, Liturgical Centre (NBCLC) in Bangalore, which he developed as a national and international centre for implementing the teaching of Vatican II, for the indigenization of liturgy and catechesis and for the reorientation and renewal of the church in its cultural and social context. For more than 25 years he was instrumental in the application of research to such areas as the 'Non-Biblical Scriptures', the changing frontiers of Evangelism, the 'struggle for a New Society', and the growth of holistic and community spirituality.

Both in the development of the NBCLC, and in his long-term residence in Anjali Ashram, Amalorpavadass laboured to shape the life, the symbolism, and the material fabric of these communities so that they expressed concretely the central insights of an inculturated and world centred faith.

In 1979 he initiated the Chair (later Department) of Christianity at Mysore University for "promoting advanced studies and research in Christianity in the secular, multi-religious, interdisciplinary and pluralistic context of India in order to promote Christianity as an academic and scientific discipline".[1] This was the first such initiative in a secular, state university in India. For 5 years he also edited the journal *Word and Worship* and since 1964, wrote or edited more than two hundred books and booklets along with more than sixty-five articles.[1a]

After completing his term as Director of the NBCLC, in 1982, Swami Amalorananda as he was now to be known, founded Anjali Ashram[2] at Chamundi Hill Road, Mysore as a spiritual, theological and artistic centre for retreats and training. A particular feature at the ashram is the monthly courses in Indian Christian Spirituality held in its uniquely Indian architecture. There he became Guru-Acharya "for thousands of seekers from all walks of life, including bishops, priests, nuns, lay people from India and abroad".[3] He also continued to teach at Mysore University, as well as concentrating much of his attention to the work of spiritual animation, initiating many thousands into genuinely Indian Christian spirituality. In 1990, tragically, he was killed in a car accident and is buried in the temple of the Ashram.

ii) Theological Testimony in Outline
Amalorpavadass pursued 'a relentless quest' throughout his life for the renewal of the church, of the whole of human society, and of individual persons. He saw this dawning in all work for social justice and liberation, through dialogue and collaboration with those of any faith, as well as through an authentic Indian spirituality. The basic process for all Christian mission and reflection in these activities was however inculturation, whereby the divine life again and again takes flesh in the local realities of human existence. Despite the imposition of false Christian identities – in some patterns of missionary or church work – such inculturation was for him totally necessary and inevitable Moreover this process has the longest tradition in Christian history. He based this conviction in the key doctrines of Creation,, Incarnation,

and Redemption., which are themselves all acts of inculturation be maintained.⁴

For Amalorpavadass, the universality of such inculturation, embracing all God's creative and liberating activity, rests in the universal presence of God in the life of *all* peoples. God is guiding all human society to a new world, he believes, within all of history and in all shared aspirations for humanity. Such a universal revelation has become definitive in Jesus who interprets and fulfils all human existence. For the spirit of Christ is at work in all the world to bring God's kingdom, so we can recognise the presence of Christ in all cultures and all religious traditions. But Christ remains the unique model of total humanization and salvation, and the supreme sacrament for giving one's life to others. Each of us is offered by him a paschal experience by which we can be fully united with him in life and death, and new life. ⁵

Thus it is that "because the God we know in Jesus Christ is present in one universal history, the Kingdom is both within and beyond culture, and God's plan for all peoples and histories is wider, older and greater than the Church". Christians therefore always have a double heritage in their national/ethnic identity and in their Christian identity as well. So the presence of Christ is to be recognised and received in one's own language, symbolisms, art forms and customs. But because the Presence of God is always redemptive and transformative, as well as creative, all cultures and histories are subject to a prophetic critique and to Christian interpretation. The cultural and religious forms of our people's life are therefore to be both fully recognised but also re-formed. This is especially so where more than half of our peoples in Asia are forced to live in sub-human conditions, largely caused by wealthy minorities and trans-national corporations, and where the Church itself has often supported or approved acts of oppression and institutional violence. ⁶

God's universal presence to all peoples also means that the Church is wholly part of the human community and cannot he identical with God's total plan of salvation. It is called rather to be a partner in building total human community and to be thus a living sign of Christ's liberation in each country today: an instrument, along with others, of God's universal plan for humanization. The Christian community therefore receives both a general revelation as a pilgrim along with others, and a Christic eschatological revelation, as a sign. It therefore announces to all the coming unity which all can work for, and so demonstrate the all-inclusiveness of salvation. The uniqueness of the Church, comes from this universal Christian vision; and evangelism is making known the universal presence of God and the transformation which God intends. It is the overflow of a living experience of universal love in Jesus Christ, which issues in concrete signs of liberation, justice and fellowship, thus again enfleshing the Spirit of God. [7]

Amalorpavadass has no illusions as to what such a programme, and its theology, requires. Renewal and full inculturation will demand a sharp critique of the church, and the evangelization of the church; a different consciousness and identity - in liturgy, theology, and openness - and a different social commitment and lifestyle. De-institutionalized forms of community life must come along with simplified patterns of personal life. But at the heart of such a pilgrimage, Amalorpavadass always places holistic spirituality, which includes dialogue, testimony and action-in-life, and which is grounded and shaped in prayer and the life of interiority. [8] In the judgement of many colleagues both in south Asia and world-wide he has provided also a "coherent, comprehensive, and contextual theology of mission".[9]

For each of the above approaches, Amalorpavadass has provided full detail, in socio-cultural analysis, in theological study, in step-by-step procedures and the resources of extensive programmes of education and experience. These have been framed in the daily life of the communities of the NBCLC and of Anjali Ashram. His expressed intention throughout, was to animate the renewal of the Church, within all movements for renewal in India. And to do this he gave priority to the animation and organization of lay people and Religious, for the promotion of justice and human development, dialogue and cooperation, all-round inculturation and a living, Indian spirituality. In all these he believed, the Gospel must, if true to the incarnation, become experienced event, in the life of the community.¹⁰ There are few such comprehensive and concrete examples of wholly integrated spirituality, theology, social action and community life.

Endnotes

¹ See Joy Thomas "Mission in the Context of Universities", paper sent to the International Association for Mission Studies (IAMS) Conference in 2004 held in Port Dickson, Malaysia.

¹ᵃ For the fullest study of Amalorpavadas' life, work and thought see Gerwin van Leeuwen *Fully Indian and Authentically Christian* (National Biblical Catechetical and Liturgical Centre & J.H.Kok,1990).

² "The name 'Anjali' was adopted to illustrate the hospitality and love with which everyone was received in the ashram". (Catherine Cornille *The Guru in Indian Catholicism: Ambiguity of Inculturation?* Peeters Press, Louvain, 1990, 144).

³ Michael Amaladoss in *Biographical Dictionary of Christian Missions* ed. by G.H. Anderson (Eerdmans Publishing, 1998) 15–16.

⁴ See e.g. Amalorpavadass 1978a, 17, 27; 1980, 99f.; 1984b, 23.

⁵ Amalorpavadass 1973a, 39f.; 1984b, 22; 1982, 61.)

⁶ Refer to Amalorpavadass 1978, 25f., 36f.; 1980a, 92, 110; 1982, 61, 241ff.; 1984a 8ff., 35ff.; 1984b, 10, 16, 22

⁷ Amalorpavadass 1973a, 28, 43, 65f., 89; 1980a, 109; 1982, 54f.; 1984b, 13f.)

⁸ Amalorpavadass 1973a, 72f.; 1984b, 28)

⁹ John M. Prior svd quoted in https://en.wikipedia.org/wiki/D._S._Amalorpavadass, archived Feb. 2019.

¹⁰ Amalorpavadass 1973a, 89; 1978, 19ff.; 1982, 27f., 221-235; 1984a, 48ff.; 1985, 5ff.

Select Bibliography and Works Cited

For full bibliography see Sr. Esuria and Sebastian Dasan B*iodata and Bibliographical Note on D.S. Amalorpavadass* (Anjali Ashram, 1985), and Gerwin van Leeuwen *Fully Indian and Authentically Christian* (National Biblical Catechetical and Liturgical Centre, 1990, and J.H.Kok,1990) 344-353.

Primary

D.S. Amalorpavadass *Destiné de L'église dans L'Inde d'Aujourd'hui* (Fayard-Mame, 1967).

_____. *Theology of Development (*National Biblical Catechetical and Liturgical Centre, 1969).

_____. *Theology of Evangelization in the Indian Context* (NBCLC, 1971).

_____. *Towards Indigenization in the Liturgy* (NBCLC, 1973).

_____. *Approach, Meaning and Horizon of Evangelization* (NBCLC, 1973).

_____. *Adult Catechumenate and Church Renewal* (NBCLC, 1973).

_____. *Gospel and Culture (Evangelization and Inculturation* and 'Hinduisation') (Erscheinungsdatum, and NBCLC, 1978).

_____. 'The Indian universe of a new theology' in Sergio Torres & Virginia Fabella (eds.) *The emergent Gospel : theology from the underside of history : papers from the Ecumenical Dialogue of Third World Theologians, Dar es Salaam, August 5-12, 1976.* (Orbis, 1978).

_____. *Indian Culture: Relation between Culture and Religion* (NBCLC, 1980).

_____. *The Bible in Self-Renewal and Church Renewal for Service to Society* (NBCLC, 1984).

_____. *Vision, Thrust and Policy for Evangelization* (NBCLC, 1984).

_____. (ed.) *Indian Christian Spirituality* (NBCLC, 1982).

Note: collections of D.S. Amalorpavadass' works have been published by the NBCLC and include writings on 'Mission Theology' in *In search of Identity;* and writings on Liturgy, Catechetics and Bible in three separate volumes *Biblical Renewal, Liturgical Renewal and Catechetical Renewal.* Four collections have also been published in Tamil.

Secondary

Sr. Esuria and Sebastian Dasan B*iodata and Bibliographical Note on D.S. Amalorpavadass* (Anjali Ashram, 1985).

Gerwin van Leeuwen *Fully Indian and Authentically Christian* (National Biblical Catechetical and Liturgical Centre, 1990, and J.H.Kok,1990)

J. Russell Chandran et al. *Third World theologies in dialogue : essays in memory of D.S. Amalorpavadass.* (Ecumenical Association of Third World Theologians, 1991).

R.S. Sugirtharajah (ed.) Voices from the Margin: Interpreting the Bible in the Third World (Orbis, 1991).

Catherine Cornille and Valeer Neckebrouck . A Universal Faith ? Peoples, Cultures, Religions,   and the Christ, Louvain Theological and Pastoral Monographs, Vol. 9 (Peeters Press, . Eerdmans Publishing, 1992.

Cyril de Souza sdb *Catechesis for India Today: An Appraisal of the Catechetical Proposal of D.S. Amalorpavadass* (Kristu Jyoti Publications, 1994)..

Barla, John Berchmans *Christian Theological Understanding of other religions according to D.S. Amalorpavadass* (Gregorian & Biblical Press, 1999).

Cheriyan Menachery "The Meaning and the Effects of the II Vatican Council for the Inter-religious relations of the Catholic Church in India" *Journal of Religious Culture*, (Johann Wolfgang Goethe Univ., 1999).

Judith M. Brown, Robert Eric Frykenberg (eds.) *Christians, Cultural Interactions, and India's Religious Traditions* (Routledge, 2002).

Robert Eric Frykenberg (Ed.) *Christians and Missionaries in India: Cross-cultural communication since 1500* (Eerdmans Publishing, 2003).

Jan Peter Schouten Jesus as Guru. *The Image of Christ among Hindus and Christians in India*. Amsterdam: Rodopi, 2008.

PART TWO
For a 21st Century Praxis and Study

I. *The Foundational Way – The Human Life of Jesus*

Summary notes from recent writings and research – sources are added below.

Many of those in Christian churches seem to be most often concerned with how different and how 'divine' Jesus was – what the proofs of this might be and whether Jesus himself was 'God'. Yet, without the sheer quality of his *humanity* and his astounding human life we would not know the nature of true 'divinity'; we would not single out this 'antique holy man', and there would be no Christian movement at all. (This is the truth often hidden in more specialist statements that 'Christology is only possible when grounded in the historical Jesus'). The whole Christian revelation was determined by that human life which he lived out with friends and with any whom he met. Without this life-with-others within the communities of 1st century Palestine there would be *no* Christian history, *no* church, *no* doctrines or creeds, and *no* theology. Yet despite its breath-taking compassion, transformative vision and self-vindicating truth, the human life of Jesus is absent from almost all traditional Christian sources: it is omitted from the canticles, from every one of the creeds, from the festivals of the Christian year and even from almost all the New Testament letters.

> We can note first of all that there are now extensive materials on that life in discoveries and researches from the first, second and third 'Searches for the historical Jesus'. There are also now over twenty Gospels recovered

from the first and second centuries; the library of researches from the last 25 years cover a dozen shelves or more; and we have many further research results for 1st century Palestine society, culture and context. From these intensive studies new images of Jesus have also emerged in the experience and research of Asian Christians in particular: of Jesus as *Guru* or *Bodhisattva*, as *Christa*, *Shaman*, or *'Sophia' Wisdom*, *Sadhu* or *itinerant Sage*, charismatic *Healer* or *Jewish Holy One*, *Dalit* or *Minjung*, *Barefoot Prophe*t or 'Subversive', the 'Activist' ' or 'Organizer', and as 'the Crucified People'.

It is important also to see that the context in which Jesus lived out his Good News was Palestine of the 1st century CE, where the people faced daily a most brutal occupation and despotic local rulers, along with oppressive religious laws and the agonies of pervasive poverty and destitution. Amidst extreme inequalities over 90% of people were severely exploited by taxation, by Roman and Herodian injustices and by religious prescription. So many were constantly and seriously malnourished that famine often resulted. Yet in this context many Jewish people remained devout even though being often sharply divided in religious practice and belief. As for the north, it should be noted that despite being often condemned as 'provincials' or 'sinners' by many Pharisees and others in the south, rural Galileans amongst whom Jesus was raised, preserved their own faithful and simple piety. And there were wandering charismatics who offered prophetic visions, some as traditional wise ones, some as healers, some apocalyptic. Other movements for renewal and dissent such as the Essene community forged alternative Biblical interpretations, life-styles and beliefs, or like the Zealots pursued an often violent resistance.

Youth and travel

Almost certainly Jesus was born in Nazareth or in quite nearby *Betleman* (not southern Bethlehem). In any case there is no historical record of any 'Registration' or census, which then would have been logistically impossible in occupied Palestine. *Betleman* and Nazareth were located in a frontier and cosmopolitan territory close to many trade routes. The international trade city of Sepphoris was only a few miles away with links to the Asia-wide 'silk routes'. As to family, Jesus was raised with brothers and sisters in the home of a 'peasant' woman and her Rabbi husband ('carpenter' being a common nick-name for rabbis because as such they most often earned their living). Jesus would have received rabbinic schooling from his father and in nearby synagogues that covered the *Torah*, the *Shema* and the Prophets. As was usual in rabbinic teaching he learned well to study, to debate and also to be of service to others. Almost certainly too he learnt the life-style of a rabbi which divided the day equally between pursuit of a trade and the pursuit of studies.

There is strong evidence that Jesus ('*Issa*', '*Eisu*' or *Yesu*) travelled widely in his late youth and was therefore not readily recognised on his return, even in Nazareth ('Who is this man?'). Recent scholarship has investigated this fully and presents a history of Jesus travelling eastwards to India and almost certainly westwards also to Britain. In north India especially there are traditions and records of him spending years in the study of pristine Buddhist and Hindu traditions. Such travel to the east occurred often then, and was available by many of the either land or sea 'silk routes'. We know there were also synagogues already in India and Roman coins discovered show that Roman traders regularly visited. From the history now established for Christianity in India we also know that Thomas and others would soon be travelling there, as well as to further east.

Travel to the west would have been on the routes of Phoenician merchants who are known to have traded in tin from the mines of Cornwall. References in the *Talmud* affirm that Joseph of Arimathea was himself a trader in tin and the evidence from coinage of the Dubunni (a British tribe) points to the presence around 30 CE of one *Eisu*. It is no longer possible to ignore the traditions from Cornwall and Glastonbury which record that Jesus accompanied Joseph (his uncle?) at least once to Britain. They claim also that Jesus returned later, along with 'a woman in her early thirties', who could of course have been his Mother or the Magdalene. (Some versions of Druidic teachings in that period also focus on the divine justice, recompense and reconciliation brought through the life of a 'man', suggesting possible mutual influences).

Back in Palestine after years of travel and enlightening experience Jesus would seem to some extent strange to earlier friends, yet there was also clearly a renewed camaraderie. For he was a disciple of John for a period and also knew traditions of the Essenes. (We can clearly see from many of the gospels that he developed a more compassionate, modest, and inclusive ministry than either John or the Essenes). He was surely also aware of the other choices offered for Israel's reform or restoration but clearly maintained his own independence as guru, teacher, healer.

Gospel and companions

It is necessary here to emphasize that from the earliest records of Jesus' teaching and living, the foundation Gospel is *not* first the story and theology of his death. Nor is it the schema or catechism that begins by telling us to first realise our sin, to acknowledge a vicarious death upon the cross which is necessary to appease God, or to 'be saved'. Nor is it in the many doctrines concerning his 'person and work' which have developed from the early centuries of study, controversy and speculation. Rather the central Gospel, echoing his cousin, is the proclamation that *God's rule is upon us* (Mark 1.1) and that this is found in the human life that Jesus lived with other women and men. So the 'Kingdom', or 'Common-wealth', is both present and future; a new world *now,* and to be fulfilled at the end of history; 'a radically transformed way of living', both personally and corporately. This is the Way of Jesus' life-with-others that all can enter. He was thus a remarkable social prophet for his people, and although drawing on the major Hebrew prophets, he uniquely redefined the inclusiveness of the Covenant as the Commonwealth of God now come and to include all – even the last, least or loneliest.

In his counter-cultural spirituality of compassionate action he thus offered a quite new vision and practice of the Reign of God's peace and justice. In his life-style and teaching, his befriending and healing this Reign was clearly known in abundant human and social well-being for all women, men and children. On behalf of the poorest or discarded ones, and in his own authority following the murder of John, he violated Sabbath or purity laws, challenged the temple system, the wealthy and the well-fed (Lk 6:24ff.), accepted women fully as equals and overturned all patriarchal relationships. His unwavering dependence for this lived-out Gospel was upon the compassionate God who holds for us *unconditional* love and forgiveness and creates fullest human community. In the words of the great prophets which he fulfilled this is 'good news to the poor, the oppressed, to captives and the sick'; it is 'justice to the nations' and 'restoration of the land' and all this was declared, as in earlier prophets, to come upon a 'new earth'. Jesus' charismatic and revolutionary wisdom offered too the scandalous teaching that, even without *any* merit or 'righteousness' at all, God accepts, forgives and restores *all* in full equity and reconciliation. This is his Gospel of God's Common-wealth: that love is and *will be* all in all, *for* all; all then can also respond, in the diverse contexts of their daily life.

His work as 'carpenter' and Rabbi took Jesus around the villages and into people's houses where he came to know so much of their lives. He often also met friends in cafés and wine-shops or in his own home (Mk 2.1, 15; Mt 4.13, 9.28) for long discussions of the scriptures, of the lives of poorest neighbours, and of the coming 'Kingdom'. There were also times beside or on the Galilean sea, Mark alone recording at least eight journeys there as if this was an accustomed outing. Soon groups formed around him, shared ideas of God's coming Commonwealth, planned urgent reforms, and then answered his call to spend time preparing, and soon in travelling, on dry-season 'missions' with him. With his friends, both women and men, he planned ways to now live out that Common-wealth in selflessness and conviviality. At suppers and parties, at which he spends and enjoys much of his time, he seems to reveal most of himself, often becoming also the de facto host. There was extensive befriending, especially of women, who were in the end his most (only?) faithful friends and co-workers. Such relations with women were clearly warm and mutually rewarding with the evidence of the gospels placing Mary Magdalene in a quite special relationship to Jesus.

With such emerging groups his 'renewal movement' began to find an informal yet disciplined shape which included not only those artificially designated 'the Twelve' but others who sought him out or whom he had healed or restored. There were in fact the 'Twenty' or more of his closer disciples and amongst these the women named in the gospels formed a significant fellowship. With many of these he came to lead the seasonal missions during which he shared the companionship and rapport of the road with a 'partnership of equals' in which each had their own ministry. Here there was teaching and listening, joking and story-telling, silent communion, shared service and prayer. It is important to recognize that this company on the road is *the best model* of God's Commonwealth on earth we have: a grouping called to journey; a new level of fellowship and communion forged in shared work; partners on a quest and in a 'mission' for religious awakening and social restoration.

Humanity and life-style

In the view of many eminent Asian theologians this life-style and teaching is the source of a true humanity and humanization which is itself *divinization* also. Here was the fullest humanity known to us yet one with a prophetic consciousness wholly 'transparent to God'; the holy animateur working for wholeness, compassion, justice, and peace; a 'concentration' of the Logos, the Spirit and Wisdom who is everywhere present. Here is the dynamic heart of the Christian movement which lived and would live, in countless followers of this first century sage, activist, mystic, and healer; the life-with-others which itself rescues and restores us. This full humanity would become the model for God's Commonwealth now breaking in; the heart of the mythic, subversive and creative *Christ* who has been known down the centuries in the widest of human experience.

Although revered as a 'Jewish holy one' Jesus was seen to much enjoy 'secular' life on the streets and in doorways, on hillsides, seashores and in village centres. He was most often seen and heard in these 'secular' places for there he carried out nearly all his teaching, demonstrating and healing. As for the more 'sacred' places, he was sometimes thrown out from synagogues, and in the temple he sometimes threw others out! Along the way he challenged accepted customs in happily associating particularly with most unsavoury characters: the supposedly 'immoral', the scorned, the sick, the mentally ill, the condemned and the discarded. From none of these (or indeed from anyone else) did Jesus first require evidence of 'repentance' or declarations of belief, before befriending, calling, healing or restoring them. His challenge was first and wholly to a life-for-others.

He was regularly outspoken in his criticism of attitudes and practices which denigrated or destroyed human community. He therefore strongly rejected religious hypocrisy, greed for power and the accumulation of wealth. Note especially the dozens of strong criticisms Jesus made of the misuse or amassing of wealth in the gospels. And the sharp rebukes given to Pharisees and others whose actions betrayed their fine words. These were the evils he most often condemned. He called his friends to do the same and called all to first seek the Common-wealth of God where distinctions by caste or class, gender or power, learning or piety, wealth or authority have no place whatever.

This fitted entirely with the life of one who 'blessed the poorest', consoled the suffering, sought out the 'last and least', and in his everyday encounters exemplified simplicity, outspoken frankness and also modesty. Here was no emphasis on 'dogma or worship', but the model of life-style, action for others and a never-to-be-forgotten 'voice-print' of his words. These all convey the deepest conviction of truths that he has himself experienced – the ends and beginnings of life he has himself lived through. The Beatitudes in particular present the blessings and wisdoms. he has received – as himself 'poor', 'mourning', 'tamed', 'hungering', 'merciful', 'single-minded', 'peace-making', 'persecuted'...

Unique Prophet and continuing Life

Then too, in contrast to many of Israel's prophets, optimism, humour and often delight marked his speech and dealings: after all, God is setting all to rights! Justice, reconciliation and love will be victorious; the highest truth can be known in the most ordinary human actions; God's love and forgiveness are unlimited and embrace every woman, man and child; the signs of God's reign are all about us and you too can be part of those signs. 'Rejoice and be exceeding glad'... 'my joy I give to you'!

- He said none was good save God alone; and none knew God's final will but God alone. Always reticent about himself, he called himself only 'son of humanity', the Human One, and never in the earliest gospels himself claimed to be divine. Yet there was for him a 'conjunction of expectations': those gathered in centuries of anticipation and those also aroused by the surprising life of Jesus of Nazareth. He was in his earthly life a 'Son of God': remarkable in his open friendship, his incisive teaching, his courageous compassion. For ourselves we can say that he is 'a Son of God' insofar as we know his life-with-others to be the definitive (although not exhaustive) showing of God's Reign of Love amongst us, and of our intended relationship with God. We can also discern in this life, then and down the centuries, that for us he was, and is, amongst all religious leaders, the unique prophet and liberator, healer and enlightened one, forerunner, rescuer and great Friend. For this he taught and inspired, welcomed and befriended, while also regularly practising civil disobedience. Twelve different kinds of such 'illegal' actions have been listed. He was often hungry, thirsty, sometimes angry, lonely, exhausted and sorrowing, while living out this counter-cultural quality of life-with-other-women-and-men. Yet even as a victim of imperial power and religious bigotry, and identified closely therefore with Rome's or Israel's victims, he still acted out an accepting and forgiving love that endured and withstood all hostility or ignorance, all cruelty and death.

- His earthly death was, of course, the inevitable end of such a prophetic life-with-others. It was *no* predetermined 'sacrifice', *nor* a 'ransom' or 'propitiation' to a 'wrathful' God, but was instead a supreme witness to justice, revealing the injustice of men; a supreme witness to love which despite all obstacles embraces everyone. For the God of Jesus requires no such offering or 'human sacrifice' before lavishing upon us a full embrace, acceptance and forgiveness. The Gospel of grace-full acceptance for all has freed us from all needs for merit, particular transactions, ritual or dogma. Yet by its transforming love this best-of-all news raises us to respond in lives which demonstrate God's reign is upon us. For Jesus as with John, 'repentance' is not just words or rites but the sharing of food and clothes, of friendship, of justice and healing. Such a turning-around to act as if Love reigns is always costly and also involves shared suffering. But along with his subsequent resurrection, Jesus' death sealed and guaranteed the sacrificial and vivifying life he gave *to*, and for *us*. Such a resurrection was not in itself unheard of – the Pharisees and indeed Paul already believed in resurrection – but it was unique because Jesus' life inaugurated God's 'end-time'. This declared unequivocally that God's rule of justice and peace has begun and will be fulfilled; that Life and Love will always overcome death and hate.

We know now that such a life and death with others could not die. It lives on in all continuing presence of unquenchable compassion and truth, as well as in all who receive his life to be *their* life and actions. It is present too in all those who unknowingly continue that liberative quality of living for others whatever might be their faith or 'unfaith'. His life of compassion and consolation, healing and restoration was therefore not at all destroyed but has continued beyond his death, and continues now in countless women and men of all peoples, places and creeds who live out such a love.

- In Jesus' life in our world, we are therefore given the image and embodiment of the eternal people-justice, peace and love of God's Common-wealth and coming New World. This is enacted, for example, in the Eucharist when we are given the life of Jesus *to be our life*... And as for our response, the Hindu-Christian Subba Rao of India has said it is "not to worship You but to live like You, to follow You". It is to find in our own experience 'the form and features of Jesus'. In his life with others we see for our faithful following every nuance of courageous compassion, strength to challenge every injustice or abuse, and all the sources of creative human community to be fostered. Because his life is the Way, so we are to practise his life of caring and prophetic action, of befriending and conviviality, his 'partnership of equals', his tranquility *and* righteous anger. Through his life-changing companionship we are to receive for our own his offering of self in hope and service, in learning and sharing, in liberating and resisting.

Sources drawn on for these notes include:
- From the Asia-Pacific region: Carlos Abesamis, Charles Avila, Ahn Byung Mu, Michael Amaladoss, Arai Sasagu, Tissa Balasuriya, J.B. Banawiratma, (Ms..) Mary Rosario Battung, Paul Caspersz, P. Chenchiah, (Ms.) Chung Hyun Kyung, Jose Cunanan, Khin Maung Din, Nguyen Y Doan (Bao Vuong Dinh Bich), Endo Shusaku, Fung Jojo, (Ms.) Aruna Gnanadason, Thich Ngat Hanh, Ian Harris, Inoue Yoji, Kagawa Toyohiko Sebastian Kappen, (Ms..) H. Marianne Katoppo, Kim Jae Jun, Kim Yong-bock, (Ms.) Kinukawa Hisako, Koyama Kosuke, (Ms.) Kwok Pui Lan, (Ms.) Agnes Lee, (Ms.) Lee Miena Skye, Wati Longchar, (Ms.) Mary John Mananzan, Alexander Men, D.T. Niles, Levi Oracion, (Ms.) Muriel Orevilla-Montenegro, (Ms.) Park Sun Ai Lee, Aloysius Pieris, Anna May Say Pa, K. Subba Rao, (Ms.) Maria Skobtsova, Israel Selvanayagam, Sulak Sivaraksa, (Ms..) Vandana Mataji, Vladimir Solovyev, C.S. Song, R.S. Sugirtharajah, David Suh Kwang-sun, M.T. Thangaraj, (Ms.) Mai Thanh, Edicio de la Torre, Wu Yaozong, Kim Heup Young, Zhao Zi-chen, Zhu Weizhi.

(For these and others refer to *Asian Christian Theologies,*. ISPCK/ Orbis, 2001-2004).

- Other sources consulted include: José A. Agola, Charlotte Allen, Joseph A. Bessler, Marcus Borg, James L. Charlesworth, Martien E. Brinkman, Rita Nakashima Brock & Rebecca Ann Parker, Dominic Crossan, James W. Deardorf, Levi H. Dowling, H.T. Driver, David Ford & Mike Higton, Holger Kersten, Ramon Malek, Elizabeth Moltman-Wendel, Robin Meyers, Robert J. Miller, Nicolas Notovich, Leonis Price, E.P. Sanders, Jan Peter Schouten, Bernard B. Scott, Elizabeth Schüssler-Fiorenza, Nicola Slee, Jon Sobrino, Gerd Theissen, Geza Vermes, Anton Wessels.

II. *Choosing Approaches & Sources for Asian Christian Studies*

There are plain implications to be drawn from studies in the above chapters for the approach to be taken in research and teaching, writing and publication, of Christian histories and theologies for the Asian region. I have been haunted since first reading D.T.Niles in the early 1960s, by his words on the necessary "self-hood of a church", and the "secular engagement of the Asian church". These became guidelines not only in his national and ecumenical ministries but also for the Asia-wide programmes of the East Asia Christian Conference (EACC, later CCA). Here was the vigorous witness of Asian church leaders to the character of God's work in their midst; a witness which had its own unique history, identity and autonomy. For those of us called into this heritage this would then become the approach we would take in study, teaching and writing in the following decades. In considering approaches to be taken for research and teaching in Asian Christianity, the outline below attempts to show distinctions in the standpoint and methods developed on the foundation of these distinctive church histories and theologies of Asian peoples.

On first serious encounter with the range of Church history and theology in Asia's regions there may be difficulty in classifying or reconciling the many divergent approaches (and their underlying assumptions) which are presented. It soon becomes apparent that authors and agencies are clearly often standing in and viewing from, quite different contexts, assumptions and mind-frames. (See also chap.7 above).[1]

1. The Distinction made

Most often these histories and surveys clearly assume that western historical or theological concepts and methods are normative for the study of *all* church histories or theologies: Asian Church History is subsumed under European or American history of missions; or Asian theology is viewed as a contribution to, or response to, 'theology itself'.[2] We are told of 'Asian voices in', or Asian 'reception of', western traditions which are supposedly standard. All of these approaches take a standpoint which is effectively – although sometimes unconsciously – outside our Asian regions in reporting or commenting on the life and history within them.[3] Upon more study however it becomes obvious that many other authors and scholars work according to quite different approaches and assumptions. We see that they start from a recognition of the vast scale, the autonomy and self-hood, of *half the world's* Christian history. There is recognition also of the Asian foundations of Christianity itself, in scripture and thought-form, in cultural origins and in its founding leader.[4] In pursuing historical research or theological construction these scholars stand in their own (or their fully adopted) traditions, yet are able to draw on larger bodies of Asian resources, both contextualizing and localized.

Yet within these recognitions there is a fundamental affirmation that if God is the great Spirit of *all* times and places, *all* peoples and cultures, then God is also present and discernible in *each* known time, *each* particular place, in the unique and concrete lives of all peoples and cultures. As we know from the Biblical record, just as each experience of God's presence is particular and localized so also is the response required of us precisely as and where we are, in all the variety of God's diverse creation. Asian Chritian theologies are there 'embedded in and emerge from' their context.[5]

In result the former authors view the Christian traditions and movements of Asian regions as only the outgrowth or re-production of western Christianity, to be studied in and assessed by, the concepts and methodologies that have been contextualized in Europe and North America.[6] While for the latter authors we see that materials and studies are discovered or produced fully conscious of a distinctive Asian self-hood and identity. They clearly acknowledge and employ autonomous histories and theologies, expressing half the world's Christian experience, thought-forms, and imageries, and found in thousands of languages. Whatever degrees of influence, exchange or hybridity can be also discerned , here we have histories or theologies that we must recognise and entitle as distinctively 'Tribal' or 'Homeland', 'Minjung' or 'Dalit', 'Women's' or 'People's', 'Double Wrestle' or 'Inter-faith', 'Dharma' or 'Dao', 'Bamboo' or 'Samizdat', 'Laicized', 'Struggle' or 'Liberation'.

The paragraphs below reflect on implications for our present approaches to study, research and teaching or writing of those unique histories and identities of Christianity in Asian countries. The very extensive histories and theologies to be explored come from regions extending from the Ural Mountains and the Lebanese coast in the west to the Kamchatka peninsula and the Philippines in the east and to India and Austral-asia in the south. The first attempt to chart these resources from the 2nd to the 20th centuries can be found in the Research Guide to *Asian Christian Theologies* (3 vols. ed. John C. England et al. (ISPCK, Claretian, Orbis 2001-2004). A large number of the materials outlined there – along with more recent items accessioned since 2000

– are already held in the *Rita Mayne England Asian Studies Collection*, Hewitson Library, Knox College, Dunedin. [7] (See also section III below).

To illustrate the distinction made in the resources available for study, the sections below[8] give in a 'quick walk past', a selection from the range of materials available. They are therefore categorized according to whether the standpoints taken by the writers are shaped more by 'western' historical and theological assumptions *or* by more contextual, indigenous resources. This is not of course to claim that either category is somehow free from multiplying cultural interactions or 'hybridities', but simply to recognise that unique historical, ethnic and local conditions and traditions remain significant sources and determinants of identity and understanding. This in turn is based on basic theological assumptions concerning:

a) the One divine presence being discernible in *all* times and places, all peoples and all living faiths;

and b) the localized particularity which characterizes all experience of such presence.[9]

2. Assumptions and Categorization

It may initially seem polemical to categorize materials in this way, or you may disagree on the inclusion of particular items in the listings below. Even so it is possible to recognise that most if not all may have their particular contribution to constructive study when we recognise some such broad *distinctions in their approaches*. They are based on the further assumptions that :

(i) We now have greatly increased bodies of resources – in text and manuscript, epigraphy, art and oral tradition – for the study of all aspects of Asian church histories and theologies;[10]

(ii) there have been millennia of contrasting and often conflicting histories or religious traditions when comparing countries within and outside the region;[11]

(iii) there are significant differences established in various studies, more recently in Richard Nisbett's *The Geography of Thought*,[12] between 'eastern' and 'western' ways of thought and interpretation;

(iv) the creative elements of *distinctive* cultural and Christian heritages and visions are to be valued contributors to our present theological and historical studies and undertakings, whatever mutual dialogue and learning becomes possible.

In any case my categorization raises a *central* question as to how far it is acknowledged that Asian Churches do in fact have their own autonomous traditions in history and theology, and how far we may draw on these as our present resources. Of course this question then leads to other questions as to the extent of our holdings of Asian theologies and histories and also as to how far our course offerings, collections and classifications themselves demonstrate that there are such autonomous resources and visions. It is unfortunately true that many of our curricula and course offerings virtually omit the Christian heritage and the present life of more than half the world.[13]

Clearly many 'two-thirds-world' countries have a continuous Christian history from the earliest centuries, as others do for at least many centuries. This has not been widely recognised even within the Asian regions, yet Christian witness and response to the 'mission of God' there is of course as valid as, and often far older than, that in most of Europe. But it is clear that the issue is not just whether we can trace a continuous tradition from early centuries, but whether Asian peoples hold in Biblical interpretation, in liturgy, life and prophetic witness, their own cultural identity; their own discernment of what God is doing in their midst; their own Christian self-hood. This is in fact to present a quite fundamental challenge to our theological presuppositions: is there held in these assumptions a complete seriousness regarding 'the presence and work of One Living God', in *all* times… *all* places…. and *all* peoples? And a presence which always accepts and even favours diversity and autonomy?

So a basic question in our approach to studying, teaching or writing on Asian Christianities is whether we are excavating, photographing, or writing up the 'over there' story, while standing firmly within western traditions, *or* whether we are standing instead with colleagues 'there and here' as they excavate, photograph, write their *own* story there (which is also in some degree our story here)? Do we, that is, seek to place our feet in our neighbour's shoes, to sit at his desk or book-shelf? The sharp question for all Asian Christian studies is to what extent we employ the same assumptions and resources as colleagues who 'stand in their own place'. We can note the procedure of metanoia employed by anthropologists and by orientalists in recent years in their recognition of colonialist and hegemonic elements in their supposedly objective studies. Such change of heart and vision is especially required of students and historians of Asian Christianities and theologies.

So our *pre-understanding* of these issues is crucial to our research in Asian Christianity: both our theological assumptions regarding the mystery and 'mission' of God, and our assumptions about the extent, diversity, autonomy and significance for us, of the histories and theologies of Asian Churches. To repeat, these stand as *more than half the Christian world*, both historically as well as in the contemporary world. To take this extent, autonomy and diversity seriously requires I believe, that we recognise the difference in standpoint of missiologies which view the life and history of Christian communities in Asian countries from the *"sending end"*, and those which in methodology and resources *"stand in a people's own place"*. To illustrate the way in which this enables us to further understand historical and theological studies since the early 20th century I include in the 'Charting' section below examples of both approaches which I have characterized as being:

a) 'from the sending end' (western sources and methods are normative);[14]

b) 'standing in their own place' (indigenous experience and assumptions have priority).

3. 'Seeing the story whole'

I am suggesting therefore that we need more than 'mission history or studies' and more even than 'reception history' or (re-oriented) 'theologies of mission'. For have not 'Mission Studies' so frequently presupposed a coming in 'from the outside', to a religious (and social) context entirely/largely free of Christian (or 'civilized') history? And don't they almost always use our (westernizing) methods of scholarship and analysis to evaluate the religious life, resources and practice encountered? Yet surely the local presence of Christian communities is to be studied in terms of its own cultural, and Jesus-centred history and life. Is not the divine Presence of whom we seek to learn, teach and write, universally One God of *all* peoples, places, cultures and times, *already* present there/here, wherever?[15]

'*Seeing whole*', '*seeing from the other end*', means a different openness to indigenous and 'non-western' tradition; to often quite different histories of Christian experience; to prophetic and 'gospel' elements within other living faiths; and to the alternative wisdoms and theologies to which these gives birth. This means a long listening to the creative sources and contexts of Christian, religious and secular life; and to prophetic witness in our own region, our own country in particular... In the light of the study and *receiving* such as this suggests, it could then be possible to build a systematic and fully mutual collaboration to excavate, identify, interpret, critique and disseminate these traditions, as well as to add to them prophetically and creatively.

The primary purpose for all our study will be to discover and understand what our sisters and brothers of Asian (and Pacific) countries (along with those expatriates most closely identified with their experience and aspirations) have found the Spirit of God to be doing and saying in their midst, in their *own* histories and cultures, their *own* sufferings, struggles and hopes . . . Compare here the words of D.T. Niles: "a church has selfhood and autonomy because mission is always [first] to a particular place and nation; it is defined by its location, its human community, in its worship, its 'conversation' and its secular engagement. . .in *this* way it is the member of one Body." [16]

So we are challenged to move beyond, or come back from, 'history' or 'studies' of mission, even from much of missiology, wherever these presuppose an interpretive base outside the history and experience of Asian Christians themselves, in their very long history. Our working basis then becomes something like 'the Christian community within the human community',[17] 'Church-in-Asian-world' studies; 'Christian/religious tradition history in Asian (and Pacific) countries'. This is a different kind of 'pneumatology' which studies the presence and purpose of the Great Spirit in all Asia's everyday world, for which the Christian church is to be, or often is not, the faithful sign and model. The yardstick for all such study, interpretation and theology remains of course, the Life-of-Jesus-with-others. (Refer to I above). Such approaches can be seen in the work undertaken in recent decades by many seminaries, institutes, universities and regional ecumenical networks (and their fore-runners). This has built on earlier studies of particular cultural and religious traditions completed by some of the earliest Orthodox, Catholic and Protestant missioners.[18]

4. But if we are to see further the Asian church whole, and 'start locally and globally'?

This requires carefully articulated priorities, and strategies:

i) Focused attention is to be given to the primacy of *Asian* church history and archival research and study projects, along with systematic 'excavation' of writings and publications, epigraphy and artefacts, especially from periods before 1900. There must of course be systems established also for adequate bibliographic control, in classification and archives for very diverse materials as well as for the methods for its storage and retrieval.

This task is already recognized and progressing in some countries (see the series of large vols. in India; for other areas refer, for example, to the *ACTS Research Guide* vols.). It is however barely begun in some other countries. Some journals have also been attempting systematic archival work (cf. *Theologie in Context, Exchange, International Review of Mission, Bibiliographia Missionaria, International Bulletin of Missionary Research,* and the *IAMS.* website).[19] To be effective however there is required much more systematic sharing and exchange between institutes and colleges, libraries and archives, and between faculties and publishers. There must also be the recognition that theological reflection (as indeed in all work of scholarship, publication and resource-building) is always a co-operative task in which the expertise of diverse practitioners is necessary. For our half of the world also, we can discern that theological reflection always arises within a people's life in response to God's presence, and so is both always a 'public theology' [20]and always grounded in and nurtures worship.[21]

ii) Obstacles to be recognized include:

- ~ the pre-occupation of national church historians and theologians with patterns of church growth, confessional identity, proselytism and the preservation of dogma;

- ~ the lack also of localized, contextual and integrated work by 'students of mission';

- ~ the widely random and haphazard influences of 'missionary experience', western church histories, fundamentalisms, academic specialisms and available finance(!) .

- ~ the contributing problems of seminary library collections which are highly westernized; and a similar European/North American orientation in the majority of course offerings and teaching in our colleges.[22]

- ~ the consequent vast imbalance of sources, the large gaps in understanding, the fragmentation of country histories, and the scarcity of resources;

~ caused largely by pre-suppositions that the record *is* fragmentary (or heretical!) and that the resources for studying it *are* very scarce!

~ the use in church historical study of concepts and classifications which are not based upon interpretation of the 'church' as being those who *in life and action* follow the life of Jesus. (See chapter 6 above).

~ all leading to widespread neglect of over half the world's own church history, its theological traditions, and historical faith.

iii) Our studies therefore *require the assumption* that there *is* a largely continuous history of independent Christian witness and thought over more than a millennium (in some areas almost two millennia); along with the assumption that there has been a guiding vision of the life, under God's Spirit, of autonomous traditions. Diatopical and dialogical methods are to be used, presupposing new levels of co-operative research and collaboration. For this we require much more imaginative and persistent approaches in research, open also to asking different questions and to using different methodologies.

A strategic plan will be needed by which we also identify the periods, areas, and materials which require 'compensatory' attention. These would include for example 17th cent. Taiwan, Thailand or the Philippines, 18th cent. Burma or China; early 19th cent. Japan or Vietnam; along with the writings of Asian women pre-20th century, and the documentation of earlier people movements. Such a plan will necessarily also identify the locations of the extensive libraries and archives which are as yet only partially explored for historic sources, for example those at Bangalore, Shanghai, Tokyo, Manila, Macau, Hochiminh Ville, Singapore, Dunedin.

iv) So for our effective research and sharing of resources the *questions must be re-phrased* to follow some such form as this:

~ What do Christian communities in Asian countries see as the most significant sources of their own national, cultural, Christian identity?

~ What do their scholars recognise as the pivotal moments of their Christian history and their people's larger history, both religious and secular?

~ What do those on the frontiers of holistic service or mission – women or men, laity or clergy, in centres, groups or movements – understand theology-in-their-place to be?

~ What sources do such practitioners currently have for their reflection or sustenance, in service or ministry, teaching or writing?

Our approach in **Summary,** for research and teaching would emphasize:

- A theology of One Living God, *all* times, *all* peoples, *all* places;
- Autonomous traditions in history and theology – Christian self-hood;
- A different openness to indigenous tradition and social history;
- Theological discernment of 'the Spirit abroad' in secular life; a 'public theology';
- Co-operative 'Church-in-world' research in carefully selected areas;
- Beginning with urgent questions for human survival and life, 'locally and globally';
- Systematic collaboration to excavate and identify creative sources;
- Priority to Asian resources even if in 'fragmentary' histories or materials;
- Primacy to bibliographical and archival research;[23]
- Full integration of teaching and research with library, and resource-centre development.

The following section provides a more detailed charting of approaches, sources and categories for the study, teaching and writing of Christian histories and theologies in the Asian region.

Endnotes

[1] Regarding use of the terms 'East' and 'West' see especially End-note 2, chap. 7. Cf. distinctions made in recent writings by Asian theologians on 'vernacular' hermeneutics which provide particular resources for Christian re-interpretation.

[2] See H-J. Klimkeit & I. Gillman *Christians in Asia before 1500* (Curzon, 1999) 1f. regarding western forms of 'intellectual imperialism'; and also the guiding principles for the writing of Church History accepted by the 5th EATWOT Conference (Oct. 1981) as to "the incarnation of the Gospel in particular regions and cultures in contrast to a recounting of missionary endeavours". M.D. David *Asia and Christianity* (Himalaya Publishing, 1985). Cf. chapter 6 above.

[3] See 'Towards a Charting of Asian Histories and Theologies' below. Examples of historical approaches taken last century, *'from the 'sending end'*: As "History of Mission" or the "Present state of Mission": Surveys of the World Dominion Press (from 1920s on); national studies published by Christian Literature Societies (e.g. for China, 1907); many individual historians from C. Buchanan (1812/2019) to H. Newcomb (1854), and later volumes to A. Schmidlin (1933); many authors from R.K. Orchard (1959) to G.H. Anderson (1998), and later works from B. Stanley (2003) to Timothy Park (2012). On 'History of the Expansion of Christianity': many vols. from K.S. Latourette, (1945 et seq.) to S. H. Moffett (2005). On 'Perspectives, Epochs, Paradigms', for mission theology: for example Ralph Winter (1981), D.Bosch (1991), J. Bonk (2011); many current European studies from, for example, the Universities of Amsterdam or Helsinki and North American studies from, for example Yale or Fuller Universities. Series of later vols. from mission agencies and denominations and many studies included as an aspect of European or North American mission history; translation or republication of earlier studies or surveys of missionary work.

As studies of *"Responses"* to western (or 'westernizing') mission: Many vols. over the past century, from "Mission and Politics in Asia"(Speer, 1898) to "History's Lessons for Tomorrow's Missions" (WSCF 1960); from many "Histories of Mission" (cf. K.S. Latourette 1940-54...) to "Patterns of Christian Acceptance" (M. Jarrett-Ker, 1972); from "Five Great Missionary Experiments" (M. Bernard, 1989), to S. Sunquist *A Dictionary of Asian Christianity* (2001 & 2017); Biographies of individual missionaries and groups (e.g. G.H. Anderson, (ed.) *Biographical Dictionary of Christian Missions* (1998); "Reception History" ('the Munich School' (1998), A.Camps, (1999).

[4] Refer S.H. Moffett, *A History of Christianity in Asia:* Vol. 1, Beginnings to 1500 (Harper & Row, 1992) chap. 1; J.C. England *The Hidden History of Christianity in Asia* (ISPCK, 1998) Introduction; Klimkeit & Gillman (op.cit. 1999) Introduction.

[5] P. Jesudason & R. Rajkumar (eds.) *Asian Theology on the Way. Christianity, Culture & Context.* (SPCK, 2012) xiii, 4ff. & passim.

[6] We were thus told that the many traditions of 1st century presence in India, *and* in China, could only be rated legend, whereas in both cases we now have full evidence that this was so. (Refer chap.1 above).

⁷ Library: www.hewitson.mykoha.co.nz Archives: www.archives.presbyterian.org.nz/

⁸ And in the listings of 'A Charting...' later in chapter.

⁹ A recent discussion of these issues is found in Felix Wilfred *Asian Public Theology* (ISPCK, 2010) xiiff. & passim. Cf. Christos Yannaras *Orthodoxy and the West* (Holy Cross Orthodox Press, 2006).

¹⁰ Refer in particular to chapters 1-3 above, and also the following section of this chapter.

¹¹ A ready parallel is seen in the diverse histories of ⁿational *literatures* which are recognised to have clearly distinctive regional, national, even local, features. These have been shaped by particular historical, sociological and political contexts which in their diversity render them no less part of a people's experience and consciousness.

¹² Free Press, 2003.

¹³ See chap. 1 above, 'Reclaiming our Christian History'.

¹⁴ Although much of this extensive publishing has been dependent upon translations or versions of works already produced in Europe or North America, many volumes – from as early as 1608 in China (Mateo Ricci) and 1718 (ISPCK) — were published in order to make available classic Chinese or Indian sources, often with Christian reflection upon these.

¹⁵ See chap.4 in this volume. Wilfred op.cit. deals systematically with those issues for which a 'new historiography' is therefore required in the Asian region. For earlier documentation see The *Humanum studies, 1969-1975: a collection of documents* (Co-ordinator David Jenkins), WCC, 1975, and Kiyoko Takeda Cho "The Weeds and the Wheat an Inquiry into Indigenous Cultural Energies in Asia" *Ecumenical Review* (27:3, 1975).

¹⁶ See 'Watershed Theologian 2 – 'Daniel T. Niles' chap. 8 above.

¹⁷ See the important book of that title from the EACC (M.M. Thomas & D.T. Niles,1964).

¹⁸ Prominent amongst locations where these studies were begun (the earliest in the 2ⁿᵈ century – see chaps. 1 and 2 above), were Cochin (India), Edessa, and Ctesiphon (Persia), Chang an and Da Qin (China), Dunhuang and Turfan (Turkestan), Madurai, Goa, Tranquebar and Serampore (India), Nanjing, Peking, Canton and Zikawai (China), Nagasaki, Kyoto and Azumi (Japan), Malacca and Penang (Malaya), along with Batavia (East Indies) and Macau. By the late-20ᵗʰ century Catholic and Protestant research institutes or colleges were, in addition, publishing localised studies in such cities as Bombay (Mumbai), Calcutta (Kolkata), Madras (Chennai), New Delhi and Pune (India); in Kyoto, Nagoya and Tokyo (Japan); in Seoul, Daegu, and Kwangju (Korea); in Quezon City, Manila, and Dumaguete Philippines); in Taipei and Tainan (Taiwan); Jakarta, Yogyakarta and Ende (Indonesia). By then also institutes for Social Concern, national Christian Literature Societies and National Christian Councils had been established in almost every country of the region. For these, the study and publication of contextual Asian resources has become increasingly

important. See e.g. P.L. Wickeri, (ed.) *The People of God Among all God's Peoples: Frontiers in Christian Mission* (CCA & CWM, 2000), D.P. Niles (ed.) *Windows into Ecumenism* (CCA, 2005), F. Wilfred *Margins - Site of Asian Theologies* (ISPCK, 2008).

[19] See further sections in this chap. for listing of periodical literature.

[20] Wilfred op.cit. xiif. & passim., also Gemma Tulud Cruz in P. Jesudason & R. Rajkumar (op.cit. 2012) 75ff.

[21] This is the strong tradition which the orthodox churches of Asia contribute to theological tasks. See e.g. Paulos Mar Gregorios *The Joy of Freedom: Eastern Worship and Modern Man*. (CLS, 1986), K.M. George *Silent Roots* (WCC, ISPCK, 1994).

[22] Note the quantitative extremes in some recent collections on Asian Christianity, from the many columns on individual western missionaries, to a sometimes complete absence of entire entries for many Asian countries.

[23] Note that this work has been well begun by members of the *Forum of Asian Theological Librarians* (since 1991) www.foratl.org.

III. *Towards a Charting of Asian Church Histories and Theologies*

To take seriously the many substantial bodies of Asian Christian histories and theologies is firstly, to recognize how very extensive the literature (and artefacts) are and how rich are the theological traditions[1] that have long been established in our region. For although Asian church history and theology have emerged as complete fields of study only in recent decades, they have themselves a full and ancient history, along with the large bodies of contemporary scholarship and writing. They exist in almost every known oral and written form, in hundreds of languages, and date from many different periods – some as early as the 2nd century – across the region between Persia, Japan and Austral-Asia.² It is also necessary to recognise the evidence of a very wide range of materials – in archaeology, epigraphy, manuscript, artefact and including folk literature – which require diverse forms of classification, translation and interpretation in such studies.

Earlier chapters here provide introductions to this long history, especially in its ecumenical and missionary thrust, and to its artistic traditions, as well as to selected periods and movements in social and theological development. This chapter outlines approaches being taken in both the study and teaching of Asian Church histories and theologies, and also offers ways of charting their periods, themes and regional characteristics. A small sample only of the extensive materials available for study is possible here, rather than any exhaustive presentation. Listings below are intended to indicate the wide range of resources that are now accessible in Asian regions, from which any number can be selected for study.

1. The History

Although twentieth century theological reflection in Asian countries may be our particular concern, this can only be understood in the context of many centuries of Christian presence in the region. Geographically this is the region bounded by the Ural Mountains and the Mediterranean Sea in the west, by the Kamchatka peninsula in the northeast, and by India and Indonesia in the south. ³ This history can be most briefly summarized by saying that Christianity had become known within a dozen countries east of Persia by the 8th century (in half of these by the 4th century) and in almost all countries of the Asian region by the 16th century. From this long presence, extensive Christian writings and memorials remain from the late antique and early medieval periods until the late modern and contemporary centuries. We are therefore offered a vast range of archaeological and architectural remains, of epigraphy and artefact, manuscript and published sources from locations as various as Trichur and Madras, Nisibis and Samarkand, Dunhuang and Xian, Bishkek and Malacca, Peking and Amoy, Kandy, Seoul and Cebu. Such wide-spread distribution was the prelude to a presence in all the centres of nineteenth and twentieth century Christian activity.

As an initial assumption it is important to recognise the distinction (see II above, end-note 3) between approaches in studying Asian Christian history which view this as a late adjunct to European or North American 'history of mission', and those which view this as the autonomous history of Christianity in 'over half the world' for two millennia, and therefore having its own unique identity and sources. The first approach retains the colonial features of Eurocentric or Americocentric writing which does not yet recognise the contextualized nature of their own formulations and which have yet to discern either the scale or diversity of Asian Christian histories and theologies or their independent identity and authority. The latter approach is based not only on historical conclusions from study of 'the other half' of the Christian world but upon the theological assumption of God's universal presence in the unique lives of all peoples. What follows is an outline for the study (and teaching) of Christianity in Asia which is based firstly on the latter assumptions and conclusions, in distinction from 'neo-colonial' methodologies.

It will be noted that in distinguishing 'the sending end' from 'standing in their own place 'the charting attempted here (see footnote 3 under section II above, as well as in further pages), retains distinctions between such categories as 'east' and 'west', oriental and occidental, indigenous and colonial/pre-colonial/neocolonial. Basis for this framework has been outlined under chapter 7 (n.2) above. But it must be stressed that although the debates on 'essentialism', 'deconstruction' and 'universalism' have alerted us to the dangers of 'totalizing' language and concepts it is not possible to attain a perspective entirely "free of the locatedness and limitations of embodied existence". Susan Bordo rightly terms this "a fantasy that I call 'a dream of everywhere'".[4] The particularity of Biblical event and history cannot be so easily dismissed.

Nor do we wish to be free of such concrete and diverse locatedness (see also section II above). In studying the histories and theologies of Asian Christian communities it is, on the contrary, fully necessary to recognise location and context – geographical, historical, cultural and religious – if we are to remain concerned for the actual lives of our people or to take *contextualizing* [5] processes at all seriously. Full study in the histories and theologies of this region reveals that Asian lands and peoples have known quite *different* cultural, social and religious histories to those of Europe, whatever degree of exchange, 'hybridity' or mutual influence can also be seen. Asian peoples have in their histories also experienced their *own* 'Reformations', 'Renaissances' and 'Enlightenments' over many centuries;[6] along with different Christian histories which demonstrate their own wide-ranging discernments, endeavours and wisdoms. These are not only heritages to be held, but also offer rich promise and hope for us now.

2. A Selection of those historians 'standing in their own place.'

See also Bibliographies to chapters 1 and 2 above and online catalogue to the *Rita Mayne England Asian Studies Collection,* Hewitson Library, Knox College, Dunedin (NZ). For further on each person or group see also *Asian Christian Theologies: A Research Guide* (3 vols.) ed. J.C. England et al. (2001-2004), and continuing reviews in *Asia Journal of Theology* and other journals listed below. [7] Further information on particular authors below can be found on such sites as www.worldcat.org, www.abebooks.com/servlet and www.used.addall.com.

Recent or earlier historical study is taken further by colleagues who begin from and draw on the independent or indigenous traditions and sources of Asian Christian communities. For most of these scholars this work has involved the recovery, even excavation, of long-neglected manuscripts publications and artefacts, often requiring also the initial classification of materials and translation from a number of Asian languages. A small selection of the *regional or national historical studies or surveys* from these authors is given below. (Date given is that of an author's first key work):

2.1 *Early studies include:*
G.S. Assemani (1719), Michael Le Quien (1740), M. L'Abbe Huc (1844), C. Buchanan (1812), J.M. Neale (1847), W. Cureton (1864), E.L. Cutts (1876), J. Legge, (1888), W. Wright (1894), A. Stein (1898), James B. Chabot (1902), F.C. Burkitt (1904), G. Malech (1910), W.A. Wigram, (1910), P. Pelliot (1914), F. El-Ghusein (1916), Saeki Yoshiro (1916), B.J. Kidd (1927), (Ms.) G. Bell (1928), John Stewart (1928), E.A.W. Budge (1928), A.C. Moule (1930), A.R. Vine (1937), (Ms.) C.P. Grant (1937), J. Foster (1939), (Ms.) F. Stark (1942), N. Zernov (1942).

2.2 *For 1945-2000:*
J. Dauvillier (1948), D. Paton (1953), C. Dawson (1955), Lutterworth / WCC studies (1960s), *One People, One Mission* (EACC, 1963), W.L.A. Don Peter (1963), J. Leroy (1963), A. Schmemann (1965), Lo Hsiang-lin (1966), B. Colless (1967), A. Atiya (1968), W.G. Young (1969), R.M. Haddad (1970), A.M. Mundadan (1970), R. Nyce (1972), V. Sitoy (1972), Min Kyung-bae (1974), M. Bordeaux (1975), Mar Aprem (1976), M.P.M. Muskens (1978), G. Every (1978), N. Lotfi (1980), H-J. Klimkeit & I.Gillman (1981,1998), Jiang Wen-han (1982), M.D. David (1985), J. Roxborogh (1987), W. Hage (1987), S. Moffett (1992), M. Zibawi (1995), K. Koschorke (1996), J.C. England (1998), K. Koschorke (1998), J. De Murat (1999), A. O'Mahoney (1999), P. L. Wickeri (2000), Mar A. Mattam (2000).

2.3 *Since 2000*
D. Lewis (2000), W. Baum & D. Winkler (2000), M. Palmer (2001), (Ms.) B.J. Bailey & J. Martin (2003), (Ms.) Kwok Pui-lan (2005), Christos Yannaras (2006), S. Rassam (2006), (Ms.) A-M. Talbot (2006), C. Baumer (2006), Mar B. Soro (2007), A. Walls & (Ms.) C. Ross (2008), N. Jabbour (2008), F. Wilfred (2008 & 2010), D.W. Winkler (2010), J. Weatherford (2010), J.A.B. Jongeneel et al. (2011), A. Dharma et al (2011), A. Treiger (2012), P. Jesudason (2012), J. Massey (2013), Li Tang (2013), Leow Theng-huat (2014), Nur Masalha & (Ms)L. Isherwood (2014) J. Harris (2015), P.C. Phan (2017).

3. Theological Studies or construction:

The very diverse forms of Christian theology which are multiplying in our countries today must also be seen in continuity with the diversity we can now study in pre-modern and pre-colonial writings. The medieval collections of hymns, poetry, treatises, homilies, chronicles, commentaries, letters, liturgies, parables, biographies, inscriptions, stone carvings, crosses, seals, and frescoes, prefigure much of the wealth of theological forms blossoming today in the region. (See chapters 1-3 above). But to them we can now add the many other contemporary forms of people-stories, manifestos, meditations, essays, declarations of conscience, testimonies, songs, dialogues, protest liturgies, and Christian arts. These are to be found in article collections and journals, in anthologies, monographs, manuscripts and bibliographies (See sections 5 and 6 below).

3.1 *Collections, Surveys, Journals*[8]

In more systematic form we have, since the mid-nineteenth century, the collected works in many volumes, of Asian Christian theologians: including those of such individual authors as

Wu Lei Chuen, Chao Tzu-chen, K.H. Ting in China;

Keshub Chunder Sen, A.J. Apassamy, M.M. Thomas in India;

L. Ch. Abineno, Eka Darmaputera, E. Gerrit Singgih in Indonesia;

Uchiimura Kenzo and Kuwada Hidenobu in Japan;

Yang Ju Sam, Kim Jae Jun, Ahn Byung Mu in Korea;

Horatio de la Costa, Leonardo Mercado, Vitaliano Gorospe in the Philippines;

D. T. Niles, Lynn de Silva, Tissa Balasuriya, in Sri Lanka;

Shoki Coe, Song Choan Seng, Huang Po Ho in Taiwan.

—not to mention the extensive collections by other contemporary authors (See further below).

3.2 *Scores of regional collections or surveys* are now available by, for example:
Cecil Hargreaves, G. H. Anderson, S. Arokiasamy, G. Gispert-Sauch, Aziz Atiya, Saphir Athyal, S.H Moffett, Franklyn J. Balasundaram, H-R. Weber, Bong Rin Ro, Vladimir Lossky, (Ms.) Henie D. Camba, Sadayandy Batumalai, (Ms.) Chung Hyun Kyung , D.J. Elwood, J. C. England, (Ms.) Virginia Fabella, Alexander Schmemann, Kim Heup Young, S.C.H. Kim, Rajah B. Manikam, L.N. Mercado & James Knight, Ron O'Grady & T. K. Thomas, (Ms.) Muriel Orevillo-Montenegro, D.P. Niles, Oh Jae Shik, Miguel M. Quatra, Anthony Rogers, S.J. Samartha, R.S. Sugirtharajah, J. Y. Tan, M.M. Thomas, Vimal Tirimanna, S.Sunquist, W.Baum & D.Winkler, Peniel Jesudason & Rufus Rajkumar.

There must be also added here the regular publications from the CCA, FABC, EATWOT, OMF, PTCA and ATA. [9]

3.3 *Journals and Bibliographies*
In almost every country of the region a range of theological journals is published (in five countries, more than twenty each).[10] Major bibliographical projects have been undertaken in at least six countries, varying in size from a booklet (Payap College, Chiangmai; or Centre for Society and Religion, Colombo) to four large volumes (the United Theological College, Bangalore). This is currently one of the most urgent tasks for many of us, so that the range and wealth of theological writings might be discovered, classified and made known. In at least eight countries, a major project has been begun for the rewriting of church histories in context (see further below).

4. *Categories and Schools of theological thought*
The following chart covers some of the chief categories discernible in Asian theologies, with particular emphasis on the nineteenth and twentieth centuries. It is offered as one guide to understanding the range and concerns of theological reflection in the region within the last 200 years. It has been possible to include only a selection of representative

examples in order to present something of the range and intentions of Asian theologies.

Note that the categories below are not presented as quite 'independent compartments', nor do they comprehend all the themes found in the work of a particular author. The purpose is rather to recognise major emphases that can be identified within the writings of a range of scholars, as well as to present something of the scale of materials available for study and application. (See introduction to 6.1. below). National studies given above, along with national bibliographies (and bibliographies already given above), should be consulted for fuller details.

4.1 *Antique and Medieval Asian writings (and art).*
Extensive bodies of these pre-colonial authors from as early as the 2nd century have been intensively studied from only the late 18th century on. (See 2.1 above).

Those who are particularly significant for us now include Tatian and Bardaisan (2nd century), Ephrem and Aphrahat (4th century), Theodore of Mopsuestia, (Mmes.) Macrina and (Ms.) Egeria (4th-5th centuries), Philoxenus of Mabbug (5th century), John Philoponos (5th-6th enturies),(Ms.) Euphemia (6th century), Mar Babai (6th-7th centuries), Patriarch Timothy I, A Lo-Pen and Adam Ching-ching (8th century), Theodore Abu Qurrah and Hunayn ibn Ishaq (9th century), Yahya ibn Adi (9th-10th centuries), Sulayman al-Ghazzi (10th-11th centuries), Subar Yeshu (11th century), Bar Hebraeus, Rabban Sauma, Ai Hsieh, (Ms.) Dokuz Khatun and (Ms.) Sorghaqtani Beki (13th century), Mar Jacob of Cochin (15th century).

There are in addition many collections of writings from the earliest centuries which remain anonymous.[11] A few of the examples we have in the first millennium C.E would include the *Odes of Solomon* (2nd century); collections of manuscripts from St Catherine's Monastery, Sinai; artefacts and relics held in Malabar museums, South India; art forms from Damascus and Nebke (Syria), Antilyas (Lebanon), and Erevan (Armenia); documents and art forms from Turfan, and Dunhuang,

Turkestan; carvings and manuscripts from Da Qin and Chang-an Monasteries, North China.

For further on these authors see Select Bibliography to chap. 1 above, in particular those volumes by Mar Aprem, C. Baumer, W. Wright, S. Brock, J.C. England, J. Foster, I.Gillman & H-J. Klimkeit, S.H. Griffith, E. Hunter, J.J. Keelathu, M.K. Kuriakose, Li Tang & D. W.Winkler, R. Malek & P. Hofrichter, S.H. Moffett, M. Palmer, P.Y. Saeki, S.K. Samir & J.S. Nielsen, J.P.M. van der Ploeg.

4.2 *Early Modern Asian Theological Writings*

The extensive late antique and medieval collections referred to above have yet to be studied as an integral part of Asian theology, although recent bibliographical work provides a solid basis for this. In the early modern period (sixteenth to eighteenth centuries), in addition to a wide range of individual works which are now known , a number of more prolific writers have emerged from recent studies, some of their theological works being also now reprinted. Although many of these authors are sometimes concerned to reproduce Latin, Greek or even English materials in vernacular versions yet all provide creative adaptations – and sometimes alternatives – to western originals.

Among those writers for whom a *series* of volumes have survived are Yang Ting Yun, (1557–1627), Hsu Kuang-chi (1562–1633), Roberto de Nobili (1577–1656), Jacome Gonsalvez (1676–1742), Philipe de Rosario Binh (fl. 1740), and Chong Yak Jong (1760–1801).

Others for whom we have selections, poems or prayers would include Vincente Hoin (b.1538), Li Zhizao (c. 1550-1630), Fabian Fucan (b.1565), Zhang Xingyao (1633-c.1725), Yi Ik (1681-1763), Gaspar Aquino de Belen (fl.1710), and Satthianandhan of Tinnevelly (c.1750-1815).

For further studies of significant works in this period see chapter 4 above.

4.3 *Contemporary Theological Work and Writings. Western forms are primary in the following:*

Numberless volumes and articles that also purport to offer Christian teaching for Asian communities have assumed as their basis the doctrinal formulations developed by the post-Constantinian churches. This of course ignores the historical processes through which Christian faith was contextualized in western countries.

4.3.1 *"Prefabricated / colonial"*

A universal validity is assumed for western formulations, which are imposed as prefabricated models in Asian contexts. This remains a colonial pattern, content with re-printings or translations of supposedly normative texts. Whatever the intention, the earlier translations of Latin, Spanish, Portuguese or Dutch writings into such languages as Tamil, Chinese, Japanese, Tagalog, Sinhala or Malay, and more recent translations of, for example, Luther's works into Korean, the translations of Barth's *Dogmatik* into Japanese, and the continuing translations of so-called "Christian Classics" into Chinese for example, fall into this category.

Many 'early modern' writings listed under 4.2. above also show these features, along with almost all publications from the Catholic presses (17th-19th centuries) at Goa, Macau, Nagasaki, Manila, Zikawei, or Peking (Beijing).[12] This is also the case with publications of Protestant presses in the same period at Tranquebar, Serampore, Chennai (Madras), Malacca, Macau, Guangzhou (Canton) and Shanghai.[13] Clearly many mission agencies and churches still understand 'mission' as being primarily the propagation of doctrines and practices already established in western Christian tradition. Such positions are often based upon a basically 'tribal' assumption that western Christian understanding and traditions are the only ones possible and remain fully normative for all others. (See also 4.3.2 and 4.3.3 below).

4.3.2 *Asia Studies the West*

This is still the basic position taken in the vast majority of institutes for theological education across the region, re-enforced also by many graduate studies undertaken in western colleges or universities. It must be noted that in fostering the teaching and writing for younger faculty members in the Asian region over many years, this has normally first involved the study of specifically *Asian* resources, histories and writings, along with a setting aside – at least meantime – of works by scholars which do not directly address these Asian resources. (These ecumenical programmes, entitled "Doing Theology with Asian Resources", were offered to staff-members of over 300 theological seminaries and faculties across the region. In them two-month local study programmes were arranged, culminating in a three-week residential seminar-workshop).[14]

A different approach is taken by scholars in the region who wish to mine western resources for their relevance to the questions arising in Asian contexts. Often fully academic in form, these writings analyse or interpret the thought of western philosophies and theologians as being, in turn, contributions to theologies within Asian contexts. Constructive examples here would be: the studies of Barth and Brunner by Kumano Yoshitaka and Mitsuo Miyata; of A.N. Whitehead by Christopher Duraisinghe, Tokiyuki Nobuhara and Hyo-Dong Lee; of Hendrik Kraemer by Peter Latuihamallo, Karl. L. Reichelt, and Damayanthi Niles; of Wolfhart Pannenberg by Suh Nam Dong, Lewis E Winkler and Koo Dong Yun; of Ludwig Wittgenstein by Mary John Mananzan and Rukmini Bhaya Nair; of Bonnhoeffer & Marx by Paul S. Chung, Poulose Mar Poulose and Suk-Sung Yoo; of Karl Rahner by Francis X. Clooney and Lawrence Ng Yew Kim.

4.3.3 *"Contributions to western theology"*

This is a default position taken by many who do welcome 'Asian voices' as additions to ongoing theological study but still assume that European or American church history or theology provide the norms or yardstick for all Christian thought and endeavour. The voices of

Asian theologians are here recognised but only as regional contributions to what are presented as being global discussions. The significance of Asian thought-forms and histories remains largely, if not completely, unrecognized, along with the wide-ranging 'Reformations, Renaissances and Enlightenments' that have shaped the cultures and societies of Asian peoples over two millennia.

Numberless *non-contextualizing* articles on 'Asian theology' in American, European and Asian theological journals could be added here, along with many monographs and collections. Then there are examples in every country of the region of writers who provide *"Asian Garments"*[15] for a theology which is still fundamentally Western, although there is an attempt to express this in local terminology or imagery. 'Asian illustrations and colour' are sometimes employed to communicate interpretations of Christian belief and history which have yet been initiated or shaped in western contexts. In other authors a quite conservative Christian understanding is presented although some terms and metaphors are drawn from Asian cultures and experience. Neither the long history of Christianity in 'the other half of the world', nor the shaping and presentation of fundamental beliefs by *Asian* contexts of culture, society or living faiths are here fully recognised.

5.   *Resources of Distinctive Asian Theologies: 19th- 20th centuries*

5.1.   *Asia rejects the West*

Refer first to 4.1 and 4.2 above, and the introduction to 6.1. below, regarding the relationship of various categories in research and writing in the work of particular theologians. For studies of former Christian theologians who firmly rejected aspects of western Christianity– in India, China, Japan and the Philippines of the 16th-18th centuries – refer to chapter 4 above and section 5.2 below.

In the 19th-20th centuries rejection has taken the form of significant, though not always systematic, rejection of particular doctrines regarded as regulative; of ecclesiastical institutions or traditions; or of socio-political relationships upheld in the post-Constantinian west. This may focus primarily:

- on the trappings of institutional Christianity, as with (for example), James de Alwis (1823-1878), Keshub Chunder Sen (d. 1884), Sadrach Surapranata (1835-1924), Paul Sawayama (1852-1887), Uchimura Kanzō (1861–1930), U Hla Bu (1897-1970), Hsu Po Ch'en (d. 1940);

- on questions of doctrine, as with (for example), Fabian Fucan (b. 1565), Ibrahim T. Wulung (ca.1800-85), Abdulla bi A. Kadir (1797-1854), José Rizal (1861-96), Pandipeddi Chenchiah (1886-1959), (Ms.) Pandita Ramabai (1858-1922), Jotirao Phule (d.1890), Isaac Tambyah (1860-1940), Isabello de los Reyes Sr. (1864–1938), Ebina Danjō (1856–1979);

- on socio-political choices, as with (for example), Dang Duc Tuan (1806-74), Mai Lao Bang (d.1945), Gregorio Aglipay (d. 1949), Aurelio Tolentino (1867-1915), Kuruvilla George (1900–1960), Wu Yao Tsung (1895–1980), I.J. Kasimo (1890–1975?), Eddy Asirvatham (1897-1969) and Amir Sjarifoeddin (1907-48);

- or on issues of Christian Identity, as with (for example), Abraham Mar Shimon V (fl.1840), Lal Bahari Day (1824-94), Alexander Solzhenitsyn (1918-2008), Upadhyay Brahmabandhab (1861–1907), Sami Hadawi (1904-2004, Ms. Sarah Grant (1922-2000), Pierre Lou Tseng-tsiang (1871-1949), Anthony Fernando (b.1932), Elias Chacour (b.1939).[16]

These are only a few of the scholar-activists who could be listed here. And there are of course many earlier authors (i.e. before 1600) who strongly rejected the assumptions and doctrines of Greco-Latin Christianity. The very long list here would extend – to mention only one or two of the most prominent: from Tatian (2nd century), to Adam Ching-ching and the Dunhuang authors (9th-11th centuries); Mar Jacob of Cochin (15th century) and other Indian authors (16th century); Fabian Fucan of Japan (17th century); Aquino de Belen and Filipino Pasyon authors (18th century). Refer here to chapters 1 and 4 above.

5.2 *Alternatives to Western formulations.*
A selection of authors whose work includes strong criticism of patriarchal, imperial or neo-colonial concepts or images, along with rejection of many aspects of European or North American theological tradition, are given below. (Dates given indicate that of notable writing by the author named; refer to sources under 2. above).

Early works – until 1945
South Asia: Roberto de Nobili (1605), Mar Gregorios (1668), Mar Thoma IV (1709), Krishna M. Banerjea (1861), James de Alwis (1863), Keshub C. Sen (1883), P.C. Mozoomdar (1883), Narayan V. Tilak (1895), Isaac Tambyah (1903), Lars P. Larsen (1907), K.T. Paul (1921), Aiyadurai J. Appasamy (1924), Vengal Chakkarai (1927), Pandipeddi Chenchiah (1938), P. Johanns (1932), V.S. Azariah (1936), Peter A. Pillai (1937), S. Kuruvilla George (1942), E. Asirvatham (1942).

Southeast Asia: (Ms.) J. de la Asuncion (1623), Lu Y Doan (1670), Gaspar A. de Belen (ca.1715), C.L. Coolen (1840), Ding D. Tuan (1842), N. Truong To (1857), Jose A. Burgos (1861), Nguyên Truòng Tô (1861), P.T. Vinh Ky (1882), Gregorio Aglipay (1898), Isabelo de los Reyes (1899), W. Shellabear (1913), Pe Maung Tin (1914), F.G.J. van Lith (1924), Frank C. Laubach (1925), T.S.G. Moelia (1933), San C. Po (1928), U Chit Maung (1939), J. Leimena (1941), Amir Sjarifoeddin (1941), Nguyen Xuan Tin (ca.1945).

East Asia: Fucan Fabian (1620), Yang Tingyun (1621), Yan Mo (1685), Creation of Heaven and Earth (ca.1800), Chong Yak-yong (1818), Li Wenyu (1887), Wang Zhengting (1907), Ahn Joong Keun (ca. 1908), (Ms.) Zhang Zhujun (1911), F. V. Lebbe (1917), (Ms.) Zeng Baosun (1917), (Ms.) Ding Shujing (1925), Wu Yaozong (1929), Kan Enkichi (1930), Nakajima Shigeru (1931), Zhao Zi-chen (T.C. Chao, 1935), Wu Lei-chuan (1936), Kim Jai Joon (1938), Xu Zongze (1940).

West and Inner Asia/Russia: Theodore Abu Qurrah (9th century), Subar Yeshu (11th century), Rabban Sauma (13th century), Bar Hebraeus (ca. 1250), Aleksey S. Khomyakov (1839), Nicolai Gogol 1836), Fyodor Dostoevsky (1864), Vladimir Solovyev (1874), Alphonse Mingana (1907), Nicolai Berdyaev (1909), George D. Malech (1910), Faiz El-Ghusein (1916), Saeki Yoshiro (1916), Nicholas Arseniev (1926), Khalil Gibran (1926), Sergei Bolshakoff (1942).

5.3 The Asian Christian Community Gathers its Resources - 19th and early 20th Centuries

Such gathering has been often pioneered by those who have discovered the work and writings of 'antique' or 'early modern' authors in such lands as Syria, India, China, Korea, Japan or the Philippines. (See 4.1 and 4.2 above). Pioneers here also include those who have rejected aspects of 'missionary Christianity' (as in 5.1, 5.2 above); those whose historical studies have uncovered the 'hidden' histories of Asian Christianities; or those who recognise the continuing significance of particular indigenous cultural and religious traditions (see 5.3.1 , below). Resources for the present work of Christian presence within Asian societies have also been found in the histories of particular peoples (see 5.3.2 and 5.3.3 below), in Biblical studies of the prophetic and Gospel witness to social justice and peace (see the majority of authors in 6.1 below), and in ecumenical experience of shared learning and struggle (6.1.1 below).

5.3.1 Encounter with Asian Traditions

On the one hand, from the mid-twentieth century there have been further attempts in *Accommodation/ Acculturation: where s*erious study of Asian tradition has led to more systematic attempts at synthesis in theological construction. These have sometimes been open to criticism however for lack of adequate criteria being applied or for their isolation from other studies already established in the particular country concerned. Prominent examples (from a large number) include Tien Liang's *The Establishment of Chinese Catholic Culture* (1959), P. David's *The Contemporary Debate on God* (1969), Yun Sung Bum's *The Korean*

Theology or Yellow Theology (1972), and Leonardo Mercado's *Elements of Filipino Theology* (1975).

On the other hand, living faiths and traditions of neighbours in surrounding society are recognised as being themselves vehicles of spiritual truth, as well as being major contributors to human community, its peace, people-justice and creativity. Major aspects of a particular culture or faith tradition are studied sympathetically in order to advance understanding of religious experience and insight. Parallels or contributions to Christian teaching are also studied. Amongst leaders of Christian communities in this period were many who sought, on the basis of their own extensive studies, a larger unity with those of other living faiths in own their societies.

There are especially rich examples of this type in some countries of the region since early centuries (see 5.2 above) with multiple examples from the mid-nineteenth century on. India offers many examples here but such leadership was found in other countries also. Expatriate writers have been active in this field in recent centuries (see 5.3.2 below) but both indigenous and expatriate scholars have rendered most significant advances. See for example:

Burma/Myanmar: U Hla Bu (1897-1970), Francis Ah Mya (1904-99), S. Pau Khan En (fl. 1995);

Ceylon/ Sri Lanka: there was James de Alwis 1823-1878), Isaac Tambyah (1860-1940), Sabapathy Kulandran (1900-1992) and Lakdasa de Mel (1902–1976);

China: those such as Fan Zimei (Fan Tzu-mei fl.1920), Francis C.M. Wei (1888–1975?) and Wang Chih-hsin (1888–?);

India: Keshub Chandra Sen (1838-1884), Vengal Chakkarai (1880-1958), (Ms.) Pandita Ramabai (1858-1922), Aiyadurai Apassamy (1891–?) and Manilal C. Parekh (1885-1967);

Japan: those such as Aimé Villon (1843-1932), Hiromichi Kozaki (b.1856), Yokoi Tokio (1857-1937) and Takahashi Gorō (fl. 1881);

Korea: those such as Choi Byung Hyun (1858-1927), Chung Kyung Ok (1903-1945), Ryu Dong Shik (fl.1975).

Malaysia-Singapore: Stamford Raffles (1781-1824), William Shellabear (ca.1863-1947), Robert A Blasdell (1892-1986).

Philippines: Isabelo de los Reyes Sr. (1864-1938), Felipe Landa Jocano (1930 –2013), Peter Gowing (1930-1983), Leonardo N. Mercado (1935-2000).

West/Inner Asia: those such as Hunayn ibn Ishaq (808-73), Meletios Karma (fl.1625), Kenneth Cragg (1914-2012), Michael Prior (1942-2004).

(See further under 6.1.2 below).

5.3.2 Studies of a particular people's history, culture, or Christian traditions.

The basic concern here has been to take most seriously the historical, anthropological, religious and sociological realities of a particular people or ethnic grouping. Such studies therefore provide the understanding of situation, event and aspiration which enables us to place and localise a people's historic experience. There too the religious insight and wisdom of centuries can be uncovered and drawn on. Full attention is therefore given to a wide variety of indigenous materials and extensive research in local or national resources has led to the recovery or establishment of indigenous histories and traditions.

These are found in the writings of, for example:

Vivian Ba (fl.1960), (Ms.) Mi Mi Khiang (1916-90), J. Maung Latt (fl.1970) – Burma/Myanmar;

Cheng Jingyi (1881-1939), Kiang Wen Han (fl.1950), Chan Kim Kwong (fl.1990) – China;

Lal Bahari Day (1824-94), A.M. Mundanan (fl.1970), James Massey (d.2015), M.K. Kuriakose (b.1948) – India:

C.L. Coolen ((1775-1873), Robert Hardawiryana (b.1926), Jan S. Aritonang (b.1953) – Indonesia;

Anesaki Masaharu (fl.1960), Kiyoko Takeda Cho (1917- 2018), Iwashima Tadahiko sj (b.1943) – Japan;

George Paik (1827-1909), Ryu Dong Shik (b.1922), Cho Kwang (b.1925), Min Kyung Bae (fl.1990) – Korea;

Richard O. Winstedt (1878-1966), Bobby E. Sng (fl.1995, (Ms.) Maureen Chew (fl.2000), John Roxborogh (fl.2010) – Malaysia/Singapore;

Horatio de Ia Costa (d.1977), Valentino Sitoy (fl. 1985), F. Landa Jocano (1930-2013) – Philippines;

Celestino N. Fernando (1914-89), Francis O. Tambimuttu (fl.1960), W.L. Don Peter (1917- 2008) – Sri Lanka;

Herbert R. Swanson (1924-2017), Seri Phongphit (fl. 1980), Kirti Bunchua (fl.1990) – Thailand;

Truong Vinh Ky (1837-98), Truong Ba Can (b.1928), Phan Huy Le (1934-2018), Phan Phat Huon (fl.2000) – Vietnam;

Qustantin Zuraiq (1909-2000), H. Dehgani-Tafti (1920-2008), Suha Rassam (fl. 2000), Rifaat Ebiad (fl.2005), Ziya Meral (fl.2018) – West Asia.

There are also histories and contextual studies published in series of volumes such as those of the I.S.P.C.K. (Indian Society for Propagation of Christian Knowledge), and C.I.S.R.S. (Christian Institute for Study of Religion & Society), of the Ecumenical Institute for Study and Dialogue (Colombo), of the New Day and Claretian Presses (Quezon City), the Communion of Christian Churches Indonesia (PGI Jakarta), of the *Kyōbunkan* press (Japanese Christian Writings), of the OMF (Overseas Missionary Fellowship) and of PTCA (Programme for Theology and Cultures in Asia).

Expatriate scholars have been especially active in this field: see for a few examples from many, the work of: Pièrre Lebbé, Timothy Richard, (Ms.) Jessie Lutz, Carl T. Smith, M. Searle Bates – China; C.F. Andrews, Stephen Neill, Kaj Baago, Richard Taylor, John C. Webster, Robin Boyd – India; Frans G.J.van Lith, Hendrick Kraemer, Frank Cooley, Karel Steenbrink – Indonesia; (Ms.) M. Cable, F.C. Copleston sj, H-J. Klimkeit, G.L. Freeze – Inner Asia/Russia; Otis Carey, Charles Germany, Stephen Turnbull, James Phillips – Japan; Charles Osgood, Richard Rutt, S. J. Palmer, Daniel Adams – Korea; Alfred Wallace, Richard Winstedt, John Roxborogh, Goran Wiking - Malaysia Singapore; Richard Deats, William H. Scott, Richard Poethig, James Reuter – Philippines; James Tennent, Graeme C. Jackson, Francis Houtart, Ulrich Dornberg – Sri Lanka; (Ms.) Francis X. Bell, Herbert Swanson, D. Swearer, Kenneth E. Wells – Thailand; William Paton, Livio Mondini, Paul Clasper, Alexander McLeish – Burma/Myanmar; Adrian Launay, J. Bouchet, Pièrre Gheddo, David Marr, P.J. Tuck – Vietnam; J.S. Trimingham, Kenneth Cragg, Sydney Griffith, Anthony O'Mahoney – West Asia.

5.3.3 *National Surveys and Studies of assembled Theologies*
These have been published in all but a few countries in recent years. (Refer 3.2 above for regional collections, many of which include selected writings according to country). Among the most useful are those by: Lam Wing Hung, Roman Malek, Philip Wickeri, Chloe Starr– China;

Robin Boyd, Michael Amaladoss, (Ms.) M. Melanchthon, James Massey – India;

Andreas Yewangoe, Jan Aritonang, Th. Sumartana – Indonesia;

A.C. van Gorder, N. Sims-Williams, Jungyang Norbu, D.E.C. Lewis – Inner Asia/Russia;

Charles Germany, Kumano Yoshitaka, Yasuo Furuya– Japan;

Harold Hong (with Kim Chung Choon), Ryu Dong Shik, Kim Yong Bock – Korea;

Batumalai Satayandy, John Roxborogh , Goran Wiking – Malaysia/ Singapore;

Rodrigo Tano, Jose de Mesa, Nonie s. Aviso et al. – Philippines;

Nicholas Abeyasinghe, Ulrich Dornberg, Aloysius Pieris – Sri Lanka;

H.K. Tong, Benoit Vermander, Huang Po Ho – Taiwan;

Seri Phongphit, Philip Hughes, Kenneth Fleming – Thailand;

Bao Dinh Bich, Thich Nhat Hahn, Jonathan Tran – Vietnam;

Naim Stifan Ateek, Nur Masalha, Anthony O'Mahoney – West Asia.

5.3.4 *Theological studies for the region as a whole*:
A large number of authors have published several *series of volumes for regional studies* in the late 20th century. Some of many which are grounded in the history and experience of national communities but which also place these in their regional context include (dates given are those of major works):

S. Kulandran (1949), Ryu Tong Shik (1960), Horacio de la Costa (1965), M.M. Thomas (1966, 1987), Emerito P. Nacpil (1968),Catalino G. Arevalo (1974), Oh Jae Shik (1974), Koyama Kosuke (1974), Pedro S. de Achutegui (1975), Takenaka Masao (1975, 1991), Tissa Balasuriya (1976), Yeow Choo Lak (1978, 1988), Carlos H. Abesamis, (1978), Samual Rayan (1978), John C. England (1981), K.H. Ting (1981), T.V. Philip (1982), Aloysius Pieris (1982), D. Suh Kwang-sun (1983), A.A. Yewangoe (1987), Jose M. de Mesa (1987), (Ms.) Virginia Fabella (1989), (Ms.) Kwok Pui-lan (1990), (Ms.) Chung Hyun Kyung (1990), R.S. Sugirtharajah (1991, 2013), S. Batumalai (1991), (Ms.) Hope Antone (1992), Franklyn J. Balasundaram (1994), K.M. George (1994), Kwok, Pui-lan (1995, 2005), Y.B. Mangunwijaya (1996), Michael Amaladoss (1997), Christopher Duraisinghe (1998), (Ms.) L. Ralte (1998), Anthony Rogers (1998), Levi Oracion (2001, 2010), Vimal Tirimanna (2004, 2007), Sebastian C.H. Kim (2008), Felix Wilfred (2008, 2010), Peniel Jesudason & Rufus Rajkumar (2012), Loh I-to (2012, D. Preman Niles (2013, 2017),

See also publications of the EACC/CCA (Christian Conference of Asia, since 1957), of the FABC (Federation of Asian Bishops' Conferences, since 1970), of ATA (Asia Theological Association, since 1970), of the Programme for Theology and Cultures in Asia (PTCA, since 1983) and of EATWOT (Ecumenical Association of Third World Theologians, from 1976).

Expatriate scholars have contributed extensively to these studies see, for example, the works of Joseph A. Mulry sj (1925), D.M. Paton (1953), J. R. Fleming (1959), J.J. Spae cicm (1960), Richard W. Taylor (1960), Peter G. Gowing (1964), Bede Griffiths (1967), Norbert Klein (1968), Kaj Baago (1968), Robin Boyd (1969), John C. England (2001), W. Henry Scott (1979), Herbert R. Swanson (1974), J.S. Trimingham (1979), Philip L. & (Ms.) Janice Wickeri (1980), (Ms.) P. Wilson-Kastner (1981), James Heisig (1983), (Ms.) Gabrelle Dietrich (1991), Sydney Griffith (1992), D.C. Lewis (2000), Wilhelm Baum & D. W. Winkler (2003), Christoff Baumer, (2006), N. Friedrich (2010), J. Harris (2015), Duncan B. Forrester (2018).

5.3.5 *Pastoral theology – questions of mission and ministry*
Where more immediate issues of ecclesiology and missiology are dealt with, it is often possible to recognise elements of a national 'Pastoral Theology', often with strongly ecumenical, missionary or historical emphasis. Prominent examples here would be *parts of* (amongst many others) the work of:

Ding Guangxun (1915-2012), (Ms.) Beatrice Leung, Chen Zemin (1917-2010) – China.

Geevarghese Mar Osthathios (1918- 2000), J.R. Chandran (1918-2000), D. S. Amalorpavadass (1932-1990) – India;

J. Ch. Abineno (1917-1995), Robert Hardawiryana (b.1926), J.B. Banawiratma sj (b.1946) – Indonesia;

Suzuki Masahisa (1912-1969), Kumuzawa Yoshinobu (b.1929), Mizuno Makoto (fl.1990) – Japan;

Roland Koh Peck Chiang (1908-1972), Yap Kim Hao (1929-2017), Batumalai Satayandy (b.1946) - Malaysia-Singapore.

Kim Jae Jun (1901-1987), Moon Dong Whan, Stephen Kim Su Hwan (1925-2002) – Korea; Catalino Arevalo sj (1925-2002), Mariano Apilado, Vitaliano Gorospe sj (ca.1940-?) – the Philippines;

Celestine Fernando(d.1984), Paul Caspersz sj (b.1925), (Ms.) Bernadeen Silva (1929-?) – Sri Lanka;

C. H. Hwang (Shoki Coe, 1914-88), Kao Chun Ming (b.1929), Huang Po Ho (fl.2015) – Taiwan;

(Ms.) Prakai Nontawasee (1926-2013), Seri Phongphit (fl. 1980), Vichai Phokthavi sj (fl.2000) – Thailand;

Nguyen van Binh (1910-95),Tran Thien Cam (b.1933), Nguyen Hong Giao (b.1937) - Vietnam

As can be seen from the contents of most journals published in the region, in terms of overall quantity this category still accounts, for the largest body of Asian Christian writing.[17] This is along with extensive article series such as those in the former journals *Tien Feng, Teaching All Nations* (until 1978 – now *East Asia Pastoral Review*), *CTC Bulletin* (CCA), *Asian Christian Review, Southeast Journal of Theology* (now *Asia Journal of Theology*), *Dialogue* (EISD – new Series 1974)), *Northeast Asia Journal of Theology (1968-82),* and many current journals. (See also concluding note below).

Some of the major contributors above to 'Pastoral Theology' have dealt with theological issues when regarded as having universal validity, but addressed from within the Asian Church. These are not so much contributions to western debates as a recognition that particular aspects of the Gospel ('that God brings God's Reign') remain central to all Christians. Of former authors – to select a few representative examples until 1970 – the bulk of D. T. Niles's writing has this character (Sri Lanka), as does that of Chao Tzu-chen (China), Nicolaus Driyarkara sj (Indonesia), J. Chetti-mattam (India), Emerito Nacpil (Philippines), Noro Yoshio (Japan), and Suh Nam Dong (Korea, until 1975).

6. The Range of Work in Asian Theologies – 20th to early 21st centuries

Refer first to sections under 5.3. above: *The Asian Christian Community Gathers its Resources.*[18]

It must be stressed here that former alternative interpretations for Christian theologies and histories are from now on being further developed and applied: in following the-life-of-Jesus-with-others in church and society, in critically appropriating Biblical truths, in recovering peoples' faith traditions and resources, in researching and re-writing national Christian histories, in encounters and dialogue with those of other Faiths, in incorporating the experience and insight of 'fringe' and oppressed communities, in recognizing the claims of nature and the environment and in the re-shaping of Christian doctrines in context. As a central concern also all these endeavours are now being increasingly recast by the stories, knowledge and wisdoms of women at every level of Christian action and reflection.

6.1 'Living Theologies'.

In presenting authors whose works particularly feature the constructive elements of contextualising local theologies, it is possible here to offer only representative examples in selected fields, from a wide range of published materials in the region. Then too the fields of research and writing most often overlap so that inter-faith dialogue and cross-textual studies contribute directly to theological construction; rediscovery of indigenous or 'native' tradition re-shapes Christian images and doctrines; new levels of dialogue with developments in the sciences, humanities and arts provide questions and insights for Biblical and theological studies; engagement in movements for societal or environmental change brings critiques of accepted concepts or assumptions; and women's studies, wisdom and stories reshape every field of theological teaching and writing. So that whether the chief 'location' for theological research or reflection may be Christian presence (and struggle) in the daily work of commerce or industry, in the interpretation of Biblical or other sacred scriptures, the encounter with enlightenments from other living faiths, or the worlds and wisdoms of women's experience, the outcomes almost always include people-justice and creative community life as well as alternative living theologies or 'theodaodharma's.[19]

'From Israel to Asia'
Theologically each of these interactions reveals a transposition of locus for the assumptions and starting-points for the work of theology. It will be recognised that many authors listed under 5.3.1-5 above have based their work within the experience of national or regional Asian communities and that re-location becomes more important from the mid-20th to early 21st centuries. In its fullest forms many colleagues describe this as 'the leap from Israel to Asia' (C.S. Song) which in research and reflection moves directly from the Biblical resources to the contexts and experiences of Asian peoples. The 'screens' of European or North American writings or traditions are therefore here left aside (at least temporarily) as the life and word of prophet and gospel-writer for today's Asian communities are more directly received. This is sometimes termed the discernment of 'Yahweh's controversy' (Koyama Kosuke) with each people, or the discernment of divine Presence, in its particular history and culture. The basic assumption here is that the spirit of God has *always* been actively present in the life of each people and that this can be also seen in two millennia of Christian history in the Asian region. A wide range of historical and contemporary sources are employed in order to recognise and employ for Asian theologies the creative resources both of that history and of contemporary Christian communities.[20]

The concern of much 'living theology' is therefore primarily 'missional or pastoral' in motivation, as a response to the suffering and hope of women and men in particular life-situations, and a discernment of 'what God is now doing in our midst.' Sections below provide selections of ongoing theological work in response to the changing contexts and endeavours in the 20th and early 21st centuries. The attempt is only to highlight a few of the more significant works in the setting of major movements which are shaping Christian life in Asian countries.

6.1.1 *Ecumenical theology and strategy*
Refer first to chapter 2 above ('Ecumenical Movements in Asia since the 3rd Century').

The development of modern ecumenical movements is most important here because of their direct relationship to local context and people's life situation in Asian multi-faith communities today. As would be expected where there are strong commitments to the *oikumene*, concerns for Christian unity are closely linked with worldly ministries in urban, rural and political situations, as well in local, as in national and regional contexts. The beginnings of later national and regional ecumenical councils can be seen in the associations in India, China, and Japan since 1828. Further consultations and local agreements once established, again particularly in Asian countries, provided the groundwork for the world conference in Edinburgh in 1910. The world-wide movement then emerging owed much in its beginnings to a global network of national leaders which included Nathan Söderblom, John R. Mott, W.A. Visser't Hooft, J.H. Oldham, Tissington Tatlow, William Temple, William Paton, Marc Boegner, Suzanne de Diétrich, Friedrich W. Siegmund-Schultze, Stefan Zankov and Hanns Lilje.

But included amongst these founding figures were also a number of outstanding Asian leaders such as V. Samual Azariah (1874-1945), (Ms.) Michi Kawai (1877-c.1952), David Z.T. Yui (1882-1936), T.Z. Koo (fl.1930), Enrique C. Sobrepena (1899-1978), Johannes Leimena (1905-1966), D.T. Niles (1908-1970), (Ms.) Sarah Chacko (1905-1954), U Ba Hmyin (1912-1982), and (Ms.) Tseng Po Sun (fl. 1940). Foundations were laid also in the building of ecumenical theology in the addresses and work of many like Kozaki Hiromichi (1856–1934?), Cheng Ching

Yi (1881–1939), Kagawa Toyohiko (1888-1960), (Ms.) J. Jara-Martinez (1894-1987), U Hla Bu (1897-1970), Zhao Zichen (T.C. Chao 1898-1979), Lesslie Newbigin (1909-1998), Kim Chung Choon (fl.1970).[21]

They would be followed by a stream of theologians and leaders who were concerned:

– to express the meaning of local ecumenical mission and Christian selfhood, among them T. S. G. Mulia (d. 1967), Kim Jae Joon (d. 1987), Lakdasa de Mel (1902–1976), R. Koh Peck Chiang (1908-72), C. H. Hwang (Shoki Coe, 1914-88), David Moses (d. 1973), U Saw Lader (fl. 1975);

– to vigorously promote regional fellowship and joint action for mission: Rajah B. Manickam (1897–?), Enrique Sobrepena (1899-1978), D.T. Niles (1908-1970), Shoki Coe (1914-88), J.R. Chandran (1918-2000), U Kyaw Than (1923-2016), Alan A. Brash (1913-2002), (Ms.) Shanti Solomon (1920-98), Yap Kim Hao (1929 – 2017);

– to articulate Christian responsibility in the secular world : K. T. Paul (1876–193 1), M.A. Thomas (1913-93), Kang Won Yong (1917-2006), T. B. Simatupang (1920-1990), John Jyigiokk Tin (b.1922), (Ms.) Lee Oo Chung (b.1923), Valentino Montes (d. 1973), Henry Aguilan (fl.1975), Takenaka Masao (1925-2006);

– or to outline the essential marks of the world-wide church and mission : L.T. Ting Fang (1891–1945?), Paul Devanandan (1901–1962), D. T. Niles (1908–1970), M. M. Thomas (1916-96), Suh Nam-Dong (1918-1984), Catalino Arevalo sj (1925-2002) (Ms.) Prakai Nontawasee (1926-2013), Kumazawa Yoshinobu (b. 1929), Aram Catholicus (fl.2010).

It is to be noted that in each case these pioneers were also acknowledged leaders of their own national church.

6.1.2 *Dialogue as mutual exploration*
The significant difference to be recognized here, from earlier approaches to those of other living faiths, is that the historical and religious experience

of a particular people and its living faith are not only fully respected, but also studied and received as offering fully authentic religious truth. Open and creative Christian response is made as representatives of different faiths together commit themselves to the mutual quest for larger spiritual knowledge, and to the fuller expression of this in work for people's justice and peace. This is then nurtured by the creative insights that are shared from each faith in an exchange, dialogue and learning which are fully reciprocal.

A growing number of scholar-activists in the region have also reported further experience and conclusions for encounters with those of other living faiths. This has come not only in 'cross-cultural studies' and in studies of ecumenical identity but also in explorations of multiple religious belonging as it serves Christian presence in many parts of the region.[22]

Among those who have led in the field of mutual exploration in the 20th /early 21st centuries there are included:

East & Northeast Asia

Sung Bum Yun (1916-1980), Ryu Tong Shik (b.1922), (Ms.)Kim Sung Hae (b. 1940), Kim Heup Young (fl.2015) – Korea;

Doi Masatoshi (1907–), Yuki Hideo (1926-2012), Takizawa Katsumi (fl.1960), Yagi Seiichi (b.1932), Jan van Bragt (1928-2007) – Japan;

Wang Tao (1828-1897), Wang Zhixin (b.1881) Zhao Zichen (T.C. Chao 1898-1979) , John C.H. Wu (1899-1986), A. Lee Chichung (1987), – China;

M. Fang Chih-jung (1926-2014), Yves Raguin (1912-1998), Song Choan Seng (b.1929) – Taiwan;

Southeast Asia

Peter G. Gowing (1930-1983), Salvatore Carzedda (d.1992),Hilario Gomez (fl.1994-8), Sebastiano D'Ambra (fl.1995)– Philippines;

Victor l. Tanja (1936-1998), Dick Hartoko (1922-2000), I.Wayan Mastra (b.1931), Gabriel P. Sindhunata (1952) – Indonesia;

E. Kee Fook Chia (1962-), (Ms.) Patricia Martinez (b.1960), Jonathan Tan (b.1969) – Malaysia/Singapore;

Augustin Moling (1924-1999), R.R. Bamrunbgtrakul (1916-2000), Maen Pondudom (fl.1985) – Thailand;

Pe Maung Tin (1888-1973), U Khin Maung Din (1931-1987), Samuel Ngun Ling (1956-) Burma/Myanmar;

Hoang Si Quy (1926-), (Ms.) Mai Thanh (1928-), N. Chinh Ket (1952-) – Vietnam.

South Asia

Paul Devanandan (1901–1962), Swami Abhishiktananda (1910-73), Jarlath D'Souza (b.1930), K.P. Aleaz (b. 1946), Stanley Samartha (1920-2001) – India;

Lynn de Silva (d. 1982), Lakshman Wickremasinghe (1927-1983), Yohan Devananda (1928- 2016), Anthony Fernando (b.1932) – Sri Lanka;

M. Nazir Ali (fl.1995), C. Amjad-Ali (1949-), James Channan (1952-) – Pakistan.

West / Inner Asia

The Dalai Lama (b.1935), N.S & F.S. Fatemi (fl. 1975), Muhyiddin Al-'Arabi, (fl.1995), Mohammed, Ovey N. (fl.1995), Elias Chacour (b.1939), Naim S. Ateek (fl.2000), Riad Jarjour (fl.2000), Michael Lerner, Osman Zumrut & Mustafa Koylu (fl.2005), Rif'at Bader (fl.2010), Nur Masalha (fl.2015).

6.1.3 *Application of Prophetic Insight to Society and Culture*
The strong tradition of social criticism within earlier Asian theologies (see 5.1, 5.2 and 6.1 above) is continued and extended in this period. Present dilemmas and jagged realities call forth declarations and stories,

letters and meditations, prayers, affirmations and poetry in a Biblical diversity of form. New areas of study and writing emerge from new levels of spiritual experience within the work and struggles of secular life. A wide range of authors already referred to have worked to relate an integral Gospel to surrounding social and cultural realities.

In northern no less than in southern regions of Asia the traditions of reflection and research within the struggles of social, people's, inter-religious or indigenous movements have made major contributions to Asian theologies. From these dynamic contexts have come insights and methodologies which often reshape earlier historical interpretations and ecclesiologies. Amongst the most significant of such movements must be mentioned *Dalits* in India, *Samizdat* authors and activists in Russia, *Dong Hak* and *Minjung* movements in Korea, *Patriotic* Christian movements in Vietnam and China, *Ecumenical liberation* movements in the Philippines.[23]

The urgent human issues that are being addressed by theologians (and activists) include: extreme inequalities in wealth, land-ownership, and access to education, and the abuses and corruption which cause these; unregulated and exploitative financial, 'legal' and employment practices; the deprivation of human rights to 'life and liberty, freedom from slavery and torture, freedom of opinion and expression, and the right to free political action; the consequences of monopolistic and globalizing trading practices, along with continuing exploitation of fossil fuels which cause severe changes in climate; and the persistence of patriarchal systems in family, work, societal and church relationships. In the fullest growth of lived theology here there is attempted a unity of life-experience, struggle and reflection, of faith and people-justice, of social and personal transformation. Many teachers of theology in faculties across the region are addressing these issues but it emerges also from many diverse groupings: from lay movements and study-centres, colleges and prisons, from activist koinonia, team ministries, and basic communities.[24]

Amongst those authors that can be included (amongst many) here are:

Rutherford Waddell (d.1932), Fred McKay (1915-2000), Richard Randerson (b.1940), Frank Brennan sj (b.1954) - Australia/New Zealand.

Claribel I. Po (1905-1994), U. Tun A. Chain (1933-), L. Zau Lat (1943-), Alan Saw U (1949) – Burma/Myanmar

Zhao Zichen (T.C.Chao 1898-1979), (Ms.) Cheng Wenzhen 9fl.1930), Ding Guangxun (1915- 2012), Zhuo Xinping (b.1955) – China;

Kwok Nai-wang (Guo Naihong, b.1940), Raymond Fung, (Ms.) Rose Wu (fl.2010) – Hong Kong;

K.T. Paul (I876-1931), M.M. Thomas (1916-96), M.A. Thomas (1913-93), S. Kappen (1924-93), I.J. Mohan Razu (fl.2015) – India.

Johannes Leimena (1905-66), Tahi B. Simatupang (1920-90),Yusuf B. Mangunwijaya (1929- 1999), J.P. Widyatmadja (b. 1965) – Indonesia;

Sumiya Mikio (1916- ?), Takenaka Masao (1925-2006), Honda Testuro (b.1942), (Ms.)Yamano Shigeko (fl.1990) – Japan;

Song Chang Keun (1898-1951), Kim Jae Joon (d. 1987), Kang Won Yong (1917-2006), Oh Jae Shik (fl.1990) – Korea;

K. Janbunathan (fl. 1980), Denison Jayasooria (b.1954), (Ms.) Dulcie Abraham (fl.2005), Stephen Tan (fl.1975), (Ms.) Chew Beng-lan (fl.1980), Sadayandy Batumalai (b.1946)– Malaysia/Singapore;

Joseph A. Mulry (1889-1945), Francisco F. Claver (1926-2010), (Ms.) Mary R. Battung (b.1943), Ed. dela Torre (b.1943) Julio X. Labayen (b.1927), (Ms.)Virginia Fabella (fl.1990), (Ms.)Mary John Mananzan (b.1937), Levi Oracion (fl.1990), (Ms.) Agnes M. Brazal (b.1960) – Philippines;

Peter A. Pillai (1904-64), Tissa Balasuriya (1924-2013), Yohan Devananda (1928-2016), Lakshman Wickremasinghe (1927-1983), J. Abayasekara (fl.1970-90) – Sri Lanka;

Shoki Coe (1914-88), John Jyigiokk Tin (fl.1940-60), Kao Chun Ming (1929-2019), Song Choan Seng (b.1929) – Taiwan;

Koson Srisang (fl.1970-80), Prakai Nontawasee (1926-2018), Mansap Bunluen (1929-2010), Bao Dinh Bich (fl.1980-90) – Thailand & Vietnam.

Fyodor Bukharev (fl.1840), Farah Antoun (1874–1922), Nicolai A. Klyuev (1887-1937), A. Solzhenitsyn (1918-2008), Alexander Men (1935-90), Naim S. Ateek (fl.2000), Elias Chacour (b.1939) – West/Inner Asia.

6.1.4 *Recovery of Indigenous Sources and Reflection*

A further strong tradition which provides both sources and expansion for Asian theologies is found in the recognition and utilization of symbolism and insight from indigenous cultural sources. In some countries this comes from the study of folk institutions or tribal traditions, of ancient archives or of oral history. In others it is the recovery of neglected areas of Christian history or writings, or the recognition of long traditions of ecumenical or inter-faith exchange. In still other countries it is the restitution and reception of life-understanding held by disprivileged or formerly discarded minorities.

In every case there is a growing awareness that the creativity of peoples' cultures is a vital source not only for reflection in our diverse theologies and action in societies in rapid social change. Central concepts of the Gospel (for example, that 'the Reign of God has begun') are affirmed here by discerning the marks of 'the life-of-Jesus-with-others' (Shoki Coe) which are already present in a people's traditions or experience. Although a very wide range of sources are therefore available for study and application there remain many fields where research has only begun.[25] Authors whose work has included the recovery of some part of indigenous sources in their own country context include:

Rainbow Spirit Elders (1997), Ruawai Rakena (1929-2019), (Ms.) A. Pattel-Gray (fl.2000) – Australia/New Zealand;

Ma Xiangbo (d.1939), Wang Weifan (1928-2015), Xie Fuya (1892-1991), Kwok Pui-lan (b.1952) – China;

A.J. Appasamy (1891-1975), Ms.) Vandana Mataji (b.1924), Wati Longchar (b.1961) – India;

C.L. Coolen (1775-1873), Philip Van Akkeren (fl.1970), Gabriel P. Sindunata (b.1952), (Ms.) S.E. Lakawa (b.1970) – Indonesia;

A.S. Khomyakov (1804-60), V. Lossky, (1903-58), A. Solzhenitsyn (1918-2008), H. Vlachos, (1994) – Inner Asia;

Uchimura Kanzo (1861-1930), Inoue Yoji (b.1927), Kuribayashi Teruo (fl.1980) – Japan;

Ryu Young Mo (1890-1981), Hyun Young Hak (b.1921), Chong Ho Kyong (b.1940), (Ms.) Chung Hyun Kyung (b.1956) – Korea;

San Crombie Po (1870-1946), Pe Maung Tin (1888-1973), U Khin Maung Din (1931-87) - Burma/Myanmar

H. de la Costa sj (1916-1977), (Ms.) M.J. Mananzan osb (b.1937), B. P.Beltran (b.1946) – Philippines;

L Nanayakkara osb (1917-82), M. Rodrigo omi (1927-89), (Ms.) Pauline Hensman (b.1922) – Sri Lanka;

Francis Wei, Zhuomin (1888-1976), Charles B. Jones (b.1937), Wang Hsien-chih (Ong Hian-Ti, 1941-1996)– Taiwan;

(Ms.) P. Nontawasee (b.1926), K. Bunchua (fl.1990), H. R. Swanson (fl.2000) – Thailand;

John Romanides (1973), M. Meerson-Aksenov & Boris Shragin (1977),G. Makdisi (1990), S.K. Samir (1994), (Ms.) S. Rabow-Edling (2006), A. O'Mahoney (2008) – West/Inner Asia.

6.1.5 *Theological Construction*
Many elements of writings referred to above obviously contribute to the building of more localized and contextual theologies but a significant body of authors explore the sources for these and the issues they

present more sharply. Along with the recognition of 'hybrid' identities or 'diasporic' locations we have in many scholars and missioners both the work of assembling present resources for Christian presence and endeavours, and the construction of Christian understanding in response to today's urgent human issues.

The common feature of this life-reflection is both the re-shaping and the application of inherited formulations or imagery as the present work of Christian presence is undertaken. It will often include a new recovery of traditional thought-forms but along with strong criticism of patriarchal, imperial or neo-colonial concepts or images as in 5.1 and 5.2 above. Accordingly a fruitful entry to all study of contemporary Asian Christian theologies is found in the writings of those who provide such critiques in the course of addressing national or regional theological and/or social issues.

A selection of writers that include such approaches follows. (The date given indicates first key works).

South Asia (India, Sri Lanka, Pakistan, Bangladesh, Bhutan):
C.R. Hensman (1958), S. Kappen (1961), D.S. Amalorpavadass (1967), M.M. Thomas (1967), N. Minz (1968), S. Rayan (1971), L. Wickremesinghe (1973), R. Panikkar (1973), P. Caspersz (1974), T. Balasuriya (1976), V.C. Samuel (1977), S. Das (1978), P. Mar Paulose (1979), C. Amjad-Ali (1982), S. Ryan (1982), A.M. Ayrookuzhiel (1983), (Ms.) P. Hensman (1984), J. Channan (1984), N. Abeyasingha (1985), A. Pieris (1986), E. Asi (1989), W. Longchar (1989), (Ms.) M. Melanchthon (1989), D.J. Moghal (1991), F. Balasundaram (1993), (Ms.) L. Ralte (1998), J. Massey & T.K. John (2013), M. Maisunagdibou (2014).

Southeast Asia (Indonesia, Burma/Myanmar, Thailand, Vietnam, Philippines, Malaysia/Singapore, Australia/New Zealand, Laos, Cambodia):
Manuel Teixeira (1961), T.B. Simatupang (1967), Khin Maung Din (1968), B.T.V. Dinh Bich (1970), T.T. Thien Cam (1970), E. de la Torre (1970), (Ms.) A.M. Say Pa (1975), Lim Mah Hui (1975), C. Avila (1976), (Ms.) V. Fabella (1978), C. Abesamis (1979), M. Pongudom (1979), L.

Oracion (1979), E. G. Singgih (1982), (Ms.) S.R. Ruiz-Deremdes (1985), A.A. Yewangoe (1985), S. Batumalai (1986), J.B. Banawiratma (1986), (Ms.) M. Orevillo-Montenegro (1987), (Ms.) M-J. Mananzan (1988), A.S. Walters (1992), S. Pau Khan En (1995), (Ms.) A.M. Brazal (1995), J. Tan (1997), N. Darragh (1995), C. Pearson (2005), J. Tran (2010).

East Asia (China-Hong Kong-Macau-Tibet, Japan, Korea, Taiwan): Kim Kyo Shin (fl. 1940), Kitamori Kazuo (1946), Sumiya Mikio (1954), Chen Zemin (1954), K.H. Ting (1957), Chi Hak Soon (1958), Shoki Coe (1966), C.S.Song (1968), Chen Nan-jou (b.1944), Kim Jae Joon (1970), Ahn Byung Mu (1972), Arai Sasagu (1974), D. Suh Kwangsun (1976), Inoue Yoji (1976), Kadowaki Kakichi (1977), (Ms.) Park Soon Kyung (1983), (Ms.)Park Sun-ai (1985), Shen Yifan (1985), Kwok Naiwang (1989), Kuribayashi Teruo (1991), (Ms.) Kinukawa Hisako (1994), Kan Baoping (1996), (Ms.) A. Wong Waiching (1997), Kim Heup Young (2003).

West and Inner Asia/Russia (Turkey, Syria, Palestine, Israel, Lebanon, Jordan, Saudi Arabia, Iran, Iraq, Gulf States, Russian Federation in Asia, Nepal, Mongolia, Afghanistan, Central Asia): E. Kadloubovsky (1954), V. Lossky (1957), A. Schmemann (1965), A. Sinyavsky (1972), A. Solzhenitsyn(1976), M. Meerson-Aksenov (1977), G. Florovsky (1979), (Ms.) P. Wilson-Kastner (1981), G. Chediath (1982), S. Brock (1987), H. Dehgani- Tafti, (1992), T.V Philip (1994), Bat Ye'or (1996), Naim S. Ateek (1999), R.A. El-Assal (1999), (Ms.) M. & R. Tobin (2002), D. Thomas (2003), S. Rassam (2006), Mar B. Soro (2007), Alexander Men (2014).

6.1.6 *Jesus Historical and Mythical*

For many of those already named above, a central concern has also been to explore sources and interpretation for the human life, and the continuing presence, of Jesus Christ, Son of Man. For some, the most significant concepts have come from research in Palestinian Judaism or in the patterns of west Asian society and culture, in the 1st century. For some, new insights have come from renewed study of the earliest gospels, including those recovered since 1870. For others the focus is upon images of Jesus Christ's life discerned within other living faiths, or in the art traditions of Asia or in Asia's people's movements for reform, justice and peace. (See section I, part two, above for some results from these researches).

The Son of Man / Human One that emerges from such intense and wide-ranging study, devotion and 'imitation' is seen to be a well-educated and courageous Galilean: Rabbi and prophetic teacher; befriender and champion of discarded or abused villagers or townspeople; companion of women; outspoken critic of religious hypocrisy and all accumulation of wealth; healer of minds and bodies; a 'holy and wise one', 'nature-lover' and mystic; both fully human but in that humanity itself also 'divine'; a presence within all truth, beauty, quest and hope.

Amongst those in the Asian regions who present images of this life-of-Jesus-with-others in particular volumes:

South Asia
P.C. Mozoomdar, Narayan V. Tilak, (Ms.) Pandita Ramabai, Sadhu Sundar Singh, Pandipedi Chenchiah, Vengal Chakkarai, D.T. Niles, Michael Amaladoss, Tissa Balasuriya, Sebastian Kappen, Paul Caspersz, (Ms..) Vandana Mataji, R.S. Sugirtharajah, Emmanuel Asi, H.L. Richard, Aloysius Pieris, (Ms.) Aruna Gnanadason, P. Premasagar, M.T. Thangaraj, K.P. Aleaz, K. Subba Rao, Jyoti Sahi, Somen Das, P. Jegadish Gandhi, George Soares-Prabhu , Fida M. Hassnain, Israel Selvanayagam, Wati Longchar, Jose Kuttianimattathil, Chaturvedi Badrinath, Jacob Mathew.

Southeast Asia
Sadrach Supranata, Robinson Radjagukguk, Carlos Abesamis, Charles Avila, J.B. Banawiratma, (Ms.) Mary R. Battung, Jose Cunanan, Fung Jo Jo, Khin Maung Din, Bao Vuong Dinh Bich, Fung Jojo, Thich Ngat Hanh, (Ms.) H. Marianne Katoppo, Manolo O. *Vano,* (Ms.) Mary John Mananzan, Levi Oracion, (Ms.) Muriel Orevilla-Montenegro, Benigno

Beltran, (Ms.)Anna May Say Pa, (Ms.) Lee Miena Skye, (Ms.) Mai Thanh, Edicio de la Torre;

East Asia
Wu Yaozong, Ahn Byung Mu, Arai Sasagu, Kim Chi Ha, (Ms.) Chung Hyun Kyung, Arai Sasagu, Endo Shusaku, Inoue Yoji, Kagawa Toyohiko, Wu Leichuan, Roman Malek, Kim Jae Jun, Kim Yong-bock, (Ms.) Kinukawa Hisako, Koyama Kosuke, (Ms.) Kwok Pui Lan, (Ms.) Agnes Lee, (Ms.) Park Sun Ai Lee, C.S. Song, Suh Kwang-sun, Yeo Kheok-Khng, Kim Heup Young, Zhao Zi-chen, Zhu Weizhi.

West / Inner Asia
Aleksandr Bukharev, Vladimir Solovyev, Sergei Bulgakov, Hassan Dehgani-Tafti, Pavel A. Florensky, (Ms.) Maria Skobtsova, Vladimir N. Lossky, John S. Romanides, John Meyendorff, Georges Florovsky, Alexander Men, Elias Chacour, Sami Hadawi, Naim S. Ateek, Ziya Meral, Wangchuk Lhatru.

6.6 *Womanist / Feminist Concerns*
Although women's work has been integrated within each section above it is necessary to focus this further, for since being key leaders in the earliest churches women have suffered centuries of male patriarchy attempting to destroy this role. Despite this, remarkable women have emerged and from these we often have biographies, writings and/or reflections from the earliest period. Along with reflection on 'feminist' issues, women have made/are making significant contributions to Biblical studies, indigenous and contextualizing theologies, societal ministries, ecumenical and inter-faith concerns. To study recent work by women we must therefore recognise the larger framework of such forebears as the two Macrinas (Cappadocia theology, 4th century); Euphemia (social prophet, Syria, 6th century); Sorghaghtani (mother of Khans, 13th century); in the 17th century, Candida Xu (China), Tama Gracia (Japan), Ota Julia (Korea), Catherine Man Tai (Annam, fl.1635) and Jeronima Asuncion (Philippines). By the late 19th century, the numbers are greatly increased, including such women as:

South Asia

By late 19th century/ early 20th century: Hindiyya al-'Ujaimi (1720-98), Chandra Lila (fl.1840), Ellen L. Goreh (1853- 1937), Toru Dutt (1856-1877), Sophia Blackmore (1857-98), Anna Satthianadhan (fl.1870), Cornelia Sorabji (fl.1890), Pandita Ramabai (1858-1922, Kheroth M. Bose (b.1865, Lilavati Singh (fl.1910).

In the 20th/21st centuries:
Sarah Chakko (1905-1954), Renuka Somasekhar (d.2007), Vandana Mataji (b.1924), Sarah Grant (1922-2000), Marjorie Sykes (1905-95), Dorothy Leith (fl.1970), Shanti Solomon (1920-98), Stella Baltazar (b.1952), Astrid L. Gajiwala (b.1957), Aruna Gnanadason (fl.2005), Dulcie Niles (b.1910), Lakshmi de Silva (fl. 1980), Audrey Rebera (fl.1980), Annathaie Abayasekara (fl.1985), Pauline Hensman (fl.1975), Bernadeen Silva (1980), Monica J. Melancthon (b.1962), Ranjini Rebera (fl.1980), Shanti Abeyasingha (fl. 1980), Nimalka Fernando (fl.1985), Violet John (fl.1985), Esther Inayat (fl. 1975), Lalrinawmi Ralte (fl. 1996), Aqeela Siddique (fl.1990), Shirin Samuel (fl.1985), Christine Amjad-Ali (fl.1995), Gulnaz Alfred rsm (fl.2005), Jennifer Jag Jivan (fl.2010), Catherine Sardar (fl.2015).

Southeast Asia

By late 19th century/ early 20th century: Leona y Florentino (1849-84), Sophia Blackmore (1857-1943), Catalina de Jesus (1867-1953), Asuncion A. Perez (1893-1967), Josefa Jarez-Martinez (1894-1987), Ana M. Clavez (1901-195, Juliana Lopez (fl.1902), Gregoria de Jesús (1875–1943).

In the 20th/21st centuries:
Daw Win Mya (fl.1970), Thramu Esther Byu (fl.2005), Claribel I. Po (1905-94), Katherine Khin Khin, (1909-95), Rebecca Shwee, (1912-91), Mary Dun (b.1941), Anna May Say Pa (1942-), Prakai Nontawasee (1926-2018), Aileeen Khoo (fl.2000), Maureen K.C. Chew ij (fl.2000), H. M. Katoppo (fl.1980), Pang Ken Phin (fl.1990), Virginia Fabella (fl.1990), Lieke Simandjuntak (fl.1980), Mary J. Mananzan (b.1937), Eh Wah (1938-), Lydia Nigidula, (fl.1980), Elizab, Agnes Brazal (1960), Ruth

Cortez (fl.1975), Mary R. Battung (b.1943), Sharon J. Ruiz-Duremdes (fl.2000), Henriette Hutubarat-Lebang (1952-), Muriel Orrevillo-Montenegro (b.1954), Hope Antone (b.1960), Elizabeth Padillo-Olsen (fl.1995), Septemmy E. Lakawa (b.1970), Mary Hayden gs (d.2017), Mai Thanh (b.1928), Amelie To Thi Anh (fl.2000), Yong Ting Jin (fl.2010).

East Asia

Flourishing in early 20th century: Chi Wang Yiwal (Chi-Oang, 1872-1946). Flourished (fl.1910-1920) Cheng Guanyi, Xie Wanying, Wang Liming, Zang Zhujun, Cheng Wanzhen, Hu Bibxia, Yuan Yuying, Zeng Baosan; Kawai Michi (b.1877), Yamada Waka (1879-1957), Kim Maria (1894-1944), Kubushiro Ochimi, Helen Kim (1899-1970).

In the 20th/21st centuries

Tai Wei-king (fl.1940), Kiyoko Takeda Cho (1917- 2018), Lee Oo Chung (b.1923), Park Soon Kyung (b.1923), Chu Mai-Fan (b.1924), Beatrice Leung (fl.1990), Isshiki Yoshiko (b.1928), Ivy Chou Su-teng (fl.1980), Oshima Shizuko (fl.1990), Lee Park, Sun-Ai (1930-1999), Cao Shengjie (b.1931), Jiang Peifen (b.1931), Wu Yifang (d.1986), Kinukawa Hisako (b.1938),Theresa Ee-chooi (1938-), Choi Man Ja (b.1943); Chung Hyun Kyung (b.1956), Park Kyung Mi (b.1959). Flourished 1980: Martha Ratnam, Maria Goretti Lau, Aiko Carter, Madeleine Kwong Lay-kuen, Lucy K.T. Loh, and Wu Fu-ya, Yamano Shigeko (fl.1990), Peng Yaqian (fl.1996),and Ahn Sang Nim. Flourished 2000-2020: Kwok Pui-lan, Chung Sook Ja, Angela Wong Wai-ching, Rose Wu, Lee Un Sun, Kim Ae Young, Choi Young Sil, Park Nam Soon, Yamashita Akiko, Yoshida Megumi Meerha Hahn, Kim Ok-youn.

West/Inner Asia

Xenia of St. Petersburg (fl.1850), Catherine de Hueck Doherty (1896-1985), Blessed Matrona of Moscow (d.1952), Emily Nasrallah (b.1931), Hanan Ashrawi (b.1946), Regina Derieva (b.1949), Vera Ghattas Baboun (b.1964), Seta Hadeshian (fl.2015), Amira Farhoud (fl.2017), Maryam Zargaran (b.1977), Salpy Eskidjian (fl.2000),

Key examples of expatriate women writers/workers in the region: Mary Wortley Montagu (1689-1762), Alice Mildred Cable (1878-1952), Constance Padwick, (1886-1968), Gertrude bell (1868-1926), Freya Stark (1893-1993), Maurine Tobin (fl.2002), Janet Gyatso, Hanna Havnevic and Helena Norberg-Hodge (all fl.2005), Ruth Kark (b.1941), Eleanor A. Daumato (fl.2010).

Endnotes

[1] Whenever the term 'tradition' is here used it has the sense not of a fixed body of inherited record but rather of a 'mediation between the past and the present', as meant by the original Latin 'traditio'.

[2] See in particular J.C. England et al. (eds.) *Asian Christian Theologies* (3 vols. ISPCK, Claretian, Oribis, 2001-2004) and bibliographies in notes 9 and 10 below.

[3] See the full outline given in chapter 1 above.

[4] Susan Bordo cited in *Feminism/Postmodernism* ed.Linda J Nicholson (Routledge, 1990) 136.

[5] The key initiator of 'contextual' categories for theological study, Shoki Coe, preferred to use the term *'contextualizing'* to 'contextual, in order to stress the continuing process that is necessary when recognising the settings and challenges of all Christian mission. See *Wrestling With God in Context: Revisiting the Theology and Social Vision of Shoki Coe* ed. by M.P.Joseph et al. (Fortress Press, 2018) 333,343.

[6] For a recent study of the issues see J.J. Clarke *Oriental Enlightenment* (Routledge, 1997) especially Parts I and IV.

[7] Most recent studies of indigenous writing appear in Ciprian Burlacioiu et al. (eds.) *Give Publicity to Our Thoughts : Journals of Asian and African Christians Around 1900 and the Making of a Transregional Indigenous-Christian Public Sphere* (Harassowitz, 2019).

[8] Note: Where names only are referred to below see also J. C. England et al. (op. cit.), *and* the volumes and journals listed at the end of this chapter, in continuing reviews in *Asia Journal of Theology and in details at* such sites as www.worldcat.org, www.abebooks.com/servlet and www.used.addall.com .

[9] Bibliographical details of these collections, of the national studies and principal authors mentioned below, are given in the vols. of *Asian Christian Theologies* as well as in the bibliographies and basic writings published by the Christian Conference of Asia (CCA), Programme for Theology and Cultures in Asia (PTCA), the Federation of Asian Bishops' Conferences (FABC), Ecumenical Association of Third World Theologians (EATWOT), and the Asian Theological Association (ATA).

[10] For these see also bibliographies published in *Exchange* (Utrecht), *Theologie in*

Context (Aachen), *International Review of Mission* (Geneva), *Bibiliographia Missionaria* (Rome), *International Bulletin of Missionary Research* (New Haven); along with catalogue for the *Rita Mayne England Asian Studies Collection,* Hewitson Library, Knox College, Dunedin.

[11] On 'anonymous' writings see chapter 1.iv above.

[12] See e.g. *Chinese Christian Texts from the Zikawei Library,* and *Sequel to Chinese Christian Texts from the Zikawei Library* ed. by Nicolas Standaert, Ad Dudink and Wang Renfang (Zikawei, 2009); and Johannes Laures *Kirishitan Bunko: a manual of books and documents on the early Christian Mission in Japan, with special reference to the principal libraries in Japan* (Sophia University, 1957). Together these bibliographies account for more than four hundred texts.

[13] From Protestant presses dating from 1711 in India and from joint publishers (notably ecumenical groups and the Christian Literature Society), already by 1877, 43 books or booklets of biblical commentary, 521 books of theology, 82 catechisms and 117 books of prayer or liturgies had been published.

[14] Refer to the annual PTCA vols. ed. by Yeow Choo Lak & John C. England *Doing Theology with Asian Resources* et seq. since 1984 (Singapore, ATESEA,); and since 2010 vols. 1-15 ed. by Huang Po Ho, M.P. Joseph & Wati Longchar (Sceptre, Kolkata).

[15] Some examples of the many who have in effect, largely taken this approach would include Pedro Sevilla, (Ms.) Melba P. Maggay, Jaime C. Bulatao (Philippines); Paul Sudhakar, Ken R. Ghanakan, K.P. Yohannan (India); Takakura Tokutarō, Furuya Yasuo (Japan); Chester S. Miao, Tien Liang, Yang Ku Cheng (China); Celestine Fernando, Ajith Fernando (Sri Lanka); Hwa Yung, Poh Boon Sing (Malaysia/ Singapore); Lee Sang Bock, Bong Rin Ro (Korea). Again, a large number of other writers have produced works in this category, being seldom in fully contextual relationship with Asian Christian sources.

[16] Entries for these, as for all other names listed here, are all found either in Asian Christian Theologies or in the R.M.E. Asian Studies Collection at Knox College, Dunedin. Note that amongst those concepts or doctrines most often rejected/omitted in teachings or formularies of Eastern churches from the earliest centuries are included: the 'fall' and 'original sin', 'eternal damnation', a 'substitutionary atonement', 'salvation' by blood sacrifice, or a Chalcedonian 'Trinity'.

[17] For example refer to other journals important for the region: *Vidyajyoti, India Journal of Theology, Chinese Theological Review, In God's Image (IGI), Dialogue (EISD), East Asian Pastoral Review (EAPR), Dharma Deepika: South Asian Journal of Missiological Research, Journal of Asian Studies (ATLA), Journal of Eastern Christian Studies, Theologie in Context.*

[18] These have been supplemented since 2000 by regional studies of (amongst others) Y. Devananda (2000), A. W. Longchar (2000), P.L. Wickeri (2000), V. Tirimanna

(2004), D. Preman Niles (2004), (Ms.) A.M. Brazal (2007), F. Wilfred (2008), P. Jesudason (2012), D.P. Niles (2017).

[19] 'Theo-dao' and 'theo-dharma' represent the alternatives to 'theo-logy' as theologians in Asia replace studies which are shaped largely by Graeco-Latin tradition with approaches shaped by the major traditions of South Asia (as with 'Dharma') or East Asia (as with 'Dao'). See for example Somen Das *Dharma of the Twenty-First Century.* (Punthi Pustak, 1996) and Kim Heup Young *A Theology of Tao* (Orbis, 2017).

[20] See the volumes from annual seminar-workshops of the Programme for Cultures and Theology in Asia (PTCA).

[21] For the Asian ecumenical history see W.R. Hogg *Ecumenical Foundations.* (Harper, 1952), H-R. Weber *Asia and the Ecumenical Movement 1895-1961* (SCM Press, 1966), England, John C. et al. (eds.) *Asian Christian Theologies: Research Guide.* Vol I, ISPCK; Claretian; Orbis Books, 2001-4), N. Koshy (ed.) *A History of the Ecumenical Movement in Asia.* (2 vols. WSCF-AP, YMCA-AP, CCA, 2003-4), D. Preman Niles (ed.) *Windows into Ecumenism.* Hong Kong: CCA, 2005.

[22] See Border Crossings: Cross-Cultural Hermeneutics ed. R. S. Sugirtharajah; Devadasan Nithya Premnath (Orbis 2007), & series of WCC vols. Wesley Ariarajah *Not Without My Neighbours.* (1999), *Your God, My God, Our God* (2012), Douglas Pratt *Being Open, Being Faithful* (2014), Peniel Jesudason et al. (eds.) *Many Yet One?* (2016), Claire Amos et al. *Who do We Say We Are?* (2016.

[23] For these see further S. Clarke *Dalits and Christianity: Subaltern Religion and Liberation Theology in India* (Oxford in Asia, 1998); M. Meerson-Aksenov & B. Shragin (eds.) *The Political, Social & Religious Thought of Russian 'Samizdat'* (Nordland, 1977); Kwon Jin Kwan & V. Kuster (eds.) *Minjung Theology Today* (Ev. Verlag, 2018); D.A. Palmer, G. Shive & P.L. Wickeri *Chinese Religious Life* (Oxford Univ. Press, 2017); N.Y. Doan *People's Theology in Vietnam* (ISPCK, 2004); H.M. Gomez & L.L. de Jesus (eds.) Commitment and Struggle (UCCP, 1997).

[24] Early collections of such materials are found in such volumes as Oh Jae Shik (ed.) *Theology of People* (CCA, 1974), T.K. Thomas, (ed.) *Testimony Amid Asian Suffering.* (CCA, 1977), and J.C. England (ed.) *Living Theology in Asia* (SCM, 1981).

[25] See e.g. the areas of Christian history for 2nd-12th century Korea, 2nd-15th century Japan or Indonesia; 4th-12th century India or Sri Lanka; 4th-13th century Turkestan, pre-Hispanic Philippines. Records are held or known for parts of these histories but full study (or even translation and classification) is in many cases yet to be begun.

Note on Further study

Although it has been necessary to drastically limit the number of authors referred to above, fuller sources for the above listings, and for other writings for possible inclusion, are given in the bibliographies included in chapters of this volume (and in the volumes listed below). Yet the field of studies is daily growing and only regular reference to periodicals and sites such as those also below will enable full study of 'living Asian theologies'.

For further on names and titles above refer to the research and bibliographic guides in:

Asian Christian Theologies ed. by John C. England et al. (3 vols. ISPCK, Claretian& Orbis, 2001-2004);

Catalogue to the *Rita Mayne England Asian Studies Collection,* Hewitson Library, Knox College, Dunedin; along with such volumes as:

Franklyn J. Balasundaram, *The Prophetic Voices of Asia.* Logos 32.3 & 4, 1993; 33. 1 & 2, 1994. Reprinted as *Asian Christian Theology* (ISPCK, 1997).

Niles, D. Preman *From East and West. Rethinking Christian Mission* (Challis Press, 2004); Niles D. Preman (ed.) *Windows into Ecumenism* (CCA, 2005);

Wilfred, Felix *Margins - Site of Asian Theologies* (ISPCK, 2008);

_____ *Asian Public Theology.* ISPCK, 2010.

Kim Heup Yong et al. (eds.) *Asian & Oceanic Christianities in Conversation.* Rodopi, 2011.

Jesudason, Peniel & Rufus Rajkumar (eds.) *Asian Theology on the Way. Christianity, Culture & Context.* London: SPCK, 2012.

Book Reviews since 2000 in such journals as the *Asia Journal of Theology* (Bangalore), *CTC Bulletin* (Chiangmai), *India Journal of Theology* (Kolkata), *Vidyajyoti* (Delhi), *Exchange* (Utrecht), *Theologie in Context* (Aachen), *In God's Image* (Quezon City), *International Review of Mission* (Geneva), *Bibiliographia Missionaria* (Rome), *International Bulletin of Missionary Research* (New Haven). For further details of authors and works referred to see also such sites as www.worldcat.org, www.abebooks.com/servlet and www.used.addall.com .

.......Along with references given in prior chapters of this volume.

www.ingramcontent.com/pod-product-compliance
Lightning Source LLC
Chambersburg PA
CBHW020732160426
43192CB00006B/205